TOWARD INCREASED JUDICIAL ACTIVISM

Recent titles in
Contributions in American Studies
Series Editor: Robert H. Walker

TOWARD INCREASED JUDICIAL ACTIVISM

The Political Role of the Supreme Court

ARTHUR SELWYN MILLER

CONTRIBUTIONS IN AMERICAN STUDIES, NUMBER 59

G P

Greenwood Press
WESTPORT, CONNECTICUT • LONDON, ENGLAND

Library of Congress Cataloging in Publication Data

Miller, Arthur Selwyn, 1917-
  Toward increased judicial activism.

  (Contributions in American studies, ISSN 0084-9227 ;
no. 59)
  Bibliography: p.
  Includes index.
    1. United States.   Supreme Court.   2. Political
questions and judicial power—United States.   3. United
States—Constitutional law.   I. Title.   II. Series.
KF8742.M53   347.73'26   81-20201
ISBN 0-313-23305-5 (lib. bdg.)   347.30735   AACR2

Library of Congress Catalog Card Number: 81-20201
ISBN: 0-313-23305-5
ISSN: 0084-9227

First published in 1982

Greenwood Press
A division of Congressional Information Service, Inc.
88 Post Road West
Westport, Connecticut 06881

Printed in the United States of America

10 9 8 7 6 5 4 3 2 1

Copyright Acknowledgment

Extracts from Max Lerner, *Constitution and Court as Symbols*, are reprinted by
permission of *The Yale Law Journal* and Fred B. Rothman & Company from *The Yale
Law Journal*, vol. 46 (1937), p. 1294.

. . . for Dagmar,
con amor . . . siempre . . .

In the last analysis, one must agree with [John] Rawls that the quest for a purely institutional or procedural solution to the practical problem of obtaining justice is futile. Every community, whether democratic or not, must rely on a rudimentary sense of fairness and equity among its members. This sense is not innate, but must rather be fostered through some system of education. The traditional American penchant for political engineering or institutional tinkering is thus profoundly one-sided; democratic procedures are almost vacuous in the absence of collectively held moral convictions.

—William A. Galston

Contents

Preface

This book was written because I have an abiding belief that constitutional theory, including the theory of judicial review, has come to a dead end. Arguments and discussions in legal and political science literature are ever increasingly rehashes of ancient controversies. The "legal realists" who brought pragmatism to law, and who dominated legal thought during the first half of this century, have never really been fully accepted in their insistence that study should concentrate upon what governmental officers, including judges, actually do, rather than what they are supposed to do or what they say they are doing.

The realists, furthermore, were idol smashers; they ripped the facade off ancient ideas about law and judging. Perhaps inevitably, a counter-revolution set in, a reversion to the type of conceptualistic thought that prevailed before the pragmatic revolution. The new thinking, however, is also incomplete: Rather than being a synthesis on strict Hegelian lines, it is in large part an attempt to resurrect the *status quo ante*. That the counter-revolution cannot —and, indeed, should not—succeed does not seem to enter the minds of many who write today about law and the role of the judiciary.

The pressing need is for new theory. This volume suggests, in Part IV, a broad outline of what a new synthesis—a new theory—might be or, rather, what it *should* be, for I recommend a new normative posture for the Supreme Court. That suggestion is an unabashed, flat-out rejection of the view that the intentions of those who wrote the Constitution should control present-day interpretation, and it is an equally unabashed proposal for greater judicial "activism"—*but only in a certain direction*. The Constitution of the United States is always in a state of "becoming," and it is past time that judges and commentators alike face up to that indisputable fact.

The first three parts of the book are necessary historical and contemporaneous discussions of the role and function of the Supreme Court, the disarray of politics, and the emergence of new "living" or "operative" constitutions. Note that I employ the plural when speaking of the Constitution. It is beyond argument that more than one fundamental law governs Americans.

This book is a long essay, in which an argument is presented and justified, but with full awareness that there will be considerable disagreement with some, perhaps much, of what is said. A preliminary statement, a probe into the dark future cast against the backdrop of what has happened in the past, by no means is it a complete or final theory. A volume now in progress, tentatively entitled *Getting There from Here: Toward a Constitution of Human Needs*, carries some of the thoughts of this book further and also builds on my recently published *Democratic Dictatorship: The Emergent Constitution of Control*. What is offered here is a bare and rather abstract analysis of what I consider to be the current crisis in American constitutionalism. I am not proffering a simple formula, but, rather, seek to pose some of the necessary questions that must be asked and answered.

Most present-day commentary upon the Supreme Court and the Constitution does not ask the correct questions and thus fails to confront the enduring problems of constitutionalism. That commentary tends to be detailed exegeses of what the Justices of that Court have said and does not inquire deeply into the question of who actually benefits from those decisions. In other words, the Court's sociological functions are not analyzed. That failure may be traced to the dominant ideology of lawyers—legalism, the mind-set that insists that law exists separate and apart from society. Law is thought to be a discrete entity, entire in itself, which is about as erroneous a view as can be held. But it dominates—more's the pity.

As always, I am indebted to many for insights and stimulation. The notes and bibliographical essay will, I hope, sufficiently indicate those who were consulted and who, in part at least, helped my thinking. Several friends have commented critically on a part of the book; they include, in alphabetical order, Dean Alfange, Jr., Jeffrey Bowman, Louis Fisher, Louis H. Mayo, and Harold Relyea. None saw the volume in its entirety, and, of course, I am completely responsible for everything said in the book.

Arthur Selwyn Miller

August 1981

Part I

THE SUPREME COURT IN THE BOWELS OF POLITICS

The very considerations which judges most rarely mention, and always with an apology, are the secret root from which the law draws all the juices of life. I mean, of course, consideration of what is expedient in the community concerned. Every important principle which is developed by litigation is in fact and at bottom the result of more or less definitely understood views of public policy; most generally, to be sure, under our practices and traditions, the unconscious result of instinctive preferences and inarticulate convictions, but nonetheless traceable to views of public policy in the last analysis.

—Oliver Wendell Holmes

The Court of the modern period has altered not only the constitutional rules but the constitutional arrangement. It has cast itself not merely in the negative, restraining role of judicial tradition, but also as a major initiative-producing agency of modern government. It has claimed a part in the governing process more imposing and more daring than any court in the past has ever claimed. And it has played that part with enough success to suggest that our traditional ideas about the range of judicial capacity may require reappraisal.

—Robert G. McCloskey

Under our system, judges are not mere umpires, but, in their own sphere, lawmakers — a coordinate branch of government.

—Justice William Brennan

1

Introduction:
The Temple on the Hill

I.

Americans like to believe that they have a government of laws, not of men. That, however, has never been more than partially true—and is even less so today than in the past. A government of laws—often called the Rule of Law —is an ideal, frequently far from the spotted actuality. At best, we have a government of men who administer laws, and who have considerable discretion in doing so. They can and do make choices from among competing principles—rather often in fact—and thereby unavoidably make a little law themselves. That is particularly so at the highest levels of government, federal and state, but it is also true of much of the humdrum activities of government officers—as, for example, in the discretion routinely exercised by prosecutors and police officers and judges in trial courts.

The higher one is in government, the more discretion—freedom from inter-dictory rules—one has. That body of "discretionary justice" may not be codified, but it is part of the "living law" of the nation. What government officers, including judges, do is much more important than what they are supposed to do or even what they say they are doing.

Woodrow Wilson knew that. He asserted in 1885 that "the constitution in operation is manifestly a very different thing from the constitution of the books."[1] So it is, and so it is with all law, whatever its source or derivation. The "law in action" routinely differs from the "law in the books." Those who have authority to interpret or administer written laws are more truly law-makers than those who enacted the original laws, whether they are constitu-tions or statutes or administrative regulations. The point is generally valid. I do not say that ours is a lawless society, but do maintain that law is much more fluid than is commonly believed. The focus of this volume, however, is not on law generally but on those few human disputes that reach the Supreme Court. This, then, is not a general theory of law and its role in the social order. The Supreme Court is a lawmaker, as well as mere interpreter, so attention must perforce be paid to how it fits into the overall legal system.

At the outset, it is important to realize that of the numberless controversies of Americans, only a minute number reach any court. That is so despite the burst of litigation in recent years. Most lawsuits, furthermore, begin and end at the trial (the entry) level. A relative handful are appealed, and of those few, only a tiny number get to the Supreme Court (about 4,500 each year). Even then, a litigant has only a mere one in twenty-five chance of being heard "on the merits"—of getting, that is, full-dress attention and treatment from the Justices. Summary "justice," summarily arrived at, characterizes most of the work of the Court. But the few dozen cases that do receive complete treatment can and do have portentous consequences. The nine Justices who sit on the High Bench are not, as Justice William Brennan reminded us in 1980, mere "umpires" of human disputes;[2] they go beyond that to promulgate what they consider to be wise public policies.

Basic to the argument of this volume is the large difference between the *formal* and *informal* Constitutions. The latter is often called the *living* Constitution. That adjective is used in this book, but since it is a word with multiple meanings, the term *operative* usually replaces it. (In Chapter 9 a further distinction is made between the Political [the formal] Constitution and the Economic [a part of the operative Constitution].)

The living or operative Constitution has at least two meanings. First, the term refers to the ways that specific constitutional clauses have evolved in their meanings through time. To mention only one example, "due process of law" today means much more than it did when the Document of 1787 was drafted and when the Fourteenth Amendment was ratified in 1868. Second, it refers to the ways in which structural arrangements in government have been altered. For instance, the federal system—the relationship between the states and the national government—today differs markedly from 1800. So, too, does the "separation of powers" in the national government, where a steady growth in presidential power has characterized the system since the beginning. Despite the theory to the contrary, the three branches of government are not equal in power, although they may be equal in dignity. The presidency is dominant.

Provisions of the formal and operative Constitutions can meet and merge, although they frequently diverge. The gap is quite wide at times. Briefly defined, the *formal Constitution* is the Document produced in the Constitutional Convention in 1787, twenty-six times amended, as interpreted—and thus updated (and informally amended)—by the Supreme Court. It sets forth what is *supposed* to take place in American government. The *operative Constitution*, on the contrary, deals with how government *actually operates* —what government officers, of all branches, do in fact. "There is a great difficulty in the way of a writer who attempts to sketch a living constitution—a constitution that is in actual work and power. The difficulty is that the object is in constant change. An historical writer does not feel this difficulty."[3] So wrote Walter Bagehot in his classic *The English Constitution*. He was only partly correct—any "historical writer" faces as many difficulties as, perhaps more than, one who writes about contemporary affairs. So much mythology clouds and obscures the past, so much is unknown simply because no public record exists, and so much of the extant scanty record is obviously incomplete that history is seen through a glass darkly. Each generation, furthermore, writes its own history, seeing in the past what it wishes to see.

Change there is in the operative Constitution; of that no doubt exists. "Of all great subjects," said John Stuart Mill, "much remains to be said";[4] surely that view is accurate for the Supreme Court and the American Constitution. Millions of words have been written about both, but they are still not fully understood. When one looks at the living reality, as compared with the paper descriptions in that immense literature, certainly one must wonder about the vast difference between them, and wonder also why constitutional scholars, generally, have failed to probe beneath the surface of the formal Constitution. Constitutional scholarship in the United States has a distinct legalistic bent; by and large it is confined to parsing Supreme Court opinions. That tendency is a type of latter-day scholasticism, not unlike the way that medieval scholars pored over Aristotle and other ancients in efforts to divine present meaning and significance from the words of men long dead. Only when the Scholastics began to view life—to count, for example, the legs of a spider—did they get away from sterile exegeses on antiquated texts. So it is with commentary on the Supreme Court: Only a few move beyond the written words in judicial opinions. When they do, all too often it is to try to discern what men long dead—those who wrote the Document—intended when they used abstract terms without definition. An essential lesson has not yet been learned: that in life one sees much of what is not in the books—at least, in the books of formal descriptions of law and the judiciary—and that the literary theory (the formal Constitution and the mythical Supreme Court) often differs markedly from brute practice.

Our focus is upon the Supreme Court and how the nine Justices operate within the Marble Palace, and upon what difference the Court has made and can make in the ways that Americans order their affairs. The Court as oracle of the law cannot be understood apart from the Constitution, whether formal or living. So scrutiny must be upon the ancient text and the institution with the self-asserted task of interpreting it. Those interpretations have at times been highly controversial, for occasionally they have cut across the grain of popular sentiment within the nation. As a governmental organ with a definite political role to play, the Court has had to pick its way through the mine fields of politics. It began, as will be seen, in 1803, when the Justices made a bold and bald grasp for governing power—and got away with it.[5] Just barely, however, as Chief Justice John Marshall conceded. Soon after the attempted impeachment of Justice Samuel Chase (who, because of his savage and partisan enforcement of the Alien and Sedition Laws and open attacks upon the Jeffersonian party, certainly deserved censure), Marshall wrote an amazing letter to Chase proposing to forgo the whole pretention to judicial supremacy in the meaning of the Constitution: "I think," wrote Marshall, "the modern doctrine of impeachment should yield to an appellate jurisdiction in the legislature. A reversal of those judicial decisions deemed unsound by the legislature would certainly comport better with the mildness of our character than [would] a removal of the judge who has rendered them unknowing of his fault."[6] (Marshall's private opinion was reflected in the fact that not until 1857 did the Court again declare an act of Congress unconstitutional. Most of the Chief Justice's shafts were aimed at the actions of state governments.)

The Document of 1787 was a highly subversive structural change in the government established by the Articles of Confederation (the first American fundamental law).[7] What had been a loose collection of states became a national union. It was John Marshall's destiny that he and the Court he led provided much of the theory for the evolution from a confederation to a "united state." Two centuries later, it has become obvious that the Document of 1787 is related to today's Constitution only in metaphorical ways. Americans have, in fact, not *one* but *three* formal Constitutions. The second and third co-exist with the first (as layers upon the 1787 parchment). The Document is the second fundamental law; it is often called the Constitution of Rights (or of Limitations); we will, for reasons that will become evident, call it the Constitution of Quasi-Limitations. It exists with the third, the Constitution of Powers that came into existence in the 1930s, and the Constitution of Control (the fourth) now coming into view.[8]

This book has a dual purpose: to both defend modern judical "activism," plus call for even more activism; and to describe the reality that lurks behind the mythology of the Court and Constitution. By *activism* is meant the propensity of federal judges, mainly but not always on the Supreme Court, to intervene in the governing process, so as to substitute their judgment for that of federal and state political officers. (Although the focus is upon the federal bench, state courts decide far more human disputes, even of a constitutional nature.)

From time to time since 1803, the Supreme Court has been harshly criticized for being too activist, not always, however, for the same reasons or by the same groups. Early on, it was criticized for upholding national over local power or, in economic terms, for furthering the interests of the moneyed and propertied over the yeomanry of the frontier. Assaults upon the Justices fall into three periods: from 1803 to the end of the Civil War; from 1885 to 1937; and from about 1948 to the present. During the first period, the question of how strong the new government in Washington should be was finally settled when Robert E. Lee surrendered his sword at Appomattox. (Not legalisms but sanguinary battle determined the crucial question of whether secession was constitutionally permissible. No one—least of all the Justices on the Court—thought that the pronouncement of a majority of nine elderly men could have been dispositive.) After 1885 the attacks centered on judical emasculation of the emergent trade union movement. Labor laws—maximum hours, minimum wages, child labor—designed to ameliorate some of the brutalities of industrialism were systematically invalidated by a Court that sat, in the words of John R. Commons, as "the first authoritative faculty of political economy in the world's history."[9] In fact but not in theory, the Justices were arms of the capital-owning class. That seemingly ended in 1937, when the Court in effect, but not openly, rewrote the economic clauses of the Constitution. Since then, and particularly since the school desegregation decision in 1954,[10] the Justices have been pelted with an avalanche of harsh criticism over some of their civil rights/civil liberties decisions. The attack is far from over. liberties decisions. The attack is far from over.

That much is familiar history and would not merit even summary restatement were it not that the three periods of assaults on the Temple may have a unifying theme. Is there a single strand that runs through the criticisms in each period, tying together those who espoused localism, who plumped for anticorporation regulation, and who decry the "permissiveness" of the Court today? The answer can only be yes. Supreme Court Justices—judges generally—have been and still are "Establishment" members whose interests and desires (*and* decisions) tend to further the interests of the class whence they came.[11] The storied Rule of Law, of neutral principles impartially applied, is largely a myth. That is a harsh accusation, but one that can and will be substantiated. Part I of this book outlines some of the evidence to buttress that accusation. The theme is taken from *The Politics of the Judiciary*, a recent important book by Professor J.A.G. Griffith of the London School of Economics. Griffith maintained, in a discussion of the British judiciary, that "the judiciary in any modern industrial society, however composed, under whatever economic system, is an essential part of the system of government and . . . its function may be described as underpinning the stability of that system and as protecting that system from attack by resisting attempts to change it."[12]

Can Griffith's observation be applied to the U.S. Supreme Court? There can be no question that until 1937 the Justices, without exception, perceived their task as protecting the capitalistic system. Even though massive social changes occurred during the nineteenth and early twentieth centuries, the judicial posture was basically always the same: protect those with wealth and property, those who controlled the levers of power in the Economic Constitution. By a neat bit of verbal sleight-of-hand, the true radicals or revolutionaries of American society—the businessmen who wrought such enormous changes—were able to pin the label of radicalism on those left behind and suffering from the ills of industrialization. The judges, including those on the Supreme Court, went along. Brandishing the Constitution and inventing new doctrines when need be, the Justices stood like King Canute, commanding the tides of social change to stop. They established themselves as a de facto Council of Elders, ruling on the wisdom and policy of socioeconomic legislation. Not that they openly asserted their power and right to rule on the wisdom of what other governmental officers did; far from it. Justice James McReynolds blurted out the truth in 1934 when he maintained: "But plainly, I think, this Court must have regard to the wisdom of the enactment. At least, we must inquire concerning its purpose and decide whether the means proposed have reasonable relation to something within legislative power—whether the end is legitimate, and the means appropriate."[13] McReynolds's statement was one of fact; it was not a plea that the Court do something else. The difficulty in that specific decision, one involving the power of the state of New York to regulate milk prices, is that he and the Court's majority had different views about what was wise. For present purposes, the important thing is that the Supreme Court by 1934, when the milk decision was issued, had in fact become a Council of Elders. At that time, the Justices's power was basically negative—they could invalidate governmental actions thought to be unwise—and it was not until the 1950s that they began to issue affirmative commands. (The point is developed in Chapter 5.)

Since the early 1940s, the Court's activism has been at least apparently that of expanding, for the first time in American history, the rights and liberties of ordinary citizens. Those left behind in the struggles of politics—they who make up, as Justice Harlan Stone once said, "discrete and insular" minorities[14]—began to receive some judicial protection. The appearance may hide a more gloomy reality. One need not be a Marxist to argue that this, too, is ultimately in the interests of those who have always been favored by the legal system—those who constitute what is loosely called "the ruling class." By helping to siphon off discontent and channel it into innocuous forms, the Court enables that class to remain on top while giving up only the barest minimum necessary to quell disastrous social disorder. As with President Franklin D. Roosevelt's New Deal, which preserved "the system" by tendering small gains to the masses without major loss to the moneyed and propertied, the Justices were a bulwark of the established order. (Ironically, attacks on the Supreme Court today and on FDR in the 1930s often come from the same sector of American society.)

If such an analysis is even partially correct and if it is true, as certainly it was, that the Supreme Court and courts generally were essential parts of a system of government that favored the plutocracy, why call for even more activism from judges? Why should one expect them to act differently from the ways they did in the past? The question is a good, even crucial, one, but full discussion must be deferred. For now, it is enough to say that, at notable times in the past, some judges (Justice William O. Douglas and Judge Frank Johnson are examples)[15] have been able to rise above class and position and to see matters whole. They tried to further the interests of parts of the "underclass" —not always, to be sure, but often enough to indicate that it is possible. That is so even though aid to the underclass ultimately helped the ruling class as well.

Theodore Roosevelt knew that "the decisions of the courts on economic and social questions depend upon their economic and social philosophy."[16] Thomas Jefferson put it somewhat differently: "All know the influence of interest on the mind of man and how unconsciously his judgment is warped by that influence."[17] Modern judicial activism, particularly that of the Court under Chief Justice Earl Warren, was a desirable development. No one, however, can validly say that the Court under Warren was trying to undermine "the system." Quite the contrary. By finally bringing the promises (often, but not always, implicit) of American constitutionalism into reality, the Warren Court helped to buttress the established order. Small gains, even cosmetic gains, perhaps they were, but they had the consequence—the latent function—of quelling social discontent. To be sure, those gains may have been only temporary—black Americans furnish the apt example—but gains they were. Their temporary nature merely illustrates the limits of law to alter deep-set social customs. A gain need not be permanent to be desirable.

The argument of this book is that *more judicial activism is both necessary and desirable, with one large qualification: activism is to be desired if it furthers the attainment of human dignity (however defined, itself a most difficult task) in America and if it helps Americans make necessary social and political adjustments as the ecological trap closes and the Age of Scarcity begins.* Federal Judge J. Skelly Wright has maintained that the "ultimate test of the Justices' work must be goodness"[18]—which he does not define. Since "the Justices' work"—their work-product—is law, Judge Wright seems to agree with legal philosopher Felix Cohen, who asserted that "the value of law depends upon the efficacy of law in promoting the good life."[19] If that is accurate (I think it is), criticism of law and of the Supreme Court must be based upon an adequate description of "the good life," however difficult that may be, and of how law and the judiciary achieve it. My purpose at this point is not to set forth a full-dress examination of the good life, except to equate it with the concept of human dignity widely enjoyed. Rather, it is to suggest that surely in the future, and even now, that discussion of The Good or goodness or the good life must encompass, of necessity, measures that will tend to further human dignity in the context of the Age of Scarcity. "He who proposes," said Aristotle, "to make the fitting inquiry as to which form of government is the best, ought first to determine what manner of living is most eligible; for while this remains uncertain, it will also be equally uncertain what government is best."[20] I posit here only that the "manner of living" that is "most eligible" must take into consideration the social milieu, leaving to subsequent discussion the details of what "living" means and should mean.

More than ample evidence is available to conclude that humankind is on the edge of a new social frontier, moving from what in the Western world generally and the United States specifically has been an Age of Abundance into one of deficiency. The future may be a shore dimly seen, but its contours, even now, admit of no doubt: The most portentous change in known human history is hard upon us. Definition of the good life must take that harsh fact into full account. It must also consider, for Americans, the extent to which imperialism—what William Appleman Williams has called "empire as a way of life"[21]—is a prerequisite to attainment of the good life by Americans.

American constitutionalism, as it has evolved in the formal Constitution, *in theory* has human dignity as its basic ideal. As will be seen, however, there has always been a gap—at times very wide indeed—between pretense and reality. The reach of Americans, in this sense, has always exceeded their grasp, even in the Age of Abundance. This book is an attempt to develop the extent to which the Supreme Court can help bridge that chasm in the troublous times that are upon us. Thin in the distance, thin but dead ahead, those troubles threaten to engulf an endangered planet.

I fully realize that overtly calling for The Good to be furthered by judges, as a part of judicial activism that pursues that end, cuts against the grain of orthodox constitutional commentary. That position of course is risky, so much so that one is likely to be castigated as a dreamer and for not thinking of law as a neutral force, impartially applied by judges—or, in the opprobrious term, to be labeled as being "result oriented."[22] The risk must be taken. The time is long past when judges, particularly those on the Supreme Court, can be viewed in any way other than as pursuing certain ends (whether articulated or not). They have always done so. The problem is to change judges, who are politicians in black robes, into officials who do more than further the interests of the class whence they came. That presents the inordinately difficult task of how to identify the men and women who are both capable of sitting in judgment on their fellow humans and can transcend class interests.

II.

One of the best known but least understood organs of government, the Supreme Court is at once a court of law, a faculty of political theory, a spokesman for social ethics, a theological institution, and a small bureaucracy. In its self-assumed power of judicial review of the actions of other parts of government—a power not expressly granted in the Constitution—it is *the* unique contribution of the United States to the art of governance. (The President, who is both Chief of State and head of government, also makes the United States unique among major nations, but that is not so much a contribution as a hindrance.) The Constitution and the Court are objects of awe, even reverence, an attitude carefully nurtured by the Justices and by lawyers—the priesthood of the American civil religion of Constitution worship. That puzzles Europeans, who do not place either law or lawyers so high in the hierarchy of social values. It amuses cool-minded Americans, who know very well that the Constitution often hampers government and is in large part a set of hortatory sentiments honored only when those who speak for the State agree, and that the Justices usually have been run-of-the-mine lawyers who campaigned for the High Bench and happened to come to a President's attention.[23]

The paucity of cases decided "on the merits" hides a larger reality. Constitutional interpretations, and even statutory constructions, mean much more than merely deciding a lawsuit between particular parties. As will be explained more fully (Chapter 5), the Supreme Court grants review of about a dozen dozen of the some 4,500 cases that come to it each year; those cases are chosen, as Charles Evans Hughes put it, "in the interest of the law, not in the interest of particular parties."[24] In the words of Chief Justice Fred Vinson in an address to the American Bar Association, "you are, in a sense prosecuting or defending class actions; . . . you represent not only your clients, but tremendously important principles, upon which are based the plans, hopes and aspirations of a great many people throughout the country."[25] For some time now—the exact date cannot be stated with precision—Supreme Court decisions have been considered statements of general principles; that is so even though it is logically impossible to infer a general principle from one particular (one case). Lawyers and judges, however, are not logicians; as *politicians*, in the better sense of that word, they do not worry about logic.

Judicial review of the handful of actions of other governmental organs, federal and state (mainly the latter), has meant different things at different times—outwardly at least. *How* the Justices operate, however, has remained much the same since the earliest days of the republic. Each October, the nine Justices, clad in funereal black, go on public display in the Temple within the Marble Palace—a baroque, high-ceilinged, smallish room. There they hold conversations (called "oral argument") with lawyers, who present their clients's claims, and there they periodically announce decisions. Most of that open activity is dull beyond measure, of interest only to the litigants, save for an occasional case that stirs the blood. Examples are Allan Bakke's successful attempt to get into medical school, President Nixon's attempt to keep the White House "tapes" secret, and the school desegregation case.[26] The *London Economist* was at least partially correct when it wrote, at the time of President Truman's 1952 seizure of the steel mills during the Korean "war": "At the very sign of a new argument over the United States Constitution and its interpretation the hearts of Americans leap with a fearful joy. The blood stirs powerfully in their veins and a new lustre brightens their eyes. Like King Harry's men before Harfleur, they stand like greyhounds in the slips, straining at the start."[27] (This is not to say that there is agreement about what "the" Constitution is; as will be demonstrated, it is much more than the Document of 1787 and its amendments.)

Little is known about the Supreme Court except for its public exhibitions, plus what individual Justices say in opinions accompanying a few of their decisions (or in some other writing or public address). Once the red velour curtain closes and the Justices disappear behind it, secrecy closes in. How they act in their inner sanctums is seldom revealed to the public. On rare occasions, the veil of secrecy is breached, and the collected papers of some departed Justices tell historians, and those who read history, some of what occurred in the past. (Publication in 1979 of Bob Woodward and Scott Armstrong's *The Brethren* provided an unprecedented glimpse of a *sitting* Court, even though some of the data related by the authors are disputed.[28] It is fair to say that the book added little to the knowledge of those who make a practice of studying the Court.)

The Justices are law*makers*, in other words, but tell those affected by their "laws" only *what* is decided; they do not reveal *how* the decisions were made. (Opinions supposedly explaining decisions are in large part justifications or rationalizations.) As a consequence, even lawyers who should know how judges operate do not know, as Chief Justice Roger Traynor of the California Supreme Court once observed.[29] Justice Felix Frankfurter said it more pungently: "The fact is that pitifully little of significance has been contributed by judges regarding the nature of their endeavor, and, I might add, that which is written by those who are not judges is too often a confident caricature than a seer's version of the judicial process of the Supreme Court."[30] A parlous situation, indeed. Deliberate obscurantism by a judicial elite makes analysis of the Court much more difficult. Nonetheless, enough is known, or can reasonably be inferred, about the Justices to enable one to reach at least tentative conclusions (and avoid expressing a caricature). The law is a species of human action, and there is no reason to believe that judges act differently from other human beings.

Does judicial secrecy jibe with democratic theory? The answer can only be an emphatic no. That, however, is only a partial picture. Many governmental decisions are secretly arrived at, particularly in the higher levels of the executive branch, and few are privy to what actually occurs in Congress. Formal votes are far from enough to lend adequate knowledge and understanding. All too often, indeed, not only the process but the decisions themselves are kept from the public—as in national security matters.[31] Americans are governed much more by fiat than the myth would have it—which is one reason why, when describing the government of the United States, it is useless and misleading to employ the word *democracy* as if it meant something precise.[32] It does not.

The Court has a gestation period of nine months, sometimes longer, but it can and does give birth to numerous decisions along the way. At the end of June or in early July, the Justices take a postpartum rest until the first Monday in October. (That does not mean a three-month vacation, for much of the summary decisions—in legalese, the denials of petitions for *certiorari* ["for review"]—can be done during the summer.) Many of the most important rulings come late in term—in May or June. Those issued earlier are the easy ones, plus the approximately 4,400 decisions not to decide (to review) a lower court decision.

The 4,500 or so decisions made each year may seem to be an onerous burden. Indeed, some of the Justices (and their minions in the legal profession) complain about the work load. Those complaints are ill founded. Most Supreme Court decisions are made rapidly and anonymously. In an acerbic shaft, aimed no doubt at Chief Justice Warren Burger, who strongly advocates reduction of the Court's work load, Justice William O. Douglas asserted in 1975: "We are far today from facing an emergency. For in all frankness, no Justice of this Court need work more than four days a week to carry his burden. I have found it a comfortable burden even in my months of hospitalization."[33] Douglas, however, was a *rara avis*, and no doubt he exaggerated a bit. The critical question to answer is this: How long does it take a Justice to decide to grant or deny a petition for review? A few minutes at most is an accurate answer. One man, no longer on the Court, once said he could do it in fifteen seconds. Each Justice has, or can have, at least three law clerks to help sort through the mountains of petitions. That means that he or she can (and does) delegate much of the work to subordinates, who write summaries of each case. The ultimate decision is that of the Justice, but the spade work has been done before the time to decide.

At times, moreover, the eight Associate Justices merely silently concur in the Chief's recommendations. He circulates a list of cases he believes to be unworthy of review. Seldom is a case removed from that list, although of course it can be. That is one means of reducing what outwardly seems to be an onerous work load. So much, one might say, for the Rule of Law in the Supreme Court. Secret, quick, and unexplained "justice" is the lot of most litigants—in all except the 140 or so cases fully reviewed.[34] Taking a case to the Court means, first, that the petitioner must have a "federal question"—one dealing with some aspect of federal law—and, second, that even if he does, he has only one chance in twenty-five of getting the full-scale attention of the Justices. Justice Frankfurter once snorted that the Justices do not sit like Muslim kadis under trees, dispensing justice by whim and caprice[35]—but can speedy, anonymous, and unexplained decisions be otherwise characterized? (This is not to say that Frankfurter was correct in his description of Muslim judicial practice. He was not.)

Refusals to rule are never explained. On occasion, however, dissents are filed, with reasons stated. In most instances, four Justices must agree to review a case—those that come up on "writ of *certiorari*." Some requests for review (technically called "appeals") are supposedly mandatory. In practice, they are treated much the same as "*certs*." That has an important consequence: The Justices have complete discretion over which cases will be given full-dress treatment.[36] Even cases falling within the Court's "original" jurisdiction—those in which it sits as a trial court—are, despite constitutional language that could be construed otherwise, discretionary.[37] That, then, is the Rule of Law in the Supreme Court: The Justices decide what they will decide, and when they do make decisions on the merits, they are not bound by pre-existing rules of law. When to that is added the fact that many opinions are written in opaque language, more than a casual resemblance between the Supreme Court and the Oracle at Delphi may be discerned.

Judges do not work too hard. Their task is no larger than what conscientious members of Congress face each year and surely is less than what high-level executive officers routinely grapple with. Chief Justice Burger, to be sure, is not alone among judges in thinking to the contrary. But even he is bearing up remarkably well. No Justice, furthermore, ever died from overwork. Indeed, they tend to live as long or longer than their countrymen. They have time for reflection and to write (or, at least, to approve) lengthy and occasionally readable opinions—opinions that frequently tend to obscure more than enlighten. That shortcoming causes confusion among lawyers and lower-court judges, who often must apply cryptic language to new situations, and is the source of much adverse comment in legal and political science journals.

There is a pragmatic reason for opinions that do not opine: Often they are the result of a process of bargaining—they are negotiated documents—which means that the writer must meet a common denominator of assent. Hence a Justice will alter or water down language that at the outset might have been clear and straightforward in order to gain the vote of a colleague or to stave off a concurring opinion. That means that the Rule of Law at times becomes, in substantial part, the Rule of Barter Economics and also that the Court is a political institution, not only in its product—its decisions—but in its internal operations.[38] Some Justices—Felix Frankfurter was an example—often engage in what one of his colleagues called "proselytizing," by which he meant that Frankfurter actively campaigned to change his colleagues's minds.[39] He even went so far as to try to influence law clerks of the other Justices as means of indirectly persuading colleagues to agree with him.[40] (To gain an inkling of how Frankfurter operated, one should read the novel *The Vicar of Christ*, by Walter Murphy. Possibly Murphy's portrait is overdrawn, but it accurately portrays the way an Associate Justice tried to manipulate a new Chief Justice and the Court. No special insight is needed to conclude that Murphy's model was Frankfurter.)

III.

The Marble Palace looms on Capitol Hill in Washington, midway between the Capitol and Senate Office Buildings. An imposing and austere structure, the Supreme Court's work place obviously was designed to reflect the dignity and solemnity of the High Bench as the highest court in the land. (Before it was built in the 1930s, the Justices sat in a small room in the Capitol.) Carved deeply in the facade of the Palace is the slogan "Equal Justice Under Law," a sentiment that expresses an ideal, not the actuality. It is dubiously valid on two and perhaps all three points—*equality* and *law* for certain, and *justice*, possibly, depending of course upon how the words are defined.

The Temple—the courtroom—is the only place to which the general public has access. Lawyers can use the library, but only if they are members of the bar of the Court. The Justices can, of course, be visited in their offices, but only with prior appointments that get one past security guards. A fortresslike atmosphere characterizes the Palace. In the Temple itself, self-important marshals scurry up and down aisles to stop spectators from whispering or taking notes. Why note taking is prohibited is an unexplained mystery; after all, reporters, who sit in an anteroom off the Temple, may do so. Solemnity, even pomposity, rules, except for one odd spectacle: Members of the bar of the Court can and do sit in a special section. Endowed with special privileges, they tramp in and out en masse when one case ends and before another begins. That disrupts the harmony and decorum of the Temple, but no one seems to mind.

Colloquies the Justices have with lawyers are for the most part classic examples of legal boredom. Some Justices have been known to fall asleep while lawyers drone on. From time to time a lawyer is interrupted by one of the "Council of Elders," to get clarification on a fine point (or, as Frankfurter attempted, to skewer him with his flashing intellect). For the most part, those on the High Bench seem to pay attention to what is being said, although no one save the Justices themselves know what is passing through their minds. One who did not pay much attention was William O. Douglas, who could often be observed busily writing and even occasionally turning his back on a lawyer and gazing into space.

How much impact those ritualized conversations that lawyers hold with Justices have on the final decision is unknown. But their importance may be doubted, except for some of the more controversial cases. Oral argument serves more of a symbolic than informing function; it gives the *appearance* of justice. Since, however, little is known about the actual mental processes of judges, some of what is said in the Temple may have an effect. As for the lawyers who appear in the Temple, their performances are frequently mediocre at best. Many come from the hinterlands and insist on arguing their own cases, even though they know little about the Supreme Court. They refuse to hire a recognized expert to appear for them. An official report rendered to the Chief Justice in 1972 maintained that "the average level of oral advocacy in the Court . . . is disappointingly low."[41] The same may be said for many of their "briefs"—their written submissions to the Court—many of which would not pass muster in a good law school class. The inadequacy of counsel likely is one of the reasons why the Justices routinely feel compelled to do what Justice William Brennan called "independent research.'"[42] In other words, they are not bound by what lawyers bring to them and thus can be self-starters to some degree. (That, again, cuts against the basic assumptions of the Rule-of-Law concept and allows even more discretion in the Justices. That the "adversary system" needs improvement has become obvious.)

Once a week the nine Justices convene in a committee of the whole to which no one else is admitted. If messages must be transmitted, the Associate Justice with least seniority is the messenger. At this writing, that is Sandra Day O'Connor, named to the Court by President Reagan. Conference activities may be the most closely guarded secret in Washington; if not the most, then surely one of the most. As a consequence, the Court may be a modern oracle, but it labors in secret its wonders to perform. (Publication of *The Brethren* breached that zone of privacy, to some degree, but it is fair to say that it merely made available to the people at large what has long been known by the cognoscenti.)

Whether secrecy is essential to the effective working of the Court is, at most, debatable.[43] Quite possibly, mystery adds to the prestige, and thus to the power, of the Court. But no one really knows, for it has always been so. In any event, the High Bench has a mystique that only rarely permits penetration of the inner sanctum. That mystique also prevents one from speaking lightly of the dignity of the Court, for courts generally, and certainly the Supreme Court, are highly revered by most Americans. That is so even though some of the Justices seem to be overwhelmed with pomposity, taking themselves much too seriously. That attitude is encouraged by the priesthood of the bar. Perhaps secrecy and pomposity serve a deep human need. As Fyodor Dostoyevsky maintained in his famous "Legend of the Grand Inquisitor," people need miracle, mystery, and authority.[44] Secrecy gives the mystery and pomposity the appearance of authority.

Of one thing we can be sure: Judges are human and, as such, prey to all of the shortcomings of the human intellect. Some try, and in trying partially succeed, to surmount those shortcomings, but all judges carry what Oliver Wendell Holmes once called their "can't-helps" around with them—as in the statement "I can't help believing such-and-such." As with all persons, judges are prisoners of their heredity and biography.

IV.

In this volume, the Supreme Court and courts generally are defended, even with full recognition of their manifest inadequacies, and urged to do even more—but only, to repeat for emphasis, in certain directions. Judicial activism has been under sharp attack in recent years—from within the legal profession, from neoconservatives, from those whose oxen have been gored by particular decisions, from those who believe that judges have forsaken "Sovereign Reason" and made decisions on fiat alone, and from those who assert that law (and judges) cannot adequately deal with many human activities. These critics, generally, miss the point. They misread history, and they do not have an adequate conception of the role of courts in a nation that trumpets it is a democracy. They display a faith in the workings of the political process (even though they never analyze that process as they do the judiciary). Journalist Anthony Lewis asserted in 1980 that what mattered in the Court is "the quality of [the Justices's] reasoning"[45]—a statement that is not even a half-truth. Even so, Lewis stated the popular—the conventional —wisdom about the Supreme Court. What matters in the Court, as in all political institutions, is who wins or loses. How the game is played is secondary to that fundamental goal.

Judges are indispensable to the American constitutional order. If the Supreme Court did not exist, it or something similar would have to be invented. A written basic law requires that one organ have the power to say what the law means when other institutions of government are at loggerheads or when some person is treated indecently by government. This book, however, is no uncritical encomium. The judiciary has flaws—some deep-seated and of long duration—both in personnel and in methods of operation. It will not do to believe in "the cult of the robe" and thus to think that today's judges perforce have a wisdom denied others. They do not. But they do have, if they are at all conscientious, time for reflection and for taking the long view about specific public policies. The best judges have been those who saw things entire and had the ability to cut through the dross lawyers brought to them, to reach the core of the human disputes assigned to courts for settlement.

It is important to realize that only the exceptional human dispute ever gets to any court, let alone the Supreme Court. Most disagreements are settled by other means. The Justices cannot reach out and identify an area for their attention; they must await the accident of litigation. Only the pathological, the "hospital" cases, reach the judiciary. Americans are notoriously legalistic and like to use courts, but even with the explosion in litigation in recent years, judicial decisions are noteworthy for their rarity rather than being quantitatively, even qualitatively, central to the governing system. Furthermore, lawsuits cost far too much and take far too much time. Most people cannot pay or cannot wait. There is too much uncertainty in a lawsuit, the law being much more fluid than the laity believes. Judge Learned Hand once said that he would avoid going to court, for next to "sickness and death," it was to be shunned.[46]

If some of the following text seems to be irreverent, that does not mean that I do not believe in the judiciary. Honoré Balzac said it well, in language that is an underlying theme of this essay: "To distrust the judiciary marks the beginning of the end of society. Smash the present patterns of the institution, rebuild it on a different basis . . . but don't stop believing in it."[47] To rebuild is vitally necessary, and to do so requires precise knowledge of what the Supreme Court has been and is (the task of Part I).

The Court is neither honored nor helped by being considered to be beyond criticism. Much of the present-day criticism, however, is destructive; the apparent aim is to trim the Justices's sails. Some go so far as to maintain in shrill tones that today's Court has been acting unconstitutionally. Others more circumspect implore the nine Justices to pursue "passive virtues."[48] Whatever the language used, those critics—and there are many—want to reduce what they perceive as the excessive power of the Justices to force their will upon a frustrated body politic. Displaying a simplistic view of the political process, they assert a touching faith in "majority rule"—precisely what has never been true in the United States.

My ultimate aim is to suggest possible ways by which those called upon to judge their fellow humans can aid in the endless search for realization of the values of the democratic ideal, cast against a necessarily brief examination of what is ecologically possible. Law in philosophic terms is, and always has been, instrumental or teleological, not an end in itself. Law is purposive human behavior; its goal is—at least, should be—human welfare (the welfare of all, not merely the few). It is to that end that the Justices should bend their efforts. That essentially calls for a new role for the Supreme Court of the United States, one even greater than that which the Justices themselves have undertaken.

The pretense is that law is not instrumental—that preexisting rules of law control (or should control) in litigation. As it is at times put, the Supreme Court should make "principled" decisions. (Exactly what a "principled" decision is, or might be, no one seems to know—or, at least, to divulge.)[49] The pretense has long been under attack (although, as has been mentioned, a counterattack has now been mounted). The Rule of Law, if it means anything, usually connotes a picture of interdictory standards of conduct to which people are supposed to adhere. Furthermore, it means that if one searches long and hard enough, the *one* relevant rule to decision can be identified. If not that, neutral principles of law can be identified and applied in adjudication.

No one privy to the facts of law and adjudication should believe that. It is a myth—the Basic Myth of American law. That some assert that they do believe it, and consequently demand that judges live up to it, bespeaks a mind either bemused by legal mythology or one that dislikes the results reached when judges proceed contrary to the pretense. Knowledgeable observers know—at least, they *should* know—that it is the Justices, not interdictory law, who speak in constitutional and other cases. Through that recognition comes the further inescapable conclusion that the basic question, the question that must always be answered in judicial and other governmental actions, is *cui bono*? Who benefits in fact from those decisions? The ostensible beneficiary likely may be quite different from the actual or real one. Answering that basic question requires, at the very least, that primary attention be paid to the social impacts, the consequences, of decisions rather than merely to the rulings themselves and the manner in which they are explained. To repeat: Who wins or loses (actually or ostensibly or both) is as important in litigation, and perhaps more so, than how the game is played. Those in the professoriate and elsewhere who do not like that concept cannot refute it, once it is conceded, as it must be, that the Court is a political body.[50] There is no one prescribed way for judges to operate. The "rules" of judicial behavior, such as they are, are not rules at all; they permit enormous discretion—the polar opposite of the orthodox notion of the Rule of Law.

Recently, it has become clear that Supreme Court Justices are themselves searching for a new role. Discussed below are both the details of what is being, and what might further be, done by the Court. It is enough now to say that it involves, at the very least, *openly* being a "superlegislature," stating norms of general applicability—that is, law or policy for people generally rather than merely settling the dispute of the parties in court. That idea is something new under the constitutional sun, at least in its openness; it does not date before 1958.[51] Also, it has brought storms of controversy swirling around the Marble Palace. Americans have never been able to reconcile the ideas of popular sovereignty and representative government with laws made by judges having life tenure, who at times decide in ways some think are contrary to "the will of the people."

V.

Toward Increased Judicial Activism has four parts. First is a history of judicial activism, accompanied by an evaluation of the main attacks on modern activism. Next comes a discussion of the disarray of the political order—of "pluralism"—in which it is argued that there is no authoritative spokesman for national values (for the "national" or "public" interest). Americans, believing the incessant propaganda about democracy, have created major problems of governance, particularly with the expansion of the franchise and of an educated populace. Third is discussion of the emergent Constitution of Control—the fourth American fundamental law—together with an examination of how such sacred documents are interpreted. Here it is posited that the Court has attained at least tacit recognition and acceptance as a "Council of Elders." Fourth, the Supreme Court and its mission under the emergent Constitution of Control is analyzed, cast against the background of the coming "steady-state" society. Perhaps of most importance, recommendations for more Supreme Court activism are made, accompanied by specific recommendations for reform of the system of judicial decision making.

Several assumptions underlie the ensuing discussion. They include:

1. The Supreme Court is now and always has been deeply immersed in politics. Indeed, it would have little meaning or function outside of politics—not politics in the invidious sense, but as the Justices being political actors interacting with other governmental officers, stating norms of conduct, and also in its internal operations. Those norms are law—the highest law, "the law of the land."

2. The Court makes approximately 140 decisions on the merits each year, as compared with the 300 to 400 public laws enacted by Congress. It is, therefore, a significant "third legislative chamber."

3. The Court has self-assumed power to say what the law is. When it does, the law so stated is not found—it does not preexist—but is created anew.

4. The Justices as a de facto Council of Elders may be likened to the oracles of ancient Greece. For the Greeks (and Romans), an oracle was a person believed to be in communication with the deity—thus, a person of great knowledge and wisdom. The Temple on the Hill is the place where supposedly wise and dispassionate men are consulted. (Was it with tongue in cheek that one commentator once asserted that "in our tripartite constitutional system, the Supreme Court Justices are 'brushed with divinity'"?)[52] They are, so the Justices (tacitly) affirm, endowed with a unique capacity to have knowledge of a set of absolute values, at times called "natural law" or "natural justice," superior to man-made principles of positive law. That has definite theological overtones, which means that:

5. The Court cannot be understood apart from its religious aspects. The Constitution is a theological document—the basic instrument of our civil or secular religion—and the Justices are the High Priests who keep it current with each generation of Americans.

6. The Document of 1787 is a politico-legal palimpsest, a parchment that still exists, upon which patinas of usage and custom—of interpretation—may be discerned.

7. Anglo-American law until the end of the nineteenth century was largely judge-made. Legislatures are latter-day institutions; they in turn have been supplanted in substantial part by administrative agencies. Americans live, as a consequence, in the "bureaucratic" or "administrative" state. Those bureaucracies are both public and private.

8. Courts, including the Supreme Court, are not central to the governing process. They are important but are overshadowed by the avowedly political branches of government.

9. The State and the legal system are closely intertwined.

10. Constitutional interpretation is distinctly not a judicial monopoly. Both Congress and the President make decisions of constitutional dimension. So, too, do the officers of the "private" governments of the nation—the giant corporations are the principal example—which in fact are correctly called "quasi-polities." (They have constitutional and legal systems of their own, separate from the political—the public—organs.) In the United States, sovereignty is shared between the institutions of public government and decentralized centers of power.

11. When rendering constitutional decisions, the Justices create the law as they go along. The question is not whether they do so, for that is beyond dispute; rather, the questions are how much? In what direction? For whose benefit?

12. The Constitution is always in a state of becoming, always being updated to meet the exigencies faced by successive generations of the American people. Each generation writes its own constitution.

13. Decisions in constitutional cases are seldom answered by the Document itself; nor can answers be found in a bootless quest for the intentions of the Founding Fathers. Those decisions are far more types of political accommodations than logical deductions from the Document.

14. Law is not a homeless, wandering ghost. It is a species of human action, created and administered by identifiable human beings. It is not so much *a priori* as *a posteriori*.

15. The United States (and the entire world) is deeply immersed in a time of continuing troubles, a time when coalescing crises inexorably point to one of the great changes in human history. Humankind is in a climacteric, not a crisis.

Each assumption obviously requires greater specificity. That will come in ensuing chapters. They are listed now merely to provide a point of departure for what follows. "The place one comes out . . . depends largely on where one starts."[53] I start with those assumptions and end with a plea that the Court do more to help bring the ideals of constitutionalism into reality. I do not pretend that much, even most, of what is said is "objective." As Gunnar Myrdal has shown, one cannot escape his valuations when writing about any social science subject.[54] Objectivity or impartiality is a chimera, as Chapter 2 shows. Myrdal also suggested the need for one to "face his valuations"—to state them. I do so in brief form: My fundamental valuation is that of human dignity on a planetary scale—the dignity of all, not merely the few. That, to be sure, is abstract, but it will be seen as less so in subsequent chapters.

2
The Mythology of the Court

I.

The Supreme Court moves in mysterious ways its wonders to perform. The mystery is deliberate, carefully nurtured by bench and bar and media. *The Brethren* and a few books written by scholars[1] have been criticized as much for breaching the wall of secrecy as for possible errors of fact. In this chapter, that notion—that secrecy serves a useful purpose—is discussed, together with some other myths that eddy around the Temple in the Marble Palace.

Lawyers (and others) pretend that what judges choose to write in their opinions accurately portrays the mental processes of judging. A by-product of that belief is the assertion, often made, that what matters about the Court is the quality of the Justices's reasoning. Scholars write long and occasionally readable articles and books, minutely scrutinizing and dissecting judicial opinions. That serves limited, albeit useful, purposes. Of most importance: since what is said about decisions is part of the environment in which the Justices operate, those writings have at least a subtle influence on them. Judges, as with other humans, crave approbation. They do not suffer criticism gladly. The extent to which they react to it cannot, of course, be known. Scholars help to set the climate of opinion. The increasing frequency that scholarly articles are cited and quoted in judicial opinions is silent testimony that at least some of what is written in legal and political science periodicals comes to the attention of judges. (That is so even though the burgeoning use of such articles coincides almost exactly in time with a widespread use of law clerks by judges. Those clerks, most of whom are fresh out of law school, write memorandums; often, portions of them are published as part of the judges's opinions.)

A second purpose of scholarly articles and books is this: Professors can by publishing them attain the status of "tenure," and lawyers can also pretend that law is a science. So hundreds of thousands of students file through law school, each propagandized with the idea that there can be a scientific study of law by reading appellate court opinions—and that those opinions are all that need be known. Law is supposedly a seamless web of internally consistent principles. Nothing could be further from the truth. Legal education, in general, is a legalized form of brain damage, routinely inflicted upon unsuspecting but willing neophytes. Law professors like to say that studying law sharpens the mind by narrowing it—as if that were the only valid goal. It is not. Lawyers should have both sharp *and* broad-gauged minds. (That belief has an important consequence for a matter discussed below—the type of person who should be named to the Supreme Court. Bad education plus narrow client-oriented practice makes the legal profession as the sole source of new Justices a poor one indeed. The pool from which talent is drawn should be widened.)

In its most insidious form, the brain damage suffered by law students takes the form of an unthinking dogma, the fundamental ideology of the profession: "legalism."[2] Under that mind-set, law is considered to be "there," separate and apart not only from the remainder of human knowledge but also from any considerations of morality. One has a good legal mind, under this view, if one can think of something tightly connected to some other thing but without thinking of that other thing. That, of course, is a manifest impossibility, but it does not deter law professors, who blithely proceed to teach law as being divorced from politics and economics. To them, a heaven of legal concepts exists, from which lawyers and judges can draw appropriate and relevant principles for the resolution of human disputes. Legalism as a belief system is not only profoundly erroneous and useless; it can be dangerous. But it exists, nonetheless. Only when a Justice is able to "rise above principle"—that is, to forgo legalism—can he operate adequately as a member of America's Council of Elders.

The consequences of unthinking adherence to legalism are multiple—and significant. Each year thousands of young men and women seek to become lawyers by taking state bar examinations. Those tests, given and graded by lawyers, are also based on the ideology of legalism. Most pass them and are admitted (studying law is more tedious than difficult). Neither they nor their peers who were admitted in the past have much more than a foggy notion of how appellate courts in fact operate and, on graduation, have no knowledge at all about trial courts—where most litigation begins and ends. Of more importance, new lawyers must immediately engage in self-education in critical matters that are brought to them—in economics, politics, science and technology, psychology, and a host of other relevant areas. Another consequence is even more important—those affected, both directly and indirectly, by what lawyers and lawyer-judges do will find their human affairs cast in legalistic verbiage; that result gives lawyers an inordinate amount of influence on public policy. This situation, together with legalism, has been called the "lawyer as astrophysicist" assumption,[3] namely, that the "generalist" training of lawyers allows any lawyer to read a text on astrophysics and launch a rocket a few days later. Law professors assert, and teach their students to believe, that all that students require is "the law"—for which read "appellate court opinions"—and if they need to know economics, an economist can always be brought in for a quick and theoretically adequate briefing. That view, at best, is a pathetic fallacy.

Should one be amused or appalled by the fact that a law student, after spending three years and several thousand dollars perusing appellate court opinions, knows only what a few judges choose to tell him? Surely the public is being ill served by the system of legal education. That likelihood, however, is ancillary to my main point—that the judicial opinion is neither a *description* of what occurred in a judge's chambers (or Supreme Court conference) nor a true *explanation* of the reasons for a given decision. At most, an opinion *justifies or rationalizes* that decision. When written in words and syntax familiar to lawyers, it is considered to be good—without regard to what was actually decided. The method, the ritual, thus becomes more important than the consequence—more important, that is, to lawyers and law professors (mainly the latter, for they make their living analyzing judicial opinions). "A court of law which achieves a desirable result by an inexact use of legal conceptions arouses more criticism from legal scholars," Thurman Arnold observed in 1935, "than one which achieves an undesirable result in a learned way."[4] That conclusion is still accurate. Oddly, felicity in language and erudite reasoning are, for many, a substitute for justice (the just result). (Law schools do not teach justice; they teach law, and a student who asks about the justice or morality of some decision is sardonically advised to transfer to divinity school.)

Professors and lawyers generally either do not realize or, if they do, do not acknowledge that "there is no there *there*" (as Gertrude Stein acidly described Oakland, California). Legalism is intellectual bankruptcy. This chapter examines some of the orthodox views about the Supreme Court. The conclusion is that there is no there *there*, that the beliefs are largely mythical and should be recognized as such, but that because of a large capacity for self-delusion, the orthodoxy is perpetuated. The chasm between pretense and reality must be bridged if the Court is to accomplish, as it should, an even greater mission than in the past. "The time is past in the history of the world," Felix Frankfurter (as professor, not Justice) asserted, "when any living man or body of men can be set on a pedestal and decorated with a halo. . . . It is not good, either for the country or the Court, that the part played by the [Supreme] Court in the life of the country should be shrouded in mystery."[5] That statement is the theme of this chapter (but I do not suggest that Frankfurter would have agreed with what is said here).

Not all believe that the web of myth should be stripped from the Court. Some consider it better to keep the Temple on the Hill enshrouded in fog—not unlike the Delphic Oracle—apparently because they think that "ordinary" Americans have neither the moral nor the mental stamina to withstand the unvarnished truth about judging. Or they believe that the Court

would be harmed if people knew what went on within the Marble Palace
Consider these statements, the first by a political scientist and the second by a
law professor: "The distinction between what the Court tells the public about
its activities and what scholars tell one another must be kept firmly in mind,"
asserted Professor Martin Shapiro; he went on to maintain that "it would be
fantastic if the Supreme Court, in the name of sound scholarship, were to
disavow publicly the myth upon which its power rests."[6] The myth Shapiro
mentioned is what we call the Basic Myth—that it is "the law" and not judges
that controls in constitutional cases.

So, too, with Professor Paul Mishkin, who asserted that there is a "strongly
held and deeply felt belief that judges are bound by a body of fixed, overriding
law, that they apply the law impersonally as well as impartially, that they
exercise no individual choice and have no program of their own to
advance."[7] That view, he admitted, may "be in part myth, [but] it is a myth by
which we live and which can be sacrificed only at substantial cost." Although
acknowledging that the truth behind the myth ought not to be obscured from
anyone wishing to learn and to take the trouble to understand, Mishkin went
on to assert:

At the same time, I see no affirmative value in the destruction of essentially sound and
valuable symbols in order to promulgate a part of a more sophisticated—and indeed
overall more accurate—general view. Such partial truths do not necessarily represent a
gain in wisdom over the more elementary general view, and the destruction of the
symbol does involve real loss. Though I know judges are human and quite distinct
individuals, I am not in favor of their doffing their robes, for I think there is value in
stressing, for themselves and for others, the quite real striving for impartiality I know
can never be fully achieved.[8]

That remark is an interesting theory, but one that is full of holes. It is the
modern counterpart to Plato's "noble lie" or "magnificent myth." In *The
Republic*, the Greek philosopher divided people into three classes—guardians (which included rulers and auxiliaries), farmers, and workers (most of the
citizenry). Rulers were to exercise supreme authority in the State, and the
auxiliaries were to be enforcers—those who carried out the orders of the
rulers. Plato sketched a Foundation Myth, under which each member of the
community was fashioned by a god. Gold was added to the composition of
those qualified to be rulers, silver to the auxiliaries, and iron and bronze to the
workers. Everything rulers did was for the good of the community. Children
were to be moved from class to class, depending on their merit and capability.
Only those with gold in their makeup could be rulers, "because there is a
prophecy that the State will be ruined when it has Guardians [that is, rulers] of
silver and bronze."[9]

Plato has been criticized for the Foundation Myth, because it suggests that
he advocates manipulation of the people by propaganda.[10] But he believed
that everyone accepted it. "It is meant to replace the national traditions which

any community has, which are intended to express the kind of community it is, or wishes to be, its ideals, rather than to state matters of fact."[11] Plato did not believe in democracy. An elitist, he advocated a type of managerial meritocracy. His conception of philosopher-rulers, often called philosopher-kings, has long endured, as witness Judge Learned Hand's 1958 comment that he would find it irksome to be ruled by a group of Platonic guardians.[12] Hand was referring to the Supreme Court of the United States. (This idea will be developed later; Hand spoke in hyperbole: If the Supreme Court "rules" in the United States, it is only in small part—far less, for example, than the President.)

At least a slight similarity exists between Plato's Foundation Myth and the Basic Myth of the American legal system. Those who believe, with Professors Shapiro and Mishkin, that truth in judging should be kept from the public are also elitists. They are willing to propagate a myth, even though far from "magnificent," or a noble lie. In this, they resemble the squid and may be said to be engaging in "squid jurisprudence"—covering the facts about the Supreme Court with a cloud of opaque black ink. Where an intellectual elite gets a warrant for keeping truth from the people is completely mysterious. Surely Americans are entitled to know not only the rules—the laws—by which they are governed, but also how those laws are made. We may live by symbols, at least in part, that help us to grapple with the problems of a mysterious and foreboding environment, but that is no argument for deliberate obfuscation. Planned obscurantism by an elite—self-appointed and who talk mainly to each other—cannot be justified. Furthermore, with the spread of higher education and with greater attention to the mass media to Supreme Court activities, by no means can it be said that the professoriate is ahead of many in the public.

That belief in obscurantism is only the first of the faults in the Shapiro/Mishkin analyses. Their assumption that the truth can be kept from the public is dubious at best. *The Brethren* proved that the Court can be penetrated, raising the question of whether it would not have been far better for the Justices to have been more open. "To recognize the truth and adjust oneself to it is in the end the easiest and most advisable course," observed philosopher Morris R. Cohen. He went on to say that of course courts "are constantly remaking the law."[13] One must concede, however, that Professors Shapiro and Mishkin stated the accepted wisdom about the Supreme Court —even though that "wisdom" is demonstrably faulty.

Another fault is that they base their views on the belief that truth in judging, openly told to the American people, would involve some type of "real loss." That belief, however, is a mere assertion, rather than a statement based on empirical facts. How do they know that harm would result, particularly since judicial secrecy and the Basic Myth have always prevailed? The Court does not seem to have been harmed by publication of *The Brethren*. Third, how a social loss would occur is difficult to fathom. What value is there in governmental secrecy? Is it "functional"? Does it serve a useful purpose? If so, what is it? The advocates of judicial obscurantism do not tell us. They neglect the insight of Lord Acton: "Everything degenerates, even the administration of justice, nothing is safe that does not show it can bear discussion and publicity."[14] As long ago as 1821, Thomas Jefferson railed against judicial secrecy: "Another most condemnable practice of the Supreme Court is that of cooking up a decision in caucus and delivering it by one of their members as the opinion of the court, without the possibility of our knowing how many, how, and for what reasons each member concurred."[15] Jefferson, to be sure, was a partisan, a strong opponent of Chief Justice John Marshall who headed the Court in 1821. He was only partially correct. Even if each Justice gave his or her opinion publicly, no one should think that what is said really expresses the thought processes of judges. In recent years the Court has been producing multiple opinions, and in at least one instance, the famous Pentagon Papers case of 1971,[16] there were nine opinions by nine Justices. The consequence, however, was more rather than less obfuscation.

Shapiro and Mishkin are inaccurate on other scores. Candor about the Court does not require that the Justices doff their robes or that the pomp and ceremony of judicial proceedings be eliminated. Rituals, even though known as such, have some merit. Impartiality would be a virtue were it attainable, which it certainly is not in any complete sense. No doubt it should be sought; in Frankfurter's words, judges should practice "an invincible disinterestness" and "not draw on [their] merely personal and private notions."[17] To him "detachment and objectivity" were indispensable. No doubt Frankfurter thought he met those exacting standards. That he did not is obvious—to all except his idolators. Not that he was alone: the human mind is a frail tool, not capable of anything approaching complete detachment and objectivity. The requirement thus becomes (as is argued at length subsequently) one of being avowedly *partial*. (The argument below concerns the means by which the Court might help attain a higher degree of human dignity in the coming Age of Scarcity. I recognize that both *human dignity* and the *Age of Scarcity* are terms that mask an enormous complexity.)

Fictions have a way of becoming pernicious. Keeping the secrets about the Supreme Court within the priesthood of the bar will ultimately destroy respect for the Court. Truth will out, late or soon, and it is far better for the revelation to come sooner and from truly knowledgeable sources. Otherwise it will dribble out, as in *The Brethren*, and distortions will be inevitable. Opening the Court to greater public knowledge will not, however, happen—at least in the foreseeable future. The High Bench is a small group—a bureaucracy. All bureaucracies, as Max Weber observed, value secrecy.[18] "Secrecy is a disease as natural to government as sclerosis of the liver is to drunks. Bureaucracies hide their mistakes like an alcoholic hides bottles."[19] The quotation is not from Weber; he would have gone further and said that bureaucrats like to hide their activities (as well as their mistakes). The Justices hide, if not their mistakes (after all, their decisions are in the public record), the mysteries of the inner sanctum. The Temple on the Hill is both a sacred place (for the secular religion of constitution worship) and a center for the difficult art of judging. Note: judging is not a science; it is an art—an art, moreover, that with the Supreme Court in recent decades knows fewer and fewer restraints. Supreme Court Justices today have, to speak generally and sententiously, broken with much of the judicial tradition. They are feeling their way onto new ground, even unknown territory, searching for a role as a part of the government of a society that is far different from that which existed in 1800, 1850, 1900, or even 1940. It is obvious that they have not yet found that role.

II.

Any anthropologist will testify that myth is one of the more interesting features of any culture. Europeans and Americans like to travel to far-off lands to study what they call primitive societies, not recognizing that their own nations are as ripe for investigating mythology. That the United States has a set of well-worn and accepted beliefs that qualify as myths cannot be doubted. A myth is a conviction based not on empirical evidence but on faith, a belief wholly resistant to critiques of logic or reason. More precisely, its dictionary meaning is "a purely fictitious narrative usually involving supernatural persons, actions, or events, and embodying some popular idea concerning natural or historical phenomena." Myths are beliefs not in consonance with reality, but not generally known as such. The human mind has an enormous capacity for self-delusion. Myths, however, should not be confused with legal fictions, which are propositions known to be untrue but which are presumed to serve beneficial ends. (The apt example of a legal fiction is calling a corporation a person, even though everyone knows that a disembodied economic entity is in fact a collectivity. In law the corporation is a person, just as you and I are, simply because the Supreme Court so decreed.)[20]

When people act or believe "as if" something were true, they are often engaging in mythological action. Americans are far from immune. Nowhere is this better seen than in a clutch of beliefs that attach to the Constitution and the Supreme Court. Elements of something akin to the supernatural may be perceived in both. Americans are a nation of Constitution worshipers and look to the Supreme Court as a high priesthood whose function it is to administer to the faithful. The Founding Fathers, some of whom helped write the Document of 1787, are the saints in America's Valhalla. That means that we worship our ancestors as well as the Document, Constitution worship, as with many religions, being polytheistic. That reverence is both amusing and pathetic. The Founding Fathers likely would be astonished at the veneration paid to them, were they to come back to life today, for they were, if anything, hard-nosed and hard-bitten men who knew the dark side of human nature and the transiency of man's institutions.

Myths may serve ascertainable purposes, but are they really necessary? Do they serve a useful social purpose? Are they "functional"? Possibly they are. As is discussed at greater length below (Chapter 10), in an outwardly secular nation such as the United States, people must believe in something, if for no other reason than that they are far from wholly rational beings. They hunger for assurance and certainty in a highly uncertain world. So they grasp something, even if that "something" is a secular institution (the Supreme Court) comprised of very human "human beings" and some bits of parchment now almost two centuries old (the written Constitution). Although such beliefs are obviously childish, they are understandable. Man as a species has suffered several intellectual shocks in the past 2,000 years, to a degree that some sort of mental and emotional crutch is apparently needed. Most fundamental is the harsh fact, not yet fully assimilated, that an anthropocentric view of life is no longer possible: Earth is *not* the center of the universe and Homo sapiens is *not* the final goal of the universe.

That fact has been slowly percolating into the human psyche for several hundred years. It is now beyond argument. In the Western world, the anthropocentric view had its genesis in Ptolemaic cosmology, which in turn was reflected in the Judeo-Christian religions. Ptolemy placed man at the center of the universe, a view that found its way from science into religion. His theories led to the view of special creation—the Adam and Eve myth. Only when Copernicus (1473-1543) demonstrated that the planets, including Earth, revolved around the sun did it become known that man was *not* at the center of the universe. Quite the contrary. That was the first of the shocks the human mind has suffered in the past 500 years. It caused John Donne to wail: "'Tis all in peeces, all cohaerence gone," the "all" being the Ptolemaic view of the universe.

That was merely the beginning. Next came Darwin, who forever shattered the conception of special creation. Then, with rapidity, came Freud and Einstein and Heisenberg, who demonstrated that humans are far from rational beings and that one must be chary about scientific absolutes. When Neil Armstrong walked on the moon and pictures were transmitted showing that Earth was a single luminous ball, floating in space whose immensity knows no bounds, the Ptolemaic conception was shattered even for Mr. T. C. Mits— The Celebrated Man in the Street. Suddenly, as time is measured, deep inside humans came the terrible knowledge, present even though inarticulated, that they truly are all alone and afraid, in a world they never made. The scientific underpinning of Western religion has crumbled. Buffeted by winds of change, now of hurricane force, humans—as a species and as individuals —must have something to grasp. A secular society that views the Constitution as at least a partial substitute for God has little other than the Basic Myth to clasp. That belief, however, is becoming so tattered and threadbare that it is almost useless. Something more is needed. (That "something," be it said, is not the frantic return to fundamentalist religious sects, now so apparent. No truly thoughtful person can believe in that attempted resurrection of long-exploded ideas. Churches as Sunday-morning social clubs, however, serve the useful purpose of helping to satisfy the herd instinct of many people. As such, they help to "socialize" those who attend.)

For many years, the Basic Myth and other myths were useful. Through the pretense that law was a neutral force, and that judges were impartial spokesmen of the law, the Basic Myth helped quell discontent. If people, that is, could think they were getting a fair shake of the social dice, they would be more willing to accept social inequities. The Myth served as a unifying, and even at times a civilizing, element in society, helping to bind people together, an intangible cement that aided in making a "united state" out of the United States.

To so unify, reference had to be made to an alleged Golden Age in the past: the time of the American Revolution. Specific men in America's history are accorded a special wisdom. Since they were "present at the creation," the Founding Fathers are central to the creation myth, and thus to the Basic Myth, of the nation. That means, in the words of Professor Michael Kammen, that there is an

awkward anomaly in American thought. Although the founders were themselves engaged in a continuous quest for modes of legitimacy appropriate to their times and needs, subsequent Americans have sought to validate their own aspirations by invoking the innovations and standards of our hallowed pantheon as unchanging verities. This nostalgic vision of the Golden Age actually conjures up an era when values were unclearly defined, when instability often seemed beyond control, when public rancor and private vituperation were rampant, and institutions frail and unformed.[21]

In many respects, that seems remarkably similar to a description of present-day America.

In their myth structure, Americans do not differ, save for the content of specific myths, from other peoples, whether "civilized" or "primitive." Part of our secular religion is to worship the Founding Fathers. Supreme Court Justices know this and frequently invoke what they say are the intentions of the Framers when interpreting the Constitution. Some scholars, learned or otherwise, maintain that resort *must* be made to what those men said to give meaning to the fundamental law today. They would settle modern problems by calling upon men long dead, men who never thought about the specific problems, to give answers. That is at least pathetic, perhaps even bathetic. But it is understandable: People of lesser minds who cannot face the immensity of the universe and of being on a tiny speck in a tiny corner of that universe must, it seems, have something to succor them. That "something" for many Americans is the Constitution and the Founding Fathers. One can be amused, as one should, by such beliefs; but what one cannot do is deny their existence—and their persistence. They exist and persist, because they apparently fulfill deep human needs. That is so even though the Basic Myth, at least for the Supreme Court, is intellectually bankrupt.

III.

The Basic Myth has several corollaries, each of which also qualifies as a myth. Included are the idea that the intentions of the Framers can guide present decisions; the notion that judicial decisions can be logical deductions from the constitutional text; the belief that judges are passionless vehicles for discovering and applying "the law"; and the view that the Justices do not rule on the wisdom of the acts of other governmental officers (but merely on whether their acts comport with the Constitution). None can withstand critical analysis; all, in final perspective, are mythical. So, too, are other views, including: the Supreme Court can be equated with any ordinary court of law; the Court usurped political power; judicial decisions have been a major factor in the growth of crime; and the Supreme Court is an extraordinarily powerful political actor. Each merits attention, but principal concentration here is upon the Basic Myth and its corollaries.

Anyone who believes that the Constitution itself or the intentions of those who wrote it can or should determine the course of present interpretation is fantasizing. Some parts of the Document, of course, admit of no argument. For example, there shall be a president who serves for four years and can be reelected only once, and he must be at least thirty-five years old when first elected. Those rigidities after nearly two centuries can and do cause major problems of governance, as is discussed in Part IV, but they are not our present concern. Beyond the never-litigated provisions are a number of clauses and requirements that are open invitations for debate, and that permit the evolution of the living Constitution. Examples: what is an "establishment of religion" (in the First Amendment)? What is "due process of law"? "Equal protection of the laws"? "Commerce among the states"? "Cruel and unusual punishment"?

These and similar nebulous pronouncements make up the litigable (interpretable) parts of the Constitution and thus provide ample opportunity for government officers—judicial, of course, but also legislative and executive—to say what the law is (what the Document at a particular time means). Our focus is upon those invitations for debate. Those clauses were left to gather meaning from experience and thus may validly be termed examples of the purposive use of ambiguity by the Framers. Those who drafted the Document not only used imprecise language, they also left unstated both who was to interpret the ambiguities and the method that was to be followed. The consequence was a tacit delegation of power to later generations of Americans to rewrite the fundamental law to make it fit the exigencies of differing times. That type of revision is exactly what has happened, although the question now, as has been intimated, is whether major alteration is necessary. In brief, has the time come for a new constitutional convention?

Neither the ambiguities of the Document nor history can be more than a datum, a point of departure from which those who make constitutional decisions proceed. Those generalities are not a set of concepts frozen in time. They permit the Constitution to be an always evolving instrument of governance, always in a state of becoming. As Woodrow Wilson put it, the Document is "Darwinian" rather than "Newtonian," by which he meant that it should be studied and understood as a process and not as a closed, internally consistent body of concepts. The laws of biology, not of classical physics, determine its course. In sum, the Constitution is now and always has been relative to circumstances. "Government is not a machine," said Wilson, "but a living thing. It falls, not under the theory of the universe, but under the theory of organic life. It is accountable to Darwin, not to Newton. It is modified by its environment, necessitated by its tasks, shaped to its functions by the sheer pressure of life."[22]

That may be seen in the operations of the Supreme Court. The Justices routinely *make, not find*, constitutional law, as Justice Byron White candidly admitted in 1966, Chief Justice Earl Warren underscored in 1969, and Justice William Brennan verified in 1980.[23] When they do so, they are, in final analysis, not bound by anything more than the ambiguities of the Constitution (which are an uncertain guide at best) and, in Warren's words, "our own consciences." As we have seen, that is conceded by scholars and also hidden by them, on the theory that the Basic Myth is better for the nation. The question for the Justices in most cases decided on the merits is "what is expedient in the community concerned"—as Oliver Wendell Holmes, speaking of law generally, said in 1881. To Holmes, that was "the secret root from which the law draws all the juices of life."[24]

The idea that the intentions of the Framers can and should guide present decisions is widely accepted, at least on the superficial level, by judges and commentators alike; it is even trumpeted by commentators who should know better. The belief is carefully nourished by the Justices themselves, for the excellent reason that invoking the shades of men who lived in America's alleged Golden Age helps to lend legitimacy to the rulings of the Court. Let no one think, however, that the High Bench is bemused by that notion. In any event, as our secular saints, the Founding Fathers are considered to have had a special wisdom. Some even think they wrought a miracle; witness the oft-quoted language of Britain's prime minister William Gladstone: "The American Constitution is, so far as I can see, the most wonderful work ever struck off at a given time by the brain and purpose of man."[25] Others believe the Document to have been divinely inspired. Gladstone's praise was fulsome, and hardly accurate, but it is believed by many. (Other English observers were far more harsh. Macaulay, for example, thought the Constitution to be "all sail and no anchor";[26] Lord Acton maintained that "weighed in the scales of Liberalism," it was "a monstrous fraud.")[27]

Americans pursue the impossible when they try to bind today's decisions by what was said in yesteryear. It is long past time to lay at rest the notion that the intentions of the Framers should guide what governments do today. First, those intentions, as well as the constitutional language itself, are usually obscure at best. When ascertainable, which is seldom, they tend to be contradictory, as Professor Kammen suggested. Second, they are of the most dubious relevance. Many criteria of constitutional interpretation exist; the "intent of the Framers" is but one of them—and far from the most important.

We cannot, of course, escape history, but adherence to it is not a duty. Nor should it be. Although the shades of men long dead are often invoked, the judge's goal is not so much to prove a point as to lend legitimacy to a given decision. The Justices can make their interpretations of the sacred text more palatable by reading things into the past that may well not have been there. Said more harshly, by purposely employing a fiction, they lead people to believe that the law rules them, not men. Far from an exact science, history at best is an uncertain muse. Each generation of Americans writes its own version of the foggy past. To follow the intent of the Framers is to be ruled from the grave. That means, in final analysis, a dictatorship of the dead over the living (or, more precisely, since those intentions are usually obscure, a dictatorship of what some judge says the Framers intended). The Founding Fathers have been buried. They did their job as well as it could have been done in the circumstances (if one accepts the proposition, itself controversial, that it was better to have a strong national government and a separate executive within it). It is folly compounded to believe that by some occult process of divination, they can be consulted to help solve today's problems and anticipate those of the past emerging future. Let them rest in their graves, and with them the idea that their "intentions" are the best criterion of present-day judgment.

Other than a few antiquarians, who may hide their dislike of *what* is being decided by the Court behind an assertion that proper judicial method is not being followed, most thoughtful observers of Court and Constitution are not deluded by the myth of the Founders's intentions. The astute legal philosopher Morris R. Cohen said it well in 1954: "The pretense that our courts are not expressing the personal opinion of the judges, but only obeying the solemn will of the people as expressed in the law"[28] is both ridiculous and tragic. It becomes even more so when it is "the solemn will" of men long dead that is supposed to control. Even though he was not at the Constitutional Convention (he was ambassador to France), Thomas Jefferson knew that; he said in 1820:

Some men look at constitutions with sanctimonious reverence, and deem them like the ark of the covenant, too sacred to be touched. They ascribe to the men of the preceding age a wisdom more than human, and suppose that what they did to be beyond amendment. I knew this age well; I belonged to it, and labored with it. It deserved well of its country. It was very like the present, but without the experience of the present; and forty years of experience in government is worth a century of book-reading; and this they would say themselves, were they to rise from the dead.[29]

The Constitution, in other words, is not a set of immutable specific truths. The legal instrument that set the nation on its course left the people without a compass to steer by; that compass has been created by nearly 200 years of custom and usage. Nor is the Document, and those who wrote it, the cause of the extraordinary affluence and power that the United States has enjoyed. Those benefits are attributable to a set of "fortuitous, nonreplicable, and nonsustainable factors."[30] The United States has grown and prospered, has waxed strong and powerful, not because of the Constitution but in spite of it.

Plumbing the past will not exorcise the pains of government. Excessive attention to what took place in yesteryear, insofar as it is knowable, serves more to obfuscate than to clarify. The time has come to "awaken from the American Dream."[31] Americans for long lived in a relative paradise, protected by two oceans and the British navy, and the beneficiaries of the enormous riches of a heavily endowed and unexploited continent. Not all profited, to be sure, but enough did to lend some credence to the American Dream. All things seemed possible. But now the burdens of living press hard upon the nation, which for the first time in its history must confront all of the problems that others less fortunate have had for centuries. To repair to the dim past, a past that never really existed, is puerility compounded. Those who drafted the Document set the nation on course, leaving as Jefferson said but one message for future generations: Solve your own problems.

Formal constitutional law develops through litigation. Someone sues another, usually a segment of public government (which itself may be the moving party), in a case that involves constitutional issues. The dozen dozen that each year receive serious attention from the Justices reveal beyond question that litigation is a poor way to make law (which they cannot avoid doing). Americans consider themselves to be highly civilized and rational beings. They believe in the magical power of words through argumentation. If people of goodwill and open minds will discuss a given problem, out of that discussion will come a decision that inures to the benefit of all. That result, at least, is the assumption. So the "adversary system" is employed in lawsuits, even though that assumption is demonstrably faulty.[32] The adversary system is a process that supposedly satisfies, to an adequate degree, this description: As a prelude to a dispute being resolved in court, the interested parties present evidence (attempt to prove their version of the facts and law) and make arguments to a disinterested and impartial arbiter who then decides on the basis of that evidence and those arguments. The system, such as it is, is a legacy from feudal days, taken over from the British legal order when most lawsuits were between private individuals, and applied to constitutional matters—which involve large questions of public policy.

That process makes some sense, but not much. The assumption of the system is more a pretense than a reality. Legal institutions are still mired in a prescientific age, operating on assumptions about the human mind that will not withstand rigid scrutiny. Justices, who usually are "narrow-minded lawyers with little background for making social judgments,"[33] make judgments on constitutional matters; they decide questions that affect all Americans, under a Constitution that has no precise guides for decision. They construe an instrument that is far more than a mere lawyers's document. Some lawyers view it as an ordinary legal document—a contract, a will, a deed—but that merely displays the invincible parochialism of a profession that cannot see the fundamental law for what it is.

Any one of the 140-odd cases chosen each year by the Justices for full-dress treatment is selected not in the interests of the litigants but to further development of the Constitution—subtly to amend it in the interests of a never-defined entity called "society." The Supreme Court cannot be a self-starter; it cannot reach out and select a public-policy problem for scrutiny. With, however, the large number of lawsuits filed in the Court each term, it can pick and choose; since those 4,500 cases cover almost the full range of issues that concern the American people, the Justices therefore can be de facto self-starters. Only litigants can trigger the Court, but they are important only for that reason. The High Bench speaks in terms beyond the immediate parties to society at large. They may not be very good at that, but lack of success does not deter them (as, indeed, it does not deter Congress or the President). The reluctance of the Justices to define *society* and delineate its interests means that their rulings can be asserted to be in the interests of the collectivity called society but can in fact benefit only a small segment of that entity.

The adversary system is a modernized and supposedly civilized version of an older tradition—trial by combat or by ordeal. When the British legal system was being formed, disputes at times were settled by combat—battles between the parties—and he who won the battle prevailed. Another variation was trial by ordeal, whereby an alleged criminal was bound and thrown into water; if he floated and lived, he was innocent. We of course do not do that. Trials have become verbalized tussles; strength of muscle has been transmuted into strength of argument. So the theory goes.

It isn't much of a theory, given the present state of human knowledge. The ideal of the adversary system is far from the tarnished reality. No knowledgeable person thinks that judges are either disinterested or impartial or, furthermore, that their decisions are based entirely, or even mostly, upon what lawyers tell them. Far from it. Decisions frequently derive from data outside of the adversary system, those data that are considered relevant and significant in accordance with the personal philosophies of the judges. Moreover, in constitutional (and usually other) matters, the Justices always have a choice between competing principles of approximately equal persuasiveness. Depending upon the ways cases are presented, all decisions on the merits could be decided either way without much difficulty. This deserves a label: the Principle of Doctrinal Polarity. Constitutional decisions are not "predetermined in the sense that they [are] predestined—their fate pre-established by inevitable laws that follow them from birth to death."[34] Judges must make choices between "two conflicting major premises . . . , one embodying one set of interests, the other embodying the other."[35] Dealing as they do with the "hospital" cases of society—those pathological disputes that cannot be settled by other means of social control—they cannot avoid making that choice. When they do, law is created—always.

A lawsuit is really an extraordinary event, one of the least used ways of settling human disputes. Most human transactions and controversies are resolved without resort to the courts. Even when lawsuits are commenced, efforts to negotiate normally continue, and the dispute is frequently settled out of court. Litigation to an ultimate conclusion is the exception. No nation, no society, can permit the slow uncertainties of lawsuits to be the norm. When, then, the socially extraordinary reaches court, and by happenstance and good fortune the Supreme Court, the myth is that the judge "declares pre-existing law, of which he is only the mouthpiece; his judgment is the conclusion of a syllogism in which the major premise is found among fixed and ascertainable rules."[36] That pretense is an obvious piece of arrant hypocrisy, perpetrated by a guild (lawyers) that has a vested interest in keeping the law mysterious.

I do not suggest that the rhetoric and rules of American society are mere shams. They are important in themselves. Although, as Chapter 3 shows, they may disguise the true realities of power, at the same time they can and at times do help to check power. My conclusion is similar to that of the historian E. P. Thompson, who in his important book *Whigs and Hunters* stated:

There is a difference between arbitrary power and the rule of law. We ought to expose the shams and inequities which may be concealed beneath this law. But the rule of law itself, the imposing of effective inhibitions upon power and the defense of the citizen from power's all-intrusive claims, seems to me to be an unqualified human good. To deny or belittle this good is, in this dangerous century when the resources and pretensions of power continue to enlarge, a desperate error of intellectual abstraction. More than this, it is a self-fulfilling error, which encourages us to give up the struggle against bad laws and class-bound procedures, and to disarm ourselves before power. It is to throw away a whole inheritance of struggle *about* law, and within the forms of law, whose continuity can never be fractured without bringing men and women into immediate danger.[37]

My point, in sum, is this: The struggle *about* law must and should continue, but that struggle cannot hope to be successful unless "the shams and inequities" of rules *of* law and their administration are exposed. We have, as Thompson said, a long way to go before a just society is created. The lawmaking proclivities of the Supreme Court, when properly directed, can help in fulfillment of that task.

Constitutional decisions are only rarely logical deductions from the text of the Document. Most—indeed, perhaps all—relationships between governments (federal and state) or between President and Congress or between government at any level and an individual are in final analysis political judgments. They are determined on the grounds of social policy; only by an intellectually indefensible fiction are they deducible from the formal Constitution. The problems the Court deals with are "delicate and imponderable, complex and tangled. They require at times the economist's understanding, the poet's insight, the executive's experience, the political scientist's understanding, the historian's perspective." Considerations of logic are not irrelevant, but they are not determinative. "Law presupposes sociological wisdom as well as logical unfolding," Justice Frankfurter once observed.[38] So it does, which means that the Supreme Court, protestations to the contrary notwithstanding, rules on the wisdom of disputed public policies (as well as the constitutional power of government).

Lawyers have a monopoly on judging, a practice that at the Supreme Court level is honored by time and tradition but little else. Justices require far more than legal competence. In addition to establishing a structure of government, the Constitution as it has evolved is an appeal to the decency and wisdom of those with whom its interpretation rests. Socially wise decisions are required, even though they may be logically arbitrary. Lawyers by no means have a corner on wisdom. The type of mind necessary for the High Bench was well described by Judge Learned Hand:

I venture to believe that it is as important to a judge called upon to pass on a question of constitutional law, to have at least a bowing acquaintance with Thucydides, Gibbon and Carlyle; with Homer, Dante, Shakespeare and Milton; with Machiavelli, Montaigne and Rabelais; with Plato, Bacon, Hume and Kant, as with the books which have been specifically written upon the subject. For in such matters everything turns upon the spirit in which he approaches the questions before him. *The words he must construe are empty vessels into which he can pour nearly anything he will.*[39] (Emphasis added.)

Although Judge Hand did not suggest where such paragons could be found, his prescription accurately portrays the demands on Supreme Court Justices. That most, perhaps all, do not fulfill Hand's requirements should cause little wonder. But what he said does point up one clear lesson: Those chosen to be Justices need not—probably, should not—come only from the ranks of lawyers. Anyone of middling competence can master the intricacies—what often are called the "technicalities"—of judicial procedure. The history of American liberties, despite assertions to the contrary by Justices Louis Brandeis and Felix Frankfurter, is far more than a matter of paying attention to procedural niceties. American freedoms are liberties in a social organization and depend more upon the milieu in which we live than upon "the law." The rights of all citizens ultimately derive from the type of society in which they live. If those rights are to be fulfilled, there must not only be attempts to further the democratic ideal but the economic capacity to do so. Legalistic niceties are only one part of such a society.

IV.

Is the Supreme Court an ordinary court of law, much like any state supreme court? The answer is an emphatic no. It is a very special type of court, and constitutional litigation is not a mere specific instance of the judicial process. True it is that the Justices have all been nurtured on case law and the adversary system. Even so, the High Bench knows no counterpart, historically or contemporaneously. "The Supreme Court is more than just an ordinary court," Justice Lewis Powell said in 1979, "It is empowered to decide whether the other two branches of government [and the states] live within the Constitution.... That's a rather awesome power and it's one that makes our system and our Court distinctive."[40] A fundamental fault with much constitutional scholarship is the attempt to force the Court to act like an ordinary court. A unique institution requires special rules and a different type of analysis, if full understanding is to come.

We should not, therefore, pretend that the Court is merely another court of law. The Justices decide questions that depend on many types of facts, their consequences, and the values that are attached to those consequences. They are questions of high public policy—of economics and politics and social ethics—and legal training cannot solve them unless law includes all social knowledge. It does not: As now taught and practiced, law is the narrow-minded pursuit of narrow, client-oriented goals. Prisoners of the ideology of legalism, lawyers have no special insight into the true nature of the issues the Court confronts. Nor is prior judicial experience a necessity for a Justice. Those called the greatest among the 102 Justices who have sat on the High Bench had little prior experience in judging. Judicial service has no discernible correlation to the kinds of problems thrust upon the Court and to the production of sociologically wise decisions. The differences between any state supreme court and the Supreme Court of the United States are not ones of degree, but of type.

That being so, it is of primary importance that the Justices have qualities that enable them to transcend the parochial and to rise above class. This prerequisite has not been true either in the past or today. If the Supreme Court is to be able to accomplish the task set out for it below, better ways of choosing those who become Justices must be found. Those who have been chosen have, without any notable exception, been individuals whose personal philosophies appeared to agree with the President. (The one possible exception was Justice Benjamin Nathan Cardozo, reluctantly named by President Hoover.) When Richard Nixon nominated four "strict constructionists"[41] (by which he apparently meant men who would be hard on suspected criminals), he was merely following a well-worn path. All know this, but, once again, the pretense is otherwise. To repeat: "The decisions of the courts on economic and social questions," as Theodore Roosevelt asserted, "depend on their economic and social philosophies"—a statement that shocked conservatives. He, however, was merely repeating one of Thomas Jefferson's observations: "All know the influence of interest on the mind of man and how unconsciously his judgment is warped by that influence." It would be absurd to press the point were it not for the myth to the contrary —the persistent and vehement assertion that judges speak (or should speak) only what the law has declared and that their personal views have nothing (or should have nothing) to do with their decisions. Justice Frankfurter was particularly intense on this score.

It is of surpassing importance to realize that no person, on or off the bench, can be completely impartial or objective. Judges, despite Chief Justice Marshall's contention to the contrary, are not "mere instruments of the law."[42] They are political actors, sensitive to political considerations, and they exercise a personal will. They are far from impassive or dispassionate oracles. All have axes to grind.

Not that they admit as much. Neither they nor their votaries are quite willing to acknowledge that it is the judge speaking and not the law. So they assert, as did Frankfurter, the need for "invincible disinterestedness," and they call for properly "reasoned" opinions. Judge Learned Hand was one of the few to state publicly what all lawyers know, or should know, and what many in the public apparently know intuitively. When invalidating governmental acts, said Hand, judges

do not, indeed may not say that, taking all things into consideration, the [act] is too strong for the judicial stomach. On the contrary, they wrap their veto in a protective veil of adjectives such as "arbitrary," "artificial," "normal," "reasonable," "inherent," "fundamental," or "essential," whose office usually, though quite innocently, is to disguise what they are doing and impute it to a derivation far more impressive than their personal preferences, which are all in fact lie behind the decision.[43]

(Judges are hardly as innocent as Hand would have it. Holmes once said that judges are naive, unsophisticated people who needed a touch of Mephistopheles. One wonders what company he and Hand kept. Judges tend to be hard-nosed realists, fully aware of what they are doing, and in fact wanting to do it.)

Fundamental to the Basic Myth is the view that judges and the law are or can be impartial or objective or neutral. That such a nature is an impossible dream should be obvious and admitted by all, but is not. Professor Judith

Shklar maintained that judges themselves are fearful of outright acknowledgment of their power and discretion.[44] E. P. Thompson believes there is value in the form of justice, even though the substance is absent.[45] Add to that the desire of lawyers to retain the secrets of their trade. Of even more importance, consider the capacity of the human mind for self-delusion. People *want* to believe something, such as the idea that judges are impartial, so it *is* believed. Such a belief bespeaks a deep psychological need for certainty and assurance and a concomitant desire to think that misfortunes of life are attributable to an impersonal force (the law). That serves the needs of the moneyed and propertied, as Thompson asserted, for they can maintain that their good fortune is also derived from forces external to them.

Even such a perceptive observer and one-time judge as Thurman Arnold thought it was better to adhere to the ideal (the myth) and not admit that the emperor is striding around in his birthday suit. Arnold thought the ideal to be of "tremendous importance." Without a continuing pursuit "of the shining but never completely attainable ideal of the rule of law above men," he asserted, "evolved solely from reason, we would never have a civilized government. If that ideal be an illusion, to dispel it would cause men to lose themselves in an even greater illusion, the illusion that personal power can be benevolently exercised."[46] (That approximates Thompson's views, quoted above.) But Arnold was not correct. Personal power is precisely what judges do exercise. People may differ on whether they act benevolently. But what they cannot validly dispute is that it is the will of the judge and not the law that controls constitutional decisions. In another context, Chief Justice William Howard Taft once plaintively asked: "All others can see and understand this. How can we properly shut our minds to it?"[47] Indeed, how can anyone? Surely enough is now known about the human mind and how it acts to conclude that those who do so are deluding both themselves and those they influence.

This conclusion emphatically does not mean that the rule of law is repudiated entirely. What is meant is that law is *instrumental*. "The teleological conception of his function must be ever in the judge's mind."[48] The jurisprudence of the Supreme Court has always been goal seeking, purposive, teleological. The Justices as lawmakers—as legislators—differ little in practical effect from those who are in the formal legislature. If what Congress does is law—and no one disputes that—the same may be said for the Court. The rule of law in both instances surely is the rule of men, but it is law nonetheless.

Social and natural scientists agree that objectivity is a chimera. Examples are easily found. Said sociologist Louis Wirth:

In human life the motives and ends of action are part of the process by which action is achieved and are essential in seeing the relation of parts to the whole. . . . Whatever may be the possibility of complete detachment in dealing with physical things, in social life we cannot afford to disregard the values and goals of acts without missing the significance of many of the facts involved. In our choice of areas for research, in our selection of data, in our method of investigation, in our organization of materials, not to speak of the formulation of our hypotheses and conclusions, there is always manifest some more or less clear, explicit or implicit assumption or scheme of evaluation.[49]

That statement fits law and the Supreme Court exactly.

Plato distinguished between rigorous *apodictic* knowledge and *decisional* knowledge.[50] By the former he meant a kind of axiomatic knowledge in which a valid syllogism culminates in a necessary conclusion and in which the mathematical equation A equals B permits predicate B to add nothing to subject A. He doubted whether such knowledge was really possible except within a framework of decisional knowledge, which recognizes as unavoidable and indeed considers as appropriate value judgments grounded on value preferences, choices, alternatives—again, a neat fit for the Supreme Court. It speaks apodictically, but engages in decisional knowledge.

So, too, in the physical (the "hard") sciences: Nobel Laureate Percy W. Bridgman maintained that "even in pure physics . . . it is becoming evident that the problem of the 'observer' must eventually deal with the observer as thinking about what he observes."[51] He did not believe that the personal element could be divorced from the study of physics. Michael Polanyi agreed, arguing that fact is inseparable from value and that the natural sciences cannot be severed from the humanities. "The ideal of a knowledge embodied in strictly impersonal statements now appears self-contradictory, meaningless, a fit subject for ridicule. We must learn to accept as our ideal a knowledge that is manifestly personal."[52]

Similar conclusions may be found in Karl Mannheim's monumental *Ideology and Utopia*, a study of the sociology of knowledge. Mannheim maintained that personal evaluations should not be excluded, for they cannot be; a new type of objectivity should be sought through critical awareness and control of those evaluations. That view has particular relevance for constitutional law, which in large part is political theory expressed in lawyers's language. The Justices in their decisions manipulate juristic theories of politics. Said Mannheim on impartiality in politics:

When we enter the realm of politics in which everything is in process of becoming and where the collective element in us, as knowing subjects, helps to shape the process of becoming, where thought is not contemplation from the point of view of the spectator, but rather the active participation and reshaping of the process itself, a new type of knowledge seems to emerge, namely, that in which decision and standpoint are inseparably bound together. In these realms, *there is no such thing as a purely theoretical outlook on the part of the observer*. It is precisely the purposes that a man has that give him his vision, even though his interests throw only a partial and practical illumination on that segment of total reality in which he is enmeshed, and towards which he is oriented by virtue of his essential social purposes.[53] (Emphasis added.)

That should be enough to validate the point: if impartiality is not possible in either the social or the natural sciences, how possibly can it be achieved in the art of judging? No way exists. "Chaos," Gunnar Myrdal has said, "does not organize itself into cosmos. We need viewpoints and presume valuations."[54] Indeed we do. The lawyers's mentality constructs only closed and static systems of thought and thus must always face a true paradox—that of having to incorporate into the legal system new laws and policies, which arise out of the unsystematic interactions of living forces that make up the chaos of the "controlled anarchy" called "pluralism"—the political order. Lawyers have not yet learned what Woodrow Wilson knew many years ago—that New-tonianism (closed and static systems) is simply not a true portrayal of how laws, including that of the Constitution, develop.

Law as Darwinian process means that choices among competing values must routinely be made. Even in their analyses of the facts of cases, judges's value preferences again intrude. Facts do not speak for themselves, the cliché to the contrary notwithstanding. In Reinhold Niebuhr's view, "Every judgment of fact is a judgment of value." Facts are not self-sustaining, "float-ing in nonentity."[55] "A single fact in isolation," Alfred North Whitehead main-tained, "is the primary myth required for finite thought, . . . for thought unable to embrace totality. This mythological character arises because there is no such fact. Connectedness is the essence of all things. . . . No fact is merely itself."[56] If that is accepted, as it must be, that means that the Basic Myth is also shattered, as Jerome Frank often said, by the idea of "fact-skepticism," as well as "rule-skepticism."[57] In other words, although people may not dis-agree about what the facts of a given constitutional case are, it is the inter-pretation one places on them that is important, together with the selection of facts into a hierarchy of importance. Professor Aviam Soifer, quoting Albert Einstein, told us that "It is the theory which tells us what we can observe."[58] That comment means, as will become more evident in subsequent discussion, that it is the theory—the major premises—from which Supreme Court Justices proceed in seeking to explain or justify their decisions that is all important.

V.

The intellectual bankruptcy of the Basic Myth is manifest. Its twin pillars are, first, the preexistence of external rules of law that judges can identify and apply and, second, the idea that judges act with an invincible impartiality. Neither reflects reality. Once that is seen and fully accepted, the problem becomes one of outwardly pursuing certain goals. For the Supreme Court, we will see in the next chapter that those goals for most of American history involved the protection of the moneyed and the propertied. Even the recent interest of the Justices in civic rights and civil liberties can be similarly evalu-ated. Those decisions are also a type of class legislation, for by helping to siphon off discontent they enable Establishment values and positions to be retained, while giving up very little.

To emphasize exactly what I am saying about the Basic Myth: I do not deny that rules of law exist, although as Oliver Wendell Holmes saw long before he became a judge, they too can be and usually are class biased and nonneutral.[59] Nor do I deny that law has a pervasive influence on the way that people order their affairs. Much of the "given" in society—that which is taken for granted or is axiomatic—is law. Law is the name given to the ways that people order their affairs. The focus, however, in this volume is upon the *constitutional* decision, as announced by the Supreme Court, and not on the run-of-the-mine, routine decisions of lower courts or on the rule of law as an accepted principle of social order.

To summarize: (a) the Supreme Court deals only with the exceptional case; (b) these cases are chosen not in the interests of the litigants but to develop the Constitution; (c) in effect, then, each such decision is a class action, with the class being defined as the entire nation; (d) the Constitution is always being created anew, updated by official decisions from not only the Court but also the President and Congress (and some of the decentralized centers of power in the nation); (e) in making decisions, the Principle of Doctrinal Polarity operates; (f) the Court, generally, reflects "Establishment" values; and (g) it is one thing to state a rule, but another thing to enforce it. The Justices, having no administrative power of their own, in effect delegate to others in government the power and duty to translate their general commands into operational reality. That those delegates at times are balky and at other times read the abstractions of the High Bench in different ways should occasion no surprise. It is on this lower level of administration that people confront government and where, indeed, the Court's decisions may receive only nominal compliance. The Justices have no way to police the enforcement of their decrees. The most they can do is to hope that others read—and heed.

The most important question to ask of any Supreme Court decision (or any other governmental action) is this: *Cui bono?* Who actually benefits? Beneficiaries can be both *apparent* (or ostensible) and *actual*. In the next chapter I do not suggest that these categories are necessarily mutually exclusive, but do say that the question must be asked and answered on both levels.

3
The Court in History:
Storms Around the Temple

I.

"We are very quiet here," Justice Holmes once wrote to a friend, "but it is the quiet of a storm center, as you know."[1] So it is: The relative silence in the austere Marble Palace is deceptive. Controversy has long swirled around the Supreme Court, beginning in 1803 when the Justices boldly and baldly insisted theirs was the power "to say what the law is"—that law being the Constitution.

Holmes sat during the second of three major periods of quarrels in the Court's history. The first dates from 1803 to the end of the Civil War. The basic question then, outwardly at least, was nationalism versus localism. How strong was the central government to be? The Document of 1787, itself a structural alteration in government (away from local autonomy under the Articles of Confederation), became under the leadership of Chief Justices John Marshall and Roger Taney the legal basis for a strong national government. After the Civil War, the focus switched to the growing power of business, which had rapidly begun to collectivize itself, and whether either government, federal or state, could regulate the corporations. In general, the answer was no, and another dispute surfaced, lasting until 1937. Sitting as an ultimate faculty of political economy, the Justices made economic policy for the nation. In another bald and bold grab for governing power, they swept away much regulation of business. Laissez-faire principles of economics were discovered and read into the Constitution—not without opposition, to be sure, a resistance that crested during the Great Depression of the 1930s and that forced the Court to recede from economics. Those questions were politicized and left to the avowedly political branches of government.

Searching for a new role, the Justices found one in civil rights and liberties, which for the first time in American history began to receive systematic judicial protection.[2] The de facto Council of Elders for issues of political economy became one of social ethics. The Justices sought to protect some individuals from the growing power of the State. For example, the court in 1954 acknowledged, for the first time, that the Constitution meant what it said—that it contained principles of legally concretized decency for black Americans.[3] A civil rights/civil liberties explosion erupted. Harsh criticism again surfaced, mainly from those who contended that the Justices went too far in "legislating" and thus did not act "judicially." Although Court protection of human rights has been slowed with a change in personnel on the High Bench (mainly appointees of Richard Nixon), a third assertion of raw governing power still prevails. The Justices maintain that theirs is the power to state "the law of the land" when construing the Document, which means that they now candidly acknowledge that they can "amend" the formal Constitution by judicial decree. It is this posture of judicial aggression, by and large accepted by most Americans and most politicians, that provides a point of departure for an even more enlarged role of the Court in the future.

During the second period of controversy, the basic issue was whether the Constitution permitted government to countervail the growing power, economic and thus political, of giant business—what were then called the "trusts." Before the Civil War, business was small and local and usually not incorporated. "Technological imperatives"—John Kenneth Galbraith's term[4]—after the War permitted (according to Galbraith, required) the growth of corporate enterprise, both in numbers and size, a development substantially boosted when the Court by some process of divination discovered in 1886 that the corporation was a constitutional person and thus entitled to protection under the "due process of law" clauses.[5] Two clauses exist, one limiting the federal government and the other the states: "no person shall be deprived of life, liberty, or property without due process of law." That cryptic language, coupled with corporate personhood, allowed the Justices to read freedom of contract principles (not mentioned in the Document) into the "liberty" aspect of the clauses. The liberty of corporations, with their enormous assets, became equated in law with that of natural persons. Anyone should have been able to see, and indeed many did, that the equation was badly skewed in favor of the corporations. That did not deter the Justices, nor did it stop the corporate bar (the American Bar Association). It was a classic example of a long period of "class legislation" by the Court—for the rich and powerful and against the poor and weak. (The judicial discovery that corporations were persons was made without request from counsel—*sua sponte*, as lawyers say. That is proof positive that the Justices can, at times at least, be "self-starters"; once a case is filed and accepted for full review, they can proceed in wholly unexpected directions. When it wishes to do so, the Court can act independent from counsel and even the adversary system.)

Since the late 1930s and 1940s, the question often has been whether members of disadvantaged minorities with little or no political strength can employ the courts to achieve goals denied by the political process. Judges have become the target of new political pressure groups, the last resort of those left behind in what is seen as a bankrupt political system. This has led some commentators—for example, Professor John Hart Ely—to recommend that the Court have an expanded role, but only to the extent that decisions are made to insure that the system of representative government is working properly.[6] I believe this to be a far too limited conception of what the Court can and should do.

The long-standing quarrels over the Court pose this question: Is there a consistent thread running through both the Court's decisions and the opposition they have generated? Superficially, perhaps, the answer is no. That, however, is hardly accurate. If we remember Professor Griffith's conclusion that the function of courts in modern industrial societies is to underpin the stability of the system and resist attempts to change it, the beginnings of a theory at once more accurate and more complete emerge. It is this: The interests of the State, and of those who in fact (although not in theory) control the State, have always been and still are preeminent.

Can that hypothesis be validated? The clear answer is yes. The Court since its formation has rendered decisions critical to development of the *formal* Constitution. Of perhaps more importance, however, is what it did *not* decide (and in fact never reached the Court)—what, that is, was left to the political branches of government—and what it did with certain statutes, principally the antitrust laws. Analysis must be on the levels of both the formal and the operative Constitutions. Of necessity, it will be brief. My conclusion is that the Court, surely in the past and even today, is in fact an instrument of the "ruling class" (or "ruling classes").[7] It is not a neutral institution; nor is the law it enunciates neutral. The interests of the stronger, as Plato said in *The Republic*, prevail: "Justice or right," said Thrasymachus, "is simply what is in the interests of the stronger party."

I realize that is a harsh accusation, and I do not wish to be simplistic. Nonetheless, no other conclusion seems tenable. It cuts against the grain of the liberal theory of law—the view, dominant for several centuries, that general rules, applied impartially and even-handedly, would result in effects that benefited all. That is the American faith; that, too, is the Basic Myth discussed previously. No one has for long been able to counteract the force of Thrasymachus's (possibly cynical) argument. I do not say that judges historically, openly, and overtly sought the doctrine that aided "the stronger party"; the process was much too subtle for that. However, in a class-divided society, which was and is the United States, the social basis for the liberal theory of law and legal institutions simply did not and does not exist. The further suggestion, derived from Holmes, is that there is no overall coherence in the (formal) law. Coherence comes only (Holmes did not say this) when one looks beyond the statements of formal doctrine and asks: *cui bono?*

As was related in Chapter 1, the living or operative Constitution deals with what actually takes place in government, not with what is supposed to occur. To understand it requires answers to this question: *Who* makes *What Deci-*

sions, How, and with what *Effects* (in whose interests)? Our concern lies in the "who" (the Supreme Court), the "decisions" (the 140 or so made on the merits each term), the "how" (which we have noted is far from fully known), and the "effects" (the theme of this chapter). The "who" of that complex question of course entails more than the Court, constitutional interpretation being distinctly *not* a judicial monopoly. Therefore, the "who" discussion encompasses the interactions of the Justices as political actors with other political actors (both those in public office and some in private life).

An understanding of the task of the Supreme Court and its impact on the social order requires that both the formal and the informal—the operative—Constitutions be considered. At times the Justices fuse the two constitutions into one by making part of the operative fundamental law a precept of the formal. Examples include executive privilege, which since the *Nixon* tapes case[8] is now constitutional doctrine (before 1974 it was a political accommodation), and "reason of State"—the ability of the government, particularly the President, to take emergency action even though the Document of 1787 does not expressly provide for it.[9]

"No answer is what the wrong question begets," Alexander Bickel asserted[10]—not quite correctly. The wrong question begets wrong (not no) answers. Can there be any doubt that the correct question is: who benefits in fact from Supreme Court decisions? The answer seems clear beyond peradventure; of course that is the proper question, but its answer is obscured by the myth structure already discussed and by the propensity of historians to dwell on the positive in America's past. The latter phenomenon might be called the "Parson Weems" or "fairy tale" school of historical writing.

The answer given here—after some general statements about Constitution and Court—is that those who benefited, in the past and now, are those who loosely constitute the ruling class of the nation—the moneyed and the propertied, the well-born and the well-placed. To repeat: coherence in constitutional law may be found only in terms of the social impact of constitutional decisions; when that is done, the ultimate, if not the initial, beneficiaries have not varied since July 4, 1776.

II.

The Constitution of 1787—the sacred Document—is many things. After ratification by nine states, a new form of government was established, one fundamentally different from that under the Articles of Confederation. The first government took office in 1789, and American constitutional history dates from that year. When Americans speak of the Constitution, they refer not only to the Document but also to the judicial version of it—to *constitutional law*: Hence an "immaculate conception" view of American history, and hence the neglect of the colonial era and of the experience under the Articles, save for the convention of 1787 and for *The Federalist Papers*—propaganda designed to help ratification of the Document.[11] Indeed, little is studied about the Constitution, in college or law school, before 1803, the date of *Marbury* v. *Madison*—the linchpin of all the Supreme Court has done since.

In the *Marbury* case, Chief Justice John Marshall seized an otherwise inconspicuous dispute (could Marbury be a justice of the peace?) to assert the power of the Court to give meaning to the Constitution. With one stroke, he plunged the High Bench deeply and irretrievably into the mainstream of American politics. Nothing in the Document allocates that power to the Court. Marshall and colleagues grabbed it, thereby neatly amending the Constitution by judicial decree. President Jefferson was incensed, even though he (and his Secretary of State, James Madison) were the nominal winners. They lost the crucial point: The Court not only became the institution to put content into ambiguous constitutional language, but, of even more importance, it also soon became a nationalizing influence in public policy. That role was contrary to Jeffersonian principles. It should be remembered, however, that Jefferson as President also became an exponent of national power (as in the Louisiana Purchase), which means that his opposition to Marshall was political rather than principled.

The formal Constitution is also a set of apparent limitations on government. The 1787 Document established a federal government of limited, delegated powers, with all other powers reserved to the states. The Bill of Rights, added in 1791, is also a limitation—at first on the national government only but by twentieth-century lawmaking by the Supreme Court, limitations on the states also. Those proscriptions on what government can do, although often couched in absolute terms, are by and large not so much commands as admonitions. As interpreted through the decades, they have always been relative to circumstances.

The Document has survived less because of intrinsic merit than because of two factors: ambiguity in many of the terms, permitting much play in the constitutional joints; and the enormous wealth of an undeveloped continent, which was rather quickly exploited by fair means and foul. Ambiguity allowed adaptation of constitutional language to changing conditions. That characteristic should be given a label, with initial capitals for emphasis: the Principle of Constitutional Relativism. Under the operations of that principle, to take but one example, economic institutions were created that could not have been in the minds of the Framers. Neither the giant corporations nor the trade unions were known in 1787. As the nation changed from one of small shops and agriculture to one with corporations dominating the economy, those new entities were assimilated.

The Constitution endures also, because some of its *unambiguous* terms have been substantially altered through time. Two examples suffice. First, the Document states that Congress has the power to declare war, but Presidents since George Washington, and particularly beginning with Franklin D. Roosevelt and continuing to the present, have used military force when considered necessary without Congressional authorization.[12] Second, the First Amendment plainly states that Congress shall make no law restricting freedom of speech and press and religion, but that amendment has been interpreted to mean "some" laws and also to apply to the state governments. A dualism runs through American constitutional history: The concept of limited government against the reality that government has always been precisely as strong as conditions warranted, as perceived by the effective powerholders in the nation.

Even more significant *structural* changes in government have been made in the operative Constitution since 1789. For example, the states are not today nearly as strong vis-à-vis the federal government as they were originally. There has been a steady accretion of power in the presidency and the executive branch of the federal government, with an accompanying diminution of power in Congress.

Supreme Court Justices assert a peculiar ability, known only to them, of divining not merely the intentions of the Framers but principles of a higher law that lurk somewhere in the interstices of the Document (or apart from it). At times they employ principles of *natural law* or *natural justice*—the terms are not synonymous—to write their ideas of good or wise public policy into the Constitution. Not that they do so outwardly. While stoutly and consistently stating that their power is solely that of determining whether governmental action squares with the Constitution, they nonetheless go beyond the words of the Document. Rather like the maid in Byron's *Don Juan* who, "whispering 'I will ne'er consent'—consented," the Justices decide whether acts of government are socially well advised, while strenuously denying they are doing so. (Perhaps that contradictory behavior is one of the reasons for judicial secrecy, the Justices believing that, as Charles de Gaulle once said, "there can be no prestige without mystery.")[13]

The meaning is clear: Courts, and of them the Supreme Court, are deeply in politics. The starting point for viewing the Court should be "what any fool could plainly see if his eyes were not beclouded by centuries of legal learning, that judges and courts are an integral part of government and politics, would be meaningless and functionless outside of government and politics, and are, therefore, first and foremost political actors and agencies."[14] They are political actors, because they make law—public policy—and they are agencies, because in their internal operations ("judge and company," as Jeremy Bentham put it)[15] they are organized and they operate politically.

III.

"The law," Chief Justice Earl Warren once observed, "floats in a sea of ethics."[16] Whether or not that is so may be doubted. But what cannot be doubted is the proposition that much more than legal education and practice are required to interpret the Constitution. John Marshall—not the first, but surely the first great, Chief Justice—knew this well. He dominated a rather humdrum court of law and transmuted it into an important organ of government. His knowledge came not from legal learning or practice. His career had been that of a man deeply interested in politics. Marshall did practice law, but that was not his primary interest.

Thirty-four years as Chief Justice, Marshall left his imprint on constitutional law so indelibly that it lasts to this day. An exponent of national power, he and his colleagues issued decisions that lent consitutional legitimacy to an enormous expansion of federal powers. Those decisions supported the perhaps even more important protection of "vested rights"—that is, property rights—by which the hold of the moneyed and propertied on government was solidified.

That is an odd type of ethics, favoring the few over the many. Can law, and Supreme Court practice, have changed so much in the period between Marshall and Warren? The answer has to come on two levels, as we will see. To anticipate subsequent discussion: the law ultimately still favors those— the class—it has always favored, and that is so whether law emanates from legislatures or administrative agencies or courts.

The United States began its history when the Founding Fathers subverted the Articles of Confederation in the 1787 convention. There merely to amend the Articles, they created a government structurally different, a government under a Constitution that posed, and still poses, more questions than it answered. During the first period of heated controversy over Supreme Court lawmaking, the critical question often was presented in terms of whether the Document had established a league of relatively autonomous states, with a weak national government, or a unified nation. No one really knew the answer to that question—not in 1787, when the issue was largely ducked; not in 1789, when President Washington took office; not in 1803, when the Court plunged into politics; not in 1815 and 1819 and 1821, when the Justices successfully challenged the power of state supreme courts and also greatly extended the affirmative powers of Congress; not in the "nullification" dispute during President Jackson's tenure, when South Carolina tried to defy the government in Washington; and not in 1857, when the Court in the infamous *Dred Scott* case invalidated a Congressional statute for the *second* time. From the early nineteenth century to the Civil War, the Justices's most important work dealt with review of the actions of state governments. Even then, the power of law to shape the course of American destiny was minimal. Only by an unthinking conceit can lawyers believe that legal commands can settle or resolve the festering sores of human society. Only a bloody and bitter civil war settled on the battlefield the question of whether the United States is indeed one nation.

As time is reckoned, the three-quarters of a century from 1789 to 1865 is less than minuscule; it is insignificant. Nevertheless, it was a period of consummate significance for the United States—a time when frail and unformed institutions were tested; when the Supreme Court, which itself had a dubious birthright (as *the* interpreter of the Constitution), strove to help unite a disparate group of alleged sovereignties perched on the shoulder of North America and existing at the sufferance of the then superpowers (France and Great Britain). Marshall's legacy was a series of decisions, extended by the Court under his successor Roger Taney, that were nationalizing in effect and that protected vested rights and consequently provided the legal basis for the Constitution that blossomed after Appomattox. Of perhaps more importance, however, were the disputes the Court did *not* decide—such as the Louisiana Purchase, the Nullification Controversy of 1832, the systematic confiscation of Indian property, the pervasive use of violence without Congressional authorization, and the slow birth of an industrializing nation.[17]

John Marshall was a master politician, combining seeming caution with boldness to achieve judicial results and to mold the High Bench into an important instrument of governance. He was aided, of course, not only by other judges, but by an "inner republic of bench and bar"[18] and also by the support of the business class. They made up the "constituency" of the Court and thereby helped to give it legitimacy in the formative years of the republic. A problem of today's Supreme Court is that its historical constituency has all but vanished. A new one must be found. That is so even though (as will be shown) the moneyed and the propertied still are the ultimate, but not the immediate or manifest, beneficiaries of Supreme Court decisions.

Marshall's decisions were relatively few by modern standards, but their significance remains. They include, but are not limited to, the following: *Marbury* v. *Madison* (1803), *Fletcher* v. *Peck* (1810), *Martin* v. *Hunter's Lessee* (1816), *Woodward* v. *Dartmouth College* (1819), *McCulloch* v. *Maryland* (1819), *Cohens* v. *Virginia* (1821), and *Gibbons* v. *Ogden* (1824).[19] (Marshall wrote the Court's opinion in each of those cases except *Martin*, where he disqualified himself; *Martin*, however, was written by Justice Joseph Story, a man who held views similar to the Chief Justice.) These few examples are enough to illustrate that some of the most vexing social and political problems reach the Court in the guise of private disputes. Marshall began a process that everyone now understands—that a private lawsuit in constitutional questions is merely a way of getting some major political problems before the Justices, which means that such suits are about as private as the actions of the United States Senate.

Our saga begins with the thrice-told tale of William Marbury. The *Marbury* case came at a particularly disputatious period in American history, a time of rancor and contention and bitterness in politics that makes modern political battles seem tame by comparison. Thomas Jefferson had been elected President in 1800. When he took office in 1801 he was confronted with some "midnight appointments" John Adams had made just before leaving office, among them those of Marbury and others to be justices of the peace. Jefferson did not want to honor the appointments, and James Madison, the

Secretary of State, refused to give Marbury the necessary commission. (John Marshall was Secretary of State when Marbury's appointment was made—and also Chief Justice, which should have been, but was not, a clear case for Marshall to disqualify himself.)

On such historical oddities great matters depend. When Marbury sued Madison to get the commission that was rightfully his (Marshall admitted as much in his opinion), he relied on the Judiciary Act of 1789, which permitted "original" suits to be brought in the Supreme Court. (In other words, the Court acted as a trial court rather than as an appellate tribunal.) The case, at least superficially, presented a painful dilemma for Marshall. If he agreed with Marbury and ordered delivery of the commission, Madison likely would have ignored the order. That would have been a body blow to judicial prestige (and to the interests of the Federalists, Marshall's party). But if Marshall did not uphold Marbury, Jefferson's party would have had an apparent victory.

The seeming dilemma was neatly turned into a Solomonic victory: Marbury was said to be entitled to his commission, but the Court could not order its delivery. Why? Marshall determined that Congress could not enlarge upon the original jurisdiction of the Supreme Court; those powers had been set out in Article III of the Document and were frozen in time. Nowhere in that Article was it stated that the Court could issue the writ Marbury requested. The victory, however, was only apparently Jefferson's, for in so holding, Marshall established the principle that the Court could determine the nature of federal powers and, indeed, the meaning of the Document itself.

In retrospect, that determination is one of the most remarkable feats in the annals of government. Nowhere does the Constitution give the Court the power of judicial review of Congressional statutes, and on the technical point, nowhere does the Document state that Congress cannot enlarge upon the original jurisdiction of the High Bench. Marshall's opinion was logically faulty, but the important point is that the Court got away with its assertion of governing power. The Chief Justice well knew, however, that the Court could not routinely second-guess Congress. He knew, for example, that a 1793 decision of the Court, *Chisholm v. Georgia*,[20] holding that a citizen of one state could sue another state without the latter's permission, was speedily overturned by the Eleventh Amendment. Even more to the point, he obviously was frightened by the attempted impeachment of Justice Samuel Chase in 1805. If ever a Justice deserved impeachment, it was Chase. He was obviously partisan and savage in his enforcement of the Alien and Sedition Laws of 1798. Marshall's fear led him to write Chase the amazing letter (mentioned in Chapter 1) in which he suggested scrapping the idea, expressed in the *Marbury* case, of judicial supremacy. That letter displayed no strong belief that judicial judgments were to be final. Chase's impeachment, however, failed by a narrow margin, and Marshall's views remained intact.

Much has happened since 1805. The Court has solidified its position, invented new doctrine, and taken on new roles. It is now accepted by friend and foe alike as *the* spokesman for constitutional values, so much so that many believe a constitutional amendment is necessary to reverse a Court ruling on the meaning of the Constitution. (An unsettled question, however, is the extent to which Congress can remove some constitutional disputes from the Court's jurisdiction—for example, in matters such as school prayers, busing to achieve racial integration in public schools, and the right to an abortion.)[21] Charles Evans Hughes, later to become Chief Justice, once asserted in a well-known sentence: "We are under a Constitution, but the Constitution is what the judges say it is, and the judiciary is the safeguard of our liberty and our property under the Constitution."[22] Hughes was only partly correct. First, it is the *federal* judiciary that tells Americans what the Constitution means (that question was unsettled in Marshall's time), and, second, the Constitution at times is what the President says it is and at other times what Congress says it is. The *Marbury* case is justifiably famous, because it presented a great question of constitutional law, great not because it involved complicated legal or technical questions, but because it embodied issues of high public policy, public good, and ultimately public morality. High policy is what *Marbury* is all about.[23] The answer, then, about who is to interpret the Document was answered by John Marshall's daring grasp for power. The Court became, but only after a period of controversy, the voice of the *formal* Constitution. Marshall succeeded in considerable part, because he was astute enough not to strike down another Congressional statute during his tenure. Only in 1857 was a second national law held invalid (in the dreadful *Dred Scott* decision).[24]

The criticism heaped upon *Marbury* by some politicians, mainly Jefferson, was relatively minor compared to the vituperation that erupted when the Court tiptoed its way to becoming the ultimate arbiter of the relative powers of the federal and state governments. *Fletcher* v. *Peck* (1810) began that extended battle. There the Supreme Court for the first time struck down a state statute, as being contrary to the Document's provision that no state can make a law "impairing the obligation of a contract." *Fletcher*, however, dealt with a grant, fraudulently obtained, by the Georgia legislature of lands that today encompass most of Alabama and Mississippi. A subsequent session of the Georgia legislature sought to cancel the grant, only to be told by the Justices that the first grant was a contract within the meaning of the Constitution, and, furthermore, that even though fraud was involved, since the land had been sold to innocent purchasers, the grant could not be cancelled. How innocent those buyers were in fact is by no means certain, but the decision stuck, and the "Yazoo land fraud' became a celebrated case in Supreme Court history.[25]

After the failure to impeach Chase, the Court's work in constitutional matters was apparently that of striking a balance between the claims of nationalism against those of localism. I say "apparently," because there are other, possibly better, ways of collating the decisions: the protection of property and liberty, harmonizing majority rule with minority rights, or making "democratic" institutions jibe with the "security of property, contracts, and commerce." Those who espoused localism were, in general, also those considered to jeopardize property rights—vested rights—and the freedom of people with money to do what they wanted with it. That idea meant exploitation of an untouched continent. The true unifying theme of the period was the power of a burgeoning plutocracy versus that of the yeomanry—the creditor class against the debtors. Alexander Hamilton had foreseen that precise need. In *Federalist No. 78* he wrote in polite yet revealing language that a life-tenured judiciary could be an "excellent barrier to the encroachments and oppressions of the representative body." He saw the judiciary as a "safeguard against the effects of occasional ill humors in the society" and as "mitigating the severity, and confining the operation" of "unjust and partial laws." Without question, he feared the debtor class and wanted to stymie it with an "independent" judiciary. What he did not say was that he expected judges to be taken from the creditor class and to reflect the values of that class. (That view, indeed, is the underlying philosophy of Marshall's opinion in the *Fletcher* case.)

Drafters of the Constitution were men of property, zealously interested in protecting it and in the liberty to increase it. They did not believe in democracy (however defined). Indeed, John Adams waxed choleric about the possibility of a "democratical despotism."[26] He was not alone: the Framers wanted government by "the wise, the good and the rich,"[27] which they tended to lump together as one aristocratic group. The Document thus was a counter-revolution to the ideas of the Declaration of Independence, particularly those dealing with equality, which was aimed at controlling excessive governmental power. As written, the Document *seemed* to establish a government too weak to protect the rich, the moneyed, and the propertied. The Bill of Rights, added in 1791, was essentially an afterthought, although the Fifth Amendment's provision for the protection of "life, liberty, and property" by "due process of law" was an important adjunct to further the Hamiltonian prescription. Something more was needed if the "wise, the good, and the rich" were to receive the protection they believed was necessary. Producing that "something" became a major function of the Supreme Court.

The Framers well knew that they were creating both a new political government and a means of economic control (or, as is detailed in Chapter 9, both a Political and an Economic Constitution, although only the former was written). Some famous language of James Madison, in *Federalist No. 10*, is relevant:

... the most common and durable source of factions has been the various and unequal distributions of property. *Those who hold, and those who are without property, have ever formed distinct interests in society. Those who are creditors, and those who are debtors, fall under a like discrimination.* A landed interest, a manufacturing interest, a mercantile interest, a moneyed interest, with many lesser interests, grow up of necessity in civilized nations, and *divide them into different classes, actuated by different sentiments and views.* The regulation of these various and interfering interests forms the principal task of modern legislation, and involves the spirit of party and faction in the necessary and ordinary operations of the government.[28] (Emphasis added.)

Exactly: the men of property against those without it. A class society. I do not suggest that *property*, the word used by Madison, was (and is) not a complex concept. Of course it is. Indeed, to Madison, property did not mean the plutocracy only. In this same essay, he emphasized that the "first object" of government was the protection of the faculties that give rise to property and not the property itself, and elsewhere he wrote that a person had "an equal property in the use of his faculties and free choice of the objects on which to employ them." Nevertheless, he clearly made a distinction between different "interests in society." Those divergent interests, as Part II shows, have now led to the manifest inability of government to function properly; selfish factions in "the zero-sum society" have become close to paralyzing government.[29]

Men of property were also the creditors, manufacturers, merchants, and bankers. Against them were arrayed those with little property and the debtors. Tensions between the two classes provide an organizing principle for the study of the development of much of American constitutional law. They also provide a similar principle for controversies over the Court. Hamilton's insight that the judiciary would be crucial to the protection of the landed and moneyed class was followed early on and indeed has been followed throughout American history. The United States, the myth to the contrary, has always been a class society. That is so even though, then and now, some mobility between classes is possible. Social mobility, however, is fast becoming much more difficult in the modern era, as the Age of Economic Scarcity takes over.

Alexander Hamilton wanted, and got in the *Marbury* case, a way to block Congress—particularly the House of Representatives. (If there was *one* Founding Father, it was Hamilton, whose views on government and economics have prevailed throughout American history.) Congress, however, posed no real threat to the plutocracy. Its laws by and large either protected that group or advanced its interests by affirmative legislation. State legislation and even state judges were a different matter. There the security of property was jeopardized, and there the Supreme Court, stepping gingerly in the early nineteenth century, began to build the legal foundation for unifying the nation by outlawing state actions protecting local interests—thus, according to the Justices, acting contrary to the Constitution (or federal statutes).

The questions of the actual power of the Supreme Court and of whether it could review acts of state governments (in the main, state supreme court decisions on "federal questions") were fudged by the Founding Fathers. That gap was quickly filled by the first Congress in the Judiciary Act of 1789, which in effect amended the Constitution (by statute) and thus gave the Supreme Court the means to be supreme over state courts and legislatures.[30] The Act was the focus of much of the controversy during the first stormy period of Court history. Its importance to development of the nation cannot be over-estimated: Insofar as any law can alter human affairs and institutions, it has had as significant a role as any other Congressional action in history. Justice Holmes observed in 1913 in a famous passage: "I do not think the United States would come to an end if we lost our power to declare an Act of Congress void. I do think the Union would be imperiled if we could not make that declaration as to the laws of the several states."[31] Holmes, who fought for the North in the Civil War, was a nationalist pure and simple. Although Holmes may not have been correct as of 1913, for by then the unifying forces of modern technology had bound the nation tightly together, in the early nineteenth century the situation was different.

The Holmes statement is the essence of John Marshall's jurisprudence. Beginning with Marshall, the Supreme Court has provided the political theory for a unified nation. The decisions of the Court may not have been—better: *were not*—the prime mover of national unification, but they did lend con-stitutional legitimacy to what businessmen, using the techniques of the early Industrial Revolution, were doing to the social structure. To mention only one example, the federal system has since 1789 been so greatly changed that the states today are little more than administrative districts for centrally established policies. A marriage of entrepreneurship to science and tech-nology produced the forces that led to constitutional change in fact. The slow creation of a national economic system, aided and abetted by Supreme Court decisions, has resulted in a national political order as well. So Holmes over-stated the importance of the Supreme Court. (Furthermore, he did not answer some critical questions: Why is "the Union" so important? What values does it further? Are there other, possibly better, ways of ordering affairs? As with Hamilton and Marshall and Lincoln—and about everyone else today—the value of national unity to Holmes was self-evident.)

Whatever impact Court decisions may have had, Section 25 of the Judiciary Act of 1789 surely ranks among the most significant of all statutes. Under its terms, the Supreme Court was authorized to review final judgments of state courts on "federal questions"—anything that involved the central government. Could Congress validly do that? Today the answer is taken for granted. In John Marshall's time, it was far from settled. The Marshall Court sustained Congress's power, after a judicial battle the ramifications of which are still being felt. John C. Calhoun well knew the import of Section 25, asserting in 1827 that the "existence or nonexistence" of the Section "would make an entire change in the operation of our system." If that Section did not exist, "the practical consequences would be, that each government [federal and state] would have a negative on the other, and thus possess the most effectual remedy, that can be conceived against encroachment. Under this view, this provision [Section 25] becomes one of the deepest importance."[32] It still is. Calhoun, however, spoke too late: Marshall's Court had already settled the legal point. No useful purpose is served by speculating on what might have been—on, that is, what the United States might have become had Section 25 not been in the law books and had the Supreme Court not seized upon it to aggrandize national power.

If we assume, however, as assume we must, that law (both legislative and judicial) does make some difference in social affairs, the Supreme Court's *appellate* power over state supreme courts was of immense importance to the "property class." The Justices were quick to protect the interests of that class. Aided by the Judiciary Act and the Constitution's principle of "federal supremacy" ("This Constitution, and the laws . . . which shall be made in pursuance thereof . . . shall be the supreme law of the land; and the judges in every state shall be bound thereby"), the Justices facilely amended the Constitution by judicial decree. They sought, and got away with, the notion that they were supreme in interpreting the Document, even though Justice Joseph Story once "cheerfully admitted" that state judges were as capable as they were in construing the fundamental law.[33] Nationalists all, the Justices married aggrandizement of federal power to protection of the creditor class.

Not that it came easily. Calhoun's views are a circumspect version of deep and bitter feelings that divided, and to some extent still divide, the nation. In terms of economics, the question was whether men of wealth and property could protect themselves against the "backwoodsmen" of the frontier. In terms of law, the issue was whether the United States was indeed one nation or a Balkanized collection of entities loosely bound together, with each having the power to go its own way. In briefest terms, could the United States be a large Switzerland? The answer: here, as always, economics prevailed and was written into law. Under both Marshall and Taney, the Court wrote on a relatively clean tablet. The Justices were free to place their notions of wise public policy into the Constitution. An essential problem, then and now, was whether others would listen and heed. It is one thing to state a norm, to say that the Constitution means such-and-such, but another thing to get that statement translated into political and social reality. In final analysis, the Court cannot command in the sense of forcing obedience with sanctions to back up its commands: it can issue exhortations and hope that others abide by what is decreed. Small wonder, then, that although the Justices did have and still do have freedom to decide what they want, they must make an assessment of how their decisions will be accepted. Not unlike the Pope, the Court has no way to use force, but like the Pope, its pronouncements can and do have a high degree of influence—a *growing* influence, for Americans are increasingly turning to the Justices as a de facto Council of Elders. Since in the United States legality tends to be equated with morality,[34] Supreme Court judgments have considerable moral force. The moral influence of a Supreme Court decision can, when coupled with its high visibility in the nation (gained through the mass media), have a substantial impact upon the conduct of Americans. (For example, the 1973 decision in the abortion cases[35] now allows hundreds of thousands of women to be aborted legally each year.)

Problems of federalism, of the relationship of state and federal governments to each other, have vexed the Court for most of its history. Today, however, because of economic and technological factors that eventually are reflected in law, the problem is only superficially difficult. Some, not long dead, thought otherwise. Attorney General Robert H. Jackson (soon to become a Justice) wrote in 1941 that "The whole subject is one of great delicacy and recurring vexation. To draw the line truly is . . . 'subtle business, calling for great wariness. . . . Especially is wariness enjoined when the problem of construction [of the Constitution] implicates one of the recurring phases of our federalism and involves striking a balance between national and state authority in one of the most sensitive areas of government.'"[36] Forty years later, Jackson's observation is far from accurate. Even in 1941 it was not particularly true. Over the years since 1789, the Justices have seemed to labor over questions of federalism, but their products since then have been remarkably similar. They may think they are "umpiring the federal system," but the clear line of constitutional development has followed economics: It has been centripetal, not centrifugal. Few substantial constitutional questions are presented by "our federalism";[37] those that do get Court attention are settled on the basis of political theories of the Justices. Political accommodations are the rule. Whatever the original intent may have been, cooperation rather than conflict is the core principle of the federal system. It could scarcely be otherwise: A nation with a federal income tax, with giant multistate and multinational corporations dominating the economy, and with external commitments and desires that straddle the globe and reach far out into space cannot brook the anarchy of original federalism. Today's Supreme Court, under the influence of Justice William Rehnquist, has on occasion struck blows for "states's rights,"[38] but they are of little effect and surely will not turn the course of politico-economic development around.

It was not always so. During the formative years of the republic, bitter feelings often surfaced over the growing power of the government in Washington. Accusations that "a judicial tyranny was silently creeping in on us"[39] were widely asserted by those who espoused localism. The Court was a bastion for the privileged, who feared the debtor class that often had control of state legislatures and thus was the target of that class as well as those who honestly believed in "states's rights." Obloquy was heaped upon the Justices to a degree that makes present-day assaults seem mild. "A most monstrous and unexampled decision," Judge Spencer Roane of Virginia's highest court snarled about an 1821 ruling (*Cohens* v. *Virginia*) that the Supreme Court had power to review state supreme court decisions in criminal matters. "It can only be accounted for by that love of power which history informs us infects and corrupts all who possess it, and from which even the upright and eminent judges are not exempt."[40] But Marshall and colleagues prevailed, and that "monstrous" decision is accepted today by one and all.

From a modern perspective, Roane's vitriolic outburst was misdirected. The Marshall Court, it is true, asserted the power to review state supreme courts; at that time, however, Congress's power to regulate the appellate jurisdiction of the Supreme Court surely would have upheld a Congressional statute that would in effect have overruled the *Cohens* decision. After all, it was only a few years before—in 1798—that the Eleventh Amendment had been promulgated, reversing the Court's ruling in *Chisholm v. Georgia*. Had Roane directed his splenetic attacks at the political process, would he have gotten acquiescence from Congress? By no means is the answer clear. That he chose to assault the Court reveals, by hindsight at least, that politics in 1821 had already bypassed the proponents of states's rights.

Acceptance of the principle of *Cohens*, however, is one thing, undeviating obedience another. Supreme Court decisions, particularly in the past thirty years,have helped partially to cleanse the Augean stables of impropriety in criminal law administration, but the pattern of compliance is spotty at best. Marshall was really not interested in the fate of those caught in the toils of the law. Rather, he wanted to establish once and for all that the Supreme Court of the United States was indeed supreme in areas within its constitutional competence. *Cohens*, thus, is the counterpart to the even more significant *Martin v. Hunter's Lessee* in which the Court, speaking through Justice Joseph Story, held that the High Bench could review decisions of state courts in civil matters—such as ownership of property—as long as a "federal question" was involved. *Martin* and *Cohens* are the twin pillars of the principle that underlies Justice Holmes's statement about the Court (quoted above). In *Martin*, which also came from Virginia, the Supreme Court reversed the state court. Story knew the dangers involved and proceeded with extreme caution. The Court merely issued the decision and opinion. No effort was made to order Virginia to do anything. Was it cowardice or statesmanship that motivated Story? Many believe the latter, and indeed it is difficult to think otherwise. In any event, the Court got its way, and if *Martin* (and *Cohens*) helped to de-Balkanize the nation, then it is statesmanship.

What had been tentative in 1816 and 1821, and even was true as recently as 1956 when the Warren Court bowed supinely to the truculence of Georgia's highest court in a capital punishment case (*Williams v. Georgia*),[41] has by 1981 become so accepted that the Burger Court could blithely overrule Minnesota's supreme court on a question of state law.[42] That little noted decision has large portents. With only Justice John Paul Stevens dissenting, the Court upheld a Minnesota statute forbidding sale of milk in plastic containers even though it had been ruled unconstitutional by the supreme court of the state. Since the matter involved application of the United States Constitution, said Justice William Brennan for the Court, the High Bench in

Washington could independently determine the validity of what Minnesota's legislature had done. No one was surprised. No latter-day Spencer Roane denounced the Supreme Court. What Marshall and Story and colleagues had started has now become holy writ. Political scientist Theodore Lowi asserted in 1979 that the United States had become a "united state."[43] So it has. Nowhere is this better seen than in the way that the Justices review questions of "our federalism."

IV.

The United States is the only nation that permits private lawyers and lawyer-judges to settle problems of the constitution of its government. Matters of high policy—of national public policy—have frequently turned on the accident of litigation. In the early 1930s, for example, monetary policy was decided by the Supreme Court, by a 5-4 vote, in a lawsuit between private parties that involved the sum of $15.60.[44] That bemused some Europeans, who simply could not fathom how Americans could allow lawyer-judges so much political power (*one* judge in the 5-4 decision). In economic matters, judges no longer have such power, not because it was taken from them, but because of a silent, although incomplete, self-abdication.[45] The Justices in 1937 altered their posture in those political questions that matter most—those dealing with economics—and ceased to stand like King Canute commanding the tides of social change to halt. That was a strategic retreat, with the Court admitting it knew little about economics—but not before it affirmatively validated the system of political pluralism by constitutionalizing the power of labor unions. Just as in 1886 the Court recognized the corporation to be a constitutional person, and thus entitled to the protections of the Document, so in 1937 the Justices agreed with Congress that labor, too, could organize collectively and bargain with business. They did not go so far as to call the labor unions persons under the Constitution, but in most respects the effect is the same. The unions attained "back-door" constitutional legitimacy. The key decision came in 1937 when the Court sustained the Wagner labor relations law.[46] A few years later, in 1944, political parties received the same treatment.[47] The unforeseen, second-order consequences are now becoming obvious: Political pluralism is now in a state of theoretical bankruptcy.

No need exists to trace all of the threads of judicial policymaking in the nineteenth and early twentieth centuries. *Cohens* and *Martin* established the basic principle, and a few illustrative decisions show the pattern. In terms of political (constitutional) theory, the fundamental question was one of federalism. The United States was born a federated republic—a group of individual states, each claiming sovereignty and each with two "ambassadors" to Washington (the senators). Federalism originally was "dual," with the states and federal government on a roughly equal basis. (If one was "more equal" than the other, it was the states.) In terms of economics, the ultimate questions were protection of property (against the debtor class) and the liberty to expand that property. The Supreme Court dutifully protected property and helped, usually by doing nothing, in the exploitation of a virgin continent.

Federalism means diversity, or at least the opportunity to pursue diverse goals in the several states, but that did not last, even though many—perhaps most—people then and now probably favor it. Economic and technological factors that sooner or later were integrated into Congressional statutes and Court decisions so altered the social milieu that splintered sovereignty could not last. A national common market, eventually dominated by giant corporations, developed and was superimposed on a decentralized political order. Something had to give and did give: the original conception of federalism, although it must be emphasized that it still lingers on in the formal Constitution. In the operative Constitution, the federal system has been so altered that it bears little resemblance to that which existed in 1789.

In theory, the Document of 1787 established a national government of only limited, expressly delegated powers. That type of government, however, was inconsistent with sentiments of nationalism (the ideology of the dominant propertied class) and did not provide adequate protection for those with money and property. Perceiving this, Alexander Hamilton organized the Federalist party—the first political party in the nation—to help make the central government stronger. John Adams cooperated, by appointing Marshall to be Chief Justice. Marshall made the Court supreme in a Hamiltonian government.

Marshall's appointment was something of a historical accident. President Adams had offered the post to John Jay, who had been the first Chief Justice but who resigned to be governor of New York. Jay refused, both because of health reasons and because, as he wrote Adams, the Court lacked "the energy, weight, and dignity which are essential to its affording due support to the national government."[48] That shortcoming was rectified by Marshall during his thirty-four years on the High Bench. Would our history have been different had Jay accepted? Or would it have been different if Jefferson, the newly elected President, had been able to name the Chief Justice? Adams nominated Marshall on January 27, 1801—less than six weeks before Jefferson took office. No one really knows the answers to those questions. What may be said with assurance, however, is that the office today has "energy, weight, and dignity," and it would be inconceivable for a lame-duck President today to be able to place a person on the High Court.

McCulloch v. *Maryland* (1819) and *Gibbons* v. *Ogden* (1824) are two of the most significant Marshall opinions—clever exegeses of debatable constitutional language. With consummate daring, he rewrote the Constitution in each. The Court, to be sure, does not have a roving commission to revise the Constitution at will; what it can do, and indeed what it has done throughout American history, is to alter the fundamental law incrementally. Constitutional law changes by slow accretion, not by a mighty volcaniclike explosion.

Only by viewing the sweep of American history can the net effect be seen in the application of formal norms to differing situations. Specific constitutional clauses have evolved through time, and structural alterations in the division of governmental powers have occurred, both of which make up the operative Constitution.

In *McCulloch*, two questions were involved: Could Congress incorporate a national bank, and if so, could Maryland tax it? Neither power is mentioned in the Constitution—how, then, to resolve the questions? With speed and dispatch, Marshall had no difficulty in upholding Congress and in voiding the tax. Writing on a clean slate, his opinion is both a lengthy essay in Hamiltonian economics and politics and the most influential statement of a theory of constitutional interpretation the Court has ever uttered.

Marshall's initial task was to determine how a government with only limited powers could do something not expressly provided for by the Framers. He could, of course, have held either way. But he was a nationalist, first and always, and so started with the inarticulated premise that Congress's powers should be expanded. That objective was accomplished, rather neatly, by the discovery that Congress also had "implied" powers. Article I of the Document gives Congress authority to make "necessary and proper" laws to carry out its delegated powers. Marshall refused to define *necessary* strictly. In words that opened the way for later expansive interpretations, the Chief Justice asserted that "we [the Supreme Court] must never forget that it is a *constitution* we are expounding, . . . a constitution intended to endure for ages to come, and, consequently, to be adapted to the various *crises* of human affairs." (Emphasis is Marshall's.)

That is an interesting sentiment and would be even more interesting had Marshall always employed that type of reasoning and had a national bank actually been necessary. (To this date, Americans do not have a true *national* bank, for Congress soon repealed the enabling statute. Not until the twentieth century was the Federal Reserve System established, and it is a hybrid—a "public-private" entity that knows no counterpart in other nations.) Our interest, however, lies in judicial method—how Marshall approached the case and how he reasoned his decision. His reading of "necessary and proper" made it the elastic clause of the Constitution, paving the way for later stretching of the Document. Only a few years before, in the *Marbury* case, John Marshall conveniently ignored the fact that he was expounding a constitution and treated the Document as any ordinary legal instrument (such as a contract or a will). In 1803 he was a strict constructionist; in 1819 he was a judicial activist. In other words, he varied his technique to suit the case at bar and to get the result he wanted. That agility may have been statesmanship—a marriage of litigation and legislation—but certainly it was also judicial casuistry. Furthermore, in striking down Maryland's tax on the national bank, Marshall again invented the law. Casually ignoring the fact that the tax was discriminatory, since it was aimed at only a branch of the national bank and not all banks, he struck down more than he had to. Nothing in the Document forbids states from taxing the nation. Surely, too, the states, having the reserved powers of government, should be able to tax as they choose—up to the point where the tax actually impedes a function of the national government. A uniform tax would not be such an impediment; discrimination would be.

One would have to be gullible to believe that Marshall did not fully realize what he was doing. *McCulloch*'s theory of interpretation became an open invitation for succeeding Justices to be free in their choice of technique. They can approach cases narrowly or broadly, in their absolute discretion, there being no such thing as *the* judicial method. Much that has occurred in exegeses of the Document may be traced to Marshall's signal in *McCulloch* that the Constitution is indeed a living instrument of governance. "Let the end be legitimate, let it be within the scope of the constitution, and all means which are appropriate, which are plainly adapted to that end, which are not prohibited, but consist of the letter and spirit of the constitution, are constitutional." With those words in his *McCulloch* opinion, John Marshall rewrote part of the Document: "necessary and proper" became "appropriate," *as determined by* the Court. He also gave his successors on the Court *carte blanche* in determining the reach of the Constitution.

Marshall's Court consistently followed Hamiltonian principles of strong centralized government, striking down state actions jeopardizing the authority of the "general government." A platform of constitutional legitimacy was built in cases such as *Gibbons* v. *Ogden*, where the interstate commerce power of Congress was expanded to void a steamboat monopoly granted by New York. Seemingly unimportant, the decision gave Congress full authority—again, as determined by the Court—over what constituted commerce and also helped to create a national common market economically. Hamilton, pure and simple: he had written in *Federalist No. 22* that the interstate commerce power's purpose was to suppress the "interfering and unneighbourly regulations of some states," regulations that, "if not restrained by a national controul," would prove to be "serious sources of animosity and discord."[49]

Two other points should be emphasized. First, the Court kept to itself the power to decide whether Congress's decisions about commerce were correct, a power that later Justices often used. Second, the principle and expansive theory of *Gibbons* provide support for modern social welfare legislation. In net, therefore, one need not be considered cynical to conclude that Chief Justice Marshall "delivered" to those who put him in office when he wrote the opinions in *McCulloch* and *Gibbons*. Surely, it was not by a mere fortuity that President Adams, no lover of "democracy," placed Marshall on the Court. The Chief Justice's philosophy coincided with those who wanted freedom to develop, often with federal aid, a continent that had lain fallow for eons. He and the Court he dominated were de facto arms of the business class, which was the preponderant political force in the new nation.

Consider in that connection a trio of contract decisions also authored by Marshall. *Fletcher* v. *Peck* and *Dartmouth College* v. *Woodward* are the best known, but *Sturges* v. *Crowinshield* is also important.[50] Under the formal Constitution, no state may enact a "law impairing the obligation of contracts," but nowhere are the key words—*law*, *obligation*, and *contract*—defined. Judicial interpretation of that clause in the pre-Civil War period had major consequences. The early decisions "aligned on the side of nationalism the economic interests of corporate organizations."[51] They were audacious rulings and had much to do with what we will later call the American Economic Constitution.

Fletcher, already mentioned, deserves larger treatment. Corruption in the United States is as American as apple pie. Scandals of fraud and bribery, and other examples of criminal behavior, have characterized the nation since the beginning. American history can be—indeed, has been—written around the theme of corruption. The Yazoo land fraud provides early and apt illustration. (It should not be considered an aberration.) The Georgia legislature was bribed to sell 35 million acres of western territory at $1\frac{1}{2}$¢ an acre—about all of what is now Alabama and Mississippi. The bribers included two U.S. Senators and three prominent judges, including one Justice of the Supreme Court. A furor erupted, and a later session of the legislature cancelled the grant. (Congressman John Randolph described one of the bribers as "a man of splendid abilities, but utterly corrupt. He shines and stinks like a rotten mackerel by moonlight.")[52]

With such obvious corruption, one might think that the grant could legally have been cancelled. Not so: in 1810 Chief Justice Marshall, drawing on a memorandum by Hamilton, found in *Fletcher* that the land had come into the hands of "innocent purchasers," and therefore Georgia could not constitutionally cancel the original sale. Again, he rewrote the Constitution, and again, as in *Marbury*, he narrowly defined the Document. Marshall took a principle from the private law of negotiable instruments—the "holder in due course" rule—and elevated it into a constitutional doctrine. One is reminded, when reading about the Yazoo fraud, of the perhaps apocryphal account of the Duke of Wellington after the battle of Waterloo. At an English garden party, he was approached by an old dowager, who, on seeing him, peered up and croaked: "Mr. Peabody, I presume?" "Madam," the Duke snorted, "if you believe that, you will believe anything." If Marshall believed that the ultimate purchasers were innocent buyers without knowledge of the fraud, he would have believed anything. They were not. Furthermore, the suit itself was feigned; both Fletcher and Peck wanted and got the same result.[53] A legislative grant is hardly a contract. But the decision stuck.

Fletcher is important for two reasons: First, it was the first truly important time that a state statute was voided by the Supreme Court. Two earlier invalidations were of minor importance. That historical milestone is far overshadowed by the reasons Marshall conjured up to justify his decision. The statute, he said, was invalid "either by general principles which are

common to our free institutions, or by the particular provisions of the constitution of the United States." The controversy over those "general principles" continues to this day, both on and off the Court. Witness, for
example, a 1943 statement by the Court: "Behind the words of the constitutional provisions are postulates which limit and control."[54] Presumably,
those postulates are best known to Supreme Court Justices, although Justice
Hugo L. Black, among others, simply refused to concede that principles
separate from the Constitution itself existed. Marshall's view has prevailed,
although perhaps not to the extent that his colleague Justice William Johnson
wanted in *Fletcher*: "I do not hesitate," said Johnson, "to declare that a state
does not possess the power of revoking its own grants. But I do it on a general
principle, on the reason and nature of things; a principle which will impose
laws even on the Deity." That is the only time a Justice seemed to say that the
writ of the Court could run even against the Supreme Being. Some *chutzpah*,
one might say.

Marshall invented the law in *Fletcher*, just as he had done in *Marbury* and
as he would do in other cases. He did not apply preexisting law, for there was
none. Nor did he advert to the intentions of the Framers (later in *Dartmouth
College*, he casually brushed aside those intentions). Marshall began the
process of not only creating law as the Court proceeded; by relying on
"general principles" outside of the Document, which are nowhere written
down, he gave the Justices a de facto roving commission to determine the
wisdom of given governmental actions. Settling a question of constitutional
law by alluding to principles of "natural law," he and Johnson were brave but
not foolhardy. They well knew that they had the support of the ruling class.

Judges have never been known for humility. Marshall's intellectual arrogance was earlier matched, perhaps exceeded, in 1612 when King James
called Lord Chief Justice Coke and other English judges before him. Differences had arisen over the King's authority to try cases himself. According
to Coke, he told James that the common law, not regal fiat, should settle a
controversy over land.

Then the King said, that he thought the law was founded on reason, and that he and
others had reason, as well as the Judges: to which it was answered by me, that true it
was, that God had endowed His Majesty with excellent science, and great endow-
ments of nature; but His Majesty was not learned in the laws of England, and causes
which concern the life, or inheritance, of goods, or fortunes of his subjects, are not to
be decided by natural reason but by the artificial reason and judgment of law.[55]

(That is Coke's version; others put it differently—that he really knuckled
under to James—but the legend, if that it be, has endured.)

But what is "the law"? The law is what the judges say it is. The Rule of
Law—the "artificial reason and judgment of law"—is, under both the
common law of Coke's era and American constitutional law, the Rule of

Judges. The law enunciated by the Supreme Court in constitutional (and other) cases, in Marshall's time and now, is not *a priori*; it was and is *a poste-riori*. Judges, lawyers all, reason as do practicing attorneys, beginning with desired results and thinking backwards—from effect to cause. As lawyers, judges became accustomed to justifying legal positions favorable to their clients. It would be difficult, and probably impossible, for a person to slough off the mind-habits of his professional career. Chief Justice Marshall knew that his critics were bothered both by the lack of adequate reasoning in his opinions and the results themselves. His "heretical reasoning" was "pronounced most damnable."[56] That led him to counter with a statement not unlike Lord Coke's: "Courts are mere instruments of the law," he maintained,

and can will nothing. When they are said to exercise a discretion, it is a mere legal discretion, a discretion to be exercised in discerning the course prescribed by law; and when that is discerned, it is the duty of the court to follow it. Judicial power is never exercised for the purpose of giving effect to the will of the judge; always for the purpose of giving effect to the will of the legislature; or, in other words, to the will of the law."[57]

Marshall could not have believed that statement, at least in its literal sense. Seizing an otherwise obscure case to issue a political pronouncement, his was a transparent effort to counter criticism of his decisions. He well knew, as Thomas Jefferson bitterly said, that the Constitution in final analysis is "merely a thing of wax," which the Court "may twist and shape into any form" it pleases.[58] He knew also that the High Bench, as a political organ, could strengthen its position in the nation by the appearance of preexisting law dictating the decisions. He realized that the Justices had no constituency in the sense of elected officials and thus had to pick their way with care. Their constituency at that time was informal, but nonetheless powerful—those we have called the moneyed and propertied.

A century and a half later, a more candid and perhaps greater Chief Justice, Earl Warren, speaking from a much more secure judicial vantage point, said in his valedictory: "We [the Supreme Court], of course, venerate the past, but our focus is on the problems of the day and the future as far as we can foresee it." The Court, Warren went on, has the awesome responsibility of often speaking the last word "in great governmental affairs." "It is a responsibility that is made more difficult in this Court because we have no constituency. We serve no majority. We serve no minority. We serve only the public interest as we see it, guided only by the Constitution and our own consciences."[59] That Warren was not exactly correct—the Court does not often have the last word and it does have an informal constituency—does not detract from his implicit rejection of Marshall's position. (In Warren's day, as in Marshall's, the public interest is an undefined concept. By no means can the judges's consciences be guided by "the will of the law." Political actors, they must have a correct appreciation of social conditions and a true appraisal of the actual effects of conduct. That is a tall order. It may be an impossible dream—but that we will not know unless and until the Justices make the attempt.)

With one exception, during his thirty-four years on the High Bench, Marshall's views prevailed in constitutional cases. He knew what he was doing. He knew that he and his colleagues were de facto representatives of the ruling class. When to *Fletcher* is added *Dartmouth College* and *Sturges*, the pattern became clear. Those decisions came at a "peculiarly opportune time":[60] 1819. *Dartmouth* involved the question of whether Dartmouth's charter from the King was a contract that, even though the American Revolution had established a new government, could be altered by the New Hampshire legislature. The answer from Marshall: no, in yet another decision of far greater significance than the precise issue. The immunity of business corporations from state control was established. Even Marshall admitted that the result was "not in the mind of the Constitutional Convention" when it adopted the contract clause. By assuming the answer to the exact question at issue—was the charter a contract?—he went on to invalidate New Hampshire's law. The sanctity of contracts was held to be above both ethical considerations and the public welfare—contracts as defined by the Court. Economic stability was promoted; the assurance to investors that rights granted by state legislatures would be secure greatly facilitated development of corporations. Surely, however, it is also true, to quote the pungent language of Professor Wallace Mendelson, that Marshall's contract decisions "encouraged the flagrant corruption of state politics and reckless waste of natural resources that marked the nineteenth century. . . . Judicial protection of fraud in the Yazoo land scandal paved the way for the Robber Barons and their Great Barbeque at the expense of the American people."[61]

John Marshall, to employ a label of present-day opprobrium, was clearly "result oriented."[62] (I do not suggest that he differed from any other person who ever sat upon the High Bench.) That description, of course, means that his opinions were not "principled" in fact, although some may argue that they were in theory. As is discussed later (Chapter 4), a demand, which many make, for principled or reasoned opinions is a bootless quest. "The requirements for principled decision," Professor Martin Golding maintains, "are: (1) that a reason for the disposition of the case be given; and (2) that the case be so decided because it is held to be proper to decide cases of its type in this way."[63] That analysis is not very helpful. It is far better to acknowledge, once and for all, that John Marshall—and all other Justices—have exemplified the advice given by Lord Mansfield, the great English judge, to an officer who had been appointed governor of a West India island. The officer was concerned about his ability to sit as a judge and decide cases (he was not a lawyer). Mansfield soothed him with this counsel:

Be of good cheer—take my advice, and you will be reckoned a great judge as well as a great commander-in-chief. Nothing is more easy; only hear both sides patiently—then consider what you think justice requires, and decide accordingly. But never give your reasons;—for your judgment will probably be right, but your reasons will certainly be wrong.[64]

Marshall did give reasons, such as they were, but there was more than a slight element of fiat in his conclusions. The reasons were the window dressing, the rationalization, the justification couched in lawyers's language. Justice William O. Douglas in his autobiography *The Court Years* quoted Chief Justice Hughes as advising him, "You must remember . . . [that] at the constitutional level where we work, 90 per cent of any decision is emotional. The rational part of us supplies the reasons for supporting our predilections."[65]

V.

What Marshall began, the Court under his successor Roger Taney con-tinued—particularly in 1851 when it promulgated the so-called Cooley Rule, the case being *Cooley* v. *Board of Port Wardens*.[66] In attempting to strike a balance between the relative powers of federal and state governments over commercial activities, the Justices managed to come out on top. It was they, not Congress as the Document stated, who would define which commerce could be regulated by the states and which demanded a single uniform rule, although they did not put it so bluntly. They said this:

. . . the power to regulate commerce, embraces a vast field, containing not only many, but exceedingly various subjects, quite unlike in their nature; some imperatively demanding a single uniform rule . . . and some . . . demanding that diversity, which alone can meet the local necessities. . . . *Whatever subjects of [Congress's power over interstate commerce] are in their nature national, or admit only of one uniform system, or plan of regulation may justly be said to be of such a nature as to require exclusive legislation by Congress.*

In economic terms, that remark meant that the idea of a national common market was boosted, and in political (constitutional) terms, another milestone in judicial supervision of the economy was erected. The result was forcefully stated by Justice Robert H. Jackson in 1949:

Our system, fostered by the Commerce Clause, is that every farmer and every craftsman shall be encouraged to produce by the certainty that he will have free access to every market in the Nation, that no home embargoes will withhold his exports, and no foreign state will by customs duties or regulations exclude them. Likewise, every consumer may look to the free competition from every producing area in the Nation to protect him from exploitation by any. Such was the vision of the Founders; such has been the doctrine of this Court that has given it reality.[67]

After the wartime hiatus, others continued to expand judicial power. The "vision of the Founders" was transmuted into doctrine by a Court dominated by Justice Stephen Field (a Court that William Howard Taft once called "a lot of mummies").[68] In this, the second period of controversy over the Court, the Justices determined that that "vision" meant that the economically strongest—the burgeoning corporations—required constitutional protection. In accomplishing this, they were helped by the corporate bar. Lawyers convinced the Court, if indeed any convincing was needed, that business enterprise was highest in the scale of values the Constitution sheltered. With the Industrial Revolution in full swing, corporations waxed strong and influential after the Civil War. A new form of property, consisting of promises (stock certificates, debentures, corporate bonds, and the like), came into being and began to outweigh ownership of land. Those who held it received judicial protection. The fall-out from that period of economic development under the sheltering umbrella of the law, constitutional and otherwise, is still being felt.

One might ask whether the Court had a truly large impact on the social order. The Justices legitimized what some others (those with wealth and property) were doing. Did they in fact have other real choices? If they did, would it have made any difference? Some observers, including Felix Frankfurter, think so. "In law also men make a difference," Frankfurter wrote before joining the Court, "it would deny all meaning to history to believe that the course of events would have been if Thomas Jefferson had had the naming of Spencer Roane to the place to which John Adams called John Marshall. . . . There is no inevitability in history except as men make it."[69]

Well, maybe. Frankfurter assumed that the Supreme Court had real political power. Is that view accurate? Or is it lawyers's history? The latter is more probable. Men may make a difference, but even so, one must locate the men who were not on the bench rather than those who, like Marshall, made judicial decisions. Who were the true movers and shakers of American society? One has to have a mind befogged by legal learning to believe that the Justices were more important than the men of property. John Marshall's judicial essays in political economy made him more a surrogate for others than a prime mover. What Marshall started has been followed by his successors.

Only by overweening conceit can lawyers believe that the Supreme Court was, and is, supremely powerful *in society*, even though it is at least theoretically supreme over other courts. Much more important to the American people, then and now, are the uncontrolled actions of businessmen and *their* surrogates in government and also of affirmative governmental efforts to stimulate economic growth. Orthodox thinking speaks in terms of a laissez-faire State in the nineteenth century. The orthodoxy is wrong on at least two counts: First, the laissez-faire State was not weak; it was precisely as strong as conditions and circumstances required. "It acquired substantial colonial empires, waged wars, held down internal disorders, and stabilized itself over long periods of time."[70] Second, governmental intervention into economics had the support—nay, the demand—of leading politicians, who—again—in fact "represented" the men of wealth and property. Railroads were subsidized (which started the transportation revolution), national banks created (for a time, at least), and the economy tinkered with through a primitive form of economic planning: "treasury fiscal operations, the deliberate use of tariffs to divert the allocation of resources into desired lines of development, and government subsidies to certain industries (fishing, small arms, and . . . grain and silk production)."[71] In brief, that was Hamiltonianism triumphant—the Hamilton of the *Report on Manufactures* (1791)—although it is true that federal activity before the *Report* took a similar path. Largely influenced by Hamilton, the first tariff act (1789) justified duties as necessary for revenue and "the encouragement and protection of manufactures." President Washington's first address to Congress declared the safety and interest of the people required that they should "promote such manufactures as tend to render them independent of others for essential, particularly military, supplies." That statement could have come directly from Adam Smith's *The Wealth of Nations*, where it was maintained that defense is more important to a nation than opulence. (More, it is echoed by modern Presidents, such as Ronald Reagan. The more things change, the more they remain the same.)

Most affirmative governmental action was never litigated. Politicians and businessmen were busily altering the face of America, thereby creating new social conditions that in due course produced disputes—some of which eventually reached the Supreme Court. By the time they did, however, the real power of the business community was overwhelming—far too much for the Justices to battle, even if they had wanted to do so. Emphatically, they did not; they were content in their role as surrogates.

Hamilton's *Report* is one of the great documents of American history.[72] Now largely forgotten, it is in many respects as important as the Constitution itself. Much of it, in letter and spirit, found its way into public policy and thus helped set the tone for the way the nation developed. Said Hamilton: "infant" industry should be encouraged, if necessary by protective tariffs. That made the *Report* "the nearest thing to planning for the future economy of the country"[73] that has ever been produced. Hamilton did not follow the new dogma of individual self-interest—Adam Smith's *Wealth of Nations* had been published in 1776 and was already widely accepted—but relied on a guided economy. Government was to stimulate and help—and thus to guide—but was not to control. Hamilton envisaged association or cooperation between industry and agriculture and government. Political and economic power were to be meshed. (That blend has produced, almost two centuries later, an indigenous form of corporatism. The United States, far more than most people realize, is a Corporate State.)[74] Federal aid to development, helped when need be by an expansive judical reading of Congress's taxing and spending powers, provided much of the impetus to exploitation of the continent.

Save for an occasional decision on state power to regulate commerce, the Supreme Court had little to say about this. Economic policies were made by the political branches of government, the Court having not yet taken on the role of aristocratic censor of what the politicians wanted. That came later, during the second period of controversy over the Court. A combination of seemingly endless land plus capital from Europe and a quiescent labor force enabled the United States by the time of the Civil War to plunge fully into the Industrial Revolution. By the midnineteenth century, the new nation rivaled Great Britain in manufactures and commerce. Advantages of incorporation, such as limited liability of stockholders, led to rapid formation of business corporations; from about 300 in 1800, they multiplied at a fast pace. In the decade of 1850-60, more were formed than in all previous American history.[75] Society was being transformed. The point here is twofold: First, economic development was in large part the result of a partnership between private enterprise and government. Second, those political actions seldom resulted in constitutional disputes being thrust upon the Supreme Court. Judges did eliminate governmental actions, mainly from the states, inimical to economic growth, but they intervened not at all in measures designed to promote growth. What is called the Economic Constitution in Chapter 9 was being formed.

After the Civil War the businessman seemed to strike out on his own. But only seemingly. Government aid continued, but less so in an overt way. Assistance came, however, from a legal system and the law itself that were skewed in favor of business. Tort law—the law of civil wrongs—is an example. Judges invented principles of "assumption of risk," "contributory negligence," and the "fellow-servant rule" to insulate business from the dreadful costs of industrialization. Those costs were paid by the workers. When, furthermore, laborers joined together—in a sense, to incorporate themselves —as did business, they ran into police officers, judges, and the private armies of business (the Pinkertons). Supreme Court Justices who were quick to protect the intangible property rights of investors in corporations just as quickly, and quite as firmly, refused to recognize an intangible property right of the worker in his job. The combination of public and private power was, for many decades, too high to surmount.

The struggle continued. Men desperate for work and for a living wage did not give up the fight. The immediate targets were state legislatures, which in the late nineteenth and early twentieth centuries began to enact maximum-hour and minimum-wage laws. Those efforts ran into the impenetrable roadblock of a Supreme Court that readily and often voided those laws.[76] The time from 1886 to 1937 has aptly been called a period when laissez-faire fairly represented "an ideology of capitalism that shackled popular-rule ideology, ordaining in effect that popular rule was all right so long as popular institutions chose to do nothing."[77] A few economic regulatory measures did survive, mainly in the public utility area. The Court in the Temple on the Hill was the ultimate protector of economic privilege.

To recapitulate, during the first period (to the Civil War) of controversy, the judiciary stayed out of the way of the federal government. Whatever Congress wanted, Congress got, with only two exceptions: the *Marbury* case and the *Dred Scott* case. Not so for state legislatures: there can be little question that "the conservative, propertied interests turned to the courts for protection against what they considered radical and unconstitutional legislation, seeking to have such laws invalidated as invasions of national authority or as violations of constitutional prohibitions upon the states."[78] As has been suggested, the Supreme Court could have held either way but did not, because it viewed itself in Hamiltonian terms as the protector of vested rights. The irony is that the true radicals were not those who got legislatures to act, but the very businessmen whose interests were protected. Marrying enterprise to technology, they so altered the nature of American society that it bore less and less resemblance to that which existed in 1787 or even 1800.

The brutalities and inequities of an industrializing nation were such that an allegedly free nation could not long tolerate them. So countervailing forces to industry power came into being, slowly at first—and for a long period unsuccessful in changing the course of constitutional development. That failure can particularly be seen in the development of the Fourteenth Amendment, added in 1868 purportedly to help the freed slaves. Section 1 of the Amendment, its most important part, reads:

All persons born or naturalized in the United States, and subject to the jurisdiction thereof, are citizens of the United States and of the State wherein they reside. No State shall make or enforce any law which shall abridge the privileges or immunities of citizens of the United States; nor shall any State deprive any person of life, liberty, or property, without due process of law; nor deny to any person within its jurisdiction the equal protection of the laws.

Cryptic language, that: several terms and words were left undefined—*privileges or immunities, person, due process of law, equal protection of the laws.* The Amendment was an open invitation—in legal terms, a tacit delegation of power—to the Supreme Court to put content into those words.

That is precisely what the Justices have done, but only over the years—and even then incompletely (the term *privileges or immunities* still has little substantive content). Soon after 1868 business interests attempted to have the Amendment interpreted to protect them. They grasped something that was added to the Document to aid freed slaves so as to stave off legislation that was the product of the rising Granger and Populist movements. Not an easy task, that, and the first efforts failed.[79] The Justices simply could not stomach the proposition that the corporation was a person within the meaning of the

Amendment and that it could invoke the due process clause. But ultimately the corporate interests prevailed.

It was a two-step process: First, the corporation—a formless economic entity—had to be designated a person within the terms of the Amendment. That step came in 1886 when the Court unanimously, and without hearing argument on the question, announced that the Justices all agreed that a corporation was the same in law as a natural person.[80] That was an immense mental leap, but the second step was even greater: the Justices were called upon to rewrite the "due process" clauses of the Document. That they did, and judicial review took a large leap forward. Whereas in the early years of the republic, many of the economic decisions of the Supreme Court dealt, as we have seen, with contracts and commerce clauses, now the Court had *carte blanche* to put meaning into the "life, liberty, and property" that was protected by due process of law.

Historically, *due process* meant "due procedure"—the means by which government acted. Business, however, wanted more—the invalidation of the content, the substance of what government was doing that affected it. Readily admitting that they had had their "day in court" (due procedure), they had to persuade the Justices to revise due process to mean *what* was being done. The Court obliged through a blinding flash of revelation and by a process of divination known only to it. The Justices discovered that due process had another dimension, aimed at the content or substance of regulation. Surely that was not in the minds of the Founding Fathers, and it was certainly not in the minds of those who drafted the Fourteenth Amendment.

The lesson is clear. Put bluntly, as of that time, the Court became the judicial arm of the corporate community.[81] The businessman's surrogates in the corporate bar were able to convince the businessman's surrogates on the High Bench that principles of laissez-faire economics were part of the liberty protected by the due process clause of the Fourteenth Amendment. That view lasted until 1937, at which time economic policymaking by the Court was informally abjured, but "substantive" due process did not die (it was employed, for example, in the abortion cases of 1973). The meaning of the new reading of due process, in economic terms, was that corporations were free from even nominal governmental regulation. Private enterprise prevailed. Fortunes for some grew beyond the dreams of avarice; the plutocracy proliferated. On the other hand, a nation that encouraged and subsidized manufactures permitted most of the people to live drab and dreary, even desperately poverty-stricken, lives. No widespread sharing of wealth came with the burgeoning commercial activity.

Politically, the men of wealth and position were dominant, controlling all branches of the federal government. Nonregulation meant that the Robber Barons received the benefits of government assistance—overt in the form of subsidies, covert in the form of a legal system tilted in their favor—without having to pay for them. That situation, to be sure, had always been true in some degree. But with the invention of substantive due process, what had been a consequence of politics was elevated into constitutional doctrine. That "amendment" to the Document is the most important addition to formal constitutional law ever made. When judges can scrutinize the *content* of legislation under the ambiguities of the due process clauses, they obviously are a powerful instrument of governance.

Despite protestations to the contrary, in final analysis substantive due process decisions are rulings on the wisdom of legislation. Perhaps a persuasive case can be made for the proposition that deciding on the wisdom of legislation was nothing new, that the Justices had always done so while covering their actions with a counterpane of constitutional verbiage. No doubt that was so for many of the decisions of the early nineteenth century. One factor, however, was new when the Justices had their flash of revelation: A concept of "rationality" was read into the fundamental law. Only laws that met the test of "reason," that had a "rational basis," stood constitutional muster. This had two consequences: First, seeming constitutional absolutes could be and were diluted by the Justices. Second, the Court kept to itself the power to determine what was reasonable in the circumstances.

That history is familiar, and needs no present restatement. The Fourteenth Amendment, one of three antislavery amendments, soon became a shield for corporate business. The former slaves were forgotten, as the Justices blandly and blithely "amended" the Amendment. With the at least tacit support of most white Americans, they ended the First Reconstruction when they invented in 1896 the "separate but equal" doctrine.[82] Even then, no one— certainly not the Court—enforced that watered down version of the original promise. Black Americans rapidly became both separate *and* unequal, in a condition of feudal peonage little better than slavery. The *apartheid* of separate but equal remained in the formal Constitution until 1954 and still exists in the operative Constitution, which provides for most blacks both separateness and inequality.

Blacks were not the only ones suffering from the brutalities of industrialization. Many whites also suffered, especially new immigrants streaming in from Europe who made up a large manpower pool for new industries. Choosing to forget that, as Hamilton had said, "the power over a man's subsistence amounts to a power over his will,"[83] the Justices announced that "liberty of contract . . . cannot be unreasonably interfered with."[84] Now, there is nothing in the Document about either liberty of contract or unreasonable interferences. Nonetheless, the Court found it easy to equate the right of an employee to quit his job with "the right of the employer, for whatever reason, to dispense with the services of the employee."[85] Any legislation that disturbed "that equality is an arbitrary interference with the liberty of contract which no government can justify in a free land."[86] That is an interesting sentiment, but one that completely neglected to see that needy men cannot be free and that the employer, because of superior economic resources, had the whip hand.

Even so, the Justices set themselves up as a little lunacy commission to decide whether legislatures had acted *reasonably*, a term they never defined, in actions such as maximum hours and minimum wages.

Reading their ideas of wise social policy into the Constitution, ideas that coincided with those of the plutocracy, the Justices were not so much blind to the dismal facts of life among the working class as indifferent. They simply did not care. One of them, Samuel F. Miller, knew that; in an off-bench statement, he tersely summed up the point: "It is vain to contend with judges who have been at the bar the advocates for forty years of railroad companies, and all the forms of associated capital, when they are called upon to decide cases where such interests are in conflict. All their training, all their feelings, are from the start in favor of those who need no such influence."[87] In 1980 Professor Lester Thurow, in his important book *The Zero-Sum Society*, made a similar observation: "In the past, political and economic power was distributed in such a way that substantial economic losses could be imposed on parts of the population if the establishment decided that it was in the general interest. Economic losses were allocated to particular powerless groups rather than spread across the population."[88] As the primary judicial instrument of the Establishment (at that time), the Court invented constitutional law that legitimized those disparities in "economic losses."

The cases are many, but the constitutional principle is clear. Even though, as John D. Rockefeller said at the turn of the century, "large-scale organization had revolutionized the way of doing business and . . . individualism had gone, never to return,"[89] the Court insisted that the workingmen be individualists. History has its ironies and its policy inconsistencies: Those with capital could collectivize themselves and get constitutional protection, but those with only their labor to sell could not. Consistency, however, is distinctly not a constitutional requirement, either for Congress or for the Supreme Court.

Laissez-faire, furthermore, was a moral principle. Poverty and economic failure were equated with sin and decadence, wealth and business success with virtue. It was the heyday of "Social Darwinism," a time when the biological theory of survival of the fittest was transferred by Herbert Spencer and others to human affairs. "The fittest" were those who won the economic battles; their values were transmuted into constitutional law by judges invariably taken from that very class.

Tracing all of the lines of judicial development in the post-Civil War period is possible only by finding, long after the fact, regularities and uniformities in the tangled tapestry of history that may not have existed. There can be no dispute, however, over the Court being the economic sovereign, the oracle that enunciated ultimate economic policy. Giant corporations flourished, with the help of government, and today they dominate the economy. Private collectivism came into existence, ironically in the name of individualism. The great "trusts" flowered, particularly after the Supreme Court rewrote the

Sherman antitrust law. About the same time, the frontier closed—a social fact that has had enormous consequences, not least of which is the fact that the nation turned its vision outwards and suddenly became deeply and irretrievably immersed in world affairs.

The Sherman Act, enacted in 1890, was a Congressional effort to enforce competition—freedom of contract—on a business community that was rapidly combining and collaborating. It was one thing for corporate lawyers to help write liberty of contract into the Document when the problem was one of the workers against business, but it was another thing to try to force the businessmen to be free in their contracts with each other. Corporate officers strenuously objected when the law was passed, for in terse constitutionlike language, it made illegal "every contract, combination in the form of trust or otherwise, or conspiracy in restraint of trade." Plain enough, one might think: surely "every" means "all," and that is what the Court held in early decisions interpreting the Act. That course was not to last. With aplomb and dispatch and another flash of revelation, the Justices discovered in 1911 that Congress did not mean what it said. They promulgated "the rule of reason" in antitrust cases.[90] That rule meant the Court not only amended the statute by decree, but it again set itself up as a lunacy commission to determine which combinations and cabals were reasonable. Because statutory, not constitutional, interpretation is involved, Congress of course can overrule such judicial decisions, but that seldom happens. (By hindsight, given the immense influence, even control, by business over the legislature, it is remarkable that the Sherman Act ever got on the lawbooks.)

Today, the Sherman Act is little more than a sheathed sword in the government's arsenal.[91] Not only was the statute gutted by the Court, but the executive and Congress have insured that even its diminished stature has no real effect. This is accomplished by not strictly enforcing the law and by Congress not appropriating funds sufficient for effective enforcement. The law has become an empty charade, a classic example of the appearance of regulation without the substance. Corporations are far larger today than they were in 1911, so large that the assets of some of them overshadow most of the nations of the world.

In other areas the Justices were equally supportive of corporate capitalism. During the Pullman strike of 1894, for example, the Court upheld an injunction against the workers. The case In re Debs[92] saw the Court finding a way to rule even though no statute permitted them to do so—exactly contrary to the law as it then stood and as it is now (as the Senate's Watergate Committee learned in 1973 in its suit to obtain the Nixon tapes).[93] About the same time, the Justices discovered, through an intuition apparently known only to the five-man majority, that a federal tax on incomes was unconstitutional.[94] (That decision required the Sixteenth Amendment to reverse.)

The invention of substantive due process, however, did more to transform the Court than anything since the Marshall era. (It ranks with the Marbury case and also, as will be shown, with the emergence during the past thirty years of the "Court as commander.") Aided by the priesthood of the bar, which viewed itself as guardians of the sacred Document, the Justices determined that almost any intervention by government into economic affairs was "unreasonable" and, therefore, constitutionally infirm. In a series of decisions that spanned forty years—from 1898 to 1937—only occasionally did political action to ameliorate the brutalities of the emergent corporate society escape invalidation. Most of the decisions were decided, as Justice Holmes said in 1905, "upon an economic theory which a large part of this country does not entertain."[95] Holmes went on to point out that some valid regulations of business did exist. The Constitution, he said, "is not intended to embody a particular economic theory, whether of paternalism and the organic relation of the citizen to the state or of laissez-faire." But his colleagues would not listen, or if they did listen, they did not heed. Only when the misery of the Great Depression and massive social discontent surfaced were judicial minds that had seemingly been set in concrete changed. (Worth noting is the probable inaccuracy of Holmes's history. Modern historians, beginning with Professor Charles Beard, have maintained that "a particular economic theory" was envisaged by the Framers.)[96]

During the four-decades period, the Court and corporate bar promoted the growth and wealth of business and thus of the moneyed and propertied class. Lawyers, with overweening hubris, saw themselves as self-appointed Platonic Guardians, with the mission of protecting the republic from the onslaught of barbarians—that is, the people generally. "Popular" sovereignty was discarded in fact, even though the theory remained, in yet another instance of the gap between the formal and the operative Constitutions.

Rather than a dark and sinister conspiracy, it was all open. Consider, for example, an 1892 statement by John Randolph Tucker to the American Bar Association:

Can I be mistaken in claiming that Constitutional Law is the most important branch of American jurisprudence; and that the American Bar is and should be in a large degree that priestly tribe to whose hands are confined the support and defense of this Ark of the Covenant of our fathers, the security of which against the profane touch of open and covert foes is the noblest function and the most patriotic purpose of our great profession.[97]

(It was no accident, as Chapter 10 shows, that Tucker spoke of the Constitution in religious terms.) Tucker was not alone in extolling the merits of lawyers or in uttering such sanctimonious balderdash.

The lawyer stands in the mainstream of the wealth that flows from government, or with government aid, to corporate enterprise. Rather than true professionals, lawyers are legal mechanics, avidly pursuing Mammon, and willing to accept any client with adequate wealth. Thorstein Veblen knew this well;

he saw the legal profession in 1899 as nothing more than a type of employ-ment "immediately subservient to ownership and financiering. . . . The lawyer is exclusively occupied with the details of predatory fraud, either in achieving or in checkmating chicane, and success in the profession is therefore accepted as marking a large endowment of that barbarian astuteness which has always commanded men's respect and fear."[98] Theodore Roosevelt was even more cutting: "Many of the most influential and highly remunerated members of the bar in every center of wealth make it their special task to work out bold and ingenious schemes by which their very wealthy clients, individual or corporate, can evade the laws which are made to regulate in the interest of the public the use of great wealth."[99] (The lawyer as hired gun still dominates a guild that likes to call itself a profession.)

My point may be simply stated: Both bench and bar, as Reginald Heber Smith, himself a lawyer, said in 1919, collaborated in transforming a legal system that had the merits of a legal claim as its ideal into one in which the availability of financial resources became the criterion of whether justice was done. Lawyers, on and off the bench, showed "an ignorance of, or indif-ference to, the disadvantages under which the poor have struggled."[100] Years later, Gandhi was to remark that the greatest obstacle to social change was the "hardness of heart of the educated"—precisely what Smith saw in the bar and precisely what, in large part, still exists. Smith was no radical or revolu-tionary; he was a pillar of the Boston legal establishment. Yet his conclusion, stated in 1919, is valid more than six decades later: "The administration of American justice is not impartial, the rich and the poor do not stand on an equality before the law, the traditional method of providing justice has operated to close the doors of the courts to the poor, and has caused a gross denial of justice in all parts of the country to millions of persons."[101]

The implications of Smith's analysis may be easily stated. In the words of Professor Jerold Auerbach, "much of the legal system . . . was designed to control poor people."[102] It still is. If one accepts Aristotle's definition of politics—"the trouble between those who are favored by fortune and those who are not"—it may readily be seen that a nation that dispenses justice for a fee (which many cannot afford) principally benefits those who can pay. That leaves law for the many "an impotent sham" (as Smith said). Only during the past few years have some, but not all, of those left out in the struggle for fortune been able to get legal service. When they do so, it usually is far from the highest quality. The best legal brains represent the already affluent.

That the law was a means to control the poor and the disadvantaged may clearly be seen in Supreme Court activity in the mid-1930s that struck down much of President Roosevelt's New Deal. Eviscerating governmental pro-grams designed, at least outwardly, to help the poor, the Justices in a series of decisions (often by a 5-4 or 6-3 vote) employed what Robert H. Jackson called in 1941 "the lawless use of law." (By that Jackson must have meant that a law higher than and separate from the Constitution itself exists and is ascertainable. If so, that is a startling proposition, one that poses difficult and complex questions of the nature of law and of constitutions.) In the guise of private lawsuits usually involving not more than a few dollars, the entire American economy was haled before the Supreme Court. FDR did not lose all of the cases, but many New Deal acts were invalidated in opinions that reflected the values of the pre-Depression period. In one group of cases, those involving the refusal to pay off paper money in gold, FDR did win, but by the narrowest of margins and over embittered dissents which "adopted the whole philosophy and terminology of the creditor class and assailed Acts of Congress as 'spoliation of citizens' and 'repudiation' of obligations, and concluded: 'the impending legal and moral chaos is appalling.' "[103]

Europeans were incredulous. All save some American businessmen and their minions among lawyers could see that five men (at times, six men) should not be allowed to veto what the people so desperately needed. What was truly "appalling" was not "impending legal and moral chaos," but the consummate stupidity and intellectual myopia that failed to perceive that the New Deal was an essentially conservative movement, designed not to change but to save "the system" by buying off discontent having a high revolutionary potential. Not only the majority of the High Bench but federal judges elsewhere struck at New Deal programs in a frenzy of judicial power that knows no historical or subsequent counterpart. The (evil) genius principally responsible for the composition of the judiciary was Chief Justice William Howard Taft, whose influence over all levels of the federal bench was lasting and all-pervasive.[104] He was largely responsible for the bloc of Justices who sat as Economic Sovereign during the 1920s and 1930s, judges whose philosophy was not far from Taft's. Taft refused to resign when he reached age seventy, even though he had previously said that that was the proper age for retirement. He distrusted President Hoover, suspecting him of "liberal" tendencies. Taft wrote: "I am older and slower and less acute and more confused. However, as long as things continue as they are, and I am able to answer in my place, I must stay on the court in order to prevent the Bolsheviki from getting control. . . . The only hope we have of keeping a consistent declaration of constitutional law is for us to stay as long as we can."[105]

Probably Taft was senile, or almost so, when he wrote that letter. Be that as it may, he well knew that when he spoke on the Supreme Court it was not in terms of law but in accordance with his personal predilections. Anyone who in the late 1920s could seriously write about a fear of the Bolsheviki controlling the Court cannot be considered to have had full possession of his faculties. Or if he did, surely his bigotry and bias should have disqualified him from the bench. Life tenure for judges has its merits in making them as independent as possible from politicians, but it also has shortcomings, as the Taft letter exemplifies. (This argues either for a fixed term—say, fifteen years—for Justices or for them to be better chosen.)

Under Taft's influence, life tenure became a means by which five Neanderthal judges were able to thwart the reasonable economic desires of the people. Said Robert Jackson: "The alternations of our national moods are such that a cycle of liberal government seldom exceeds eight years, and by living through them the Court could go without decisive liberal infusions. So well has this strategy worked that never in its entire history can it be said to have for a single hour been representative of anything except the relatively conservative forces of its day."[106] Not until FDR's second term was half over did he get to name a new Justice. Taft's reactionaries heeded his advice, clinging to their positions as Justices and thus as overseers of socioeconomic policy.

That was too much for Roosevelt to stomach. After his lopsided electoral victory in 1936, he produced a plan to add six new Justices to the High Bench. But he used the wrong tactics, charging the Court with inefficiency. When it was quickly shown that the Justices kept abreast of their work load, the plan collapsed but not, however, before a furor broke out. The President was accused of wanting to "pack" the Court. That, no doubt, is exactly what he wanted to do. Knowing full well that personal philosophy, rather than interdictory law, controlled Court decisions, he wanted a Court that would sustain the New Deal. Roosevelt's plan, although legally valid, was politically not feasible. (Congress has constitutional power to designate the number of Justices, save that it can reduce the Court only when vacancies occur.) FDR lost the skirmish, but he won the campaign, possibly because he knew (as Theodore Roosevelt once said): "I do not know much about law, but I do know how to put the fear of God into judges."[107] (The "Court-packing" plan, moreover, was not novel. During President Grant's administration, he was able through Congressional connivance to name two new Justices and thereby obtained a reversal in the important legal tender cases.)[108]

Whether or not the Justices, notably Owen J. Roberts, had "the fear of God" put into them, it is true that in 1937 the Court suddenly began to reverse itself. The Justices were blessed with a new insight into the meaning of the economic clauses of the Constitution. Roberts learned by an intuition known only to himself that due process of law did not mean what he and other Neanderthals had previously thought. Suddenly he joined the "liberal" dissenters to make up a majority that constitutionalized Keynesian economics (the New Deal). What had been invalid in 1936 became valid in 1937. The Court deftly beat a strategic political retreat (and immediately began to search for a new role). The reactionary Justices went down to a snarling and vindictive defeat, even though Roberts's conversion in all probability saved the Court. Not for much longer would people, leading lives of less and less quiet desperation, have tolerated five elderly men barring urgent governmental efforts to combat the Depression. The Neanderthals had listened too long to the economic theories of the dominant business class, theories that had led to the deepest depression in American history. They asserted that misery must be suffered, because their reading of the Document, but not the Constitution itself, forbade governmental aid to alleviate distress. One is reminded of the British government during the "great hunger" (the potato famine) in Ireland, when officials refused to intervene even while people starved to death, because—so they said—of certain economic "laws." Such a "let them eat cake" attitude of those in positions of power cannot long be sustained in any nation that calls itself democratic. Sooner or later, the people would have revolted—as they did in Ireland. (There is another political lesson to be drawn: The Court cannot long be out of phase with the *zeitgeist*—the temper of the times—which both restricts and, paradoxically, enlarges its power.)

Roberts made the famous "switch in time that saved nine." It first surfaced on March 29, 1937,[109] a date of equal importance to 1803 (when the *Marbury* case was decided), and the Court has not been the same since. (The Court has not been *outwardly* the same, that is, for the same question—*cui bono?*—and the same answer—the moneyed and the propertied—remain to the present.) The issue in 1937 was familiar: Could the state of Washington validly enact a statute regulating wages of women workers? On precedent alone, the law surely was dead, for it was much the same as a New York statute invalidated in 1936.

Justice Roberts's intellectual flipflop came after FDR's landslide victory in 1936 and before March 1937. Just how he suddenly was able to see new constitutional light has never been revealed. But he did, with the result that the oracle in the Temple on the Hill now permitted minimum-wage legislation. "Freedom of contract," as invented by the Court, was quietly buried. "What is this freedom?" Chief Justice Hughes asked. His answer: "The Constitution does not speak of freedom of contract. It speaks of liberty and prohibits the deprivation of liberty without due process of law." With that, Hughes swept aside forty years of Supreme Court decision making. But he went even further, maintaining that liberty is not an absolute under the Constitution. It is, said Hughes, "liberty in a social organization which *requires* the protection of law against the evils which menace the health, safety, morals and welfare of the people." He then went on to assert that "liberty under the Constitution is . . . necessarily subject to the *restraints* of due process, and regulation which is reasonable in relation to its subject and is adopted in the interests of the community is due process."[110] (Emphasis added.)

A portentous statement, that. Hughes changed the nature of liberty in America[111] and altered the role of the Supreme Court. Still sitting as a little lunacy commission, he and colleagues "amended" the Constitution as it had been interpreted by emphasizing "the interests of the community." Although not defined, the word *community* could only have referred to the "unmoneyed and the unpropertied," those theretofore not given constitutional protection. Law was asserted to be "required" to protect against the evils of industrialization. Liberty is in "a social organization." The political theory for a benign form of collectivism began to be formulated.

With his defection from the Neanderthals, Justice Roberts in effect became a one-man Supreme Court, a tribunal that in early April 1937 upheld the

Wagner labor relations act (and thus constitutionalized labor's right to act collectively).[112] Other reforms were speedily validated—for example, social security and unemployment compensation.[113] Social discontent was siphoned off in the American version of the welfare state. I do not suggest that the New Deal, even when validated under the formal Constitution, cured the woes of economic depression. Not until a war economy came, and World War II erupted, did the United States emerge from the swamp into which laissez-faire policies had lured Americans. The larger lesson is implicit: A close *overt* government-business partnership became the norm. It still exists and shows few signs of breaking up.

The Justices did not abdicate entirely. Their high and lofty position in government remained. After a few years of tentative probing, they shifted gears and became the first authoritative faculty of social ethics in the world's history. For the first time in American history, human rights came to center stage and received judicial protection. "Discrete and insular minorities" left behind in the political struggle turned to the courts. Led by black Americans, the judiciary became the object of pressure group tactics,[114] in effect not dissimilar from the way that Congress and the bureaucracy are importuned. The Justices responded, slowly at first and then with a rush. With that response was born the third period of controversy over the Court. Conservatives and neoconservatives now attack it, at times with a venom close to that which assailed John Marshall. The critics are purblind. They do not perceive that the Justices, once again, are helping to drain off social discontent, helping to create a permissive albeit innocuous society, and thus making it possible for those who have always ruled to continue to do so. Some of the disadvantaged are accorded constitutional gains, to be sure, but on the whole those advances, if not merely cosmetic, are the minimum price that must be paid to retain social cohesion.

VI.

We are enjoined by high school civics and history texts to view America's past as pristine. It was far from that; blots on the record run back to pre-revolutionary times. One deserves special mention: slavery. As written in 1787, the formal Constitution protected the slave system—underscored by the Supreme Court in the *Dred Scott* case in 1857. Not until the Thirteenth Amendment was rammed through the states after the Civil War did blacks attain even ostensible freedom and even then at most they merely exchanged the bonds of slavery for the less visible but nonetheless shackling fetters of an informal system of feudal peonage. (Lincoln's Emancipation Proclamation was a mere gesture and, indeed, one that had no basis in law.) The promise of the formal Constitution (outlawing involuntary servitude) was denied by the operative fundamental law. That condition in time became intolerable, particularly when black Americans were drafted and forced to fight, and perhaps to die, in freedom's name during World War II.

Efforts to get legislative aid for freed slaves were abortive, and executives were indifferent at best, savagely repressive all too often. Of necessity, therefore, if black Americans were to work within "the system" to better their dreary condition, they had to turn to the judiciary. No other official avenue was open. Most white Americans simply did not care about, or even think about, the millions of men and women of African descent. The first attempts to get judicial protection were futile. Judges enforced the dreadful *Plessy* rule to the extent of segregating blacks but did not enforce it to make equal facilities available. The performance of the formal Constitution fell far short of the promise. Nor was that all. In addition to a failure to enforce the "equal" part of the *Plessy* doctrine, government in America enacted Jim Crow laws to insure black separateness. Vicious brutalities of lynch mobs (seldom punished) and a system of "white man's justice" kept blacks "in their place." The indecencies of a true caste system in a nation that trumpeted its freedom and democracy were the rule. Black Americans, accordingly, had little reason to respect white man's law, as made by legislatures and applied by administrators and interpreted by courts. The Civil War Amendments (Thirteenth, Fourteenth, and Fifteenth) were a living symbol of manifest injustice to those Americans who had not been born with skins the color of sallow pink so prized by those who wielded, and still wield, effective power within the nation.

The Constitution, for many years, was an insult, all the more so because its authoritative interpreter—the Supreme Court—had no difficulty in integrating feudal peonage into the Document. With *apartheid* the rule, it is by hindsight extraordinary that blacks remained quiescent for so long. It is even more extraordinary that they perceived in the courts an opportunity to better their condition. Targeting the courts was necessary—no other option, save that of violence, was available—but hardly promising. Judges responded, although not at first, to the pleas of Negroes to be treated decently. Their success had an unforeseen but significant heuristic effect. Others of the disadvantaged began to seek, with increasing success, a measure of redress from long-endured wrongs. A constitutional revolution occurred. Blacks got formal equality, and judges found a new role as arbiters of social ethics. The key decision is *Brown* v. *Board of Education*, which tolled the death knell for "separate but equal" in the formal Constitution.

Only twenty-seven years span the time between the *Carrie Buck* case[115] and the *Brown* decision, but that brief period marks an enormous leap forward in the formal Constitution and perhaps even in the operative fundamental law—although the latter is by no means clear at this writing. In the *Buck* case, Justice Holmes sneered that it was the usual last resort of constitutional arguments to plead that the Fourteenth Amendments's equal-protection clause had been violated. His statement came not in a race case, but in one in which an alleged feeble-minded woman fought Virginia's compulsory sterilization law. In effect, Holmes told Carrie Buck and others that life is unfair, and the Court would do nothing about it; he also merged the formal Constitution with the operative. His opinion is the absolute nadir of a man widely considered to be one of the greatest judges. It approaches the "race purity" laws of Nazi Germany.

The *Buck* case is legalized fascism. In Virginia. In this century. It has never been overruled or repudiated. As reported in 1981:

> Between 1924 and 1970, over 7,200 men and women in Virginia mental institutions were involuntarily sterilized in the name of eugenics to prevent "the increase of feeble-minded, morons and criminals." Many of them were neither mentally ill nor retarded. Instead, they were sterilized for being "misfits," "loose women," or "incorrigibles." They were told that the sterilization was an appendectomy, circumcision or other surgery, and that they would not be released unless they consented to the operation.[116]

The Virginia statute, passed in 1924, allowed state hospitals to sterilize anyone "afflicted with hereditary forms of insanity that are recurrent, idiocy, feeble-mindedness or epilepsy." Although Carrie Buck was said to be feeble-minded, it is doubtful she would be so adjudged today. Virginia's authorities, moreover, seem to have gone far beyond the letter of the law and tried to eliminate every kind of antisocial behavior by sterilizing unwed mothers, prostitutes, petty criminals, children with disciplinary problems, and welfare recipients.

With that type of background, it is remarkable indeed that the Court in 1954 could completely rewrite past interpretations of the equal-protection clause. Not that it was a sharp and abrupt break; the faint beginnings of the human rights movement began slowly, even antedating the abdication of the Justices in economic matters (in 1937). Even the Neanderthals could not stomach Alabama's callous treatment of the Scottsboro Boys, so in 1932 the Court for the first time held that defendants in criminal trials on capital charges were entitled to a lawyer.[117] If they could not afford to employ one, the state had to furnish one. By modern standards, that was the smallest of steps. But it was significant. Slowly but inexorably, maltreatment of black Americans gave way to a higher standard of decency in the way government officers dealt with them. Since this development is crucial to understanding the Court's modern role, a few highlights of the road to *Brown* v. *Board of Education* should be mentioned.

The first crack in the *Plessy* separate but equal doctrine came in 1938, in the *Missouri Law School* case.[118] There the Court ruled that Missouri's plan to pay for legal education of Negroes in another state was constitutionally infirm. The Justice did not overrule *Plessy*; nor was Gaines, the plaintiff, ordered to be admitted to Missouri's lily-white law school. Rather, the Court said that the state had to build another law school for all qualified blacks. A small victory, no doubt, but significant: the equal protection dike had been breached. A step was taken on the road to decency. Separateness was still permitted, however. The Supreme Court led the way, for neither Congress nor the President did anything to crumble America's caste system. Not that the change was abrupt or all-encompassing. A trickle remained a trickle for several years, but bit by bit the formal Constitution was modified by the Justices. Today, it not only guarantees equality in treatment but may even be edging toward a (probably temporary) preference for blacks.[119] The operative Constitution has not been altered nearly so much, however. For some blacks it has, but for most, it has not; they are still imprisoned within the invisible walls of an informal caste system.

The first truly major stride in racial equality came in 1941 when FDR ordered nondiscrimination in employment by war contractors. The victory did not come easily. Roosevelt had donned his "Dr. Win-the-War" hat, throwing aside his "Dr. New Deal" chapeau. He had no real interest in bettering the conditions of black Americans. Only the threat of a Negro march on Washington compelled the President to issue the order. Even then, it was seldom enforced; after the war, it became a dead letter[120] (until the Civil Rights Act of 1964). Its importance lies less in the fact of what was actually accomplished, but more in the threatened march that evidenced a new Negro militancy. Neither President Roosevelt nor the American people became more sensitive to the long-denied rights of blacks. Politicians react to pressure; seldom does principle control.

Whether the Justices were aware of the growing discontent of America's submerged 10 percent and, accordingly, read the *zeitgeist* in ways to protect blacks (and thus help to avoid social turmoil) cannot be stated with certainty. Surely, however, the Justices were (and are) privy to the facts of social and political life. They do not live like cloistered monks, and the Marble Palace is distinctly not an ivory tower. Surely, too, they knew that the war was being fought by conscripts, most of whom came from the lower strata of society. If men are required to fight and at times to die for their country, surely there is a reciprocal obligation by the country to them. That concept is not written in black-letter type and thus is not part of the "positive" law. Nevertheless, to repeat what the Court said in a different context in 1943, "Behind the words of the constitutional provisions are postulates which limit and control."[121] One such postulate, as seen by hindsight, is the need to treat those called upon to sacrifice for their country in a decent manner.

So it was that in 1944 the Court took a giant leap forward when it ruled that the Democratic party was so linked to government that it could not keep blacks from voting in primary elections.[122] Another, possibly even larger, step came in 1948 when judicial action was held to be "state action" within the terms of the Fourteenth Amendment, and, therefore, racially restrictive covenants in deeds of real property could not be enforced. When they can afford it, blacks can now buy their way out of the ghettoes—provided, of course, that they can find willing sellers. The decision, *Shelley* v. *Kraemer*,[123] is also significant for its implicit acknowledgment that courts are part of the political process. Before 1948 the pretense had been otherwise. Although *Shelley* has not become part of the operative Constitution, it nonetheless sits in the law reports as a time bomb that can literally cause an explosion in private law. Should its principle be fully enforced, any discrimination on racial grounds by a private party—for example, a social club—would be invalid. The only need is for someone to be a willing plaintiff and challenge the discrimination in court. (Neither the Justices nor the majority of Americans are as yet willing to extend *Shelley*).

Shelley was an equal-protection case, illustrating how a score of years could alter a Supreme Court from its dreadful *Carrie Buck* decision—not in fact, however, for the case has never been overruled, but in the expansive view taken of equal protection. Then in 1954, after some intermediate steps, came the bombshell—*Brown* v. *Board of Education*—and neither race relations nor the Supreme Court have been the same since. *Plessy* was overturned, and blacks at least seemingly got a new birth of freedom. Certainly, they did insofar as the formal Constitution is concerned.

Brown not only marked a crashing beginning of the Second Reconstruction; it also provided impetus to other groups left behind in the political arena to try to get judicial recognition of rights long denied. For example, residents in cities unequally represented in state legislatures won a famous victory in 1962 when the Court, over an impassioned dissent by Justice Frankfurter, found that that situation presented an equal-protection question.[124] Two years later the "rotten boroughs" of the nation were eliminated in one stroke: one person/one vote was enshrined in constitutional doctrine.[125] Other groups followed—women, juveniles, illegitimate children, aliens, to name only a few.[126] A civil liberties/civil rights explosion took place in the formal law. The Court was the catalyst, and Congress and the executive followed.

Nothing comparable can be found in American history. The words of the Document remained the same, but were given a different meaning. As spokesmen for social ethics, the Justices openly read their ideas of good public policy into the ancient Document, interpreting the cryptic phrases to help insure that government acted in accordance with "evolving standards of decency."[127] That course of the Court has not yet been run. In fact, it may be barely starting. Even the present Court, loaded with Nixon appointees, is "activist" when it wishes to be (as in the 1973 abortion decision). Other values are being furthered, including an effort, not always successful, by Justice William Rehnquist to resurrect principles of federalism. (In that, Rehnquist may be said to have led the way to the policies that President Ronald Reagan is, at this writing, attempting to have enacted into law.)

The Court's present posture and thrust are developed in subsequent chapters. Some factors, however, raise questions to anticipate later discussion:

1. Why did it take so long for the human rights revolution to occur? No one can accurately say that the nineteenth century was truly an open society for most people. Before World War I the protections of the Bill of Rights and the

Civil War amendments existed mostly in theory and for the favored few. "More and more problems of government are being presented to and handled by federal courts as questions of constitutional law."[128] That statement by Archibald Cox is at least partially correct.

2. A result is selective intellectual fury (the subject of Chapter 4). The dissenters from the Court's recent work, in the main, are those of neoconservative views. Disciples of Edmund Burke, the defender of the *ancien régime* during and after the French Revolution, these commentators[129] see barbarians at the gate of the city, led—astoundingly—by men and a few women in black robes whose predecessors were principally interested in fending off the *demos*. A strange development, that, which poses once again our basic question: *cui bono?* Who in fact are the beneficiaries of recent Supreme Court activism and permissiveness? I suggest now, and expand later, that there are two types of beneficiaries—the ostensible and the actual —and that the ultimate beneficiaries are the same as always: those who control the levers of power in "the system."

3. The Justices have lost their historical constituency of the moneyed and propertied, who simply are too dense to see that drawing off social discontent really benefits them. No longer do businessmen view the Court as their ultimate guardian against adverse regulation. Instead, they seek to manipulate the political process (and are generally successful).

4. A new constituency may be emerging, as yet inchoate. The Court as Supreme Court and the Justices as High Priests rank highest in esteem among all governmental officers. The controversies that swirl around the Temple on the Hill come from those whose oxen have been gored by specific decisions and those who fear what John Adams once called a "democratical despotism."

5. The Justices are continuing to rewrite the Document. They have always helped to update it to help the nation meet conditions faced by succeeding generations of Americans. In so doing, they make up the law as they go along; as Felix Frankfurter, when a professor at Harvard, said in 1937: "People have been taught to believe that when the Supreme Court speaks it is not they who speak but the Constitution, whereas, of course, in so many vital cases, it is *they* who speak and *not* the Constitution."[130] Some still profess outrage at such a notion, but there is little they can do about it. Given the litigious nature of the American people, the Court will continue to be the oracular voice of the Constitution.

6. In recent years, the Justices have begun to decide not only the case before them but untold other cases yet to come. When they do so, which is not always, they promulgate norms of general applicability—legislative pronouncements. The overt practice dates only from *Cooper* v. *Aaron* (1958),[131] the decision concerning Governor Orval Faubus's effort to prevent racial integration of schools in Little Rock, Arkansas. Under *Cooper* and progeny, the Justices assert, and get away with asserting, that their decisions are "the

supreme law of the land." That makes them in fact and in theory a continuing constitutional convention, with an open-ended commission to write their views into constitutional law. It also provides the springboard for an even greater role for the Court.

7. The Justices are more than leaders of a vital national seminar on societal values.[132] They have more than a teaching function, but rather are a power organ in a governmental structure. By no means are they the dominant branch of government, but equally surely, they can, in many areas within their area of constitutional competence, do things that neither Congress nor the President is able to do.

These and other matters are alluded to, and discussed, in ensuing chapters. Our next inquiry is into the selective intellectual fury that has greeted some of the Court's products in recent years.

4
The Court Under Siege

I.

Social events can have wholly unexpected side effects. One such event was the Negro drive for equality that culminated in *Brown* v. *Board of Education* and progeny.[1] When the Court after long deliberation held that black Americans could not be prevented from attending all-white schools solely because of their color, few—perhaps, no one—fully anticipated the heuristic effect of the decision. *Brown* gave the Justices a new sense of power and of the ability to prevail in exercises of it; other disadvantaged Americans saw in the Court a means for redress of long-felt grievances.[2] This chapter discusses the reaction to those new demands and suggests ways to evaluate both the attacks and the demands. (Chapter 5 develops "the Court as commander"—how it has proceeded from *Brown* to a wholly new posture in the governmental structure.)

Brown was, and is, an enormously significant milestone on the long and tortuous road toward decency in treatment of the Americans who are of African descent. The trek is far from ended; in fact, it has scarcely begun. Under the formal Constitution, blacks have attained "equal justice under law"; but the operative Constitution differs: In the more important of the two fundamental laws, they are still second-class citizens. Furthermore, there is an eroding commitment among white Americans to better their status.[3] In a perceptive essay, Professor Aviam Soifer has shown that the Supreme Court's commitment is diminishing[4]—not in so many words, of course, but by a subtle alteration in interpretive technique. Now the Justices inquire into the motive or intent of government officers, looking behind action that appears to discriminate to determine whether those responsible intended to do so. Again, and in a different context, the Justices have established themselves as a commission to read the minds of legislators and administrators—not, this time, for the "reasonableness" of their actions, but, rather, for what they intended. This is accomplished by placing the burden of proof upon those who contest the action to show discriminatory intent or motive. Since the mind-set of those who take such actions is seldom, if ever, written out, it is next to impossible to prove an intention to discriminate.

Two points are apparent: First, the Supreme Court is part of the swing to conservatism in the nation; we are witnessing "the end of liberalism"[5] as it has been known, particularly in race relations. Second, Supreme Court decrees, which become part of the formal Constitution, are not necessarily translated into social reality (the operative Constitution). The latter point poses the question of whether the power of law, and of judges, is sufficient to alter deep-set mores and prejudices. Can, as William Graham Sumner flatly denied, "stateways" change "folkways"?[6] That is the basic question *Brown* poses. By no means is it fully answered yet.

But, first, consider the spinoff effects, pro and con, of *Brown* and progeny. The decision epitomizes the Justices's new role as an authoritative spokesman for social ethics. In the main, that was accomplished through extension of the equal-protection principle, sometimes closely tied in with Hughes's new version of due process of law (noted in the previous chapter) to other groups —voters in the "rotten boroughs" of the nation; those caught up in criminal law administration; other ethnic groups, even including American Indians; women; the poor; illegitimates. Even more, the Justices went on to give expansive meaning to First Amendment freedoms of speech and of the press; to loosen the laws on pornography; to recognize the right to an abortion; and to all but eliminate the law of libel for "public figures." Some, but not all, of these things fall within the category of "status rights,"[7] for they are less the rights of individuals as such than as individuals as members of groups. Traditionally, constitutional rights were personal—individualistic—but in the past three or four decades, a concept of status has emerged in constitutional law. In this, the Justices tacitly recognize that the United States is a highly organized nation. The implicit meaning of these rulings is that a person is significant not as an atomistic person, but more and more as a member of a group or groups. "For a variety of reasons," said Professor Michael J. Phillips, "the 300-odd-year march of the sovereign self and its detached, egoistic, manipulative posture toward both man and nature may be reaching its limits."[8]

Status rights can and do conflict with traditional *personal* rights. It is this, among other reasons, that has caused such a sharp, even bitter, reaction to the Court's rulings during the era of Chief Justice Earl Warren. By acknowledging social needs and dealing with them, to the extent that the judiciary can alter human affairs, the Justices unloosed a counter-revolution. A second spinoff from *Brown* is an assault on the Court not only by bad-mouthed know-nothings but, of more importance, by sophisticated professors (and others) of conservative persuasion.[9] (Those commentators are, generally, votaries in the cult of Frankfurter worship.) In addition, the Court lost its historical constituency of the businessman, of the moneyed and propertied. The assaults and the accompanying loss of powerful support has resulted in an embattled but still fighting and far from defeated group of Justices. They appear fully to realize, to employ Professor Frankfurter's words in a different context, "that public life is warfare."[10] Skilled politicians all, even though few ever ran for public office, Supreme Court Justices know at least intuitively, and probably consciously, that if the Court is to remain as a major organ of political power, they must be willing to battle for it. The Court cannot be an instrument of power by sitting idly by and having responsibility thrust upon it. Since it is largely in control of its own agenda, it must—more, it does—fight for the power to make important public policy decisions.

The focus of interest in this chapter may begin with a truism: Rights, of whatever type, do not exist in a vacuum or in a "heaven of legal concepts." The Supreme Court, since it is a political organ, must and does operate in the political arena. If one asks the question "Why the civil rights/civil liberties revolution of recent decades?" and attempts to suggest an answer, one is at once confronted with a problem of staggering proportions. There is, as Professor Ernest Nagel has told us, no such thing as a simple *and* complete answer to explain any human phenomenon.[11] Human affairs are too complex, too interwoven with imponderables and unknowables of life, to permit more than tentative guesses. Keeping that in mind, I should like to suggest a working hypothesis as a means to help answer the basic question just posed: Modern emphasis on human rights, of whatever type, is a result in large part of Americans living in their "Golden Age."

That proposition in itself is one of great complexity, but only brief discussion can be given here. Every nation, every people, have a golden age. Writing in the eighth century B.C., the Greek Hesiod pined for a lost paradise. (Is the analogy to the Adam and Eve myth apposite?) According to him, our age (the "Iron Age") is the fifth of a series that has been declining from the first—the Golden Age. In the Golden Age, a superior race of people "lived like gods without sorrow of heart. . . . They dwelt in ease and peace upon their lands with many good things, rich in flocks, and loved by the blessed gods." Then came the Silver, Brass, and Heroic Ages, each progressively more deteriorated than its predecessor; and finally the Iron Age. In this age, said Hesiod, men "never rest from labor and sorrow by day, and from perishing by night; and the gods shall lay sore trouble upon them."[12] (He did not foresee the coming of the Technological Age, which promises some relief from labor, but that is another and, again, extremely complex matter, not directly relevant to the present discussion.)

My point is simple and directly contrary to Hesiod—the Golden Age for Americans was not in the dim and distant past, not, that is, at the time of the Revolution and the birth of the nation. Rather, it was the period, only a few years long, from 1945 to about 1970. During that quarter-century, the United States was the effective sovereign in world affairs. The dollar was king, American military might supreme, and nations large and small recognized— although, as with the Soviet Union, they did not always agree with—the preeminence of America in world affairs. All things seemed possible, and indeed many were, both externally and internally. The economy grew at a steady pace, and the economic pie became so large that more people than ever before were able to sup at the groaning tables of opulence. It was the era of *Pax Americana* in world affairs and of seemingly endless economic growth. Of course there were some warts on the body politics—the viciousness of McCarthyism betrayed a latent uneasiness; two undeclared, and inconclusive, wars were fought (the second was really a defeat); and early portents of the ecological trap became visible when the Paley Commission issued its report on natural resources in 1951.[13] But McCarthy died and with him much of the nastiness of government repression; by 1970 it became obvious that the war in Vietnam was being lost. At the same time, environmental problems became acute. When the price of petroleum skyrocketed in 1973 (and since), the era ended with a barely suppressed whimper. Some still do not believe the age of American dominance is over, never to return, but it is.

The civil rights/civil liberties revolution fits the time span of the true American Golden Age almost exactly. When economic growth slowed perceptibly, the counter-revolution to expansion of status rights set in, even in the formal Constitution. The social milieu in which human rights flourished was and is being so altered that serious questions can now be raised about their longevity. If law, including constitutional law, reflects the social climate—the *zeitgeist*—surely a persuasive case can be made for the proposition that the human rights revolution was a consequence of America experiencing its Golden Age. If it is true that that age has ended, at least in economics, surely one can accurately forecast a diminution in recognition and enforcement of those rights. That is precisely what seems to be happening. Rights, personal or status, have not been abolished, but it is becoming ever more obvious that their exercise will be less and less possible as the ecological trap closes.[14] In a time of diminishing expectations, there is a substantial zero-sum element in the enforcement of human rights.

II.

Criticisms of the Supreme Court today take three main avenues: First, the Court is said to be undemocratic. From that belief is derived the proposition that it should not make policy—at least, not much policy—for a nation that is (or calls itself) a democracy. Next, the opinions of the Justices are asserted to be improperly "reasoned"—that they are based on "fiat," not reason. Finally, Justices are said to lack an adequate system of informing themselves about the complexities of the disputes brought to them.

Each criticism has at least some merit. On the whole, however, they fall of their own weight, mainly because they are superficial. At most, they are unhelpful. At worst, they may be cloaks for hiding dislike of the results reached by the Court behind a cloud of verbiage about judicial method and democracy. It is important to understand why the three-pronged attack is faulty. I am not suggesting that the Court is either honored or helped as being considered to be beyond criticism; of course it is not. But equally true, the criticism, when it comes, should be constructive rather than destructive. Much of today's brouhaha over the High Bench is destructive. The aim, so it seems, is to cut the Court down from its lofty pedestal, so that the elected politicians will have practically free rein over public policy. (The critics never mention that representatives of "the" people, and the bureaucracy, have control over most public policy today—a condition that is not at all likely to change.)

The attacks are led by a gaggle of professors who worship at the shrine of the late Justice Felix Frankfurter—who may not have been a great judge (he was not) but who managed to wield an extraordinary amount of influence in the law schools and political science faculties. Votaries in the cult of Frankfurter adoration castigate the Justices for being too "activist," for, that is, substituting at times their judgment for that of politicians. Activism, however, is very much a sometime thing; it is not often employed, although some of its uses have high public visibility. As with Frankfurter, the critics advocate judicial self-restraint, a quiescent judiciary that leaves litigants to try to influence the political process to further their ends. But that is precisely what is wrong: The political process, for a number of reasons, is not fulfilling the demands or aspirations of numerous people and groups.

Failure of the critics to recognize that fact fatally flaws their arguments. Some who know the inadequacies of politics maintain that, rather than resorting to judges, people should try to improve the way that politics operates—and thus gain their goals. That is pure Frankfurterism: He—naively? because he was a super-patriot?—believed that if politicians do not respond, they should be voted out of office. In 1962, in one famous example, he told voters in urban areas in Tennessee that they should not invoke the Constitution to get rid of the rotten-borough system; rather, they should go to the state legislature and ask that it enforce the state's constitution—in other words, ask that legislators from rural areas vote themselves out of office.[15] That was an extraordinary position, to say the least, displaying either complete ignorance about how politics operates or a willingness to exalt form over substance. Surely, it was the latter, for he was a consummate politician, both before and after he went on the Court.

Frankfurter was not so persuasive, however, that he could make his views prevail in many decisions during his tenure. The case that so exercised him in 1962, *Baker* v. *Carr*, classically displayed his relative impotence to marshal his colleagues to march to his tune. *Baker* still aggravates many of the Court's critics, but not, it should be emphasized, the people themselves, who have adjusted quite nicely to the decision and its progeny—the one person/one vote command that the Court decreed in 1964.[16] Typical among the attackers is Raoul Berger, whose widely publicized 1977 book, *Government by Judiciary*, was a frontal assault on both the *Baker* and *Brown* rulings. Berger asserted vehemently that the Court acted unconstitutionally in both.[17]

Another critic is a prominent neoconservative, Professor Nathan Glazer, who believes that the Court "is engaged in a damaging and unconstitutional revolution"; that "the courts truly have changed their role in American life"; that they "now reach into the lives of the people, against the will of the people, deeper than they ever have in American history"; and that a "free people feels itself increasingly under the arbitrary rule of unreachable authorities." This, Glazer maintained, "cannot be good for the future of the state."[18]

Berger and Glazer are far from alone; they are typical of those who are assaulting the Temple on the Hill. Were their views accurate, it would be a damning indictment of the Court. But they are not, although they do have a modicum of validity.

Consider the first accusation—that the Court, an oligarchic institution, should not make policy for a democracy. That has a beguiling appeal, but is based on some erroneous assumptions. It is not the correct question. Calling the Court oligarchic, as Frankfurter and his followers have, is merely the beginning of wisdom or understanding. If another question is asked—is *any* part of American government "democratic"?—and answered, it may be possible to advance further and even to approach a correct answer. Such a conclusion can come, however, only after some acceptable definition of democracy is proffered. (The Court's acerbic critics never do that.) One should, furthermore, carefully distinguish between democracy and constitutionalism. If the former is considered to be rule by "the people" (which is a manifest impossibility), the latter requires some restraints on policies so enunciated (by the people or their representatives). We should never forget, Professor Walter F. Murphy has cogently argued, that the United States is a *constitutional* democracy.[19] Powers and actions of politicians, which supposedly reflect the wishes of the people, are limited by the values of constitutionalism (of which more anon). As Professor H. N. Hirsch has shown, Frankfurter built his theory of judicial action on that of Harvard professor James Bradley Thayer as interpreted by Oliver Wendell Holmes. "The essential assumption of Thayer's theory," Hirsch observed, "was the necessity of judicial self-restraint in the face of 'reasonable' policy decisions by popularly elected legislatures. The crucial—but inarticulated—premise of this assumption is that the United States is in fact an open polity, in which the political process accurately and fairly reflects all citizen preferences."[20]

Frankfurter simply misunderstood Holmes, even though he was a close personal friend of Holmes and indeed idolized him. Grant Gilmore pointed out the failure of Frankfurter to know what his idol stood for:

Holmes is a strange, enigmatic figure. Put out of your mind the picture of the tolerant aristocrat, the great liberal, the eloquent defender of our liberties, the Yankee from Olympus. All that was a myth, concocted principally by Harold Laski and Felix Frankfurter, about the time of World War I. The real Holmes was savage, harsh and cruel, a bitter and lifelong pessimist who saw in the course of human life nothing but a con-

tinuing struggle in which the rich and powerful impose their will on the poor and weak. . . .
In this bleak and terrifying universe, the function of law, as Holmes saw it, is simply to channel private aggressions in an orderly, perhaps in a dignified fashion.[21]

Others have reached conclusions similar to Gilmore's, for example Gary Jacobsohn: "For the liberals . . . Holmes' skepticism (and the constitutional philosophy that it entailed) was an important weapon in the fight against the Spencerian interpretation of the Constitution. It was this happy alignment of skepticism on the side of liberalism that greatly attracted Frankfurter to Holmes. Beyond this political attraction lay a deep and abiding personal affection."[22] The difference between Holmes and Frankfurter was one in which the idolater never perceived (or, if he did, refused to acknowledge) that Holmes didn't care, but Frankfurter cared passionately about many things. That the Thayer-Holmes-Frankfurter conception of Supreme Court power is inadequate becomes manifest in the ensuing chapters.

Who *does* have power to determine when governmental action transgresses the Document? (That differs from Frankfurter's position: He was concerned with who *should* have that power.) Writing in 1651, Thomas Hobbes maintained, quite correctly, that "All laws, written, and unwritten, have need of interpretation."[23] That is accurate for laws however derived—from legislatures, from administrative agencies, from courts, and, indeed, from the Constitution itself. Since the time of Chief Justice John Marshall, lawyers have become accustomed to thinking that it is the function of judges to say what the law is. That view, however, is simply not accurate with respect to the Constitution—or, for that matter, any other type of law. Power to interpret is a shared power; officers in each branch of government make constitutional decisions routinely. So, too, do officials in state and local governments, who often must consider the applicability of both the federal and their own state constitutions. In addition, those who control the "quasi-polities"[24] of the nation—the private governments—have a role in updating the fundamental law; that role is best seen in the operative Constitution and in what will later be called the Economic Constitution.

Each time Congress enacts a statute and each time the President acts, an assumption is made about its constitutional validity. Sometimes that assumption becomes overt: an inquiry is made and an opinion rendered. Usually, moreover, political decisions emanate from the operations of the "subgovernments" or the "iron triangles" in Washington—the cooperation between Congressional committee, executive bureau (or President), and affected interest group.[25] These decisions, too, are at least tacitly constitutional. A quasi-polity—a corporation, for example—can and does make decisions of such import that they affect the entire nation and that, as a consequence, have some type of impact upon the ordering of power within the institutions of the formal Constitution; they, therefore, may be viewed as constitutional.

That the courts do not have a monopoly on constitutional interpretation should be obvious. Each branch makes decisions that alter the operative, if not the formal, Constitution. The Court does so routinely, by a process of continual updating of cryptic language—so, too, with Congress, but possibly on a lesser scale of magnitude. The Judiciary Act of 1789 has already been mentioned as one such statute. Others include the Sherman antitrust law of 1890, which set forth in spare constitutionlike language the type of economy that Congress presumably wanted. Other examples are the Employment Act of 1946, under which the federal government expressly assumed responsibility for the economic welfare of Americans; the Civil Rights Act of 1964, the most important statute dealing with the rights of ethnic minorities and of women; the War Powers Resolution of 1973, which diminished the President's power to commit troops abroad; the Budget and Impoundment Control Act of 1974, which altered the balance of power between Congress and President in budgetary matters; and the National Environmental Policy Act of 1969, a commitment to improve the quality of American life.[26] These statutes deal with and tend to alter the structure of government and thus are constitutional. Others could be mentioned, notably the establishment of the Federal Reserve Board as an autonomous administrative agency with centralized control over monetary matters and the Humphrey-Hawkins Act of 1978, which is the beginning of a system of formal, centralized economic planning.

Those statutes will suffice as specific instances. Each is of fundamental and far-reaching significance, much more so than most Supreme Court decisions. To them should be added, however, a general pattern of uncontrolled discretionary governing power that is delegated to administrative agencies through the medium of many statutes, so much so that "the bureaucratic" or "administrative" State has been created.[27] The public administration has become a power center of its own, entirely within the operative Constitution but with the approval of the formal Document (through statutes and Supreme Court acquiescence).

Add the President, who since the days of George Washington has taken military and other actions not provided for in the Constitution (or the statutes). Many Chief Executives have used military power without express sanction of Congress. During the first weeks of the Civil War, Abraham Lincoln acted in ways that amply evidence the proposition that the President can alter the Constitution. At first, Lincoln's acts changed the operative Constitution, but when some were challenged in court and upheld by the Supreme Court, they then became part of the formal Constitution. The basic principle in the use of violence is "Reason of State," under which Presidents can and do act to protect the security of the nation. The principle exists even though not mentioned in the Document.[28]

Another example is "executive privilege," by which Presidents keep data secret not only from the people but also from the courts and Congress. Again not mentioned in the Document, it too has been recognized by the Supreme Court (in the case involving the infamous Nixon tapes).[29] Modern Presidents, furthermore, assert an independent power to interpret the Constitution and thus not to enforce laws they consider to be unconstitutional. They tend to equate "the" United States with the President and thus challenge Congress.[30] Not yet has a Chief Executive openly defied the entire Supreme Court— Andrew Jackson's alleged statement that "John Marshall has made his decision, now let him enforce it" is probably apocryphal and in any event did not concern a Court order about presidential power; Lincoln's refusal to obey an order of Chief Justice Taney in a habeas corpus case was never taken to the full bench (Taney rendered his opinion as an individual judge "on circuit").[31] Today's immediate issue is over the validity of the so-called Congressional veto,[32] which Presidents since Franklin Roosevelt have denounced as unconstitutionally impinging upon executive prerogatives. The Supreme Court has not yet ruled upon it. When it does, as it may in the near future, it strains credulity to believe that the loser—President or Congress—would not comply with the judicial ruling. Moreover, unless the Court's order *directly* involves the President, he can, by ignoring the decree, effectively render it impotent. The power of enforcement is executive; there is no way short of a lawsuit aimed at a contumacious official that the Court can enforce compliance. There may be, in sum, postulates behind express constitutional provisions that limit and control, but there also are principles, lurking somewhere behind or above the Constitution, which for the President at least enable him to expand his powers.

One need not labor the point: Constitutional interpretation is distinctly not solely a judicial task or prerogative. Any comprehensive view of the course of constitutional development must consider much more than the Temple on the Hill. Even so, our interest lies mainly in the Constitution and the Court. What must be kept in mind, however, is that if one asserts that the Supreme Court is not a democratic organ of government, one must also remember that even the supposedly democratic institutions are subject to the same criticism.[33] That they are not by the disciples of Frankfurter is evidence of a failure in constitutional scholarship.

Most constitutional interpretations are routine, are made by judges and politicians, and are usually final. The Supreme Court deals less with the ordinary than with the extraordinary, and of the latter, only those matters that are really exceptional receive attention from the Court's critics. Only a half-dozen or so rulings of more than ordinary magnitude are rendered each year by the Justices. That small number means, it is important to emphasize, that under any of the familiar definitions of democracy, the branches said to represent the people usually prevail, simply because there is no judicial review of their actions. (To cite only one example, the Veterans Administration makes some 12 million decisions each year, each important to a person, but judicial review is a rarity.) A lawsuit is an aberration, even given the litigious nature of the American people.[34] No nation, including the United States, ever litigated its way to prosperity or to military victory. That is not to say that in the tiny number of human disputes the Supreme Court fully considers the consequences are not large in importance. The High Bench has tackled some seemingly intractable social problems—not always with success —problems that get to it, simply because usual methods of social control have broken down.

Only the socially pathological gets to the Temple on the Hill. Limiting themselves to those "hospital" cases, the Justices select problems for full review that, generally, transcend the individual litigants—those that provide opportunities to develop general principles of law. I do not suggest that the 4,400, more or less, other petitions for review are not important or meritorious. Of course, many are. But the Justices have limited time and must husband their resources. Moreover, some issues may be considered to be too sensitive for immediate attention. An example is the present Court's refusal to rule on the rights of homosexuals.[35] During the 1950s the Justices put off, for spurious and flimsy reasons, deciding the constitutionality of miscegenation laws. By 1967 the social climate had so changed that a ruling was made, striking down those laws.[36]

At times the Justices flee into an undefined hideaway, best known to them, called "political questions" and thus refuse to decide some questions.[37] They had several opportunities, for example, to deal with the Vietnam "war," but did not do so. Or they can say that the plaintiff has no "standing"—that is, does not have the requisite status to challenge a governmental action. The Court in this manner bypassed two chances to rule on Connecticut's anti-contraceptive law. Not until 1965 did it find that their previous refusals could be shunted aside.[38]

When the Justices decide not to decide, they invoke self-imposed limitations—which by no means are rigid requirements. They have discretion to determine if they will follow their own rules of whether a dispute presents a constitutional "case or controversy" within the terms of Article III of the Document. Despite outward appearances seemingly to the contrary, they usually move with care. The norm is either a refusal to rule at all or, when the Court does issue a decision, to uphold governmental action. At times, however, the Justices bravely plunge into the fray, as in the abortion cases of 1973.[39] Decision there could easily have been avoided, simply because the gestation periods for the females had long since run by the time the Court ruled. But decide it did, even though the cases could easily have been called "moot" (which is another self-imposed limitation).

Once a case is accepted for full review, the Principle of Doctrinal Polarity comes into play. No clear-cut, easily predictable answer exists. Parallel lines of argument are presented by counsel, each of which could be persuasive. Choices the Justices make between conflicting arguments render their decision unavoidably creative—lawmaking. A little law is made, and the Constitution "amended," with every decision.

Most commentators, on and off the bench, who attack the Supreme Court for being *undemocratic* do so without vouchsafing a definition of the word; they assume, as if it were self-evident, that Congress and legislatures are democratic. Even if they acknowledge the undemocratic character of legislative action, they nonetheless assert that the proper goal is to make them more responsive to the wishes of the people.[40] (They never say how this can be done.) Those intellectual positions doubtless are comfortable, but they do not withstand rigorous scrutiny. They do not comport with reality.

In its composition, the Supreme Court is an oligarchic institution. That is—at least, it should be—beyond dispute. Only one possible way exists by which it can validly be said that the Court is democratic—by the criterion of whether its decisions further the concept of human dignity that is the essence of democratic theory. That, however, is anathema to members of the Frankfurter school, who call it "result orientation" (apparently, one of Frankfurter's neologisms), by which is meant that who wins or loses is a, perhaps the, primary desideratum. Claiming interest in the "process" and not the "consequences," they view Supreme Court decision making as a matter of ritual rather than of substance.[41]

Any attempt to reconcile or to attack the Court's operations as jibing or not jibing with democratic theory is based on two untenable assumptions: that *democracy* has a commonly accepted meaning, and that other organs of government are democratic under that definition. Neither assumption holds water. George Orwell once said, quite correctly, that the word *democracy* has "several meanings which cannot be reconciled with one another."[42] Not only is there no agreed definition, he went on, the effort to make one is resisted from all sides. Surely that opinion is accurate. At least 200 definitions of the term exist.[43] In many respects, Professor Bernard Crick has observed, to call any government democratic "is always a misleading piece of propaganda."[44] But the word *is* used, even though it is emotion charged, and it behooves those who attack the Court for not being democratic to do more than make the flat assertion or the unverified assumption that elected bodies are democratic. At the very least, they should set forth their theory of democracy and evaluate whether any segment of government comports with it.

My position is that what counts are the *effects* of political, including judicial, action. Who wins or loses in the political arena is of ultimate importance, for democracy surely must be considered to be more than a set of procedures for reaching decisions.[45] Procedures are good when they produce good results. That is basic (and central to the argument of this volume; we return to the point from time to time). Others disagree, to be sure. An example is Justice Hans A. Linde of the Oregon Supreme Court, who maintained in 1976: "the last few years have reawakened our appreciation of the primacy of process over product in a free society, the knowledge that no ends can be better than the means of their achievement. 'The highest morality is almost always the morality of process.'"[46] That position is profoundly erroneous. There is far more to law and to morality than "process." Prescription of a ritual, a procedure, for official actions to take is possible only when there is common acceptance of the ultimate ends—the goal values—of society. As Yves Simon put it, in a democratic State "deliberation is about means and presupposes that the problem of ends has been settled."[47] That statement, however, is precisely what is *not* true in many troublous areas of constitutional litigation, and what will become even less true as the ecological trap closes.

No doubt exists that those who wrote the Document of 1787 feared a "democratical despotism." A republic was created, as evidenced by those permitted to vote. Only white males had the franchise, and then only those with property, for President and other official positions, and the actual election for the President and Vice-President was placed a step away in the Electoral College. United States Senators were elected not by the people, but by state legislatures. The people, as such, were not trusted. (Direct election of senators came only in the twentieth century, but the Electoral College still exists.)

To be sure, the franchise has been greatly expanded since 1787. Property qualifications have been eliminated, and women and freed slaves can vote. The voting age has been lowered to eighteen. Voting has indeed been "democratized"—which itself has had a significant effect: To the extent that primaries in fact determine presidential candidates, the United States is the only nation that permits the people to choose not only those who are to govern but also the candidates.

The point stressed is this: Democracy, however defined, is at most an ideal, something to be striven for, rather than an actuality. We may wish the democratic element in government to be greater, but there is little discernible desire for government *by* the people. Technology is available today whereby national referenda could be speedily conducted, through use of television and computers, on any important public policy issue. That technology is not likely to be employed, if for no other reason than that one must beware of trying to put all of the apparent implications of metaphysical formulations into effect. No democracy could long endure if it strictly followed "the will of the people," rather than the leadership of the enlightened few, or if it left to abstract external standards (the law), rather than the discretion of the few, the determination of substantive policies. Certainly, no nation has ever done so. The London *Economist* observed in December 1980 that "in 1960-80 America became a nation of laws instead of men. The country had previously thrived by being exactly the opposite, although its lawyers wrote books pretending it wasn't."[48] That statement may be extreme, but certainly there is at least a kernel of truth in it. The metaphysic of democracy calls for majority rule, but that has never existed and, indeed, cannot and probably should not exist. It is exactly because the theoretical tenets—the metaphysic—of democracy are taken seriously today that the American political order is in disarray.

To emphasize our main point: no useful purpose is served by calling the Supreme Court *undemocratic* unless other organs of government can accurately be termed *democratic*. Enough is known about the presidency, Congress, and state and local governments to conclude that it is idle and perhaps mischievous to call any of them democratic. Each exemplifies "the iron law of oligarchy." "Who says organization says oligarchy," asserted Robert Michels in 1911,[49] an insight into human behavior that was true then and now. Every group, of whatever size, is controlled or dominated by a few. That includes the nation-State itself. The most voters can do is to elect an elite to govern them, an elite that, when in office, often pursues goals separate from "the will of the people" or even from the promises made to the electorate during campaigns. To mention only one illustration: today, about 75 percent of Americans favor some type of handgun control, but there is no chance it will be enacted into law.

Congress exists mainly to put the decisions of pressure groups and the experts into statutory form (and of course to give the appearance of representative government and thus to placate the people). Congress does not represent "the people"; indeed, "the people" do not exist as an entity. Instead, there are a series of disparate groups, a congeries of publics. Congress represents groups. Since Arthur Bentley wrote *The Process of Government* in 1908, the prevailing philosophy of many political scientists is the "group basis of politics."[50] In politics as in economics, it is the group, the collectivity, not the individual that is important. Elites controlling interest groups compete for governmental action. That is the system, such as it is, of *representative democracy*—the term most used. The consequence, Professor Grant McConnell has shown, is that

a substantial part of government in the United States has come under the influence or control of narrowly based and largely autonomous elites. These elites do not act cohesively with each other on many issues. They do not "rule" in the sense of commanding the entire nation. Quite the contrary, they tend to pursue a policy of non-involvement in the large issues of statesmanship save where such issues touch their own particular concerns.[51]

Existing in a state of antagonistic cooperation, interest groups battle each other. They also often cooperate, as was particularly true during America's Golden Age (1945-70). By 1980, however, it had become obvious that politics is a zero-sum game; with the end of the Golden Age, not all can win. The system is out of kilter.

As with Congress, so with the President and the bureaucracy. The Chief Executive may speak in terms of the national or public interest, but he has to operate within the limitations of a political order dominated by groups. He is constrained by the same forces that bind Congress. Only nominally does he represent "the people." His main interest is to further the concerns of the State and thus of those who control the State.[52] (The word *State* is an abstraction, designating a disembodied entity, albeit a real one, separate and apart from the people—society—and even from government—which is the apparatus of the State.)

Rather than asking the wrong question—is the Supreme Court democratic? —the problem is one of fulfilling James Madison's prescription:[53] "If men were angels, no government would be necessary. If angels were to govern men, neither external nor internal controls on government would be necessary. *In framing a government which is to be administered by men over men, the great difficulty lies in this: you must first enable government to control the governed; and in the next place oblige it to control itself.*" (Emphasis added.) The Framers chose to splinter the powers of government, to create separate institutions sharing power. Lawmaking is high among the shared powers. Each branch makes law, and each has a veto on at least one of the other branches. The President can veto acts of Congress (which in turn can override vetoes). Congress has developed a system, extraconstitutionally, of "legislative vetoes," by which it can negate specific executive actions. Moreover, Congress can refuse to enact the President's recommendations into law. In theory, the Supreme Court can decide whether any act of either political branch squares with the Constitution. Who, then, checks the Court? Congress, in many respects, has the whip hand. It has constitutional power to regulate the appellate jurisdiction of the High Bench, although it is controversial just how far that power goes. Furthermore, it can enlarge, or reduce (when vacancies occur), the size of the Court (that has been done in the past). The President cannot veto judicial decisions in a formal sense, but he can do so informally, by simply refusing to enforce them. The Court may propose, but the politicians dispose. The check on the Justices, then, is not "legal" but "political"; as such, it is as real as are the legal checks on the other branches.

To ask the Madisonian question—how can government be obliged to control itself?—is to miss at least half of the equation. It leaves out the crucial further question: in whose interests should the government be controlled? Or, put another way, in whose interests should affirmative governmental action be directed? We have seen that in the past the moneyed and propertied were the principal beneficiaries of all governmental activity, including the judicial. Is that still true? The answer, quite surely, is yes. Something, therefore, is required to control, both negatively and as to its affirmative actions, the political branches of government. That "something" must be outside of or external to them, for politicians do not police themselves. In the American system, that can only mean the Supreme Court: If it and judicial review did not exist, it or something similar would have to be invented.

The critical problem is accountability—of those exercising power having to answer in another place for their actions. Accountability has two dimensions:

the familiar negative one of placing limitations, such as due process of law, on government; and the less familiar but equally important one of trying to insure that justice for all is affirmatively achieved. Morton Mintz and Jerry S. Cohen have shown in their monumental *Power, Inc.* that a pervasive lack of accountability in the negative sense characterizes American government, both public and private (they do not discuss the affirmative side of the concept).[54] Outside of the workings of the political order itself, which can but often does not make power wielders accountable, the courts are the sole organs of legal (that is, official) social control that can do the job. That they are not very good at it should be obvious to all.

That courts are oligarchic matters little. Probably, it is better that way. Once one accepts the premise that external checks are required on the workings of politics, and also that the ballot box is not sufficient to that need, a widely competent, independent judiciary that is insulated from the immediate political battle seems to be not only the best but the only way to achieve "democratic" goals. As the highest tribunal, the Supreme Court of course has to speak with some authority, to make sociologically wise decisions, and thus can help to keep the formal Constitution abreast of new conditions. The Court must also have the competence—in judges and lawyers—to deal with enormously complex problems and a system of operation that enables it to do so. (At the moment, one should not be sanguine on that score.) Most of all, the Justices should be independent in fact not only from the politicians, but also from those who operate or greatly influence the operation of the levers of power in the nation.

The Court sits as an authoritative faculty of political theory and social ethics, "charged with the evolution and application of society's fundamental principles":[55] So the popular wisdom goes. Thus when the Justices further the human rights of the disadvantaged, they also seem to act in consonance with the deepest values of the American system. That, however, is only a partial picture. When one looks at what the Court does and who in fact benefits from those decisions, rather than merely to the Court itself, surely it is accurate to say that although the Court does aid some of the disadvantaged and thus comports with democracy in the immediate effects of some of its decisions, it is also an Establishment institution pure and simple, reflecting Establishment values.

This analysis suggests that the fundamental question to be asked and answered in any discussion of democracy and the Supreme Court is: *cui bono?* Who benefits from Court decisions? We have seen in Chapter 3 that the Court historically was a bulwark for those with money and property. Does the human rights revolution of recent years mean a different beneficiary now exists? Has a silent constitutional revolution occurred?

An answer must be on two levels: First is the *ostensible* beneficiary, such as black Americans. But the probe must cut deeper: Of longer-range importance are the *hidden* beneficiaries, those who profit from the stability of the constitutional order. The essential question thus becomes: what is the sociological function of the recent enhanced protection of personal liberties?

Suggested above is the idea that judicial cognizance of human rights roughly coincides in time with the true Golden Age of the United States. Certainly, as Professor Paul L. Murphy has shown,[56] the Bill of Rights existed far more in theory and symbol than in actual practice before the 1920s. No serious effort to protect civil liberties and civil rights came until the federal government criminalized certain forms of expression and belief during World War I. Not until well after World War II had been won, however, did those liberties and rights find any kind of systematic protection in the formal Constitution. Perhaps, as has been suggested, it would have been impossible to fight a major war, relying principally upon conscripts, without at least a tacit promise of bettering the condition of the survivors after the war. (That seems to have been true in Great Britain, as the defeat of Winston Churchill at the end of the war evidences.) Be that as it may, the judicial willingness to enforce the Bill of Rights and the Civil War Amendments did not come until the late 1940s and early 1950s.

In many respects, that new posture not only coincided with America's Golden Age, but was a second-order consequence of the Court's previous willingness to rewrite the economic clauses of the Document in the late 1930s. A major by-product of that constitutional revolution was the rise of new social groups to prominence and power, accorded constitutional status (as with labor unions) but not personhood by the Court. Groups theretofore deeply submerged in society began to demand more. The trade union movement flowered. Black Americans, long under the thumb of a rigid caste system, insisted that they, too, were persons under the Constitution and entitled to its protections and benefits.

These reasons, which overlap, do not exhaust all possible explanations of a historic alteration in Supreme Court decision making. But they doubtless helped to create a new social climate, an emergent *zeitgeist*, that found expression in Court rulings, presidential actions, and Congressional statutes. Freedom flourished as never before in America. Those social phenomena— the Golden Age, the rise of new groups, possibly a payoff for participation in a savage war fought in the name of democracy—merely *permitted* new liberties and rights to be recognized and to burgeon. Not yet explained—the question is simply not asked—is the social function that protection of human rights serves.

All political, all social, phenomena have functions, whether acknowledged or not. In *The Pathology of Politics*, Professor Carl J. Friedrich went so far as to maintain that dysfunctional—some would say aberrational—matters such as violence, betrayal, corruption, secrecy, and propaganda have definite, identifiable functions, "notably that of facilitating the adaptation of a system or regime to changing conditions occurring either in the system or in the social substructure, or in the outside environment."[57] That proposition is not argued here, except to say that if such objectionable behavior can be "functional," surely a series of Supreme Court decisions can be similarly analyzed.

Judicial decisions are political epiphenomena. As a political institution, the Supreme Court's function is to produce decisions that are both system maintaining and system developing. "A political function," Friedrich asserted, "is the correspondence between a political process or institution and the needs or requirements of political order."[58] Any political order requires not only stability but a means of orderly change, and that is so even for nations with written constitutions. The Supreme Court facilitates both stability and change. It tries to create a constantly shifting equilibrium as new problems emerge. As it confronts both the body politic and other organs of government, the High Bench lawmaking proclivities have, furthermore, both "manifest" and "latent" functions.[59] Manifest functions are the outward or obvious ones: Can, for instance, a young man parade around a public building in California wearing a leather jacket emblazoned with the slogan "Fuck the Draft" during the Vietnam conflict, without running afoul of the criminal law? The answer the Court gave: yes, he can; the First Amendment protects even that type of "speech." So Cohen, the young man, could not be punished: He was the manifest beneficiary, the recipient of the Court's manifest function.[60] That situation, to be sure, is an extreme case, but it serves to illustrate the point. Manifest functions—in the *Cohen* case, the protection of wide-open, robust speech—are of great importance. They, however, must be seen in connection with latent functions—those that do not immediately meet the eye but that may be of greater importance.

Using that distinction between functions, what may be said about the High Bench's libertarian decisions of recent years? Two conclusions seem evident: First, the manifest function of the Court has been to help bring disadvantaged minorities into the mainstream of American political life and thus to protect the individual in his personhood against arbitrary governmental acts. Well and good, one might say, and certainly, that conclusion is where most analysis ends. Only the manifest function of the Justices receives attention from scholars and commentators.

That attention is not enough. Necessary also is an effort to determine whether the Court had a latent function as well. Forget for the moment about the obviously obnoxious Cohen, and remember Professor John Griffith's previously quoted conclusion: "The judiciary in any modern industrial society . . . is an essential part of the system of government and . . . its functions may be described as underpinning the stability of that system and as protecting that system from attack by resisting attempts to change it."[61] Who, then, are most interested in stability and keeping the system from fundamental change? The answer, although complex, must perforce be brief.

The main point has already been adumbrated—that Court decisions protecting civil rights and liberties are a means whereby hydraulic pressures of social discontent are, in part, relieved, siphoned off, and in effect neutralized.

If that hypothesis is valid, the ultimate beneficiaries (of the Court's latent function) are essentially the same as those who throughout American history have profited from the operations of the constitutional order: the "ruling class" (the moneyed and the propertied). The Justices acknowledge the need for some social change, which they facilitate with rulings that come at the least possible cost to those who control and rule. They are thus interested both in protecting the status quo and in accommodating new demands without excessive social cost to the class whence they came.

I do not call the latent function of the Court a dark and conspiratorial maneuver by a hidden power elite (the ultimate beneficiaries). The process is far too subtle for that. But it can hardly be denied that human liberties receive protection only to the extent that the vital interests of the State are not jeopardized. These "interests" have to mean the vital interests of those who control and who profit most from the activities of the State. Both ostensible and ultimate beneficiaries have benefited in recent decades from Supreme Court decisions. Can there be much doubt about who profits most? Hardly: they who constitute the amorphous "ruling class," its hangers-on, and *apparatchiks*. So, whether conspiracy or not, the result seems utterly clear: "Them as has, gits"—now as in the past.[62]

The latent function of the Supreme Court simply exists, as a consequence of the development of the constitutional order (including, as will be seen, both the Political and Economic Constitutions) and as an illustration of what Holmes long ago saw in his 1873 remarks about the nonneutrality of law. Although not a conspiracy, it is part of the ethos of the American nation and the American experience. With a goal of social stability, it has a self-appointed major prophet in Professor B. F. Skinner (and perhaps a patron saint in Pavlov, who discovered the conditioned reflex). Said Skinner in *Beyond Freedom and Dignity*: "What is being abolished [in modern America] is autonomous man—the inner man, the homunculus, the possessing demon, the man defended by the literature of freedom and dignity. His abolition is long overdue. . . . A scientific view of man offers exciting possibilities. We have not yet seen what man can make of man."[63] Skinner was neither joking nor speaking in hyperbole. Although he himself is harmless—doubtless he believes that his work is furthering the cause of humankind—others may well seize upon his ideas and apply them. "Gobineau was a harmless intellectual crank, but out of his harmless theory of the intellectual superiority of the Aryan race came National Socialism. As Keynes noted: 'The political fanatic who is hearing voices in the air has distilled his frenzy from the work of some academic scribbler of a few years back.'"[64]

I do not call the Justices "political fanatics"; nor is it even implied that they have read or are cognizant of Professor Skinner's views. What I do say is that the Justices are unwitting participants in a pervasive system of mind manipulation. They engage in what Professor Charles Lindblom has called a "structure of persuasive interaction in competitive . . . politics"; they are part of an authority system that involves, said Lindblom, "government by persuasion."[65] Almost 150 years ago Alexis de Tocqueville in his classic *Democracy in America* forecast that social mechanisms then at work in democratic society would eventually tend toward more and more control over the citizenry. Said he: "An immense and tutelary power" will "extend its arm over the whole community." The ultimate consequence will be that it "compresses, enervates, extinguishes, and stupefies a people."[66] Americans are now acting out Tocqueville's prediction in what will later be called the emergent Constitution of Control. The goal is "predictable" man, manipulable man, the person who conceives of freedom in terms of doing what one is supposed to do. Can this statement be far off the mark?

In the past generation, there has been a fundamental shift in the way government and other organizations control the lives and behavior of individuals. No single method and no single phrase adequately describe it—it is both too subtle and too pervasive—but it represents a radical change in the way people are treated and in the relationship between the citizen, his employer, the state, and the state's institutions. In general, it is a shift from direct to indirect methods of control, from the punitive to the therapeutic, from the moralistic to the mechanistic, from the hortatory to the manipulative. More specifically, it is reflected in the replacement of overt and sometimes crude techniques—threat, punishment, or incarceration—with relatively "smooth" methods: psychotropic drugs; Skinnerian behavior modifications; aversive conditioning; electronic surveillance; and the collection, processing, and use of personal information to institutionalize people outside the walls of institutions.[67]

My suggestion is that the Supreme Court is aiding in that "fundamental shift" by making decisions that often have the latent function of drawing off discontent.

A permissive society is being built—indeed, has been built—not solely by judicial decisions, of course, but helped by them. Americans now enjoy the highest degree of freedom in the nation's history. Life-styles are changing; marijuana and other mind-changing drugs are commonly used; alcohol consumption is on the rise; abortion has been legalized; the press and motion pictures have been freed from even blatant obscenity and pornography; the press is practically in a preferred position of privilege; rights long denied blacks and women, children and illegitimates, among others, receive some protection. All these conditions and more may be likened to Aldous Huxley's "soma pills"; they have the latent function of keeping the masses relatively quiescent. National advertising and political indoctrination, usually employing the mass media, have become all too familiar. The human mind is being conditioned, but at a price. The cost of permissiveness is more control, particularly in economic activities, and the price for increasing governmental controls over economic and similar activities is a State-approved permissiveness. Huxley brilliantly forecast the development in his anti-Utopian novel *Brave New World*, although he thought in 1931 that it would be 500 years away. He was correct in his prediction, but, as he later admitted, his timing was off.[68]

The Supreme Court's role in this development, of course, is not stated as such. It may even be that the Justices do not themselves fully realize what they are doing. Perhaps they focus only upon the immediate litigants, and how a decision may affect them one way or another, and thus concentrate on their manifest function. In our analysis, that function is to further civil rights and liberties. There must, however, be more. Justices are not intellectual eunuchs; they are acculturated by their heredity and biography—as are all persons. So they must know, at least subconsciously, that those decisions have a latent function as well. If the biographies of some Justices are any criterion, those men knew full well precisely what they were doing. Chief Justice Taft, as has been mentioned, is an example.

If this analysis of the Court's dual functions is even partly correct, talk about democracy and the High Bench is futile—with one proviso: If the Court makes decisions that have the manifest function of furthering human dignity, whatever the latent function may be, then—and only then—can it be called a democratic institution. The Supreme Court will be truly democratic when both the manifest and the latent functions of its decisions are widely perceived as advancing the cause of human dignity.

III.

Those who plump for "reasoned" opinions, with regard for the results, are at least superficially on the right track. Ideally, the Justices should speak in measured tones, using language and arguments that convince even the theretofore doubtful. One devotee of that position, Professor Henry Hart, said it as well as anyone (albeit in words of high-level abstraction): The Court appears "predestined in the long run, not only by the thrilling tradition of Anglo-American law but also by the hard facts of its position in the structure of American institutions, to be a voice of reason, charged with the creative function of discerning afresh and of articulating and developing impersonal and durable principles."[69] To Hart, reason is the life of the law; it is a matter of indifference who wins or loses in litigation before the Supreme Court.

Abstractly, that view has a certain appeal. Those who sit in Academia, far away from the sweaty mob, easily construct theories of desirable judicial behavior without reference to the facts of life. Hart spoke about "hard facts," without identifying them, and only in the context of the Court's position in government. He did not refer to the facts, hard or even much harder, of the conditions of life with which litigants routinely deal. His was a call for a verbally consistent edifice of durable principles of law, something that, as physicist Percy Bridgman has shown, is not possible even in the natural sciences.

There is a beguiling attraction to Hart's view that the aesthetics of judicial opinions are much more important than the results reached. He, however, asked for the impossible. But since his ideas are shared by many others, perhaps a majority of those who comment on the Court, some attention must be paid to the charge of judicial "unreason."

The ideal, as stated by Hart, is seldom if ever reached, possibly because no one knows for sure what reason means with respect to the judiciary. Surely,it is more than the bastardized type of logic that characterizes legal discourse. That is so even though logic does have some part to play. Surely, too, the word *reason* is one of multiple meanings. Surely, moreover, that for litigants and for most people, the overriding criterion about any lawsuit is: who wins or loses? The public cares about results and is not interested in the ways that judges explain them. Judicial opinions are read and dissected by a small minority of the professoriate, law and political science, and they are read by lawyers in other cases when they attempt to gain persuasive arguments from precedent. Few lawyers are directly concerned with constitutional questions; when they are, they give no evidence of wanting anything more than support for their clients's positions.

Even a high visibility decision such as the abortion cases of 1973 reflects the indifference of the people to the opinion and their great and continuing interest in the result. Under no criterion does the majority opinion of Justice Harry Blackmun exemplify an exercise of Sovereign Reason, but the people cared not for that. They wanted to know only one thing: When, if at all, could a woman obtain an abortion on demand? The Court's product is evaluated, no doubt in accordance with the personal philosophies of those who think about it, not in the manner in which judges explain or justify its genesis. Hart and many others do not like that fact, but there is nothing they can do about it except complain. Complain they do, in stentorian tones and with varying degrees of bitterness. This does not mean that Blackmun should not have written a better opinion. Indeed, Justice Potter Stewart, concurring in the abortion cases, did so; he reached the same result as Blackmun, but explained it better.

Nor should Blackmun's opinion be taken as being essentially different from the mass of opinions issued since 1789. Judges since the beginnings of the republic have displayed an element of fiat in most of their explanations of decisions. Since choices in constitutional cases always are made between conflicting principles, judges have discretion unfettered by anything except their consciences (and, possibly, that ultimate tribunal: the court of public opinion).[70] The Justices's choices which when made also create law, are in last analysis dependent upon their social and economic philosophies, impartiality being either a delusion of the simple minded or a banner of the opportunist and the dishonest. (Professor H. N. Hirsch's psychobiography of Justice Frankfurter convincingly shows that Frankfurter's oft-stated "invincible disinterestedness" masked some strongly felt prejudices.)

Some writers—Professor Ronald Dworkin is an example[71]—assert that a distinction exists between judges and legislators, with judges having the duty to reach the *one* correct answer in human disputes while legislators have more freedom and discretion and need not concern themselves with whether the result they reach is *the* only one. Dworkin can hardly be correct. His position is based on a jurisprudential cosmology that has never existed and, indeed, because of human frailty cannot exist.

Impartiality being a chimera, the call for *reason* in judicial opinions, as if the word meant something specific, falls of its own weight. Since everyone carries his intellectual "can't-helps" around with him, the truly important aspect of judicial opinions is the premise, often not articulated, from which the judge proceeds in his explanation of his decision. What is the source of these premises? Judges seldom, if ever, enlighten us on that score. There should be small wonder that the premises are often diametrically opposed. Judges differ in what is considered to be "expedient in the community concerned." Holmes said it well: "Every important principle which is developed in litigation is in fact and at bottom the result of more or less definitely understood views of public policy; most generally, to be sure, under our practices and traditions, the unconscious result of instinctive preferences and inarticulate convictions, but nonetheless traceable to views of public policy in the last analysis."[72] Holmes wrote that in 1881. Nothing that has been discovered or learned since undercuts the accuracy of his views, whether for "private" or for "public" (constitutional) law. What, then, can the call for reason mean? What value does it have? Perhaps reason does have a place, a valuable place, but, if so, only after premises are revealed.

Justice Potter Stewart made precisely that point in a dissenting opinion issued in 1963:

The Court's opinion is lengthy, but its thesis is simple: (1) The withdrawal of citizenship which these statutes provide is 'punishment.' (2) Punishment cannot constitutionally be imposed except after a criminal act and conviction. (3) The statutes are therefore unconstitutional. As with all syllogisms, the conclusion is inescapable if the premises are correct. But I cannot agree with the Court's major premise—that the divestiture of citizenship is punishment in the constitutional sense of the term.[73]

Stewart's candor is important for another reason; it shows that once a premise has been chosen, reason (as logic) can be employed. (The Stewart opinion also evidences that premises themselves are not the product of reason—that they are based on something else [faith? predilections? philosophy?], but few, if any, of the Court's critics delve into that important matter.)

Reason in the sense of well-structured opinions in which conclusions follow by inexorable logic from the premises is therefore possible, but only after the most important intellectual step has been taken: the identification and articulation of the premises, the basic assumptions from which a judge proceeds. Those assumptions, it merits iteration, come from a judge's heredity and biography more than from the presentations of counsel through the adversary process. Lawyers, of course, know that, for they often go "judge shopping" or even "forum shopping." Judges are not fungible; it matters a great deal to the litigants who wears the black robes of office and hears a given case. All knowledgeable persons know this, but the pretense is otherwise. One example illustrates the point (many more could be given). When Frank Snepp, ex-CIA agent, wrote and published *Decent Interval*, the government promptly sued him for breach of contract. All CIA employees must sign an agreement to get agency clearance of anything written for publication. Snepp had not cleared *Decent Interval*. The forum chosen by the government— there is leeway in this—was the federal court in Alexandria, Virginia, presided over by Judge Oren Lewis. "Roarin' Oren," as he is called, has a known bias for the government in litigation, which he showed at the trial. The Court of Appeals for the Fourth Circuit also tends to tilt toward the government. Snepp lost all the way—up to and including the Supreme Court. The Court faced with two conflicting premises—the First Amendment and the contract —without much apparent thought speedily chose the latter. The opinion for the Court, issued *per curiam* (no signed opinion but six of the Justices agreeing), displays a complete lack of coherent reasoning. Nowhere is it explained why a contract can be held to waive First Amendment rights. (The decision is also important, because it shows, once again, that the State wins when the magic words *national security* are uttered.)[74]

Reason cannot be an end in itself. Law is not "there," a separate and discrete entity apart from the warp and woof of society from which judges can select their basic principles in the sense that only one tenable principle exists. The corpus of law contains a multiplicity of premises. Entwined with politics and economics and with the deepest aspirations of the people, the law is a human institution created and implemented by humans, with a consequent panoply of human shortcomings. Far from being akin to a laboratory science, it is not a science at all, but a series of temporary accommodations to deal with different situations. It is not antecedent, but always in a state of becoming. Those who demand reason as being the life of the law fail to comprehend that law, as with all human institutions, is a slender reed that reflects the power configurations of society at a given time.

The call for reason also means that felicity in language is substituted for the quest for justice—the just result. That call is an integral part of the advocacy of process over substance. The means become the end. Some commentators even go so far as to assert that in so many words. Witness Professor Richard Funston: "Opinions based upon reasoned principle . . . are necessary to the very self-preservation of the Supreme Court. Assuming that the institution is worth preserving, Justices must sometimes sacrifice what they conceive to be a desirable result, if they cannot logically justify that result. In other words, procedure may be as important as substance; means more important than ends."[75] That position simply will not do. No one, to be sure, advocates opinions that do not opine. Nor should one. The end of law, however, is justice (or human welfare), not mellifluous language. Liked or not, the meaning is clear: Who wins or loses in lawsuits is as important—more important?—than how the game is played. That, at least, has been the practice of the Supreme Court throughout American history.

Funston's demand is intellectually untenable, even though leading scholars tend to support it.[76] Professor Ronald Dworkin, for example, maintained that legal norms, to be defensible, must be supportable with good reasons. He said that if laws do not have foundation in good reasons, they cannot be differentiated from the personal preferences or prejudices of the lawmaker. He, however, did not suggest what "good" reasons might be; nor did he say when lawmakers (of any category) ever acted in the way that he prefers.

Judges are enjoined to make their opinions models of rationality, but few take the trouble to analyze what that means, and no one has done it satisfactorily. For most commentators, rationality seems to be a conception of reason that leads to the discovery and application of rules (or principles) to disputes and thus permits logical justifications of the results. That definition is not enough. Another dimension should be seen—reason as creativity. That creativity is the essence of the Justices's activities in interpreting the Document. This concept does not mean, Professor Paul Diesing has pointed out, that "creativity is . . . formless [or] indescribable." It can proceed according to principles. But the irreducible point is that "ultimate ends, the basic aims of life, cannot be selected or evaluated by rational procedures; they must be dealt with by arbitrary preference, or intuition, or by cultural and biological determinism."[77] Those ends or aims are the premises of judicial decision making.

In constitutional lawmaking, "the basic aims of life" are the very meat of the decisions. They are dealt with by fiat ("arbitrary preferences") or by personal predilections ("cultural and biological determinism"). That fact should be clear enough to anyone who takes the time to see and makes the effort to understand. But it was precisely on that point that Felix Frankfurter went astray: "In his correspondence with [Henry] Stimson," Professor Hirsch related, "Frankfurter once again assumes that reasonable men cannot disagree about goals, but only about means to their goals."[78] That assumption was his basic error, one that makes his theory of judicial self-restraint fatally flawed. After nearly two centuries of Supreme Court operation, surely enough has been learned not only about the Court but about the mind-habits of humans to realize that reason never has been and cannot be an end in itself. Creating the law as they go along, the Justices make choices by which they attempt to manage a segment of the future.

The plea for reasoned opinions at best is unattainable. At worst, it calls for unexplained choices between conflicting major premises and then running the chosen premise through a judicial logic machine. That situation may not be bad in itself, but it is hardly enough. In addition to the need for adequate explanation of one premise over another, it is also necessary to state why reasons are good or bad. That latter question cannot be answered by con-

centrating on the logical consistency of the opinion, but only through evaluation by an independent set of external standards. The Court's critics seldom
favor us with a discussion of why reasons are good or bad, save on the level
of abstraction that makes the explanation meaningless. Even more, another
question—*which reasons?*—is as important or more so than the employment
of reason itself. "The heart has its reasons that reason itself does not
know,"Pascal has told us. The simple (rather, simple-minded) reliance on
rationality as the proper end of judicial activity found an effective answer in an
observation of the late film director Jean Renoir: "You see, in this world,
there is one awful thing, and that is that everyone has his reasons."[79]

"Everyone has his reasons": How, then, is one set to be considered to be
better than another? The question is at the heart of the proposals to be made
in this volume. Reasons for judicial decisions, we argue, should be evaluated
not in terms of whether they are logically consistent or because they are
extensions of precedents—although both have their value—but in terms of
the realization or nonrealization of an explicit set of values. Consequences
that follow Supreme Court decisions are important, indeed surpassingly so.
My suggestion is that the values to be sought by the Supreme Court should be
subsumed under the overarching concept of human dignity, of justice for all
rather than for the few. I concede, quite readily, that those goals are immensely complex and also that people will disagree on their definitions. Even
so, their explicit acceptance by the Justices seems to be wholly desirable. If
that idea is accepted, reason can of course be used to help achieve them. In
other words, and to leave no grounds for misunderstanding, I am proposing
that judges be avowedly result oriented, with the results being those that are
within the ambit of human dignity. Chief Justice Earl Warren once said that
the law floats in a sea of ethics; if that statement is true, as I believe it is (or
should be), the place of reason in constitutional law is basically similar to that
which it has in ethics. Goldsworthy Lowes Dickinson said it well in 1901:

It is the part of Reason, on my hypothesis, to tabulate and compare results. She does
not determine what is good, but works, as in all the sciences, upon given data. . . .
noticing what kinds of activity satisfy, and to what degree, the expanding nature of this
soul that seeks Good, and deducing therefrom, so far as may be, temporary rules of
conduct. . . . Temporary rules, I say, because, by the nature of the case, they can have
in them nothing absolute and final, inasmuch as they are mere deductions from a
process which is always developing and transforming itself.[80]

Dickinson could have been talking about the development of American
constitutional law, particularly in the past three or four decades.

To conclude: I am not advocating arbitrary decisions. I simply believe that,
as a matter of logic, they are unavoidable, unless and until societal goal values
can be identified, clarified, and articulated. When that is done, and obviously,
it is indeed a tall order, reason can be useful. As matters now stand, the

development of American constitutional law illustrates that the storied Rule of Law is really the Rule of Men and fallible men at that. We need judges who can make sociologically nonarbitrary decisions, and who would not blink at the fact that at times they are logically arbitrary. Until that fundamental need is fulfilled, insofar as mortal men can fulfill it, the Supreme Court will neither be understood nor subjected to the type of critical analysis so vitally necessary.

How, however, are the Justices (and others, for decisions are not made solely by the judge but by "judge and company") to determine when a decision is sociologically wise (that is, nonarbitrary)? That question, perhaps the most difficult of all, involves the third major criticism of today's Supreme Court.

IV.

Do the Justices have a means of adequately informing themselves of the complexities of the cases brought before them? Do they, the lawyers for litigants and the law clerks who serve the Justices, have the competence to understand those complexities? Can they evaluate or predict the social consequences, both immediate and long range, of alternative decisions? Are the Justices limited to the data brought to them by counsel? In short, is the adversary system sufficient to the need of making sociologically wise decisions?

The quick answer to the last question is no. One, however, should not rush to judgment about either the question or that answer. The Justices cannot, of course, make decisions without information, but if one compares the Court to either Congress or the executive, it quickly becomes apparent that all three operate on the basis of incomplete data. A recent carefully documented study concluded: "Appellate judges must make decisions on the basis of incomplete information, as all who hold important decision-making positions must."[81] If that is accurate, as surely it is, the problem of governance is much broader: How can anyone in a position of high responsibility, public or private, obtain data adequate to the need? Congress enacts some 400 public laws each session; it is sheer fantasy to believe that an individual Member can be or is privy to the facts of all of them or even most of them. Furthermore, those who are most knowledgeable in Congress still do not have a full comprehension of relevant information. As for the President, he of course must rely on his staff, and they on the bureaucracy, with the result that the Chief Executive is the prisoner of whatever data his subordinates choose to bring to him. No man can personally be fully apprised of the details of all of the problems that come to the Oval Office. The conclusion is clear: Governmental decisions, including those of the Supreme Court, are often arrows shot into the sky, to fall to earth those who shot them know not where, and with consequences, both first and second order, that cannot be predicted with any certainty. The fumbling and bumbling that go into the primitive type of economic planning now accomplished by the executive branch in cooperation with Congress is ample testimony to prove the point. As for the system of private governments of the Economic Constitution, it is truistic that, to use only one example, executives of automobile companies either had faulty information or used bad judgment (or both).

So seen, the oft-made accusation that the adversary system is a poor vehicle for informing judges is placed in proper perspective. There can be no doubt that it is inadequate. But is it any less so than the informing process for the outwardly political branches of public government (and the officers of private governments)? If one accepts the proposition that the need is for wise sociopolitical decisions, is the Court less wise than Congress or the President (or the Chief Executive Officer of, say, Chrysler)? The answer is obvious: The politicians (the term is not used invidiously) on the High Bench have as much insight as do politicians elsewhere. Possibly, they at times have more, for in theory at least the judges have time for reflection and are insulated from the pulls and tugs of the electoral process. The usual lawsuit does not require an immediate reply.

The conclusion about wisdom can be turned around: Governmental wisdom is a sometime thing, more fortuitous than planned and more dependent upon imponderable external forces than exact knowledge of social conditions—wherever public policies are promulgated. Certainly, any fair assessment of what Washington hath wrought during the past three decades would not reveal lesser wisdom in the Justices than in those who strode the corridors of power in the White House or the Capitol. "The best and the brightest" enmeshed the United States in the unspeakable Vietnam "war," a policy to which Congress quickly and unthinkingly agreed. Whatever may be thought about recent judicial decisions, nothing can parallel that dreary record of stupidity and mendacity, not to say illegality. Not only was Vietnam the most dreadful foreign adventure in American history, the fallout from it still poisons the economy and the political arena. Sagacity in government, whether public or private, is in very short supply.

True enough, the adversary system has flaws that must be corrected, and soon, if the Supreme Court is to remain an important segment of government. There are two basic shortcomings: how the Justices inform themselves and the competence of "judge and company." The discussion at this point is, of necessity, brief.

That judges are not adequately informed by counsel has long been known. In 1924 Judge Benjamin Nathan Cardozo (later to go on the Supreme Court) noted: "Some of the errors of courts have their origin in imperfect knowledge of the economic and social consequences of a decision, or of the economic and social needs to which a decision will respond."[82] Holmes said much the same in 1881: "judges . . . should openly discuss the legislative principles upon which their decisions must always rest"[83]—a statement in which he echoed Jeremy Bentham in the early nineteenth century. In 1954 Justice

Frankfurter sighed that "How to inform the judicial mind . . . is one of the most complicated problems."[84] The pretense is otherwise: As reflected in judicial opinions and textual commentary alike, it is widely assumed, and possibly believed, that the traditional methods of bringing data to judges through the normal operations of the adversary system are adequate.

They are not. The system is a verbalized trial by combat in courtrooms, in which opposing lawyers seek to persuade purported impartial judges of the validity of their clients's positions. Under the orthodox view, an appellate judge receives "briefs" from lawyers (pamphlets that set forth arguments of the adversaries), can refer to "the record" (what went on in the trial court), and can glean knowledge from oral argument (conversations in open court with lawyers). He can also use "strict" judicial notice, by which is meant that he can consider other data provided it is a matter of common knowledge. An appeals judge is supposed to accept the facts as found by the trial bench and then apply the law in a "principled" manner, using the tools of reason. Put into a formula, the task may be stated in this way: $R(ules) \times F(acts) = Decision$ (more briefly, $R \times F = D$). Little creativity is possible; the rules supposedly preexist, and the facts are said to speak for themselves.

We have already shown the inadequacy of that model of judicial behavior. It is based on unsupportable assumptions, including: (a) that lawyers are not only fully competent to deal with complicated socioeconomic problems, but also are approximately equal in competence; (b) that the Justices are also fully capable of handling those complex matters; and (c) that truth in the judicial sense comes from the clash of opposites, in the arena of the courtroom. The Court, in sum, is in theory supposed to be a miniature "marketplace of ideas,"[85] out of which not only truth but the common good emerge. None of the assumptions comports with reality. Each is based on faith alone, a faith that the system is working adequately.

That is not enough. We may not be able to improve the system, however much it needs it, but we should know that it is an imperfect tool. The adversary process "works," mainly because the Justices often go outside the boundaries of what lawyers bring to them to find additional data and because they are willing to make blind guesses about the societal impact of their decisions. Thus far at least, the public has been willing to put up with manifest faults, just as the public seems willing (or perhaps apathetic or in despair about) a general lack of competence in lawyer-judges (and counsel) to make socially wise decisions. How long that acquiescence will continue cannot be forecast. What can be said without fear of contradiction is this: The system requires substantial modification.

Some sporadic recognition of that very point has come from the Justices themselves. At times they will do, as Justice William Brennan once admitted,[86] "independent research"—either by themselves (which is seldom) or by use of law clerks. They do not consider themselves bound by only the information presented by counsel. An example is Justice Harry Blackmun's opinion in the abortion cases (1973), in the writing of which he took judicial notice of many data not presented formally. How often that, or something similar, occurs is unknown. Few studies have been made of the flow of information to the Court.[87] Enough is known, however, to conclude that although the personal research by a Justice is aberrational, independent inquiry by law clerks is routine. That raises difficult problems of fairness. If the Justices develop data on their own, lawyers for neither litigant can contest them, nor can they present contrary arguments. On rare occasions, the Court even decides a question not even argued by counsel (an example is the 1886 ruling that a corporation is a constitutional person).[88] There is nothing unlawful about that, but it does raise questions of propriety—but only to the extent that the orthodox conception of the adversary system is considered to be an end in itself. If that system is viewed, as it should be, as a mere vehicle, albeit an old-fashioned one, for triggering the Court, questions of the propriety of both independent research and decisions made without request tend to fade away. (Are there other, better ways of energizing the Court? Should there be? The answer on both counts is yes.)

In addition to the research by the small bureaucracy each Justice has, and the bureaucracy of judge and company that is the adversary system, the Justices of course draw upon their personal knowledge and experience. Indeed, they cannot escape doing so. It is not at all unknown for judges to discuss pending cases with others (friends and trusted confidants).

The Supreme Court engages in two types of decisions. First, and most known, is the settlement of the dispute between the immediate parties. Will Marbury get to be a justice of the peace? Will Bakke get into medical school? Will Gideon be given a lawyer paid for by the state? For this dispute-settlement function, the Justices require only particular ("adjudicative") facts, those that deal with the parties before the Court and their dispute. Adjudicative facts come from the lawyers. The Court resolves the dispute and in so doing makes a little general law. It is law, however, only to the extent that the decision is usable in later litigation as a basis for predicting what the Court will do. (That type of use is the Holmes-Cardozo "prophecy theory of law"—a forecast of what a court would do with a given dispute.) In terms of broad legal theory, a lawsuit produces only the "law of the case," for technically, only the parties at bar are bound by the judicial ruling.

For the Supreme Court, no one really believes that others are not bound by it. The few cases given full treatment each year are considered to state a general principle, even though it is logically impossible to infer a general principle from one particular. Doing so in itself would make the Supreme Court an important organ of governance (in the establishment of public policy), but there is more, much more: In recent years it has (at times, but not always) taken on a broader, overt lawmaking function. The Justices expressly assert that their decisions are "the law of the land" in a general sense and are getting away with it, which means that they not only settle the immediate dispute but make law for generations of Americans yet unborn. They state a "general norm," not unlike a Congressional statute, purporting to bind everyone. When done, the Justices must pay attention to more than mere adjudicative facts. "Social" or "legislative" facts become crucially important, for they are making law for people generally. Society at large is impacted. Therefore, the roles of judicial notice, of independent research, of the personal experience of the Justice, and of his personal philosophy become much more significant. Lawyers know this, for often they bring immense amounts of "nonlegal" data to the Court in an effort to provide a factual basis for their clients's claims. When they present such data, and it is accepted by the Justices, it means that the Court is a fact finder.

That runs counter to the accepted wisdom about the role of appellate judges, who are supposed to accept the facts as found by the trial court. It also evidences the proposition that the facts of a dispute are as important, perhaps more so, than the law to be applied. Legislative facts are presented at times to the Court, but at other times the Justices find them for themselves, although it must be said that some of the "facts" so found are actually untested assumptions.

The Supreme Court's practice of stating general norms in explicit language does not antedate 1958, when it unanimously decided *Cooper* v. *Aaron*, the Little Rock school desegregation case.[89] I do not suggest that prior decisions, as noted above, were not considered to have *in effect* a broader meaning. *Cooper* is important, because it was the first time the Justices *openly* asserted that a lawsuit between two litigants could result in a general norm, a legislative prescription, a rule binding on all similarly situated. In practical effect, but only to the extent that the practice is followed, *Cooper* amended the Constitution by making the Court's legislative role legitimate.

Such rulings are extremely controversial. Whether the Court is straying beyond the bounds of proper judicial conduct is the question. Many think so, although it is difficult to determine whether those critics are disapproving the results reached or the fact that they were made in a sweeping, "legislative" manner.

The Supreme Court, thus, is a "commander"—a topic that is explored in the next chapter. Our present interest lies in the lesser but still important question of whether the Justices are adequately informed about the intricacies of the problems brought to them. The answer must be no, a fact that at times is candidly acknowledged by the Justices in cases involving "administrative law"—that is, judicial review of the decisions of the bureaucracy: In that area, which is in many ways as significant as constitutional interpretation, the Justices will defer in some complicated matters to the putative superior expertise of administrative officers. That is also a frank recognition of the lack of competence in judges in some questions, for example, those dealing with scientific and technological problems.[90]

V.

To summarize: the three-pronged assault on the Supreme Court is too superficial. Each criticism has some merit, but taken together they do not cause the bastion of judicial review to crumble. (We will return later to the affirmative arguments for judicial activism, *in a certain direction.*) Those who attack the Court seem to be more interested in getting judges out of policy-making than in improving the ways courts operate. They advocate judicial self-restraint. Possibly, theirs will be the ultimate triumph. That it should not be is one of the messages of this book.

5
The Court as Commander

Four major milestones mark the almost two centuries of Supreme Court activity. Three have been discussed: the 1803 power grab in the *Marbury* case, the invention of "substantive" due process after the Civil War, and the abdication of the Justices as ultimate economic policymaker in the 1930s and 1940s. The fourth, and possibly the most significant, is now clearly evident: Since 1958 the Court at times has been an *affirmative commander* as well as a *negative naysayer*. On occasion the Justices tell other government officers what they *must* do to have their actions jibe with the fundamental law, rather than what they *cannot* do. The Court has become a commander; this chapter outlines that portentous development.

At the outset, I recognize the semantic problem: A naysaying decision can be considered to mean that the Justices chose affirmatively to pursue certain values. For example, by striking down a statute—say, one providing for minimum wages and maximum hours in employment—the Court in the 1890-1937 period could be said to have made a "must do" pronouncement on corporate rights, to further business expansion even at the expense of the working class. The problem of course exists, but my point is different. The Justices in recent years have begun openly and expressly to command, by issuing opinions couched in language of affirmative duty laid upon political officers. In these instances, there is no need to infer a command (as in the employment decisions), for it is flatly stated in plain language.

That role is a constitutional revolution of the first water. Again, it was not announced as such: The Court moved in an entirely new direction without fanfare and, seemingly, because it tried to make the new posture a mere variation on what had gone before, it was doing only what judges had long done. That stance is far from true: Nothing quite like it had been seen in American history (nor in the experience of any other nation). The Justices became a de facto Council of Elders. By asserting the right and the power to say what the law *is* (as in the *Marbury* case) they have, through time and because of widespread acceptance, become able to say what the law *should* be. Rather than being "mere umpires," they are now able, in Justice Brennan's words, to be "lawmakers—a coordinate branch of government."[1] The implications of that development have not yet been seen; there is little reason to think that the Court will not attempt to carve out an even larger role for itself in the future.

There is another way of looking at the development. During the heyday of the (second) Constitution of Rights (of Quasi-Limitations), the Court chose to emphasize certain rights of personhood they attached to economic collectivities, by denying government the power to intervene into economic matters. The Justices spoke in terms of individualism and of laissez-faire. Today there is at least a tacit recognition that the basic unit of society is the group, which has had the consequence that a concept of status is emerging in constitutional law. A major task of the Court is to effect the nexus, within the scope of constitutional values that they identify and articulate for and by themselves, of the individual between the groups (including the nation-State itself) of a bureaucratized society. That development means that the Court has collectivized constitutional law.[2] An aspect of that development is the propensity, by no means always employed, to issue decrees couched in language of affirmative command. The Justices are attempting to preserve the values of individualism in a group-dominated nation. To do so, they have had to invent new ways of looking at old problems. They know, in some manner, that the stability of "the system" depends on siphoning off social discontent. Since those in positions of authority, both public and private, are not likely to police themselves, and thus to alter the system in at least minimal ways, the Court steps in and does so. When that is done, the Justices act as surrogates for those who benefit most from the system. One example illustrates the point—*Green* v. *School Board*,[3] a 1968 decision involving school desegregation. There a unanimous Court used language of positive duty:

Brown-II [the second, implementing decision of *Brown* v. *Board of Education*] was a call for dismantling of well-entrenched dual systems tempered by an awareness that complex and multifaceted problems would arise which would require time and flexibility for a successful resolution. School boards such as respondent [in *Green*] then operating state-compelled dual systems were nevertheless *clearly charged with an affirmative duty* to convert to a unitary system in which racial discrimination would be eliminated root and branch. (Emphasis added.)

Green, thus, goes far beyond the traditional decisions of the Supreme Court. Nowhere before that time can there be found language in Court opinions charging administrative officers with "an affirmative duty" to do something. An express command aimed at school officials, *Green* means that the Justices have openly entered the political arena, overtly taking part in the travail of society. The movement is from adjudication (settling only the dispute of the parties at bar) to legislation (stating rules for the public at large or at least for all similarly situated to the parties in court). It is a constitutional revolution of the first magnitude. There were forerunners to *Green*, to be sure, but none that used the express words *affirmative duty*.

The Court makes no pretense in such decisions. In philosophic terms, the Justices have become telocratic and openly admit as much. The rules of law they promulgate are overtly instrumental—goal seeking. Americans have long believed that the United States is nomocratic—rule governed. That belief, that Basic Myth, has now become more than threadbare; it simply is not true. In constitutional matters the emperor has no clothes. A government of laws, not of men, has seldom characterized the United States.[4] To the extent it does so today, it hampers rather than helps the resolution of public-policy problems. Telocracy, furthermore, has always been apparent in the Court's work, the question being not whether it has been so but, rather, which purposes it was pursuing. There is, however, a difference between yesteryear and today, in two ways. First, the Court is now openly and outwardly purposive, and second, it has broadened the reach of its decisions to cover many more people.

The Justices choose constitutional questions to decide, not in the interests of the litigants but to develop the general law. Chief Justice Fred Vinson reminded lawyers in 1949 that "you are, in a sense, prosecuting or defending class actions; . . . you represent not only your clients, but tremendously important principles, upon which are based the plans, hopes and aspirations of a great many people throughout the country."[5] A class action is legalese for one plaintiff suing another in his own name and for all others similarly situated. *Brown* v. *Board of Education*, for example, was a class action. The litigant was Miss Linda Brown of Topeka, Kansas; but her suit was brought for a general principle and not for specific, immediate relief. (That relief, of course, was also sought, but was not the primary motivation.) Vinson's remark was an oblique acknowledgement of the Court as legislator, for often those "others similarly situated" do not even know of the lawsuit. Surely, that was true in the abortion cases and in the controversial *Miranda* ruling (concerning the rights of a person caught up in administration of the criminal law). Although the Court has recently moved to tighten use of class actions, Vinson's point is that all constitutional cases permit judges to rule generally while appearing to do so only specifically. They are, thus, "backdoor" class actions[6] and therefore not subject to the limitations imposed on true class actions by statute and judicial decisions. The Justices, not being logicians, have no difficulty in stating a general rule in the context of one particular. The lesson here should be obvious: The Justices, generally, set their own rules, both in procedure to be followed and the substance (the rules) to be applied; they have constitutional *carte blanche* and can go as far as they want to go—or, rather, as far as the political process permits them to go.

II.

By fits and starts, with some Sisyphean backpedaling, the members of the High Bench are pursuing—overtly—their ideas of justice. They do not seem to be bound by preexisting rules. The consequence, as might be expected, is obvious: Ideas of justice, of good public policy, differ among the nine Justices. Nothing is new about this, except the open admission by some of the Justices that they are lawmakers and a dawning recognition that the conflicting interests of a pluralistic society must be accommodated. That they are far from successful in the latter goal is revealing testimony of the short-comings of pluralism itself as a form of political order.

The differences between the outward attitude of Justices in yesteryear and those of today are suggested by the following episodes, the first related by Judge Learned Hand about Justice Holmes and the second personal to myself. Said Hand:

Remember what Justice Holmes said about "justice." I don't know what you think about him but on the whole he was the master craftsman of our time; and he said, "I hate justice," which he didn't quite mean. What he did mean was this. I remember once when I was with him; it was on a Saturday when the Court was to confer. It was before he had a motorcar; and we jogged along in an old coupe. When we got to the Capitol, I wanted to provoke a response, so as he walked off I said to him, "Well, sir, good-bye. Do justice!" He turned quite sharply and he said, "Come here, come here." I answered, "Oh, I know, I know." He replied, "That is not my job. My job is to play the game according to the rules."[7]

Holmes had the nineteenth-century view. (It is interesting to compare that episode with his 1873 candid acknowledgment that the rules were not neutral [previously recounted].) He simply did not care about trying to help rectify some of the injustices of the world. "Savage, harsh, and cruel," as Professor Grant Gilmore described him, he was willing as a Justice on the Supreme Court to aid "the rich and powerful [to] to impose their will on the poor and weak."[8] His was a harsh and gloomy universe, although he well knew that playing the game "according to the rules" gave judges great leeway, he was unwilling to make the mental leap into considerations of justice and fair play.

The modern, albeit publicly unacknowledged, conception is that of Justice Hugo L. Black, a man whose cosmology made him an inheritor of the ideals of the Enlightenment and who saw in the Court—not consistently, to be sure, but often—a means whereby something more than the nebulous Holmesian rules could be employed. In 1959 I had an opportunity to speak with him in his chambers in the Marble Palace. The room was piled high with books, almost cascading off his desk, most of which dealt not with law as technical doctrine but with philosophy and history and economics. Black, a gracious man, spent an hour discussing the work of the Court and his role. With some reluctance, I finally got up to leave, for he obviously was a busy and hard-working man. As we walked to the door, I turned and shook his hand, and asked a final question, "What, sir, do you conceive your basic task to be?" I don't know what I expected, but what came back was this: His eyes blazed, his right hand shot into the air, and without hesitation he fervently said, "To do justice!"

It would be wrong, of course, to infer too much about either episode. Black's answer to my question, nonetheless, does seem to epitomize the new jurisprudence of the Court, the open desire, not always followed, to do justice or achieve fairness in individual cases—and thereby to promulgate a general norm or norms of justice as fairness. It is not an invariable practice. Some members of the present Supreme Court are proceeding at times in the opposite direction.

Justice William Rehnquist is perhaps the intellectual heir of Holmes in his attitude. Consider in this connection the *Rummel* case,[9] decided by a bare 5-4 majority in 1980. In an opinion written by Rehnquist, a Texas law was upheld that made a life sentence mandatory when a person was convicted of three felonies. Texas's criminal law is notoriously harsh. Rummel's three offenses involved a total sum of $229.11 (forgery, wrongful use of a credit card, and not fulfilling an air-conditioning contract). The life sentence, Rehnquist concluded, was not a cruel and unusual punishment proscribed by the Eighth Amendment. Maintaining that he was proceeding according to the rules and that the relevant rule was the Texas law, Rehnquist quite forgot (or simply ignored the fact) that the rule—the Texas law—was the very question at issue.

Some Justices today do not pretend, as did Rehnquist, that constitutional law is a game to be played—in Holmes's words—"according to the rules." Unabashedly making law, they often seem to strain for the "just" result. The problem is that no one, on the High Bench or otherwise, has yet produced a workable definition of what *justice* means in the context of Supreme Court lawmaking. Hence the sharp splits on the Court, as in the *Rummel* case, and as in the well-known decision concerning Allan Bakke's application for admission to the University of California medical school. The school had a policy of preferential admissions for blacks and other disadvantaged people. When the *Bakke* case[10] got to the Marble Palace, the Justices again narrowly split and produced a Solomonic decision: Bakke was to be admitted to the school, but in the future race could be used as one of the criteria of admissions. The result was that white Americans (represented by Bakke) as well as black Americans (the disadvantaged generally) were each given at least a partial victory. My point is not to argue the pros and cons of the *Bakke* decision, but to suggest that it, and others, reveal a marked propensity even on the "Burger Court" to follow Justice Black's *cri de coeur*: "Do justice!"

By no means is telocracy—avowedly pursuing a given goal and doing justice—publicly admitted by the High Bench. The pretense still exists that Holmes's prescription of nomocracy prevails. A failure to see through the pretense, to accept what judges say in their opinions at face value, at times leads learned scholars into serious errors of judgment. Bertrand de Jouvenel, the well-known French political theorist, is an example:

Nomocracy is the supremacy of law; telocracy is the supremacy of purpose. Modern [i.e., Western] institutions were developed around the central concept of law. Individual security is assured if the citizens are not exposed to arbitrary acts of the government, but only to the application of the law, which they know. . . . The guarantees of such a regime are precious. But institutions of a judicial type are not [designed] for action.[11]

He went on to say: what "distinguishes contemporary government is its vocation for rapid social and economic progress. . . . Once government activity has a relatively precise goal, the regime's inspiration is telocratic and political forms necessarily reflect this."[12]

De Jouvenel was not then speaking of the Supreme Court of the United States, but his views are nonetheless relevant. He displays a faith in nomocracy, in the supremacy of interdictory law. That supremacy, however, is precisely what has never been wholly true in the United States (or elsewhere). He doubtless is correct in describing contemporary government, but surely he errs in asserting that it is a new development. Telocracy is novel only in the express acknowledgment of it by all branches of government. Law since the earliest colonial days in America has been instrumental—goal seeking, that is, or telocratic. Professor Morton Horwitz's conclusions about the common law are equally accurate for constitutional law:

By 1820 the legal landscape in America bore only the faintest resemblance to what existed forty years earlier. While the words were often the same, the structure of thought had dramatically changed and with it the theory of law. Law was no longer conceived of as an eternal set of principles expressed in custom and derived from the natural law. Nor was it regarded primarily as a body of rules designed to achieve justice only in the individual case. Instead, judges came to think of the common law as equally responsible with legislation for governing society and promoting socially desirable conduct. The emphasis on law as an instrument of policy encouraged innovation and allowed judges to formulate legal doctrine with the self-conscious goal of bringing about social change.[13]

That statement, particularly the last sentence, reads remarkably like what the Supreme Court and other courts have been doing for at least a generation.

The change, thus, is not from nomocracy to telocracy, but in the open avowal of social goals pursued by officers in all segments of government. Congress, for example, by enacting the Employment Act of 1946 expressly called for policies that further the economic well-being of the people. Other statutes have delegated authority to agencies and bureaus to help fulfill that very purpose. The President's annual budget and economic messages to Congress are a conscious effort to tinker with the economy for telocratic purposes. The Supreme Court has had a major role in the new (open) posture—first, by validating new powers of Congress in socioeconomic affairs (the so-called constitutional revolution of the 1930s); and second, by rendering decisions that are themselves telocratic. "It is of the very nature of a free society," Justice Felix Frankfurter once maintained, "to advance in its standards of what is deemed reasonable and right."[14] Today, it is deemed reasonable and right, even necessary, for the government in all branches to pursue social welfare ends. The pretenses of the past have been cast aside. Law has become obviously instrumental. To be sure, disagreement occurs (at this writing, for example, in the details of President Ronald Reagan's economic programs), but it, at least outwardly, is about means rather than ends. Very few, that is, dispute that government has some role to play in socioeconomic affairs; even the Reagan "supply-side" economics is being promoted as a means of helping all of the people (not only the affluent, who would be the immediate beneficiaries).

The legal theory for the new posture was suggested many years ago by Leon Duguit: "Any system of public law can be vital only so far as it is based on a given sanction to the following rules: First, the holders of power cannot do certain things; second, there are certain things they must do."[15] Formal constitutional law from 1789 to 1937 involved the "cannot do" of that formulation, not always to be sure but often enough to make the Constitution one of "rights" or of "limitations." Since 1937 the "must do" aspect has been slowly emerging.

When the Court validated the New Deal in the 1930s and 1940s, it confirmed, rather than wrought, a revolution in American government. The High Bench caught up with the political branches of government. Each branch became an active participant in the travail of society. At first, the Justices were not fully aware of what they were doing, but the new form of government—the emergence of an operative Constitution of Powers—quickly made it evident that even judges could neither stay aloof from nor forever block the tides of social change sweeping through the nation. Writing in 1908, Woodrow Wilson perceived the need for a common purpose among those who govern. Once it is conceded, as surely it must be, that courts are an integral part of the governing process, his comment is particularly apt: "Government is not a body of blind forces; it is a body of men, with highly differentiated functions, no doubt, in our modern day of specialization, but with a common task and purpose. Their cooperation is indispensable, their warfare fatal."[16] Although Wilson was speaking of President and Congress, his observation fits the Supreme Court as well. Judges are not so much independent from as cooperators with other branches of government. Rather than being separate and apart, they stand squarely in the mainstream of politics when they act to lend constitutional legitimacy to what politicians want to do. Even when they declare some actions of political officers invalid, judges have an ongoing political function to perform.

An understanding of the flow of constitutional decisions, from the Supreme

Court and elsewhere, requires inquiry into trends of doctrinal development in both the formal and the operative Constitutions. Trend analysis involves starting in the past, discussing interim developments, and projecting into the future. That can be done on several levels—of the evolution of specific constitutional principles, of the structure of government itself, and with respect to the relationship of government vis-à-vis the citizenry. The latter is our present focus.

The fundamental trend, as has been said, is from ostensible nomocracy to avowed telocracy. In politics, the change is from the negative, nightwatchman State to the positive State; in economics, it is from laissez-faire to regulation "in the public interest"; and in law, the Rule of Law has been redefined from a seeming static system of immutable principles to a dynamic, openended stream of decisions. Each merits discussion, not separately but together.

Less than a half-century ago the American people crossed over one of the great constitutional watersheds of their history. In what was aptly termed a constitutional revolution, judicial approval was accorded to what most people wanted: governmental intervention in socioeconomic affairs so as to provide —at least, attempt to provide—minimum economic security.[17] The positive State came into existence under a third operative fundamental law—the Constitution of Powers. Government overtly became responsible for more than minimum internal order and external security; it assumed obligations of a social-service or welfare nature. We have already mentioned a possible reason for the development: a "pay-off" for fighting a sanguinary war. We have also noted that the new posture of government coincided almost exactly in time with America's true Golden Age (1945-70).

Whether the new commitments of government can long endure is by no means certain. Its politics, seemingly settled in the post-World War II period, are becoming unraveled. That condition may be attributed to the slowing down, even cessation, of economic growth, to the depletion of natural resources, and to the rising demands of people in the former colonial areas of the world. So it should come as no surprise that tensions, verging on violence, concerning welfare programs are being felt, for we are witnessing, in John Kenneth Galbraith's terms, the "revolt of the rich against the poor"[18] as a type of counter-revolution to the increasingly insistent demands of the underclass (both in the United States and elsewhere). Professor Lester Thurow has labelled the new politics "the zero-sum society," by which he means that in a slow- or no-growth economy, any important economic benefit for one segment of society requires a concomitant sacrifice elsewhere. Hence the zero-sum game: it is one in which all cannot win. "In the past," Thurow said, "political and economic power was distributed in such a way that substantial economic losses could be imposed on parts of the population. . . . Economic losses were allocated to particular powerless groups rather than spread across the population. These groups are no longer willing to accept losses and are able to raise substantially the costs for those who wish to impose losses upon them."[19] The groups include blacks and other ethnic minorities, workers, women, and consumers. Powerful business interests still exist, and the result is creeping political paralysis. Whether and how that Gordian knot of the American political economy can be cut may well be the central constitutional question of the day. (Our interest in this book lies in the extent to which, if at all, the Supreme Court can help in that monumental task.)

Galbraith and Thurow, without doubt, are correct. Their message is well worth pondering, for what they are saying is that the telocracy that has characterized government for the past several decades may no longer be possible. The economic pie is shrinking, of that there can be no real question. Even so, whatever the outcome of the struggles that have already begun and are certain to continue, the commitment of government to general economic security remains. Congress still sets broad policy guidelines, the administration of which is left to the bureaucracy, and the judiciary cooperates. How long that posture will continue is uncertain. One thing, however, seems sure: There will be no reversion to the *status quo ante*, to the Golden Age of the 1945-70 period. Americans are entering the age of limits, of frugality, of scarcity. The ecological trap is closing. There can be little doubt that the next decade and beyond will be "a harsher, more exacting, and more perilous age."[20]

So telocratic goals pursued by government may well have to change. (I do not propose to discuss the point further, save in the context of Supreme Court decision making.) The social milieu is being rapidly altered. Does that mean that the instrumentalism of the Justices, so evident since 1937, will be altered so that different goals are pursued? Can human dignity, defined as the realization of basic human needs, survive and be enhanced in a "steady-state" economy? Can, in other words, the Court help effect the transition from the now-defunct Golden Age to "the lean years"[21] with a minimum of stress on existing institutions and expectations? That question is the problem that now stares all governmental officers, including those in the Temple on the Hill, squarely in their faces, and it is a problem with which they will be concerned as the future unfolds. No quick technological fix, or any other similar remedy, is available. We are in for it, deeply and irretrievably, and it behooves all who care—and only saints and fools do not—to help in the extrication of humankind from the crisis of crises—the climacteric—it now confronts. Judges cannot be immune from that effort.

The problem emerges at the very time that the theory of the Rule of Law, historically nomocratic, is being redefined to encompass a telocratic dimension. Constitutional law was traditionally procedural, telling government how it must deal with the citizenry. It has now taken on a goal- or purpose-seeking aspect. Not always, to be sure, but enough to conclude that nomocracy no longer is an adequate conception of the role of law and legal institutions. This is not to say that some of the traditional view is not kept; of course it is. But it must operate side by side with the new instrumentalism. The United States, thus, has assumed the task, vastly more difficult than enforcing a law known to all (the orthodoxy), of deciding what the law ought to be and of making desirable changes.

Perhaps the clearest expression of the new Rule of Law came in 1959, in the Declaration of Delhi of the International Congress of Jurists (a group of lawyers from countries outside the Soviet bloc of nations):

> The International Congress of Jurists . . . recognizes that the Rule of Law is a dynamic concept for the expansion and fulfillment of which jurists are primarily responsible and which should be employed not only to safeguard and advance the civil and political rights of the individual in a free society, but also *to establish social, economic, educational and cultural conditions under which his legitimate aspirations and dignity may be realized.*[22] (Emphasis added.)

To the extent that the spirit, if not the letter, of the Declaration is accepted, and it is by an entire range of American governmental programs, the Rule of Law has come to mean, in Aristotle's terms, *distributive* justice as well as *corrective* justice. Government, as Duguit said, "must do" certain things of an affirmative nature.

How, if at all, has the Supreme Court responded to that version of the Rule of Law? The Justices, first, have not announced any spectacular shift in so many words. When, however, some of their recent decisions are viewed in terms of effects, of social consequences, rather than as examples of doctrinal exegesis, it is clear that the Court has indeed accepted at least some parts of the new Rule of Law. Furthermore, the Justices have contributed to the settlement of some of the immediate aims of Americans. It will be recalled that Yves Simon once observed that in a democratic society, "deliberation is about means and presupposes that the problem of ends has been settled."[23] The Justices have contributed to developing consensuses on troublous matters such as race relations, abortion, the church-State relationship, the immersion of the nation in world affairs, and other critical public policy issues. I do not suggest that they have solved them. Far from it. In those and other areas, the Justices have moved to catch the conscience of the American people and thus to stimulate and keep alive a continuing seminar on vital constitutional matters. If democracy means anything, it means a continuing dialogue among the citizenry on matters of public concern. The Justices both lead and participate in that dialogue.

The precise turning point to constitutional telocracy can be identified in Chief Justice Charles Evans Hughes's 1937 opinion in a minimum-wage case, *West Coast Hotel Co. v. Parrish.*[24] To Hughes, liberty meant "liberty in a social organization," which required the use of law to ward away the evils of industrialization. From being a limitation on governmental power, the due process clauses of the formal Constitution thereby became at least an invitation, and perhaps a command, for political action to ameliorate human distress. The command, if that it was, was couched in discreet terms. The idea lay dormant for almost twenty years. Not until 1955, in the second, implementing decision in *Brown* v. *Board of Education*,[25] did the Justices screw up their courage to tell other government officers: "Do this." In that instance, the command was to integrate black children into public schools "with all deliberate speed."

Hughes's opinion in *Parrish* permitted government to do something to further the cause of the disadvantaged—that is, to use law purposively. It also, as Professor Edward S. Corwin phrased it, changed the due process clauses from limitations on legislative power to "an actual instigation to legislative action of a leveling nature."[26] At what point does an "instigation" become a command? There is no way to answer that question. At some time, however, between 1937 and 1955 a new perception of their role was accepted by the Justices.

The *Parrish* decision, with others, permitted the birth of the (third) Constitution of Powers, for the Court had constitutionalized massive interventions into the political economy by Congress and state legislatures. That third fundamental law still remains as part of the operative Constitution; it is a layer on the palimpsest that is the Document of 1787. Not that the (second) Constitution of Rights (of Quasi-Limitations) was completely shunted aside and supplanted. The point is that it now had to share top billing with the third Constitution.

III.

It is "an axiom of statesmanship," Henry George once observed, "that great changes can be brought about under old forms."[27] So with the Constitution: the formal words remain the same, but only as a facade, beneath which lies a radically different living reality. The emergence of a Constitution of Powers meant that structural changes came without amendment of the Constitution of Rights. Two of them are well known—the shift in the federal system toward a consolidation of national power and the increased flow of power within the "general government" toward the presidency (and the bureaucracy). Nor was it a sudden development; much of American history evidences the slow beginnings of both changes. By 1950 it had become clear beyond doubt that both were permanent alterations in the allocation of governmental powers. (That is so despite some recent attempts, as in the 1976 decision in *National League of Cities* v. *Usery*, to resurrect historical federalism.)[28]

Neither federalism nor the rise of executive hegemony will be discussed here. My interest lies in what has happened and is happening to the Supreme Court. The Justices have moved on several fronts to meet the challenges of the modern era. They have not remained quiescent, but have become an active participant in the arena of politics. Examples are easily found: racial segregation; apportionment in state legislatures (and the House of Representatives); the rights of women, of aliens, of children, of illegitimates; administration of the criminal law. Taken together, they tend to validate—not entirely, to be sure, but at least partially—McGeorge Bundy's comment that "The fundamental function of the law is to prevent the natural unfairness of society from becoming intolerable."[29] At the core of many recent decisions of the Court are the equality principle, writ large, and a concept of justice as fundamental fairness.

Under the new jurisprudence of the Supreme Court, it acts as a commander, not in the sense of having enforcement power of its own (which it does not), but by stating norms that purportedly bind the entire nation. By becoming a commander—and getting away with it—the Justices have made it possible for them to assume an even larger role. What that role might be is adumbrated later. It suffices for now to state that the Court as legislator is not fully accepted. People throughout the United States do look to the Temple on the Hill for guidance, if not for ultimate resolution, in some of the more troublous problems that confront them, but anguished protests emanate from those whose oxen have been gored by the very idea of the Court as commander. Those objections will likely fade away. The Justices's position as a constituent part of government, a necessary part of government, is too solidified to be altered. The Court is needed, badly needed, by a fragmented and alienated populace that is trying to navigate the white rapids of the climacteric of humankind that lie dead ahead. I do not suggest that, now or later, the Court can or will do this alone. That is a manifest impossibility. But the Justices can light a candle rather than standing aside and cursing the darkness of the coming Age of Frugality.

IV.

The new judicial posture that has been built in the last generation or so involves the concept of "positive freedom." To explain it requires reference to a long forgotten English philosopher, Thomas Hill Green, who wrote in the latter part of the nineteenth century. To him, the notion of positive freedom "reflected the rediscovery of the community as a corporate body of which both institutions and individuals are a part, so that the idea of collective well-being or the common good underlies any claim to private right."[30] Ponder that statement for a moment. Can there be much, if any, doubt that claims to "private right" do give way in modern law and policy to ideas of "collective well-being"? The "community" has indeed been rediscovered. It may be seen in the rise of the State to preeminence, in the successful assertions of national security as justifications for governmental action, in invocations of the public (or national) interest by successive Presidents, in the "entitlements" that more and more Americans consider to be their right—in all of these areas, and more, the notion of individual autonomy has been supplanted by an inchoate type of collectivism. Despite much rhetoric to the contrary, few dispute the need for the change, and fewer would wish to revert to the storied days of individualism (which existed, for most, more in the myth than in the reality). It should be remembered that individualism, far from being inherent in the human experience, is a latter-day phenomenon, not older than the French Revolution. Even as a theory or a philosophy, it is now either dead or dying, both in social affairs and in law. The autonomous man does not exist as such.

The development may be seen in American constitutionalism in the newly emergent concept of status rights, of rights, that is, that derive from one's membership in a group (or groups) and not because of some inherent, metaphysical notion of personhood. An "indivisible" nation pledges "liberty and justice to all." That may be a mere slogan, a symbol, but we must always remember that, as Holmes said and Frankfurter often repeated, "we live by symbols."[31] The symbol today is of collective well-being—of welfare, if you will. Green provided the philosophical basis for positive government, for social insurance programs that supply the economic means for more people to be free (if they wish). The duty of government in this conception is not so much to maximize individual liberty in itself—as an end in itself—but, rather, "to insure the conditions for at least a minimum of well-being—a standard of living, of education, and of security below which good policy requires that no considerable part of the population shall be allowed to fall." Analysis of governmental programs since the 1930s shows how closely they approximate that requirement. One need only refer to the Declaration of Delhi to see how some legal thinking coincides with Green's. It needs to be remembered, however, that Green wrote at a time when economic growth appeared to make his proposals possible. The history of most of this century is also one of economic growth. Modern governmental programs thus were created during an Age of Abundance, well before the incipient Age of Frugality, and thus well before the zero-zum society became apparent. That, of course, makes the task of government immensely more difficult. It is a task, furthermore, that now has encountered serious intellectual opposition, from neoconservatives generally and from articulate wishful thinkers such as philosopher Robert Nozick and economist George Gilder.[32] Both Nozick and Gilder want to create what they fancy was the world of yesteryear—a free market, non-statist society—or, if not that, to move toward that end. That they cannot and will not succeed should be obvious to all.

No one in government, certainly not the Justices, has ever openly avowed that Green was the patron saint of the Constitution of Powers. Indeed, it would have been odd had anyone done so. Green was an obscure academic scribbler, little known outside of England. His ideas, however, have percolated through other, perhaps lesser, minds to be seized by men of action who had never heard of him and who had no interest in abstract ideas as such. But there can be little question that Green's views on freedom as a social, not individual, right are dominant. He wanted to reunite the individual with the social order of which he is a member, and without which his existence has no meaning. He saw that individualism was running its course, a temporary phenomenon limited in time and space to a few centuries and the Western world. He also knew that organizations—the collective body, including the nation itself—were the new order. Therefore, individual freedom is, paradoxically to some, protected by legal and other institutions that can only be provided by the community. We have thus outlived the Robinson Crusoe myth. "When we speak of freedom as something to be so highly prized," asserted Green, "we mean a positive capacity of doing or enjoying something worth doing and enjoying, and that, too, something that we do or enjoy in common with others. We mean by it a power which each man exercises through the help or security given him by his fellow men, and which he in turn helps to secure for them."[33] In a phrase, that is a formula for benevolent collectivism—precisely where Americans are now, at least in the ideal. The ideal, to be sure, has not been achieved for many; with the incipient Age of Frugality, pehaps even fewer will get it.

How has the Supreme Court lived up to Green's conception? Only indirectly, as the following examples illustrate. Taken together, they display a marked tendency toward overt telocracy on implicit Green lines. Their numbers may be small, but they are of fundamental significance, both because they reveal beyond doubt a new and significant role for the Justices and because they are the principal targets of the Court's modern critics. To generalize: these illustrations show that the Court is willing for the first time in American history to give constitutional protection to some members of some "discrete and insular" minorities; to a rather substantial but still not complete extent, the Constitution has been extended to "We, the people . . . ," the opening words of the Preamble.

Race Relations

The Negro problem, Gunnar Myrdal maintained in his classic *An American Dilemma* (1944), is really a problem in the hearts of white Americans. Except for a brief period, from about the mid-1940s to the late 1960s, whites have been willing to keep blacks in either a formal or an informal caste system. When slavery was abolished by the Thirteenth Amendment, the First Reconstruction began. It met an early death, first in politics and then by judicial decrees that limited Congress's power to enforce the Civil War amendments. In the infamous *Plessy* v. *Ferguson* decision of 1896 the Justices legitimated a caste system, wrapping it in the sugar coating of "separate but equal," even though everyone knew that blacks were both separate and unequal in fact. Under the operative Constitution, blacks were kept "in their place." Peonage was widespread, a form of bondage scarcely distinguishable from slavery.

That could not last, at least in the formal law. No nation that trumpets it is a democracy with "equal justice for all" can indefinitely keep a large part of the populace submerged in a status that provided little hope, except for an occasional fortunate escapee, to get out of it. But last it did until World War II. As has been noted above, the United States, like Great Britain, could hardly conscript men to fight and at times to die in the name of freedom and democracy and then return them to ghettoes at the end of hostilities. Nor could blacks be further denied an opportunity for education and thus for fuller participation in American life. As we have seen, blacks who were not called into service could not be denied employment in war industries. That led to President Roosevelt's executive order barring racial discrimination in employment. FDR, a true Machiavellian, made a virtue out of necessity.[34]

The main breakthroughs for bettering the status of America's "untouchables" came in the Supreme Court—in the white primary cases, in *Shelley* v. *Kraemer*, and then in *Brown* v. *Board of Education*.[35] The facade of constitutional law has not been the same since: Others took their cue from black Americans and made the Court an object of pressure-group tactics. The reach of the equality principle has been extended to other areas. A Supreme Court, supposedly dispassionate, become compassionate. Men, women, and children, with little or no political influence, found in the judiciary a way to redress long-felt grievances. Federal appeals Judge J. Skelly Wright said it well: After pointing out that "great social and political problems [are better] resolved in the political arena," he went on to say, "But there are social and political problems which seem at times to defy such resolution. In such situations, under our system, the judiciary must bear a hand and accept its responsibility to assist in the solution where constitutional rights hang in the balance."[36] We have already mentioned that the Justices used express language of affirmative duty in the late 1960s in an effort to eliminate racial discrimination "root and branch." What remains for blacks is not the principle in the formal Constitution, but its application in other cases and in the operative Constitution. The Court may promulgate a general norm—a rule of law—but unless it is accepted and obeyed by people generally, it tends to become, if not a dead letter, less and less significant.

Until they discovered that discriminatory motive or intent was not only important but had to be proved by those alleging discrimination, the Justices have been remarkably consistent in furthering the cause of human dignity for black Americans. The basic change, subtle but important, surfaced in 1971 but was underscored in 1980 in *City of Mobile* v. *Bolden*.[37] In *Bolden*, black citizens of Mobile, who make up one-third of the city's population, argued that their vote was unconstitutionally diluted because of the city's at-large system of electing the three City Commissioners who govern the city. The system, established in 1911, freezes blacks from effective political participation. Six separate opinions were filed; Justice Potter Stewart, speaking for a plurality, rejected the claims. Adverse action on an identifiable group was not enough, said Stewart; there must be proof that a challenged action was undertaken "at least in part 'because of,' not merely 'in spite of,' its adverse effects upon an identifiable group." Professor Aviam Soifer has ably summed up the implications:

It is as if in 1980 black citizens no longer constitute a discrete and insular minority. A black citizen's constitutional claim will not prevail unless he can demonstrate precise intentional discrimination against himself as an individual or some specific and intentional discriminatory treatment of blacks. Otherwise, the promise of the fourteenth and fifteenth amendments, and the civil rights revolution, has either been satisfied or is properly left to the politicians. As we enter the 1980s, it is presumed that we all compete fairly. When no bad guys can be connected to evil discriminatory deeds, the Court apparently simply assumed that we all enjoy equal and fair opportunity.[38]

The *Bolden* decision, then, makes the Court, as Justice Thurgood Marshall said in dissent, "an accessory to the perpetuation of racial discrimination." His point is well taken: How possibly could Stewart and others who upheld the Mobile system not have seen what should be obvious to all?

The meaning, for black Americans, seems clear beyond doubt: The formal Constitution is merging with the operative fundamental law. Under both, the blacks are slowly reverting to second-class citizenship. Under the living law of American constitutionalism, the promise of *Brown* v. *Board of Education* and progeny has never been realized. Ghettoes remain; black unemployment is the highest in the nation. Blacks do not receive, as in Mobile, their fair share of city services. As for unemployment, one study concluded: "The data fail to provide support for the popular belief that there has been a significant increase in the proportion of middle and upper income black families in recent years. If anything, these findings suggest that the proportion of such families may in fact have declined, that the economic gains of many blacks may have eroded under the combined effects of recession and inflation."[39] Many whites want to believe the contrary, but the facts do not bear them out. True, a larger number of blacks have been able to gain economic and even social rewards. But most do not, and they are joined by ever-increasing numbers of Hispanics and poor whites.

The social consequences may well be considerable. Will blacks and other disadvantaged long acquiesce in a condition of operative *apartheid* and a growing willingness of the Supreme Court to uphold it? Justice Marshall ended his dissent in the *Bolden* case with a warning that may be prophetic; he said that a "superficial tranquility" created by "impermeable" and "specious" requirements that discriminatory intent must be proved may be short-lived: "If this Court," he concluded, "refuses to honor our long-recognized principles that the Constitution 'nullifies sophisticated as well as simple-minded modes of discrimination,' it cannot expect the victims of discrimination to respect political channels of seeking redress." Indeed, it cannot. When the political avenues are barred and the Supreme Court does not respond, is there any other way that victims can peacefully work within "the system"? None is apparent.

I do not wish to push the point further at this time. It is enough now to say that the Court's new posture of issuing commands of affirmative duty not only poses difficult, as yet unanswered, questions but, for blacks at least, is by no means a one-way street. The public at large may agree with—at least, not disagree with—the Court as commander, but scholars and commentators, and judges themselves, have not answered questions such as these: Where does the Court get its constitutional right to issue general rules?[40] How are they to be enforced? Is the President, who is constitutionally charged with the duty of taking care that the laws are faithfully executed, under a duty also to "execute" the decisions of the Court? Are Supreme Court decisions of the same rank as a statute as far as Article VI of the Document is concerned (making the Constitution, laws, and treaties the supreme law of the land, binding judges in every state)?[41]

As for the President, if he does have a duty of executing judicial decrees, is it merely "moral" or "political"? Or does it go further, carrying the implication that someone can go into Court to make him enforce a judicial decision? Recall that in *Cooper* v. *Aaron*, the Court maintained that its decisions are "the law of the land." If that statement means what it says, a Supreme Court decision is akin to a statute under Article VI, and the logical implication is that the President must enforce the decision. Even though the writ of the Court can now run against the President (as in the *Nixon Tapes* case), no one has yet tried to trigger the Court to get an order that the President carry out that duty. The short answer to the question, then, is that it at best is an unsettled constitutional question; at worst, no one can get the Court to act.

Another question is this: If the Court decision is "law," can someone not before the bar of the Court (that is, someone who was not a litigant) be held in contempt of court for not obeying the asserted general norm? The immediate litigants certainly can, for the Court's statement of a general norm usually is also a specific decree aimed at them. Legal theory, however, does not at present consider it a crime nor does it make a person defying the Court subject to contempt charges—even though he may be within the scope of the actual or "back-door" class-action ruling. To illustrate: if the Court holds that prayers cannot be recited in public schools in a case coming from, say, Ohio, by no means would school officials be subject to punishment for not adhering to it in, say, Montana. Nor does legal theory yet meet the challenges of federal judges acting as administrators, as, for example, in Judge Frank Johnson's sweeping mental hospital and prison rulings in Alabama.[42] Johnson in effect established himself as de facto head of both systems, telling state officials to rectify admitted grievances on pain of emptying the hospitals and jails. Those decisions pose crucial questions about the power of federal judges, but are beyond the scope of this essay. Suffice it merely to note that Johnson's orders are the logical extension of the role of the Supreme Court as commander.

As the Justices continue open acknowledgment of their new role, those and other questions will have to be answered. Judicial power has been enhanced. Perhaps, however, mounting criticism of the Supreme Court, added to an awareness of the intractability of many questions, may cause the Justices to pull back. They have done so, as noted above, in cases involving black Americans—not always, to be sure, as the Solomonic decision in the *Bakke* case shows and as the decisions sustaining "affirmative action" in employment evidence.[43] The Court is developing a new constituency—the "great unwashed" of the populace. Whether that new base of support will be enough for the Court to strike out and recognize claims for human dignity depends, however, upon whether those who are the ultimate (the hidden) beneficiaries of judicial action (the elites of the nation) are sufficiently acute to perceive that human rights decisions are in their interests also. On that score one should not be sanguine: What Gandhi called his greatest problem—the hardness of heart of the educated—is matched, perhaps exceeded, by the inherent inability bordering on stupidity of many of the moneyed and propertied to realize where and how their long-range interests can best be served.

In final analysis, what the Court can or cannot do for blacks and others depends on the social milieu. I have written elsewhere[44] that the ecological trap is closing and that Americans will be fortunate if they are able to escape realization of Arnold Toynbee's doleful forecast: "In all developed countries," he asserted in 1975, "a new way of life—a severely regimented way—will have to be imposed by ruthless, authoritarian government."[45] We can hope Toynbee was wrong, but there can be little question that the world is moving quite rapidly toward a steady-state economy and that two centuries of unprecedented technological and economic development are drawing to a close. Those two centuries—almost exactly the life span of the American republic —have left an indelible mark on the minds of modern Americans. Many still believe in the inevitability of continuing progress, although few take the trouble to define that ambiguous word. The Justices and all politicians will have to operate in a social context well described by economist E. J. Mishan:

> Modern economic growth, and the norms and attitudes it establishes, have produced a highly complex industrial and urban organization, albeit one that is increasingly vulnerable largely because the spread of affluence, the diffusion of the products and processes of technology, and the sheer rapidity of change, have combined, unavoidably, to undermine the influence of the complex of institutions and myths that invested all preindustrial civilizations with stability and cohesion. The existing libertarian order in the West is no longer rooted in a consensus that draws its inspiration from a common set of unquestioned beliefs. The legitimacy of all its institutions is perpetually under assault. Social order is visibly disintegrating.[46]

In some respects, Mishan is saying the same thing as Lester Thurow in his idea of the zero-sum society. When to both is added one further factor, not mentioned by either, it may be seen that the ecological trap is not only closing, but it is producing a high potential for social tension, even violence.

That factor, stated simply, is this: When the expectations of a significant group of people (say, black Americans) are raised so that many believe the rhetoric of democracy and equality, and then those expectations are dashed as they have been (blacks, again), not only is the political order in disarray (as Thurow said), but the economic system cannot fulfill those demands (Mishan and Thurow). The result is a high probability of violence (which in turn will produce harsh repressive measures).

The challenge for American political institutions is obvious: to develop another "common set of unquestioned beliefs." It is here that the Court can be of substantial help. Of course, the Justices cannot do it alone. But if the disintegration of the social order that Mishan perceived is to be halted and turned around, the Justices cannot shirk participating in the task. The same sort of attitude that permitted the Supreme Court in 1954 to grasp the nettle of racial discrimination should, it will be argued below, prevail for other polycentric social questions. Americans should demand no less from the black-robed Justices who work in the Temple on the Hill.

Legislative Reapportionment

To repeat: *Brown* and progeny, both judicial and legislative, successfully altered the formal Constitution and even during America's Golden Age, the operative Constitution, because an economy of abundance characterized the United States. With economic growth slowing or even ending, the consensus that held the nation together since 1945 is falling apart. A spin-off from *Brown*, the legislative reapportionment cases, has made this disintegration both possible and inevitable. It has made the black vote, insofar as blacks vote in a bloc, of great importance in political campaigns (particularly for the presidency). The apportionment decisions, mandating "one person/one vote," came at the precise time that whites began to flee to the suburbs from the large cities. Not by mere chance did Raoul Berger,[47] among others, single out *Brown* and *Baker* v. *Carr*, the key apportionment decision, for particularly harsh criticism. *Baker* and aftermath, buttressed by the Voting Rights Act of 1965, made bloc voting crucial in key cities.[48] People long bereft of political power can now make their weight felt, particularly in presidential elections where the Electoral College is still used. (The College "works" only because of widespread acceptance of the notion, not at all in accord with the intentions of the Framers, that electors vote in accordance with the popular vote.)

Baker emanated from an especially pernicious situation in Tennessee, where the state legislature contrary to the Tennessee constitution had failed to reapportion the legislature for sixty years. That situation meant that voters in rural areas had a grossly disproportionate number of representatives. After several attempts to have the system declared unconstitutional had failed, the practice became so bad as to offend a majority of the Justices. So in 1962 they ruled that an "equal-protection" case had been made out. Two years later the Court went the full distance and decreed that voting districts had to be as nearly equal in population as possible, both for state legislatures and the federal House of Representatives. The principle was subsequently applied to local governments.

Again, a furor erupted, led by academic disciples of Justice Frankfurter, who thought that the Court had not properly reasoned its decisions and had not exercised a proper amount of self-restraint. Oddly, however, and contrary to the reception of *Brown*, the apportionment decisions have been placidly accepted by the public and politicians alike. Frankfurter thought that the voters in Tennessee should ask state politicians in effect to vote themselves out of office. Even a federal judge who was once a law professor should have known better. He carried his mistaken views about judicial self-restraint to absurd lengths. Another dissenting Justice, John M. Harlan, waxed even more choleric in 1964: He grumbled that the one person/one vote decisions

give support to a current mistaken view . . . that every major social ill in this country can find its cure in some constitutional principle, and that this Court should "take the lead" in promoting reform when other branches of government fail to act. The Constitution is not a panacea for every blot upon the public welfare, nor should this Court, ordained as a judicial body, be thought of as a general haven for reform movements. . . . This Court . . . does not serve its high purpose when it exceeds its authority even to satisfy the justified impatience with the slow workings of the political process.[49]

That statement is simply not adequate. Not only did Harlan seek to differentiate a "judicial body" from the "political process," which for the Supreme Court is at best fallacious, he also maintained that his colleagues had exceeded their authority. That assertion is not true. Nowhere is it prescribed, in Constitution or statute or rules of the Supreme Court itself, what the authority of the Court is. Since almost the beginnings of the republic, that authority has been what the Justices say it is, and what, politically, they can get away with. Frankfurter and Harlan, furthermore, badly misread the social tea leaves in their impassioned dissents: People have accepted the Court's rulings in reapportionment areas, whether "reasoned" or not. Ideally, it doubtless would be better if the political process were adequate to manifest and long-denied needs. But at times it is not, as Harlan had to concede. How possibly could he and Frankfurter have thought that politicians would reform themselves and voluntarily give up some of their power? Surely, Judge Wright's statement, quoted above, is closer to the realities of the constitutional order. Be that as it may, for present purposes the lesson of *Baker* and progeny is clear and unmistakable: They classically exemplify an affirmative constitutional duty imposed by judges upon the political branches of government. Since 1964 state legislatures have been restructured, at times after a direct command from a judge. Compliance has occurred. At this writing, another round of apportionments is taking place as a result of the 1980 census. The rotten boroughs of the nation have been easier to eradicate, therefore, than racial discrimination—which is a lesson to be pondered when one thinks about the political power of the courts.

The suggestion here is not that the products of state legislatures, after reapportionment, differ markedly from the past. It is far too simplistic to believe that legislators vote on a rural-urban split. The reapportionment decisions did little to cure the ills of the political process. One of those ills, yes, but a relatively minor ailment when seen in perspective. But the significance of *Baker* and subsequent decisions lies in the creation by the Justices of an affirmative duty on the part of politicians to do certain things, simply because the Justices so read the Constitution. That they—the Justices—have prevailed is itself a large lesson in politics as the art of the possible, a lesson that surely can be applied elsewhere.

Other Examples

No need exists to multiply the examples where the Justices have acted as commander. Sometimes their command is couched in permissive language, as in an 1980 decision allowing patents to be issued for the creation of new forms of life. At other times, they are direct and pointed. *Miranda* v. *Arizona* (1966) is an example of the latter. One of the most criticized of all recent decisions, it set forth a "code" of conduct for officers to follow when someone is arrested. Affirmative duties were imposed on police officers throughout the nation, even though the lawsuit nominally merely concerned Miranda and the state of Arizona. He was important to the ruling only because, as with divers others before and after him, he was necessary to trigger the mechanism of the Court.

Another example is the well-known and controversial ruling in the abortion cases (1973), where the Court decreed that a woman had a right to an abortion dependent upon the length of her pregnancy. A trimester system was established, under which abortions cannot be prevented during the first three months, while during the second three months a steadily increasing societal interest in the viability of fetuses made abortions regulable by the states. During the final three months, abortions are permissible only in extreme circumstances. Again, a set of general rules was promulgated, and again, the litigants were unimportant.

Judges in other courts, both federal and state, caught the cue from the Supreme Court and occasionally, but far from always, issue commands. We have already mentioned Judge Frank Johnson's mind-boggling decrees that Alabama's treatment of mental patients and prisoners violated the Constitution and thus had to be remedied by complicated administrative procedures established by Johnson. In Boston Judge Arthur Garrity declared the school system to be in receivership and ordered busing to achieve racial integration.[50] As for the states, an outstanding example came in New Jersey, where its supreme court ordered the legislature to enact an income tax to improve schools on pain of having them closed by court order.[51]

I do not suggest that Judges Johnson and Garrity or the New Jersey supreme court have been able to translate their bare-bones orders into operational reality. There is a long, long road between judicial decision and full compliance. What is important for present purposes is to see a growing willingness of some judges actively to intervene in politics and to command obedience to judicial decrees. One can agree with Professor Nathan Glazer that "the courts have truly changed their role in American life" and reach deeper into the lives of people than "they ever have in American history." But one need not—one should not—agree with Glazer when he maintains that this is "against the will of the people."[52] Some people, yes, but certainly it is the people themselves, many of them new types of litigants (the poor, the disadvantaged, women, etc.), who are energizing the judiciary. Impotent politically, they see judges as their final hope. If that is so, and it is, activist judges may be the final, even desperate, hope of a crumbling system of American constitutionalism to save itself from its own inequities and inconsistencies.[53] The litigants believe the incessant rhetoric about democracy and the Rule of Law and call upon an oligarchic judiciary to further democratic ends. That fact may be a paradox, but it is the truth.

IV.

The Court as commander requires affirmative cooperation from other governmental officers. The Justices can pronounce, but they cannot administer. Even federal judges on lower courts, such as Johnson and Garrity, find that detailed administration is beyond their capacities. So judges must trust the goodwill of politicians to carry out their decrees. That situation of course also means that litigants, too, must trust the goodwill of politicians. No doubt it would be better were that not true. Many officers who should administer the law of the land as stated by the Court, do not; they are reluctant and often defiant. Even with the best of intentions, which doubtless many have, administrators also have to contend with possible public disapproval.

That possibility has an important meaning. The Supreme Court interprets the Constitution, but politicians, bureaucrats, and lower-court judges interpret the Court.[54] Those entrusted with administration apply oft-times obscure commands. In so doing they have considerable discretion themselves. That judicial freedom has long been known, but seldom analyzed in depth. Few have inquired into the extent to which there is compliance with the Supreme Court's rulings. Judicial opinions do not enforce themselves. In an oft-quoted statement, Bishop Hoadly said in his Sermon to the King in 1717: "Whoever hath an absolute authority to interpret any written or spoken laws, it is he who is truly the lawgiver, to all intents and purposes, and not the person who first spoke or wrote them."[55] The Justices may have "absolute authority" to interpret the Document, but those interpretations must be transmuted into operational reality by literally tens of thousands of other governmental officers who were not before the bar of the Court.

Compliance, thus, often is chancy, especially so when Court opinions are written in opaque language. The Justices, moreover, cannot possibly predict all of the factual situations that might arise in which their general norms are applied. Nor can they expect all who are affected by administrative actions to be aware of what the Court has said. So ambiguity in pronouncement, plus uncertainty in application, makes for unevenness in administration. Even in the best of circumstances, lawyers are adept at "distinguishing" cases—showing that factual situations differ in significant ways—so that even unambiguous judicial decrees can be evaded. Furthermore, constitutional decisions tend to produce new claims and thus new litigation, with the result that constitutional law has become a lawyers's paradise—a fertile area for more and more work for more and more attorneys. The truly fundamental principles of American constitutionalism are being lost in a swamp of thousands of judicial rulings— the Supreme Court alone has produced some 450 fat volumes of reports—all of which are kept in law libraries and computerized files.

To summarize: freedom in the United States is as much positive as negative. For a person to have freedom *to* participate and to attain goals central to the concept of human dignity, he must have freedom *from* both the arbitrary exercise of governmental power *and* inadequate social conditions that make it unlikely he can achieve that level. Courts do help, albeit imperfectly, in dispensing distributive justice. Their fundamental task now is to help create something wholly new: a Constitution of Human Needs.[56]

Why judges? some may ask. The short answer is that, as political as well as judicial officers, they cannot avoid the swirls and currents that engulf the body politic. But why not legislatures and administrators, including the President? The short answer is that the system of governance established by the Document is not suited to the demands of the era. It worked well, by hindsight at least, during the nineteenth and first part of the twentieth centuries. Today, however, politics are in disarray. Serious students speak of the "ungovernability of democracy."[57] History since 1789 has seen a steadily expanding franchise and the rise of decentralized groups that dominate the government and at times even challenge the State's claim to sovereignty. The name for the political order is *pluralism*. In theory, people form groups, and out of the clashes between them something called the public or national interest is supposed to evolve. That is a romantic conception of politics, far from reality (although some use it to argue that the Supreme Court should have a lesser role).[58] Political pluralism is Adam Smith economics writ large and transferred to politics. It is no more valid there than in economics.

Part II
THE BANKRUPTCY OF POLITICS

The pluralist component has badly served liberalism by propagating the faith that a system primarily built upon groups and bargaining is self-correcting. Some parts of this faith are false, some have never been tested one way or the other, and others can be confirmed only under very special conditions.

—Theodore J. Lowi

A substantial part of government in the United States has come under the influence or control of narrowly based and largely autonomous elites. These elites do not act cohesively with each other on many issues. They do not "rule" in the sense of commanding the entire nation. Quite the contrary, they tend to pursue a policy of non-involvement in the large issues of statesmanship save where such issues touch their own particular concerns.

—Grant McConnell

This is the heart of our fundamental problem. Our economic problems are solvable. For most of our problems there are several solutions. But all these solutions have the characteristic that someone must suffer large economic losses. No one wants to volunteer for this role, and we have a political process that is incapable of forcing anyone to shoulder this burden.

—Lester C. Thurow

6
Pluralism as Anarchy

I.

As the United States enters the 1980s, its political economy is in deep trouble, perhaps on the verge of paralysis. With high inflation and rising unemployment, declining industrial productivity and budgetary imbalances, the economic system staggers from year to year. No one, certainly not professional economists, seems to know what to do. The political system cannot resolve obviously urgent problems. Government is in disarray. Mistrust is widespread, not only of government but of all centers of authority. Catastrophe is in the air; something serious is out of kilter in the constitutional order. Yeats wrote many years ago that anarchy was sweeping the world, and that the worst elements of mankind were taking over. The best were experiencing a failure of nerve. He was correct.[1] Artists often have a special prescience. Well before events overtake and engulf less insightful people, the artist paints or writes or composes in themes that accurately foretell the shape of things to come. So it was with Yeats (among others, including Kafka), who foresaw today's time of troubles. Just when the State, acting through its apparatus (government), is seemingly stronger than ever, and exactly when more and more people look to it for satisfaction of "entitlements," the political order obviously cannot meet those demands. This chapter outlines the basic theory of pluralism, the dominant philosophy of American politics today, and suggests why and how it is failing. Americans are in a condition of an anarchy that is pluralism, which was entirely all right in the past, because there was only one dominant group, but which, with the proliferation of new groups with substantial electoral power, is now disintegrating.

To call pluralism anarchical requires definition of terms. In the usual view, *anarchy* means chaos and disorder, with no governing authority. That view, however, is not correct: Anarchy is a condition in which there is no single ruler or governor—no sovereign, no central source of direction and control. Like nature, politics abhors a vacuum. Lack of centralized authority simply means that local or decentralized centers of power have control, limited to be sure but nonetheless pervasive. Nowhere are humans without some type of governing authority. It takes various forms and may often (like the political order of the giant corporations) operate contrary to principles of constitutionalism, but it—governing authority—always exists. Anarchy as the absence of governing power has never characterized humankind, save perhaps for brief periods during a revolution, and, indeed, there seems to be no way that humans can escape being governed. Man, as Aristotle said, is a political animal—always has been and always will be. The question is not whether there will be government; rather it is: who governs and how and in whose interests?

By ignoring the problem of sovereignty, the Founding Fathers created an anarchical type of government. In the rhetoric, "the people" are sovereign, but the pretense does not jibe with the reality. Governing power is shared between the states and the central government, and in the latter, between Congress and the President. In its original form, that sharing could not and did not last. The movement of governing power in the United States has always been centripetal, both in the federal system and within the national government. That characteristic, however, pertains to the *formal* Constitution; the operative fundamental law differed—it became, with the rise of socioeconomic groups, more and more centrifugal. The original anarchy of the Document has, that is, been replaced by the growing power of the State, the national government, and the presidency. Formal constitutional law thus widely varies from the living law. When after the Civil War the marriage of technology to entrepreneurship produced the trusts, which in turn became giant corporations, and when in this century countervailing groups arose, the effect was the creation of a true pluralistic order. It flourished for a time because of steady economic growth. When growth ended, or at least markedly slowed, about 1970, the political economy went into decline. It has not collapsed, but there can be little doubt that it is on the verge of massive change. What is collapsing—indeed, has already done so save in the myth and in the minds of those who follow the faith of Milton Friedman[2]—is the notion of limited government and the ideology of the beneficent effects—that the clash of interest groups in the political arena will somehow produce the common good.

The emergent orthodoxy is complex. Government in theory has been or is being freed from formal constitutional shackles, but it also is the captive of decentralized centers of power. A new operative Constitution is being created: what will be called the Constitution of Control. Government has become a complicated amalgam of public and private authority systems, which seem to be separate but in fact are so closely connected that they may accurately be labeled the Corporate State. In that State, public government paradoxically is both weak and strong, weak in that its institutions must contend and bargain with private governments but strong in that it has certain inherent, reserve powers that can be called upon, particularly in times of emergency. In yet another paradox, private governments are both strong and weak, strong in that they can control their internal orders and can influence the flow of public policy with respect to their own concerns but weak in that they, too, must bargain with other private governments and are in final analysis beholden to the State for their very existence.

What, then, is pluralism? An answer must begin with the indubitable proposition that the individual—the natural person—no longer is the basic social unit of the nation. Conditions differed in 1787, when the Document was drafted: The budding notion of individualism was becoming dominant, both in economics and in law, including constitutional law. Adam Smith's *The Wealth of Nations*, published in 1776, was widely read and influential. By 1861 Sir Henry Maine in a famous passage could assert that the movement of "progressive societies" was "from status to contract"[3]—by which he meant that the individual had become dominant. Feudalism, Maine implied, had vanished. Contract is the legal instrument of a free-enterprise economy.

The suggestion is not that everyone profited, that all individuals were beneficiaries. To the contrary: The theory of individualism neatly fitted the requirements of the moneyed and propertied, those who could, because they were not necessitous, be free. Law and the legal system provided a network of protection for those with wealth and thus with political power; principles of the private law of contracts, of property, and of torts all inured to the benefit of those in positions of power. The negative, nightwatchman State existed only in theory: Its institutions protected property and wealth whenever necessary, both by a benign (for the chief beneficiaries) legal order and an operative Constitution that allowed the use of violence to quell popular discontent.

So Maine was correct in 1861 only insofar as the principle of contract could be and was employed by those with wealth and power to dominate those without it. Even had he been accurate, the social bases for individualism quickly eroded whatever support the theory may have had. The individual as such soon became economically and politically meaningless. Today, he is important only as a member of a group (or groups). The powerlessness of the individual in the age of public and private bureaucracy—which is the United States today—requires no documentation. It is a theme that runs through both scholarly literature and contemporary fiction. The individual is submerged in a congeries of groups. When that fact was finally realized, the political theory of pluralism emerged. First given expression by Arthur Bentley in *The Process of Government* (1908),[4] and, until recently, widely accepted by political scientists. Law professors and judges still maintain a belief in pluralism both as a valid description of what the political order is and what it should be. The *hope* of pluralism has been well expressed by Professor Frank Tannenbaum.

The true well-being of a society . . . lies in diversity rather than identity of interests. The greater the variety of groups, the richer is the community, and the more certain of continuous harmony. The harmony best suited to a society is one which comes from many-sided inner tensions, strains, conflicts, and disagreements. Where disagreement is universal, men can agree only on particulars, and where men can really quarrel only about particulars they have too many things in common to tear the community apart. Divergence of interests within the community . . . is the condition of healthy controversy and social peace.[5]

Well and good, one might say, except that the hope has not and is not being realized in practice. Tannenbaum's conclusion is a resounding *non sequitur.* His expression of hope has been dashed by a harsh reality. Groups abound in America, and there are conflicts, but emerging out of those tussles in the political arena are either the dominance of one group (as in the oil industry and energy policy) or watered-down compromises that represent a common denominator among affected interest groups. Public policy, from whatever source, tends to reflect those compromises. Theodore Lowi once remarked that the result is: "Groups become virtuous; they must be accommodated, not regulated."[6] (That conclusion seems to be a variation on Ambrose Bierce's definition of politics, in his *Devil's Dictionary,* as "the strife of interests masquerading as principle.")[7]

Neither consequence of the group struggle in politics is desirable. It will not do to have one group—a group that is in fact although not in theory a cartel—dominate such an important policy area as energy. Nor should the National Rifle Association be able to control national policy on gun ownership. Those examples are sufficient to illustrate the inadequacy of that aspect of pluralism. The other is concerned with the compromises that interest groups make when their goals collide. Compromise at first glance is the genius of politics as the art of the possible; it "is at least on the edge of being a virtue in Anglo-Saxon discourse. It does not solve the world's problems once and for all, but it at least provides for the world's ongoingness."[8] The Document of 1787 was an effective compromise between the states and national power, between the states themselves, and with existing economic interests. Edmund Burke argued that "all government, . . . every virtue, and every prudent act is founded on compromise"[9]—a sentiment that he did not carry into practice.

Compromise, however, is less a virtue than a convenience, or perhaps a necessity. Consider these statements, the first by Friedrich A. Hayek, the second by John H. Hallowell. Said Hayek: "Our whole conception of justice rests on the belief that different views about particulars are capable of being settled by the discovery of rules that, once they are stated, command general assent."[10] Compare Hallowell: "Compromise, as a self-sufficient principle divorced from all considerations of truth and justice, is simply, in the last analysis, the ancient Thrasymachian doctrine that might makes right."[11] The problem is that compromise—the give and take of politics—may provide solutions for the immediate parties, but it does not result in consideration of what is right or just in a broad sense. The consensus of compromise, in other words, is mainly—perhaps only—between affected interest groups; those who control those groups do not take into account an overarching public or national interest, do not, that is, make provision for social justice. The theory of pluralism is that justice will emerge from the conflicts of opposed groups; the practice is to the contrary. There are, Robert Paul Wolff has said, "some social ills . . . which cannot be cured by the techniques of pluralistic politics."[12] To deal with them, the requirement is for some way to constitute all of society as a group with a group purpose and a notion of the common good. Pluralism rules this out in theory and practice, by insisting on the group nature of society. That concept means that societywide interests do not exist, save in the purely procedural system of preserving a society of group conflict.[13] Under pluralist theory, finally, government is supposed to oversee and provide the mechanism for competition among interest groups. However, Professor Henry Kariel has shown in his important study *The Decline of American Pluralism*[14] that the referee function of government actually favors the interests of the stronger party in pluralistic conflicts and thus tends to solidify the power of those already in possession of it. That means, says Wolff, that government "plays a conservative, rather than a neutral, role in the society."[15]

Other preliminary observations are in order, each concerning the constitutional and thus the political order. Perhaps of most importance, the Constitution, as written, must operate in a social milieu wholly different from that of 1787 or 1800 or even 1850 or 1900. A new "world" has been and is being created, in large part because of the impact of technology on ancient societal institutions. The environment in which constitutional mechanisms operate has changed more in the past 100 years than in the previous 3,000 years. Social change has become part of the social order, so much so that it has telescoped time (new events occur with increasing rapidity). One must therefore, ask whether the United States today is in a crisis or a climacteric (a coalescence of crises). It is important to have a view on this. How the question is answered will determine which public policies will be promulgated and which changes in time-honored institutions are necessary. My answer, which I do not believe can be refuted, is that we are experiencing a climacteric, a sea change in the way that Americans confront the human condition, a change that is one of the most sweeping and fundamental in history. If that be so, Americans face a future, even in the short term, that will not be calm and orderly. Whether in the long term there will be progression, steady or not, toward a better society is far from certain. The notion of human progress, an age-old idea that flowered in the Enlightenment and that characterized much of American history, is dead, reeling from successive shocks to the human mind and psyche.[16] It is, perhaps, "the arrogance of humanism"[17] that allows many to believe that, as Mr. Micawber kept saying in *David Copperfield*, something will eventually turn up to rescue man, including Americans, from his follies. But whether or not that is so is not really the question: The effort must be made—*should* be made—by all who care. In that task, the Justices of the Supreme Court cannot be aloof; they should participate in the travail of society.

Next, the United States has a secular or civil religion—Americanism (nationalism; patriotism). Despite a large number of purported believers in God and the old-time religion, not only are new sects appearing but, of much more importance, society—the State—has a grasp on Americans that is truly religious in nature and intensity. It is perceived as the source of unlimited benefits. Patriotism, even in its degenerated sense of puerile chauvinism, and religious fervor go hand in hand. One need only refer to the outpouring of emotion that characterized the return of the fifty-two hostages from Iran in 1981 as well as the pride taken in putting men into space, to illustrate the point. More to the central idea, people no longer accept the promise of rewards in an afterlife; they "want it all now"—*in this life*. Karl Marx was not far off the mark when he called orthodox religion the opiate of the masses. Religion still is, even though it is not so much the faiths of the Judeo-Christian tradition as a blind, touching belief in the power of the State, operating through government, to fulfill the growing demands for entitlements. The development was anticipated: More than a century ago Auguste Comte argued in his *System of Positive Polity* that religion would be replaced by a secular worship, one with the trappings of Roman Catholicism but with society—the nation, the community—as the object of reverence.[18] For American constitutional purposes the meaning is clear: Although church and State are separated, religion and the State are closely entwined, both in the many institutions that recognize religious orthodox (even the Supreme Court is not immune) and in the secular religion of Americanism. This fact has important consequences for analysis of the Court and Constitution. If civil religion in America means, as Comte said, that the nation or the community is an object of reverence, it appears possible to construct a first step toward a philosophy of the common good.

A fundamental assumption of constitutionalism and of American democracy is that all problems are solvable by men of goodwill who approach the problems in a rational manner. This can be called the New England "town meeting" concept writ large. People, assumed to be rational, can and will through public debate and open argument arrive at decisions that further the common good (and thus their own specific ends). (Justice Felix Frankfurter, an intense patriot, fervently believed in the assumption.) The very statement of the assumption is its own refutation. It is based on the unwarranted belief that people are indeed fully rational beings and that by merely following correct procedures, by which usually is meant something like "procedural due process," correct answers will be forthcoming.

Surely, however, enough is known about human nature that it may be concluded that people are far from wholly rational, and that they tend to pursue selfish goals with little regard for others or even of what may be their true long-term interests. People are hedonists, generally, striving mainly for short-range objectives of personal pleasure and gain. The meaning should be clear: The assumption cannot be empirically verified. In the past, public debate helped to resolve many problems, but only because of the nearly unlimited resources of the nation and the consequent room for maneuver in policymaking. The assumption is based on the ideal of human character as having "certain general traits or dispositions of mind, including simplicity, honesty, openness, wisdom, humility, and generosity."[19] That posture may be possible, at least in the ideal, during times of peace and abundance, but emphatically it is not during times of stress and strife and crisis. This is not a new intellectual problem. Witness Thucydides's comments on the effects of civil turmoil during the Peloponnesian War:

Words changed their ordinary meanings and were construed in new senses. Reckless daring passed for the courage of a loyal partisan, far-sighted caution was regarded as the excuse of a coward, moderation was taken to be the pretext of the unmanly, the power to see all sides of a question was seen as complete inability to act. Impulsive rashness was held to be the mark of a man, caution in planning was a specious excuse for avoiding action. . . .

So civil war gave birth to every kind of iniquity in the Greek world. Simplicity, the chief ingredient in a noble nature, was ridiculed and disappeared, and society was divided into rival camps in which no man trusted his fellow.[20]

What has changed in the modern era is not the nature of human action during crises; Thucydides's observations would be true today (as the ecological trap closes). What has changed is the modern concept of moderation, which is far different from the ancients's view of balanced judgment and the requirement to locate a mean between extremes. Finding a mean is something more than compromise. The concept of the mean is not the present-day notion of the middle way (which usually is the modern idea of compromise). In Professor Lon Fuller's words: "For moderns the middle way is the easy way, involving a minimum of commitment. For Aristotle the mean was the hard way, the way from which the slothful and unskilled were most likely to fall."[21]

Any serious thinker in the field of political (of constitutional) theory must have a well-thought-out theory of man; else his views likely will be worthless. Professor Philip H. Rhinelander said it well:

Not only political theory and history, but also theories of knowledge, theories of value, theories of ethics, theories of art, theories of language, and theories of religion depend on assumptions about *man*. Yet the crucial underlying assumptions often remain unspecified. If there were a tacit consensus about the nature of man—if some paradigm or model of man were generally accepted today—the failure to specify what model of man is being invoked on a particular occasion by a particular writer or speaker would not be a source of serious concern. But the fact is that there is no agreement today on the meaning of phrases like "human nature" or the "nature of man," or even on whether they mean anything at all.[22]

If that be so, and I think it is, it is important to state one's concept about "human nature." I do so briefly: Mine is a Hobbesian view of the human being, as being in general aggressive, egotistical, and self-seeking. Of course there are exceptions, but they are insignificant. My view coincides with that of Professor David Ehrenfeld: "we must come to terms with our irrational faith in our own limitless power"[23]—which is another way of stating that the assumption being discussed is faulty. In his important book *The Arrogance of Humanism*, Ehrenfeld maintained: "Absolute faith in our ability to control our own destiny is a dangerous fallacy. . . . But belief in the nobility and value of humankind and a reasonable respect for our achievements and competences are also in humanism, and only a misanthrope would reject this aspect of it."[24] The problem, then, is in the religious side of humanism—the faith in human reason and its ability to solve all human problems. The assumption, as we have stated it, of constitutionalism and American democracy is faulty.

This is not the place to pursue that line of thought in greater detail. Relevant to it, however, is the widely held belief that no ideology—no public philosophy—is necessary, and that the pragmatic approach, whatever that means, is sufficient to the need in all public-policy matters. Pragmatism, far from being a philosophy, is a poor excuse for not having one. It fails by its own test: It does not work. The pragmatic temper may be seen in "the science of 'muddling through,'" which is the term some use to describe the American policymaking process. If it was adequate in the past, it was only because a set of accidental and nonrepeatable factors allowed the nation to wax large and strong. Those factors have either vanished or are on the verge of doing so. The consequence is obvious for all who would see: We must know what we want and strive to get it. The "what we want" cannot be the narrow goals of disparate pluralistic groups within the nation, each single-mindedly pursued with little regard for others. The United States teeters on the edge of disaster on a number of fronts—possible, even probable, nuclear war; energy shortages; financial collapse; population growth; inflation combined with unemployment, to name but a few. These threats and others combine into the climacteric of humankind that is fast producing what we will subsequently call the Constitution of Control. The era of American hegemony in world affairs has ended, and we must face up to it, and fast. At the same time, the "what we want" must consider what was called "the arrogance of humanism" —the supreme faith in man's ability to control his fate. The requirement, in my judgment, is to "elevate our sights a little lower" and once again come to terms with nature.

Finally, history has its ironies. One of special relevance is that the State in America (and elsewhere) assumed obligations toward the citizenry at precisely the time that they could not be adequately fulfilled. Economically, they are realized today only by going into debt (by mortgaging the future, as unthinking hedonists are wont to do). (There is little or no realization of a new fact in human history—that, because of the extraordinarily rapid rate of social change, most Americans today are their own posterity. Therefore, those who ask "What has posterity done for me?" are really talking about themselves.) Socially, the governmental obligations are met only partially and haphazardly, as with the black-white and rich-poor (and Western world-Third World) dichotomies. With the rise of what has previously been called the "positive State," the preconceptions of American constitutional theory have been completely undermined. Just as modern giant corporations have altered the assumptions of classical economic theory and the quantum undermined classical physics, so positive or affirmative government is something new under the constitutional sun. Purchasing social harmony through welfare programs, however, is a policy that seems to have run its course. So, too, has pluralism. Carey McWilliams may well have put his finger on the shape of things to come in an article he wrote shortly before his death in 1980:

I am convinced that the Establishment—that elusive but very real force in American life—has decided that authoritarian controls must be imposed to get the country out of the mess in which it finds itself; that there is no other way to preserve the power structure. The Establishment believes that democracy is doomed in a world of shrinking resources and rising expectations, but that the structure which surrounds it can survive if we abandon some of our freedoms....
Many Americans want reassurance that the Great National Barbeque will continue indefinitely....[25]

The public till is almost empty, even though more and more demands are being made upon it. That cannot last, simply because it is absurd. Something will have to give way—something *will* give way—and that is the system of "liberal democracy" as it has been known.

II.

It will do little good for Americans to continue to indulge themselves in the fantasy that the governmental system remains about the same as created in 1787. True it is that the form and facade appear to be the same, but structural changes have occurred in basic institutions such as limited government, federalism, separation of powers, and prevention of a "democratical despotism." What endures in the original conception is what cannot be changed except by amendment and the political order that developed. The rigidities of the Document—such as a four-year term for the President, each state having two senators, the absence of parliamentary responsibility, and the like—are not our present concern. Rather, it is in pluralism as the prevailing concept of politics.

Pluralist theory is based on two bedrock propositions: First, many sources of governing power exist other than the State. Second, through the interactions of those decentralized groups, something akin to the public or national interest evolves in public policy.[26] The first proposition is valid, the second faulty. Groups do possess power over portions of the polity, even though their power may be considered as a delegation from the State, and they also interact with official government in the "subgovernments" or "iron triangles" of Washington. A subgovernment (or iron triangle) is the label for the ways in which social groups deal with government. Three entities are involved—the social group, the relevant Congressional committee, and the appropriate administrative agency. Policy tends to be the resultant of the tensions and, of more importance, the common desires of leaders of the three groups.

Those who would understand pluralism should start with Arthur Bentley's *The Process of Government* (1908). It is a classic, but as with most classics, it is more cited than read. Bentley spawned a vast literature, although not immediately. Government to Bentley is a process of adaptation and adjustments by individuals cooperating in groups. Even the judiciary is not immune: Discussing the tenure of Chief Justice John Marshall, Bentley maintained that even if Thomas Jefferson had had the ability to appoint the Chief Justice, the history of America "would have been different," perhaps, but only

from a surface view. . . . On the basis, not merely of Marshall's decisions but of all the rest of our country's history which bears on this point, we may feel sure that the interests that underlay those decisions, if they could not have gained expression through Marshall, would have gained it in some other way. The power was not in Marshall, but in the interest groups he so adequately recognized and allowed to come so smoothly and speedily to their due dominance in the government. And per contra, if the interest groups had been actually different from Marshall's reflection of them, his decisions would have been but temporary obstacles and would have been overwhelmed, not by any virtue in some other constitutional theory or reasoning, but by the power of the underlying interests which pump all the logic into theory that theory ever obtains.[27]

That opinion, to be sure, is far from the orthodox view of the role of law and of the Supreme Court—expressed, for example, by Felix Frankfurter. But Bentley's views cannot be gainsaid. As we have previously said, Marshall "delivered" to the class whence he came. Had he (or someone else) not done so, those who held effective power in society would still have triumphed.

Pluralism "worked" during the nineteenth century for one simple reason— the domination of one group: the moneyed and propertied class, often coupled with the growth of corporate business. What Bentley perceived in 1908—the clash of several groups—was not so much a description of things past or then present, as a forecast of things to come. The twentieth century has witnessed, in Kenneth Boulding's terms, the "organizational revolution,"[28] many of which were constitutionalized by the Supreme Court in the 1930s and 1940s. Farmers, labor unions, veterans, among others—

these newly emergent groups, exercising political power, were able—albeit imperfectly—to ameliorate some of the brutalities of industrialization. Alexis de Tocqueville described the severities imposed on workers: "I am of the opinion, on the whole, that the manufacturing aristocracy which is growing up under our eyes is one of the harshest which ever existed in the world."[29] Harsh, then—the 1830s—and even harsher later. That "manufacturing aristocracy" was also able to dominate all branches of government.

Pluralism in any ideal sense never existed until America's Golden Age of plenty. Then it flowered not because of inherent merit or because the common good emanated from the system, but because the Age of Economic Abundance was such that it could not fail. The group basis of politics quickly became accepted dogma, both in political circles and in Academia. However, because politics had been divorced from economics in the universities—no longer was "political economy" studied—and in the theory of the Constitution, no one made the connection between unparalleled growth and the political order. That situation was taken to be the natural order of things, the due of every American, inherently good. The Supreme Court by and large went along: The Justices stoutly refused to agree with Bentley; they would not and will not acknowledge that economic power is political power and that governance—sovereignty—is shared between the organs of public government and decentralized government and decentralized centers of power. Those groups, of which the giant corporations are the principal exemplar, are said to be "private" and thus not to fall within the ambit of "state" or "governmental" action. It has always been a commonplace that the Constitution runs against governments only, and governments to lawyer-judges are the official organs of power.

Separation of politics from economics is a thin fiction, but as such, it serves a latent function of insulating officers of private governments from constitutional constraints. True it is that they are subject to some regulation from public government, but as we will see, that regulation was welcomed, even demanded, by corporate business. Furthermore, it is under heavy attack today.

III.

The American political system today is in obvious disarray, paradoxically, precisely because of the success of pluralism. Professor Tannenbaum's hope (quoted above) has not been realized in practice. The result is a growing paralysis. That paralysis is the crisis—and failure—of pluralism. The irony is that at the precise time in American history it flowered, it went into steep decline. It has become intellectually untenable. Lester Thurow concluded his important book *The Zero-Sum Society* with this ominous warning:

As we head into the 1980's, it is well to remember that *there is really only one important question in political economy*. If elected, whose income do you and your party plan to cut in the process of solving the economic problems facing us? Our economy and the solution to its problems have a substantial zero-sum element. Our economic life would be easier if this were not true, but we are going to have to learn to play a zero-sum economic game. If we cannot learn, or prefer to pretend that the zero-sum problem does not exist, we are simply going to fail.[30] (Emphasis added.)

Thurow spoke of political economy, but that is what constitutions are all about and what Supreme Court Justices routinely deal with. If his zero-sum game fails, the Constitution as it has been known will fail with it and also the political order it sustains. No one should be sanguine about the outcome, immediate or ultimate.

Given such an analysis, it may seem puerile to suggest that the Supreme Court could play an important role in helping Americans to play zero-sum economic games. But that possibility is exactly what will be argued in later discussion. First, however, it is necessary to draw attention to the twin goals of modern constitutionalism: more *efficiency* in government (public and private) and more *accountability* in those who wield significant political power.

7
Constitutionalism on Trial

I.

"The fundamental question [today]," James L. Sundquist of the Brookings Institution maintained, "is whether . . . the U.S. government can be made to work—under any leadership."[1] So it is: The very success of "democracy"—of pluralism—is its own undoing. A consequent growing political paralysis poses constitutional problems of the first magnitude. "Democracy" is not working. Government flounders from crisis to crisis, with little notion of where it is going or even of what the real problems are. "Severe institutional and structural problems" exist deep "in the traditions of American political behavior . . . [and] the constitutional structure itself," Sundquist concluded. This chapter develops some of the needs of modern constitutionalism, with emphasis on the (apparently) inconsistent goals of efficiency and accountability, cast against the background of the nature of the State in America.

Despite much loose talk, mainly from politicians and political pundits, about the perils of "statism," there have been few attempts to analyze the State in America in any systematic or comprehensive manner. Slogans and hyperbole have been substituted for careful scrutiny. My theme now is that the United States is a Corporate State, consisting of the joinder of two entities in the operative Constitution—the organs of political government and the centers of decentralized economic power (mainly the giant corporations)— into a superentity that encompasses both but with each retaining its own identity.[2]

Of necessity, the analysis here is abstract, simply because the State is an abstraction. Not mentioned in the Document of 1787, the State is not a thing; it is a construct not synonymous with either government or society. Government is the apparatus of the State, and society is that which is governed, in appearance about 230 million disparate individuals but in reality an aggregate of interacting groups. Like the business corporation, the State is an artificial being, invisible and intangible, existing only in legal and constitutional theory. But even though it cannot be seen, it is nevertheless as real as a natural person. In fact, it is even more "real," for whenever its will collides with the wills of natural persons, it *always* prevails in any matter considered important by those who wield effective power in the nation.

The overarching, pervasive social reality in the United States is the State. It is an anthropomorphic "group-person"[3] with drives and interests of its own, an "organism" (as Holmes called it),[4] albeit a disembodied one. Political and economic power co-exist in a syzygetic system. A biological term, syzygy means the joinder of two organisms with each retaining its own identity. So it is in the United States: The combination of corporation and government has produced an entity that at once permits each to keep its formal identity and that is far larger than the arithmetical sum of both—and, indeed, larger than the arithmetical sum of the private interests of the nation. Like the giant corporation, the State is more a method than a thing, in law an artificial person even though it has "no anatomical parts to be kicked or consigned to the calaboose; no soul for whose salvation the parson may struggle; no body to be roasted in hell for celestial enjoyment."[5] A legal fiction, the State as such does no act, speaks no word, thinks no thought, but exists to the extent that those who wield power in government speak for it and to the extent that men may die and property may be seized in its name. The important matter to perceive is that the economy is itself a system of power, a political order.

The point of departure for the ensuing brief discussion comes from John Kenneth Galbraith:

When the modern corporation acquires power over markets, power in the community, power over the state, power over belief, it is a political instrument, different in form and degree but not in kind from the state itself. . . . When we [economists] make power and therewith politics a part of our system, we can no longer escape or disguise the contradictory character of the modern state. The state is the prime object of economic power. It is captured.[6]

Yet, Galbraith continued, remedial action for economic problems lies mainly in the State. All look to it. That is so even though "The fox is powerful in management of the coop. To this management the chickens must look for redress."[7] In other words, the very institutions and instrumentalities that are at the center of, and indeed cause, economic problems are asked to provide remedies. A parlous situation, indeed.

If Galbraith is correct, and I think that in large part he is, it becomes important to outline the contours of the result in constitutional theory and practice—the Corporate State. My suggestion here is that not only are corporations and government closely intertwined, but that business needs the State as much or even more today than it did in the past. During the nineteenth and early twentieth centuries, subventions by government to aid business greatly helped the growth of corporate giants (the "trusts"). Moreover, corporate leaders actively advocated regulation of business by government, regulation that had the appearance but not the actuality of curbing the supercorporations. Today, a growing antiregulatory movement is aimed not so much at delegitimizing the State but at defanging it in specific areas. (The drive for deregulation is concerned mostly with cross-industry agencies, such as the Federal Trade Commission, the Consumer Products Safety Commission, and the Occupational Safety and Health Administration. Captive bureaus, such as the Federal Communications Commission, the Departments of Defense, Interior, and Agriculture, and the Federal Aviation Administration are distinctly not the targets of those who plump for deregulation.) Business needs the State for three reasons: to accord legitimacy to the power of the giant corporations, to protect the property of corporations through police and military action, and to preserve the mythology of private enterprise. The latter keeps public discontent away from business and focused on public government. The State, emphatically, will not wither away.

First, the historical context: one need not dwell on the way in which corporations waxed in number and size from the beginnings of the republic to the present, so much so that a unique institution has been created—the modern supercorporation—and a political economy dominated by these institutions. Corporate gigantism, new to this century, is one of the most important contributing causes of the Corporate State. Nor need one restate the many subventions in favor of business enterprise that were the norm in the nineteenth century and that not only continue but have increased in the present day. Economic historians have traced that path and marked it clearly. Rather, emphasis now is upon the way that law and the legal system were and are employed by the business community to further its interests. We have already shown how Supreme Court decisions had that result. The present focus is upon the entire legal system. The word *employed* is not used invidiously. There was and is much corruption in the political order, including the judiciary, but the situation is far more subtle and far more entrenched than instances of out-and-out criminality.

A close relationship has always existed between business and government, much more so than those who perpetuate myths, such as Supreme Court Justices and corporate executives, have been willing to admit. As expressed by a lawyer, "the line between public and private action is blurred, and always has been blurred, in American law."[8] The Corporate State did not spring forth, full-grown, like Aphrodite. In its present form, it is the culmination of trends that may be traced deep into American history. Some form of corporatism has always existed in the United States, the difference between past and present being one of degree rather than of kind. Today, the following definition seems valid for the United States: It is a Corporate State that has these attributes: (a) some sort of merger, actual or tacit, between political and economic power; (b) a legal nexus between the two; (c) the consequence of a metaphysical corporate body that both encompasses the two and is greater than their arithmetical sum; and (d) a diminution of the social and legal role of the individual (in other words, the domination of the group in society).

We return to fuller discussion of the Corporate State in Chapter 9 (dealing with the American Economic Constitution). It is enough now to say that the emergence of corporatism in this century presents yet another challenge to traditional concepts of constitutionalism. That, in brief, is the need for government to be both efficient and accountable. Can the Supreme Court help attain those goals?

II.

Accountability is not an easy topic, to be sure, but perhaps is more manageable than efficiency. A start may be made with two statements. First, the Constitution as drafted splintered political power to prevent its concentration in one hand—in other words, to help stave off despotism. Second, the term *accountability* is often used but seldom defined. In my definition, to be given shortly, both a *procedural* and *substantive* dimension are involved.

"If men were angels," James Madison maintained, "no government would be necessary."[9] (That is not really correct: even angels presumably dwell in an organized society, which means that some governing rules are necessary. Politics and government cannot be eliminated, even in an afterlife.) But men are not angels, so some external force is necessary to keep their brute passions in check. Madison went on to say that the difficulty in governance was not only in enabling government to control the populace but also "oblige it to control itself." That the governed can be controlled admits of no doubt, but only insofar as the governed are natural persons and not pluralistic groups. Adequate societal checks on group power have not yet been developed. In other words, accountability must in a constitutional order refer to the dimension of private governments, as well as to the organs of public government.

In the main, however, the Madisonian prescription has been directed to ways and means of government controlling itself—public government. If it is conceded, as it must be, that political power—read: government—is necessary, the question is this: How can power that is necessary be made as tolerable and decent as possible? The nation-State has always been "precisely as strong as it needed to be in the circumstances."[10] That was so even for the so-called laissez-faire (or liberal) State, which supposedly existed in the United States during the nineteenth century. Theoretically limited to a "nightwatchman" function, it was far more in fact: "It acquired substantial colonial empires, waged wars, held down internal disorders, and stabilized itself over long periods of time."[11] Despite the oft-repeated assertion that the Framers splintered political power to prevent despotism, the operative Constitution permitted, and still permits, a range of actions that are repressive. Neither the separation of powers in the national government nor the federal system have been barriers to what those who controlled or greatly influenced the levers of political power wanted to do. Some of those actions may have been extralegal, and surely some were extraconstitutional, but nonetheless they were accomplished—and with the acquiescence, silent or express, of the judiciary.

Judges either upheld exercises of extraordinary powers; or they refused to rule upon them, often calling them "political questions" not suited for courts; or the matters never got to court. Use of military forces in foreign adventures and to subdue the Indian tribes, suppression of the rebellion in the Civil War, savage repression of the "Wobblies" and other labor groups—all of these actions and more either got judicial approval or were ignored by the judges.[12]

What, then, is accountability? Ten years ago I essayed this tentative definition: "accountability, if it means anything, means that those who wield power have to answer in another place and give reasons for decisions that are taken."[13] That shorthand definition, in essence, is a procedural concept. It assumes that if the rules are followed about a fair hearing, or if, say, Congress can theoretically overrule the bureaucracy, no more is required. The assumption is that procedural regularity is sufficient to the need. I now recognize that procedure alone is not enough, and that attention must be paid to substance, to the content of governmental decisions. In other words, accountability seen as merely procedural assumes the unassumable—that there is a common acceptance of "right" moral and political ends. That common acceptance, however, is precisely what is not true of modern America: The goals of social action are frequently the very subject of dispute.

That situation makes the problem of accountability devilishly difficult. Those who exercise power must not only be checked—answer in another place—for the *way* their decisions are made but also *for the decisions themselves*. That suggests the need for an external set of standards by which the *content* of those decisions can be weighed and, if found wanting, rejected. The problem is that there is no consensus on such standards. The Supreme Court at times has discovered, in its mysterious way, such a limitation and read it into the fundamental law. That happened, for example, when the Justices during the 1890-1937 period read freedom of contract into the Constitution's due process clauses. However, that was merely *their* notion. An external set of standards presupposes that adequate consensuses on important issues have been reached by the American people, something that becomes ever more impossible as pluralism becomes more successful.

If the problem of accountability is also one of consensus, at least in part, the task becomes even more difficult. No way exists by which judges, including those on the Supreme Court, can determine the national consensus on a given issue. Even if they could, there is more to the problem of accountability. The essence of constitutionalism, if it means anything, is what Justice Hugo L. Black said: "to do justice."[14] Even much more sophisticated polling procedures, or even a national referendum or initiative petition voted on electronically through home television sets (a system that is technologically possible), would not be sufficient to the need. That need is for consensus *plus* achievement of a just society, a society in which basic human needs that make up the concept of human dignity are both sought and satisfied (to the extent that ecological considerations permit). "The public will," Felix Cohen told us, "can be as foolish and as brutal as any individual will. Regularly it is too formless and irrational a thing to serve as a foundation of law."[15] An additional component, thus, is required, a component that ultimately is ethical in nature. Said Cohen:

The instrumental value of law is simply its value in promoting the good life of those whom it affects, and . . . any law or other element of the legal order which has effects upon human life can be judged to be good or bad in the light of those effects. . . . The total valuation of law resolves itself into a judgment upon the life of human beings insofar as it is involved in the law itself or is affected by law. The evaluation of law must be in terms of the good life, and to demonstrate the nature of this standard is the task of ethics, and, more particularly, of morality. Difficult as that task is and uncertain as its conclusions have been, it is a vicious illusion to suppose that the task of the statesman is less difficult or that his conclusions can be more certain.[16]

Since Americans, as Woodrow Wilson once noted, have married legislation with adjudication and look for statesmanship in their judges, clearly the judge as statesman must consider the ethical or moral aspects of the human disputes brought to them. "An essay on the criticism of law [or judges] must be fundamentally an essay on ethics";[17] or as Jeremy Bentham put it:

Those who, for the sake of peace, seeking to distinguish politics and morals, assign utility as the principle of the first, and justice of the second, only exhibit the confusion of their ideas. The whole difference between politics and morals is this: the one directs the operations of governments, the other directs the proceedings of individuals; their common object is happiness. That which is politically good cannot be morally bad; unless the rules of arithmetic, which are true for great numbers, are false as respects those which are small.[18]

The quoted passages help to reveal the immense complexity of the accountability problem in its two dimensions: procedural and substantive.

A final point should be raised at this time: What is the proper scope of law (of judicial action)? The general principles of ethics prescribe what law and courts *ought to do*. Are there limitations on what law *can* do? Are there, in Roscoe Pound's important query, "limits of effective legal action"?[19] Law is important not because of action commanded, but because of action caused or influenced. It would be fatuous to offer a simple solution to the complexities of accountability. The problem involves the question of law observance or, to put it another way, of disobedience. At this time, I wish merely to suggest that "limits of effective legal action" are by no means fully known and also that the physical environment—in broad terms, the ecology—in which humans live (and will live) must be taken into full consideration.

Another dimension of the substance, rather than procedure, of accountability involves large affairs of State. One result of the thrust of history that catapulted the United States into the center of world politics is a little discussed constitutional crisis. Nothing less than our constitutional system is at stake. A major problem concerns the difficult, perhaps impossibility, of getting true national interest decisions in a polity that is dominated pluralistically.

"There can be no grosser mistake," observed Sir Henry Maine in 1886, than the impression that "Democracy differs from Monarchy in essence.... The tests of success in the performance of the necessary and natural duties of government are precisely the same in both cases."[20] Those "necessary and natural duties of government" are, Walter Lippmann once pointed out,[21] the defense and advancement of the vital interests of the nation abroad and order, security, and solvency at home. Can the American system insure the making of "hard" decisions, those that assert a national or public interest against private inclination and against what is easy and popular? Or is there a Gresham's Law of politics by which the "soft" decisions tend to triumph over the hard ones? Our previous analysis of the breakdown of pluralism—paradoxically, because of its very success—makes answers to those questions easy: The hard decisions are not being made.

The problem is far greater than attaining consensus in policymaking, for the decisions must reflect more than the bargaining and compromises of politics. In some way, by some means, they must be able to transcend parochial interests and reach a level of the public interest that is greater than the lowest common denominator among the interest groups of the nation. They must, that is, surmount the inadequacies of pluralism. I recognize that the term, the public interest, is controversial. Some commentators maintain that there is no public interest apart from the consensus of private interests that comprise the State. In a democracy, the two are considered to be equivalent. Once one assumes that a national interest exists apart, we are committed ineluctably to the notion that some special persons other than the "consensus takers" are better equipped to spot that separate and transcendent national interest and are thereby free to take the nation in the direction of their allegedly superior knowledge of that interest, even over the protest of the populace from whom these superior few theoretically derive their power. That scheme, to some, is dangerous, presumptive, and repugnant to democratic theory.

That view is faulty for several reasons. First, it consists of a post hoc label on the outcomes of group struggles within the nation; hence, the national (or public) interest does not exist until after the group struggle has been lost and won. Therefore, it can provide no standard for policy formation. It, moreover, tends to become a statement that "whatever is, is right" and thus to maintain that all public policy is in the national (or public) interest. Finally, it seems to be a consequence of a naive belief in a type of political Darwinism that assumes everything will work out properly if everyone pursues his own interests and is thus the political counterpart of Adam Smith's "invisible hand" theory in economics. The consensuses reached by the group struggle may or may not coincide with the national interest, but there can be no escape from the bedrock proposition that the public or national interest is something more than the results of the battles that take place in the political arena. It is "substantive" as well as "procedural."

Once one moves beyond the merely procedural—defining the public interest as the outcomes of the group struggles in politics—one is confronted with a problem of staggering dimensions. By what criteria is that interest to be identified? None exist, save in high-level abstraction. Perhaps the best statement available may be found in the magnificent generalities of the Preamble to the Constitution: "We the people of the United States, in order to form a more perfect union, establish justice, insure domestic tranquility, provide for the common defense, promote the general welfare, and secure the blessings of liberty to ourselves and our posterity." Let us extract from that well-known sentence this one word: *justice*. The Constitution was ordained and established to *establish justice* (among other goals). If that *was* the aim, is it still the goal of the United States? If so, what does *justice* mean?

It is not my purpose here to proffer a systematic definition of one of the most-used and seldom-defined terms in all of law. Others have done that, only to end in controversy. To mention only one example, John Rawls's *A Theory of Justice* is one of the most discussed books of this century; there is much in it that I find compatible, even though others have contested some of his views.[22] For present purposes, I should like only to suggest, with Professors Henry Hart and Albert Sacks, that courts as political institutions have social purposes, the main one being "establishing, maintaining and perfecting the conditions necessary for community life to perform its role in the complete development of man."[23] Hart and Sacks offer more specific guidelines for purposive judicial decision making: avoidance of social disintegration, maximization of satisfaction of valid human wants, and the fair division of resources. To me, then, justice is satisfaction of basic human needs and can be summed up in the concept of human dignity. What, if anything, can the Supreme Court do to further that concept? A few words now, and fuller discussion in Part IV.

First, accountability of those who exercise governing power, insofar as it is within the capacity of the High Bench to impose it, must encompass the affirmative dimension of justice as defined above. Second, that effort must be seen in the context of a society in which the ecological trap is closing. Courts as part of the political process cannot avoid deep and continuing involvement in the never-ending quest for social justice. However much judges have reflected, and still reflect, the wishes and values of the governing class in America, they and others in government must confront and deal with—effectively, one hopes—the growing passionate desires of people everywhere for both a fair shake of the social (and thus the legal) dice and a fair share of the planet's riches. It is too late, far too late, for there to be continuing denial of pent-up human needs. Judges, including those on the Supreme Court, can participate in society's struggles and labors: they can assist in making government officers (public and private) in the Corporate State accountable, both procedurally and substantively. I do not suggest, of course, that judges can do this monumental task alone. Far from it. My point is the lesser and apparently, but not actually, simpler one of saying that an avowed commitment to human dignity should be emblazoned on the escutcheons of those who serve on the nation's courts. That approach of course calls for both more specificity in definition and—of more importance—a basic reorientation of the judicial process. An approach to that is outlined below.

III.

There is, to be sure, much more to accountability than what was said above. We turn, however, to the equally important and perhaps more intractable problem of *efficiency*. Only a few preliminary suggestions can be set forth at this time, built around the fundamental proposition that efficiency is vitally necessary in all governmental activities.

Dictionary definitions of the word obviously are inadequate. Said *Webster's*: "1. ability to produce the desired effect with a minimum of effort, expense, or waste; . . . 2. the ratio of effective work to the energy expended in producing it, as of a machine; output divided by input." In a word, then, efficiency refers to *costs*—in funds, in human effort, in the energy used to achieve a desired result. These costs are fairly easy to calculate; engineers do it routinely. Much more difficult, however, is the question of *social costs*, which may be defined as "all direct and indirect losses suffered by third persons or the general public" as a consequence of specific activities—here, those of government. The term comes from K. William Kapp's insightful *The Social Costs of Private Enterprise.*[24] Kapp's concept has significance wider than private business, although it, too, must be considered in any evaluation of governmental efficiency. That is so not only because the United States is a Corporate State, with an Economic as well as Political Constitution, but because purportedly private enterprise in fact is a type of public endeavor. Kapp maintained that "social losses may be reflected in damages to human health; they may find expression in the destruction or deterioration of property values and the premature depletion of natural wealth; they may also be evidenced in an impairment of less tangible values."[25] So perceived, the concept of efficiency encompasses much more than economic cost. If it is acknowledged that government does and will have a continuing important role to play and if that in turn means that government should be efficient, both financial and social costs must be taken into consideration. That will require orientation of the political theory of American constitutionalism toward philosophy. Whitehead's assertion that "if science is not to degenerate into a medley of *ad hoc* hypotheses, it must become philosophical and must enter upon a thorough criticism of its own foundations"[26] is equally applicable to constitutionalism. Indeed, constitutional theory must overcome its philosophical isolation as the province of lawyers and lawyer-judges (and a few political scientists, who often are more legalistic than lawyers) and bring its fundamental assumptions in line with the present state of philosophical insight. That course means more than merely abandoning legalism as the prevailing ideology of lawyers and of those who study the Constitution and the Supreme Court. Legalism, which it will be recalled is the view that all law is an entity separate and apart from the remainder of society, is intellectually bankrupt. No more erroneous notion could be held. But it prevails. So, too, there should be abandonment of the belief, again among lawyers, in a bene- ficent natural order in social affairs and in the basic rationality of man. Phi- losophers and psychologists have long since moved on to more accurate per- ceptions of reality.

The new beginning that should come, and one that makes efficiency such a difficult goal to achieve, recognizes strong tendencies toward social disorder and disequilibrium. Law is posited on order; indeed, it is *the* principle of order.[27] But its philosophical foundations have eroded away, as Kapp told us:

the natural sciences, or at least the more philosophically minded scientists, seem to have abandoned the earlier tacit belief in a fundamental order of things in the world of nature. Thus, Whitehead points out that "science can find no individual enjoyment in nature; science can find no aim in nature; science can find no creativity in nature; it finds mere rules of succession." . . . Bertrand Russell even thinks that "the universe is all spots and jumps without unity, without continuity, without coherence or orderliness or any of the other properties that governesses love."[28]

My suggestion is not that all is disorder and disequilibrium in the American political economy, although surely it can validly be said to be in a continuing process of change. Indeed, the United States may, as was implied in Chapter 6, be suffering from too much political equilibrium. The political order may be approaching *stasis*—a static condition—precisely when the social order is rapidly changing. Rather, my aim is to show that constitutional theory—the theory of the American political economy—must encompass the dimension of theoretical frameworks that show all of the variables of social affairs and, therefore, will enable individuals and governments to make policy choices with full understanding of the probable repercussions of their actions. The meaning of this, in briefest terms, is that "social impact statements"[29] should be required before any governmental policy is promulgated, by any branch of government. (A *social impact statement* is similar to, but greater than, the environmental impact statements now required for government action.)

The further meaning is that full attention must be accorded to the concept of social value. Social evaluation is far from a new problem. In theory, it is the basis of all governmental action. That is so, because "any social policy or decision necessarily rests on a social value judgment, a social concept of social well-being, derived from social thinking."[30] There is a large problem here, however: the gap between theory and practice. Governmental action all too frequently is aimed not at social well-being but to further the interests of some identifiable interest group. Even so, the theory of *social* value is more important than *individual* preferences. It is the collectivity—the State—that in last analysis prevails. When conflicts occur between individual and social values, the latter prevails in any matter considered important to the State. That was known by Machiavelli: "It is not the well-being of individuals that make cities great, but the well-being of the community." Furthermore: "the common good can be realized in spite of those few who suffer."[31]

To sum up: efficiency as a constitutional value entails both financial and social costs, and it must consider social value. That enormous task is far from solved in the political order. One of the great conundrums of American constitutionalism, it presents the question of whether the Supreme Court can help in its resolution. To do so will require a delicate balance between efficiency and accountability. It is a task that the Supreme Court should not shirk.

IV.

Government in the United States is a paradox: It is at once powerful and weak, powerful when it confronts the individual person and weak because it seldom can make true national interest decisions. Professor Theodore Lowi believes that the consequence is "policy without law"; he thinks that "We are fast being done in by our national government, but not by its inefficiency or its corruption, its size or the irresponsibility of its senior officials. We are being done in by the very efficiency and zealousness with which officials pursue the public interest. It is not the officials who are corrupt, but their jurisprudence, which seems to render them incapable of making right decisions."[32] That view is not quite correct. We have shown above that efficiency and zealous pursuit of the public interest is simply not true of the officers in government. Furthermore, their jurisprudence, whatever Lowi means by that (which by no means is clear), is not corrupt. Rather, the political order itself—the constitutional system—makes correct decisions so devilishly difficult.

What, then, can the Justices do? Can they act as a modern "Council of Revision" or "Council of State," analogous to but not the same as what was proposed in the Convention of 1787? Can, that is, the Court serve, in Carlyle's phrase, as an "aristocracy of talent"[33] to help build a new and better jurisprudence (and constitutional order)?

Part III

THE CONSTITUTION: ITS ROLE AND FUNCTION

Every society contains within itself the forces that create its own future. The social order is always in the process of becoming, and the future inevitably must be different from the past. . . .

. . . The United States has moved well down the path toward a corporate state. Economic power is concentrated in the hands of a relatively few supercorporations that are now moving toward a dominance in the world economy to match their position in the domestic economy. Political power has shifted heavily into the hands of the executive branch of the federal government as the positive state has taken on an increasingly significant role. These two centers of economic and political power have developed a growing symbiosis.

—Daniel R. Fusfeld

In fact the very habits of mind begotten by an authoritarian Bible and a religion of submission to a higher power have been carried over to an authoritarian Constitution and a philosophy of submission to a "higher law"; and a country like America, in which its early traditions had prohibited a state church, ends by getting a state church after all, although in a secular form.

—Max Lerner

Behind institutions, behind constitutional forms and modifications, lie the vital forces that call these organs into life and shape them to meet changing conditions.

—Frederick Jackson Turner

8

A New Constitution—
Without Amendment

I.

Americans have never been able to reconcile a written Constitution with the fact of rapid social—and, therefore, legal—change. How can law be stable and yet not stand still? The question has long puzzled legal philosophers. Their answers are far from intellectually satisfactory. Just as "America still awaits a treatment that does full justice to the importance and subtlety and intricacy of the role of the Supreme Court,"[1] so it is with the Constitution. This chapter is a functional analysis of the Constitution in the United States—its purposes and its beneficiaries. What follows sets forth the perimeter of the question, but does not probe all of its subtleties and intricacies. An in-depth discussion is less necessary than a statement of general principles. The conclusion, stated now and later amplified, is that the United States is moving without announcement or fanfare into government under a *fourth* constitution—which will be labelled the Constitution of Control—that exists simultaneously with the second and third. Few acknowledge this change at present, but the change in fact, although not in basic constitutional theory, is as sure as anything can be in an uncertain world.

We begin by referring to the two types of functions previously mentioned in connection with Supreme Court decisions: Any social institution has both a manifest and a latent function. So it is with the Constitution. This chapter shows that one of the manifest functions of the Document of 1787, as amended and as interpreted by the Supreme Court, is preservation of the essential values of constitutionalism—in form, at least: The reality may and often does differ. "The function of the constitution may ... be stated," said Professor Carl J. Friedrich, "as that of defining and maintaining human rights."[2] Furthermore: "The prime function of a constitutional political order has been and is being accomplished by means of a system of regularized restraints imposed upon those who wield political power."[3]

Friedrich stated the ideal and thus presented only a partial picture. Another manifest function, surely the one uppermost in the Framers's minds in 1787 (because they failed to insert a bill of rights in the Document and thus left human rights unexpressed), is establishment of the basic framework of government (both public *and* private). As everyone knows, public governance is characterized by two divisions of powers: first, in the federal system (between the states and the national government) and, then, in the tripartite separation of governing powers in the central government. A third division, equally or even more important, was left to inference: the capacity of men to create and maintain *private* centers of governing power. That great silence in the Document had by the twentieth century produced what is called in the next chapter the American Economic Constitution.

The purpose of the Document is stated in highly abstract, familiar words in the Preamble: "We the people of the United States, in order to form a more perfect union, establish justice, insure domestic tranquility, provide for the common defense, and secure the blessings of liberty to ourselves and our posterity, do ordain and establish this Constitution of the United States of America." Note well the emphasis on *justice*, the *general welfare*, and *liberty*. The Framers did not define those terms; indeed, they have not yet been defined, save in the resolution of specific matters. Almost two centuries later, a pressing need exists for such definitions and for consensuses about them. The Document, as has been said, should be considered to be a highly subversive instrument. When ratified, it structurally changed American government to one fundamentally different from that under the Articles of Confederation. In both politics and economics, the "United States" was set on the road, which it has undeviatingly followed, toward being a "united state."[4]

To determine the latent function of the Constitution is far more difficult and controversial. The question that must be asked, once again, is: *cui bono?* Who benefited in fact from the new fundamental law? Who benefits today? "The real questions," Professor Walter F. Murphy asserted, "are who or what will benefit and how."[5] Although Murphy was then speaking about judicial decisions, his observation is applicable as well to the Constitution. We have already shown how the Supreme Court, through interpretations running back as far as 1803, was and is a protector of the rights and property of the moneyed class. Much the same may also be said about the Document itself; the Framers created not a democracy, as many fulsomely repeat, but a republic designed to isolate governing power from most of the people. (The "we the people" part of the Preamble was not historically accurate. Only in very recent years have "the people" tried to assert a greater role in governance, a fact that leads some commentators to speak portentously about the "ungovernability" of democracy.)

Another aspect of the latent function of the formal Constitution (the Document) is a number of silences. One has already been mentioned: the Economic Constitution, under which a dual system of power exists, a system that is purportedly private but that is not actually so. Another is the largely undefined powers of the President, whose office is enormously larger in power and stature than it was originally. Some of those powers have now gotten Supreme Court cognizance, for example, "executive privilege" and "constitutional reason of State." Still another is the concept of the State itself and what it means. All of these aspects, and more, are part of the operative Constitution.

This chapter, then, outlines the emergence of *three* constitutions and their simultaneous existence. These three are called the Constitution of Quasi-Limitations (the second), the Constitution of Powers (the third), and the Constitution of Control (the fourth). The first American fundamental law was the short-lived Articles of Confederation.

First, how are written constitutions altered? Most lawyers, with invincible parochialism, believe that change is possible only through Supreme Court decisions and amendment—mainly the former, for the latter is seldom employed. To repeat the oft-quoted words of Charles Evans Hughes, who later became Chief Justice: "We are under a Constitution, but the Constitution is what the Justices say it is."[6] That statement is accurate as far as it goes, but it does not go far enough. Constitutional law—paradoxically, another name for constitutional change—has been and is being made by Presidents, by Congress, by custom and usage, and even by ostensibly private organizations. The Court may flatly assert, as it did in 1803 and again in 1974, that it is "the province and duty of the judicial department to say what the law is," but those assertions not only have met stout resistance at times, they are only partially accurate. Abraham Lincoln, echoing Thomas Jefferson and Andrew Jackson, said it well: "Judicial decisions must be binding in any case upon the parties to a suit as to the object of that suit"; furthermore, "while they are entitled to very high respect and consideration in all parallel cases by all other departments of the Government," nevertheless, "if the policy of the Government upon vital questions affecting the whole people is to be irrevocably fixed by decisions of the Supreme Court the instant they are made in ordinary litigation between parties in personal actions the people will have ceased to be their own rulers, having to that extent practically assigned their Government into the hands of that eminent tribunal."[7] Again, not wholly correct: despite Tocqueville's observation that most political questions are judicialized, it simply is not true that "the people . . . have ceased to be their own rulers" and that the Supreme Court runs the government. Even so, Robert H. Jackson, soon to become an Associate Justice, wrote in 1941 that Europeans were amazed, even bemused, to observe that national monetary policy in the United States could be determined in a 5-4 decision of lawyer-judges on the Supreme Court in a case between private parties involving a mere $15.60. Be that as it may, the concept of the Constitution as law—the highest law—and, thus, peculiarly within the province of lawyers, endures. It helps to make the United States the most legalistic of all nations. Furthermore, the Constitution as fundamental law has a totemistic appeal to the people; a fetish, it symbolizes enduring values and eternal verities.

Under the influence of lawyers's views of the Constitution, viewing it as law rather than as political and ethical theory about the nature of government, Americans have become accustomed to thinking that the Court's word on the meaning of the Document is, even should be, final. Moreover, there is little recognition even among lawyers that constitutional change comes in ways other than litigation before the High Bench. That that view is not correct should be obvious to all who have not been blinded by legal learning and practice. The Constitution, quite emphatically, is not a monopoly of lawyers, and the Supreme Court should not be manned solely by lawyers.

II.

Any document, such as the Constitution, that exists through time and is still considered authoritative takes on such a gloss, through interpretation and custom and usage, that its present actual version bears only a tenuous relationship to the original.[8] The words remain the same, but their content changes in accordance with exigencies faced by succeeding generations of Americans. The Christian religion provides an illustration of the basic point. The Bible, written in ancient times under the influence of Ptolemaic cosmology—which had as its basic tenet that man was the center of the universe—has had to absorb the insights of Copernicus and others who placed man where he really is—on a small obscure planet tucked in a corner of one galaxy among millions, perhaps billions, of others—and who taught that Earth revolves around the sun. That discovery was an intellectual trauma that shattered preconceived notions of man's place in the universe. The pieces are still being picked up. When Charles Darwin cast conclusive doubt about man's special creation, the intellectual basis of Judeo-Christianity crumbled. Of course, many—indeed, a growing number in the United States—still assert belief in the old-time religion. That faith, however, comes at a time when the empirical basis for those beliefs has vanished. Parts of the Bible, as in the passage in Genesis bidding man to go forth and multiply, are under severe attack as the problems of overpopulation become ever more apparent.

No need exists at this time to discuss the insubstantial basis for believing in fundamentalist religion, save to note that in practice—as compared with its formal expression—religion is a capacious tent within which almost anything can be and is done. The point is that biblical exegesis still occurs, adapting that document to modern situations and changing conditions. So, too, with the Constitution. That characteristic is why the most important, albeit almost totally neglected, aspect of the American Constitution is its "living" or "operative" characteristics—what actually takes place, the decisions made by governmental officers, and their consequences. (Even Soviet theoreticians employ a theory of "living Marxism" to explain the twistings and turnings of the policies of the USSR.)[9]

Modern legal and constitutional theory is based upon an outmoded, repudiated cosmology; it therefore is inadequate. That basis may not be

Ptolemaic (man centered), but surely it is Newtonian—the idea that the universe may be likened to a huge clock, in which principles of balance rather than of process are said to dominate.[10] That concept causes legal writers, who in final analysis are prisoners of Newtonian mechanics and its offshoot, Cartesian philosophy, to try to construct symmetrical structures of legal doctrines, each complementing another in a "seamless web" of law. Those writers do not realize, physicist Percy Bridgman has taught, that a structure of verbally consistent principles is not possible even in the natural sciences:

> I will not attach as much importance as do apparently a good many professional lawyers to getting all law formulated into a verbally consistent edifice. No one who has been through the experience of modern physics . . . can believe that there can be such an edifice, but it seems to me that nevertheless I can sometimes detect an almost metaphysical belief in the minds of some people in the possibility of such an edifice. If one needs specific details to fortify his conviction that there is no such edifice, plenty can be found. . . . The situation . . . for the lawyer resembles somewhat the general situation for the scientist.[11]

The "metaphysical belief" about which Bridgman spoke may be traced to Newtonian celestial mechanics—the notion of an ordered universe. Enormous intellectual effort is expended to try to make law into a "verbally consistent edifice" (and to criticize the Supreme Court for not producing one). Law, however, is Darwinian; it is a process, not a clock, a never-ending stream of decisions made to meet the problems of the day. Those decisions have some, but far from complete, control over what is done tomorrow. In law as in life, verbal consistency is a sometime thing; the principle of precedent is a mere convenient tool, not an inexorable command, simply because there are dual or even multiple precedents for all proposed actions— and all possible Supreme Court rulings.

Any constitution, then, is always in a state of becoming. Not static or frozen in time; it is a river, not a lake—a river, moreover, that has only a vague course and that knows few specific, unalterable banks. Changes occur when new demands confront the nation. Some constitutional provisions, of course, are rigid, alterable only by amendment: For example, the President shall serve for a four-year term and be once reelected, and each state shall have two Senators. But even some of those seemingly immutable provisions in fact are not, as, for example, the way in which Senators have become "peripatetic" in some instances; witness the elections of Robert Kennedy and Daniel Moynihan to the Senate from New York, even though each had only nominal ties to that state. With the rise of political parties, the Electoral College has become an anachronism (perhaps a dangerous one), so as Arthur Bentley said in 1908, "The American method of electing the president is one thing in the written constitution, and another in the actual constitution."[12] Even so, for the purpose of considering constitutional change, the open-ended provisions and the silences of the Document are most important.

The constitutional river flows on; the process continues. Supreme Court decisions help to give new content to specific constitutional provisions—those deliberately couched in ambiguous terms—freedom of expression, unreasonable searches and seizures, interstate commerce, due process of law, and equal protection of the laws, among others. But those decisions are not the only means of change; it is wrong to think that the Court is the only means, other than amendment, of altering the fundamental law. Presidential actions, Congressional statutes, custom and usage, and decisions emanating from some of the "private" centers of power also update the ancient language to meet new conditions. (Not all such nonjudicial decisions, to be sure, but surely the most important ones.) This has been so throughout American history. Constitutional interpretation responds "to the politically dominant segment of society rather than to received doctrines."[13] Professor Gerald Garvey dates this from Chief Justice Roger Taney's time (1837-64), but it was equally true earlier. Said Garvey: "The judicial check, originally thought of as a limit on political democracy, would henceforth support the political check. Changes in the Law of Rules—or more broadly, in basic mores, needs, and values of society—must prevail over the Rule of Law narrowly defined."[14] In 1849 Taney made this need explicit in the *Passenger Cases*: "It will be regarded hereafter as the law of this court, that its opinion upon the construction of the Constitution is always open to discussion when it is supposed to have been founded in error, and that its judicial authority should hereafter depend altogether on the force of the reasoning by which it is supported."[15] (As we have seen, that view is not correct insofar as the mention of "reasoning" is concerned.) The Justices have never, save when they wished, been bound by precedent. Constitutional questions are always open.

The Supreme Court, nonetheless, has always worked in the main within an inherited tradition. Only infrequently does it reverse past rulings. Instead, it maneuvers around them, chipping away at them, with the Justices getting the result they wish by using what Garvey called "the high talents of a constitutional *bricoleur*." (*Bricolage*, a French term, is "the art of the do-it-yourself handyman who must solve problems given only limited tools and his own ingenuity.")[16] The Justices know that continuity with the past—at least, the appearance of it—is important, even though it is not really possible in any true sense: "today there is increasing recognition that constitutional argumentation is often little more than desperate legal acrobatics. Part of the reason is surely the difficulty of believing that meaningful continuity exists between our founding documents and our present condition."[17] Even so, the *form* of adherence to the past abides, perhaps because it helps fulfill some deep-seated psychic need.

III.

Each generation of Americans writes its own constitution. It could not be otherwise. The Document of 1787 is constantly being updated to meet new conditions. Only by a transparent fiction can it be said that today's fundamental law is the same as yesteryear's. The pretense, of course, is to the contrary. But the reality differs. Massive changes in the structure of government have taken place, and new centers of political power have arisen. Americans live under a Constitution, but the Constitution, generally, is what conditions make it. It is *a posteriori* rather than *a priori*. Rather than being a set of absolute limitations and prohibitions, as well as a structure of governance, the Constitution is a collection of relative policy admonitions.

The basic concept is *power*—political power: who exercises it, by what means, for whose benefit. "Power is participation in the making of decisions: G has power over H with respect to the values K if G participates in the making of decisions affecting the K-policies of H."[18] In another definition: power is "the capacity of an individual, or group of individuals, to modify the conduct of other individuals or groups in the manner which he desires."[19] Obviously, power is difficult to define with precision. But those definitions will do; they are quoted to lend greater understanding of constitutions. "No society in recorded history," Franz Neumann once wrote, "has ever been able to dispense with political power. This is as true of liberalism as of absolutism, as true of laissez-faire as of an interventionist state. . . . The liberal state was [not] a 'weak' state. It was precisely as strong as it needed to be in the circumstances. It acquired substantial colonial empire, waged wars, held down internal disorders, and stabilized itself over long periods of time."[20] Surely, that statement is correct: The Document of 1787 has proven to be a remarkably flexible instrument.

This is not to say that changes are not necessary, changes that can come only by amendment or by another constitutional convention. The time has come for Americans to think seriously about basic alterations in the Document. We defer fuller discussion of that point, limiting the present point to suggest the obvious: that major alterations have already occurred in the operative Constitution, which by all odds is by far the more important of the two fundamental laws (formal and operative).

Those changes require only summary attention. The main theme of this section is that the United States is moving, without constitutional amendment and, indeed, without announcement, into government under a *fourth* constitution. This has been labelled the Constitution of Control to highlight its fundamental feature—increasingly authoritarian government. Preceding it were three other fundamental laws, two of which still exist: the Articles of Confederation, the 1787 Constitution of Quasi-Limitations (often misnamed the Constitution of Rights or of Limitations), and the Constitution of Powers. Few today pay attention to the Articles, even though some who fear the power of the State advocate that they be resurrected and put into effect.[21] However desirable that proposition may be in abstract theory, it will not happen. The enormous social changes that have occurred since 1787 make it certain that the United States will not—indeed, it cannot—return to the allegedly halcyon days before the Document of 1787 went into effect. That time, it is worth remembering, was far from tranquil and unruffled; it was more a Hobbesian era of conflict and strife than a golden age of tranquility. The Articles, however, were the first American Constitution and merit present attention if only to provide contrast with the past. It is erroneous, albeit commonplace, to think of the United States as having been born with the "immaculate conception" of the Document of 1787. It was not, however much the Articles and colonial history are slighted today. Even so, the important (formal) instrument is the few thousand words drafted one hot summer in Philadelphia and some twenty-six times amended.

The second constitution (of quasi-limitations) was predominant from 1789, when the first national government was created, until about 1937. Despite some belief to the contrary, nurtured by writers's concentration on the "cannot do" aspects of government, it was far from a weak fundamental law. Actions were tolerated in the nineteenth century that bear striking similarity to those taken by governments without written constitutions: Wars were fought, with the President being the moving force (without regard to the Document's provision that only Congress can declare war); territory acquired, by purchase (as with the Louisiana Purchase by Thomas Jefferson) or theft (as with the Indian tribes); discontent among the working class was repressed, at times savagely; and largesse from the federal government was a significant factor in the growth and prosperity of business enterprise. "Manufactures" were encouraged in accordance with Hamilton's *Report on Manufactures* (1791). Government helped business to incorporate and spread itself over the nation. Government, furthermore, aided through judicial decisions (which we have previously discussed) to limit the nascent power of non-business groups, such as farmers's organizations and labor unions. Through a wondrous flash of revelation, the Justices in the latter part of the nineteenth century discovered that they could read *their* ideas of wise public policy into the Document's due process clauses.[22] The development merely accelerated, however, what had long been true: The Supreme Court's ideas of policy wisdom almost unfailingly coincided with the dominant (ruling) class.

When the Great Depression engulfed the nation in the 1930s, all but the willfully blind could see that major policy changes were needed. They came with President Franklin D. Roosevelt's New Deal. Resisting at first, the Justices followed the old view that organized capital was constitutionally valid but that organized labor was not. Again, however, a flash of revelation hit the Marble Palace: The Justices suddenly acknowledged that hydraulic forces of social discontent could not be bottled up indefinitely. Something had to give, and something did give. A new constitution came into existence, not by amendment, but as an overlay on the Document of 1787—the Constitution of Powers.

The new constitution has two aspects: First was the validation of socio-economic programs of the New Deal. A series of "thou-shalt-not" decisions became an unending process of "thou can," if wished. Next came the Employment Act of 1946, a Congressional statute that changed the nature of government in America into one of expressly assumed obligations toward the populace. The "Positive State" was born. That State is the appropriate label for express acceptance by the federal government—by government generally and thus by most of the people—of an affirmative responsibility to further the economic welfare of all of the people. It is a collective undertaking of a duty, of constitutional dimensions, to create and maintain minimal conditions within the political economy—of economic growth, of employment opportunities, of the basic necessities of life.[23] The Supreme Court did not overtly begin to call the Document the Constitution of Powers; nor did many commentators acknowledge it as such. It took the insightful Professor Edward S. Corwin to place the apt label on the new constitutional phenomenon.[24]

About the same time still another—a fourth—fundamental law began to emerge: the Constitution of Control. Again, it had roots deep in American history, but became clearly evident when the United States entered World War II. A controlled economy with a controlled citizenry was the unavoidable concomitant. What began during that War was carried on, in some degree, after the War—up to and including the present time *and* the foreseeable future. The United States today is not only the Corporate State, it is the National Security State. Illustrative examples are easy to locate: the loyalty-security program begun by President Harry Truman, a seemingly uncontrolled and perhaps uncontrollable arms race, undeclared "wars" in far-off Asian lands, brush-fire violence closer to home (as in the Dominican Republic in 1965), and a pervasive system of spying on Americans by American police and intelligence personnel.[25] As for the future, economic controls are easily foreseeable. As the ecological trap closes, some measures will have to be taken by government to manage the situation. The Age of Scarcity is upon us, and who says scarcity says authoritarianism. That is the Constitution of Control.

The result is a constitutional triad, which includes the co-existent second, third, and fourth constitutions, but which also has the fourth—the Constitution of Control—as probably becoming dominant. Government, always relative to circumstances, today and surely in the future faces new challenges and new problems of a scale and intensity not before known. The basic principle of the fourth Constitution is *raison d'etat*—constitutional Reason of State—by which is meant that those who govern will do whatever is considered necessary to insure the survival of the collective order called society (and the nation-State called the United States), no matter how repugnant some acts may be to the rulers in their private capacity as decent and moral men. Niccolo Machiavelli said it well: "I claim that republics which, in imminent danger, have recourse neither to a dictatorship nor to some form of authority analogous to it, will always be ruined when grave misfortune befalls them."[26] Just as Locke was the philosopher for the second constitution and John Maynard Keynes for the third, so Machiavelli is for the fourth.

Little doubt exists that the United States is moving and will continue to move toward a more authoritarian, regimented society. Humankind faces a number of vulnerabilities, each one of which is terrible in itself: thermonuclear war, energy shortages, dependence on nonfuel minerals, food shortages, the population "bomb," social disruption, terrorism, economic turmoil (such as inflation and rising unemployment), and the psychological problem of a failure of nerve. These conditions are coalescing, so Americans and others now confront not a crisis, but a crisis crises—a climacteric—unique in modern and probably in all history. The human climacteric marks one of the great turning points in human experience.

Since we live, in Dr. Harrison Brown's words, "in a largely synthetic ecological system, new in human experience and inadequately understood,"[27] belief systems and behavior patterns that are the products of eons of history must now be employed in wholly novel situations. It is therefore not surprising that this is the "me generation," the "age of narcissism," and that the politics of selfishness are all-pervasive. To repeat: in such a condition it does no good to ask, as some have, "What has posterity done for me?" and then blithely proceed to act hedonistically. Because of extraordinarily rapid social change, so characteristic of the modern age, people today are their own posterity. It is not only their children who must live with what is done today—but they themselves. Decisions made in the 1980s will affect most Americans alive today—for the rest of their lives. Never before in human history could it be said that the present generation is also the posterity of tomorrow. (When the Framers mentioned "our posterity" in the Preamble to the Document, they certainly did not mean themselves.) Never before have so many changes in the environment in which they live affected so many people. During most of known history, conditions were static; only in the past hundred or so years has change, at times rapid almost beyond comprehension, been built into the social order.

In constitutional terms, that rapidity of change means that society acting through government cannot avoid coming to grips with unprecedented challenges. If the past is any criterion, as to a degree it certainly is, can there be any doubt that Arnold Toynbee's doleful forecast that in developed countries a severely regimented way of life will have to be imposed by authoritarian governments will prove true?[28] This does not mean, it must be emphasized, that repressive government will come under the banner of tyranny. Quite the contrary: fascism may come but it likely will be "friendly," as Bertram Gross has said,[29] or it will be a form of "democratic dictatorship."[30] The forms of democracy will be retained but the operative Constitution will differ.

IV.

No present need exists to delineate in exhaustive detail the characteristics of the Constitution of Control. That was done in a previous book—*Demo-*

cratic Dictatorship: The Emergent Constitution of Control (1981). It is enough now to outline some of its main features:

1. *The overarching social reality is the State—the Corporate State*. In legal theory it is a real person, as real, indeed, as any natural person. That is so even though it cannot be seen or touched, has no anatomical parts, and no soul for which a parson may struggle. The State, in sum, is a "group-person," existing over and above "the multiple individual persons of which [it is] composed."[31] This fact has been recognized in numerous Supreme Court decisions, although not labeled as such, and in presidential pronouncements. Witness, for example, a little noticed but portentous statement by President John F. Kennedy in 1962: Answering a question about a "public interest" in collective bargaining negotiations, Kennedy said, "These companies are free and the unions are free. All we [the executive] can try to do is indicate to them the public interest which is there. After all, the public interest is the sum of the private interests, or perhaps it's even sometimes a little more. *In fact, it is a little more.*"[32] (Emphasis added.) Nineteen years later, in his farewell address to the nation, President Jimmy Carter echoed that sentiment: "the national interest is not always the sum of our single or special interests."[33] Carter spoke for realization of "the common good"—which he did not define. In these statements, two Presidents helped to make the State—"the public interest," "the national interest"—something over and apart from the arithmetical sum of the private interests of the nation. In final analysis, that is an organismic conception of the State as a separate, albeit disembodied, being, a corporate person, rather like calling an economic collectivity—the business corporation—a constitutional person. The political theory for the development may be traced to the German legal theorist Otto von Gierke, who enunciated the idea of groups as persons. His chief translator, Ernest Barker, pointed out the danger in such a notion:

If we make groups real persons, we shall make the national State a real person. If we make the State a real person, with a real will, we make it indeed a Leviathan—a Leviathan which is not an automaton, like the Leviathan of Hobbes, but a living reality. When its will collides with other wills, it may claim that, being the greatest, it must and shall carry the day; and its supreme will may thus become a supreme force. If and when that happens, not only may the State become the one real person and the one true group, which eliminates and assimilates others, it may also become a mere personal power which eliminates its own true purpose directed to Law or Right.[34]

Barker's fears will become increasingly apparent as the ecological trap closes and the Age of Scarcity bears hard upon Americans and American institutions. The State—the nation-State that is the United States—claims, successfully, that it has a monopoly on the *legitimate* use of force. Its will does collide with the will of natural persons at times; when it does, it carries the day. Numerous Supreme Court decisions are testimony to that occurrence.[35]

The State, moreover, is closely connected with religion (but not with the church as such); in fact, the State is a religion, a civil religion. As such, it shares with religion the capacity to impart meaning to death. As Max Weber observed, a soldier's death on the battlefield is consecrated.[36] One need only remember the incessant propaganda characteristic of most wars to see that capacity of the State.

2. *Security is the most important value.* All governments have two basic goals: internal order and external security. Various ways are available to achieve the first—through repression, propaganda, and "purchase." Each has been and is being used in the United States today. Americans, the myth to the contrary notwithstanding, have never suffered dissidents gladly.[37] Both violence and the more subtle use of law and the legal system have been employed to stifle their activities. Propaganda, as Jacques Ellul has shown, is characteristic of all governments.[38] One of the latent functions of the mass media in America is to help stifle discontent—by inculcating loyalty in the citizenry in two ways: first, by raising the specter of "foreign devils" who are alleged to have designs on American national interests; and second, by continuous uncritical plumping for the "American way," for patriotism, for the symbolism of the flag. Internal order through purchase is a product of the New Deal, the welfare programs of which had as one main goal the buying off of social discontent. Those programs were for *personal* security from the woes of industrialism and of an economic order that chewed people up and spit them out. During the Great Depression it became politically necessary to alleviate the conditions of millions of Americans. That could be done, because the nation went on a "war" footing, first in World War II and then in the continuing Cold War that has lasted since 1945, and because, as has been suggested, the Golden Age of America—the Age of Economic Abundance—emerged in the postwar period. Internal order was possible, because most Americans could sup at the groaning tables of economic opulence.

It has become all too apparent, however, that the economic pie is shrinking and that governmental provision for economic and psychic security of many Americans is on a collision course with the other security goal—national security. The Reagan budget is vivid testimony to the inconsistent security goals. Recall this statement, written just before his death by Carey McWilliams (he died on June 27, 1980):

I am convinced that the Establishment—that elusive but very real force in American life—has decided that authoritarian controls must be imposed to get the country out of the mess in which it finds itself; that there is no other way to preserve the power structure. The Establishment believes that democracy is doomed in a world of shrinking resources and rising expectations, but that the structure which surrounds it can survive if we abandon some of our freedoms.

It would be fatal to such a strategy if the man in the Oval Office had even a whiff of the demagogue about him: That would be a dangerous warning sign. What the strategy

calls for is a President who enjoys the confidence of the people—a President who is regarded as a nice guy. . . .
If a figurehead President is desirable, Reagan is the ideal nominee. As controls began to be imposed, people would not grasp what was happening until it was too late.

Ronald Reagan exudes the faith that happy days are just around the corner, that there are simple answers to complex problems. And in these troubled times, he appeals to anyone who does not want to face the unpleasant implications of an era of limits and retrenchment. Many Americans want reassurance that the Great National Barbeque will continue indefinitely, and this is exactly what Reagan offers.[39]

McWilliams advanced that scenario of a ceremonial President fronting for an authoritarian Establishment "with great hesitation." Surely, however, it must be carefully considered, all the more so for the well-publicized efforts of the President to repeal much of the New Deal (and subsequent) programs.

During the Age of Abundance, both personal and national security could be furthered without harm to each other. But the diminution of economic growth, coupled with the other crises of the climacteric of humankind, means that hard choices will have to be made. Demands for personal economic security are colliding with those of national security. The modern State, to employ Professor Harold Lasswell's apt label, is the Garrison State, one "in which specialists on violence are the most powerful group in society."[40] It is also the National Security State, which came into being in 1947 with enactment of the National Security Act. A National Security Council was created in the office of the presidency to integrate "domestic, foreign and military policies relating to the national security so as to enable the military services and the other departments and agencies of government to cooperate more effectively in matters involving national security."[41]

Security as the primary value of modern America means that the natural person is bound ever more tightly to the State (public and private governments) through the visible chains of enforced loyalty and the invisible bonds of pension plans and other techniques to insure minimal economic welfare. That has portentous consequences for the nature and enjoyment of human freedom. Said Lasswell in 1950: "An insidious outcome of continuing crisis is the tendency to slide into a new conception of normality that takes vastly extended controls for granted, and thinks of freedom in smaller and smaller dimensions."[42] I do not assert that freedoms have disappeared, but do say that there is much less human liberty in America today than we are led to believe through the use of incessant propaganda.

3. That fact will become more apparent as it is perceived that *crisis has become the norm*. Americans have indeed become accustomed to situations of continuing crisis. "It is not possible," said economist E. J. Mishan, "to avoid the conclusion that something quite fundamental has begun to go wrong with Western civilization."[43] A time of continuing crises means that, as Senators Frank Church and Charles Mathias wrote in 1974, "emergency government

has become the norm."[44] No doubt exists that humanity has begun to experience a profound social transformation. The eventual outcome may be in doubt, even though most indicators leave room for little doubt—as Mishan concluded:

> In the circumstances, only an extension of state power and a diminution of personal freedoms will prevent a disintegration into social chaos. And this process . . . is under way. The growing fears of violence, terrorism and urban disruption, the public's apprehension of the grave threats posed by the new technology, and the intensification of group conflicts within our "pluralistic" societies—all of these untoward features, traceable . . . to the technological revolution of the past century, have weakened popular resistance to the assumption of wider powers of control by modern governments. An instinct for survival is impelling the Western democracies along the road to the totalitarian state.[45]

Crisis in America has always been considered to be aberrational. Our institutions, our very underlying assumptions and ideas, are based on the view that normality is antithetical to crisis. Generally, that impression was so until at least World War I or perhaps even later. But with the Great Depression and World War II, plus the Cold War, it has become increasingly apparent that Americans have entered a new era. Crisis has become normality.

4. *The tyranny of technology.* Many years ago, at the very dawn of the Age of Technology, Henry David Thoreau maintained that "men have become the tool of their tools." Technology is both boon and bane. Its benefits are obvious but two factors of the application of technology to human problems are far from beneficial. First are the second-order consequences of apparently "good" technologies. DDT, for example, is an extremely effective insecticide, but its use has bred not only "superbugs" that are immune to it but also has had deleterious effects on many other benign species.

That effect is bad enough in itself, but of lesser magnitude than the second factor: the growing realization that control over the human mind and conduct is possible through application of new technologies. No need exists to do more than point out the problem at this time. Suffice it merely to say that with the advent of the "information society," those who control information will be able to control all individuals. Solzhenitsyn pointed out the dangers of an information bureaucracy in *Cancer Ward*: "As every man goes through life he fills in a number of forms for the record. . . . There are hundreds of little threads radiating from every man, millions of threads in all. If all these threads were suddenly to become visible the whole sky would look like a spider's web and if they materialized as rubber bands, buses, trams and people would lose their ability to move."

We must realize that what is technologically possible will be done, sooner or later. With the coming of minicomputers, through microprocessing, the question is not whether man can be made to act like a computer. That fact is technologically possible. Man has conquered nature (even though he is suffering adverse second-order consequences from that "conquest"), is on the way to conquering at least a part of the immensity of space, and is now ready to control the human mind. The philosopher for the development is Professor B. F. Skinner, who, as we have seen, sees and applauds the need for mind control: "What is being abolished," says Skinner, "is autonomous man—the inner man, the homunculus, the possessing demon, the man defended by the literatures of freedom and human dignity. His abolition is long overdue. . . . A scientific view of man offers exciting possibilities. We have not yet seen what man can make of man."[46]

Until recently, only three kinds of mind control were possible: persuasion through propaganda, torture, and "co-optation." Each has been and is being used. Propaganda, however, is expensive and often not successful. The modern State requires compliant human beings. Torture is effective, but it is merely a one-on-one procedure—too slow, too costly, and in final analysis likely to be counterproductive. Co-optation, by which brainy, upwardly mobile young men and women are drawn into the outer circles of the governing class in America and richly rewarded, is quite effective but does not provide for the mass of people. Only selected individuals are chosen. Something else is needed by the modern State under the Constitution of Control— a psychological conditioning advocated by Skinner and others. Two statements by Aldous Huxley illustrate the point:

We have had religious revolutions, we have had political, industrial, economic, and nationalistic revolutions. All of them, as our descendants will discover, were but ripples in an ocean of conservatism—trivial by comparison with the psychological revolution toward which we are so rapidly moving. *That* will really be a revolution. When it is over, the human race will give no further trouble.

The older dictators fell because they could never supply their subjects with enough bread, enough circuses, enough miracles and mysteries. Nor did they possess a really effective system of mind-manipulation. In the past, free-thinkers and revolutionaries were often the products of the most piously orthodox education. This is not surprising. The methods employed by orthodox educators were and still are extremely inefficient. Under a scientific dictator education will really work—with the result that most men and women will grow up to love their servitude and will never dream of revolution. There seems to be no good reason why a thoroughly scientific dictatorship should ever be overthrown.[47]

The suggestion is not that the Huxleyan world has already arrived, although some evidences of it are discernible at this time. Rather, it is in the form of a prediction: As the ecological trap continues to close and as the Constitution of Control becomes ever more evident, the conditioning of the human mind through the application of technology will be seen as necessary. It will be the ultimate triumph of rationality, as Roderick Seidenberg maintained in his important but neglected *Posthistoric Man*, and it will be the ultimate tyranny of technology.[48]

5. *Government under the Constitution of Control is, and will continue to be, basically different from the theory (and even the practice) of the past.* Several aspects merit mention; they are listed with little or no discussion.

   a. Elitism in government will be acknowledged.[49] Although it has always existed, the myth is to the contrary. Now, however, serious commentators, who must be taken seriously, perceive the rise of the *demos* to greater political power and decry it. Their call for elitism in government is being heeded.

   b. That recognition means that "representative government," however defined, is on its way out. Perhaps the form will remain, but lurking behind the facade is government by the elite. There seems to be no escape from the truth of Professor Marek Sobolewski's comment: "In the political process of the modern State, the relation between electors and their individual representatives . . . is of minor importance."[50]

   c. Law, including constitutional law, will ever more become avowedly "instrumental"—goal seeking—rather than interdictory (a set of "thou-shalt-nots"). The question for policymakers, generally, is not whether the rules permit such-and-such an action, but whether it is physically and financially possible. The Constitution of Control interdicts the subjects of governance, that is, rather than those who govern.

   d. Socioeconomic planning by government will become overt. Although some type of planning has always characterized the United States, the trend is toward more of it. As the Age of Scarcity arrives, it will become indispensable. The beneficiaries, at this juncture, are not likely to change; the controls that will be imposed will be for the benefit of the class that has always prevailed. That situation is nothing new, of course; in the words of the Bible: "For whosoever hath, to him shall be given and he shall have more abundance; but whosoever hath not, from him shall be taken away even that he hath."

   e. Secrecy will characterize government, particularly as foreign affairs impinge ever more directly upon domestic matters.[51]

   f. Presidential government has come to stay. Despite the popular wisdom to the contrary, Watergate and aftermath have created only the appearance of a renascent Congress.[52]

   g. Federalism as it was known is fast becoming moribund. The states have become political anachronisms.[53]

   h. The constitutional command of equal protection of the laws is more fantasy than fact.[54]

V.

That the Constitution of 1787, as amended, has been greatly altered since that time admits of no doubt. Always relative to circumstances, the American fundamental law has been and continues to be adaptable to the various crises of the American experience. As the United States approaches the bicentennial of the 1787 Constitutional Convention, it has become all too apparent that not only is the present fundamental law related to the Document of 1787 only in metaphorical ways, but that certain basic changes are needed. Perhaps it is too much to expect that another convention will be called to rewrite the Document (although some propose a limited convention to deal with matters such as abortion, school prayers, and a balanced national budget). But it should not be too much to ask that Americans confront the pressing need for some specific changes. Further adaptation, by whatever means, may not be sufficient. The Constitution of Control—America's fourth fundamental law—poses grave, as yet unanswered problems of governance.

9
The Economic Constitution

I.

A generation ago, Max Lerner observed: "The Big Corporation, Big Unionism, and Big Government live in an uneasy menage in America, with no one of them able to crush the others. A new constitutional structure of industry and government is emerging, with a new separation of powers that is more relevant for contemporary America than the classical separation of governmental powers."[1] That description is at least partially correct. Scholarly attention has concentrated on the classical concept. This chapter argues that the time has come to acknowledge in theory what is obvious in practice: Lerner's "new constitutional structure."

The structure is not really new, but the perception of it is. If we consider, as we should, the corporate systems in America to include both enterprise and union,[2] there can be no question that they have had enormous influence upon every segment of formal American government. Furthermore, those systems have so altered the ways prices are set, the way profits are made, and the very nature of property itself that the actualities of economic power bear little resemblance to classical concepts of capitalism.[3]

Lerner wrote about modern America, but his observations can be extended far back into history. In addition to the four constitutions discussed in Chapter 8, another bifurcation in American constitutionalism may be posited—between the *political* order formally expressed in the Document of 1787 and the *economic* order which that instrument left to inference. The former will be called the American Political Constitution, the latter the American Economic Constitution.[4] To most Americans, and certainly almost all constitutional lawyers, the notion of an economic constitution will seem odd. After all, constitutions deal with a political concept—power—and there is little thinking in those terms as far as economics is concerned. Power is attributed, under orthodox constitutional thought, to public government alone, although it has been known since at least 1924, when John R. Commons published *Legal Foundations of Capitalism*, that at least two and perhaps three types of power exist—physical (the State), economic (property or business), and (perhaps) moral.[5]

The Document says little about economics. A few sparse provisions relate to the power of government to tax and spend. The Framers contented themselves with stating a few fiscal issues, rather than specifying in detail the respective powers of the federal and state governments. Those generalities were left to gather content from experience. Other than the obligation-of-contracts clause and the later insertion (in 1791) of a due process clause protecting property, plus an eminent domain proviso, nothing was said about the private sector. The twenty-six amendments do not vary the original pattern. As for taxation, the Supreme Court in 1866 summed up the federal power in a few sentences: "the power of Congress to tax is a very extensive power. It is given in the Constitution, with only one exception and two qualifications. Congress cannot tax exports, and it must impose direct taxes by the rule of apportionment, and indirect taxes by the rule of uniformity. Thus limited, and thus only, it reaches every subject, and may be exercised at discretion."[6] (Since that time, the Sixteenth Amendment has permitted what was called a direct tax—that on incomes—to be levied "without apportionment.") Spending powers are even more scanty. Save for an occasional aberration, American policymakers, including the Supreme Court, have always followed principles early stated by Alexander Hamilton. In essence, Hamilton—the true father of the operative, and at times the formal, Constitution—maintained that there were no limits on Congress's power to spend.[7] That opinion is not quite correct today, as the church-State relationship indicates, but is close enough to serve as a generalization.[8]

The concept of the Economic Constitution is based upon one bedrock proposition—that the American economy is, and always has been, a system of power. An understanding of *power* as a political concept is fundamental to American constitutionalism. A slippery term, it requires definition. For present purposes, it is taken to mean the ability or capacity to make or influence the decisions of others. In other words, it is the ability to make decisions affecting the values of others, to impose deprivations or bestow rewards so as to control the behavior of others. R. H. Tawney defined *power* somewhat differently: "The capacity of an individual, or group of individuals, to modify the conduct of other individuals or groups in the manner he desires."[9] (Those definitions are admittedly abstract, but they should suffice.) I do not suggest that a person who exercises power need also be able to employ actual physical coercion over another. As Commons saw, the sanctions through which power is wielded can be, and usually are, much more subtle. They are psychological or economic, or both, and they can be direct or indirect.

Everyone acknowledges that the Document of 1787 deals with the allocation of *formal* political power and that the Bill of Rights, added in 1791, is concerned with limitations on that power. (However, the Supreme Court determined in 1833 that the first eight amendments were not limitations on the states,[10] a situation not changed until this century, and the seeming absolutes of the Bill of Rights are in fact mere relative standards.) This chapter deals with the greatest silence of the Document—the organization and management of the economy into an informal, in that they are not overtly "official," yet significant set of power relations. The Economic Constitution has two basic principles: contract and property. Contract is the legal instrument appropriate for a "free" (or, better, "private") enterprise economy, and the protection of property, according to John Locke, the intellectual father of the Constitution, was the reason for the formation of governments. ("Property," Professor Charles E. Lindblom observed, "is a system of authority established by government.")[11] Private law, therefore, is the legal system of the Economic Constitution, although at times it meets and merges with the public law of the Political Constitution. Private law is law, not because of any inherent qualities, but only because the State recognizes it as such. That means private individuals can call upon the State to enforce rights concerning property and its use; it also means, as is argued below, much more: In legalese, private law is a form of delegation of power from the State to private individuals and the organizations they form.[12]

II.

When the Roman Empire disintegrated, the Church, together with political power, attempted to exercise dominion over the remnants. The result was the Holy Roman Empire, a curious combination of ecclesiastical and political authority that in fact was neither holy nor Roman nor an empire. Out of that jumble emerged a pattern of relationships among increasingly autonomous States, each one of which claimed sovereignty over designated territory and its inhabitants. The Peace of Westphalia (1648) became the cornerstone of the modern system of nation-States (what today seems to be the natural order of political affairs, the nation-State, thus had its origin less than 400 years ago). Professor Leo Gross has said that the Peace resulted in:

a new system characterized by the coexistence of states, each sovereign within its own territory, equal to one another, and free from any external earthly authority. The idea of an authority or organization above the sovereign states is no longer. . . . This new system rests on international law and the balance of power—a law operating between rather than above states, and a power operating between rather than above states. . . . The idea of an international community becomes almost an empty phrase, and international law comes to depend upon the will of states concerned with the preservation and expansion of their power.[13]

Within this system, each nation-State is a separate geographical unit with one, and only one, goal: the pursuit of its own interests. Not until the nineteenth century, however, was the process completed in Europe, and in the post-World War II period, more nation-States have been formed than ever before (some of which are little larger in size or influence than the city-States of medieval times). That much of history is familiar and needs no further restatement.

The United States came into existence by spinning off from being a colony of Great Britain. The peace treaty of 1783 gave it formal legal status as a nation-State, although, as British activities up to and including the War of 1812 demonstrate, America was in fact something other than truly sovereign. That position, however, was in its external relations and of no interest to the present discussion. My basic point is that the new nation, "conceived in liberty and dedicated to the proposition that all men are created equal" (as Lincoln erroneously put it in his Gettysburg Address), had all the attributes of sovereignty *internally*. True it is that political power was split in the federal system between the states and the general government, but the nation, as expressed in the Constitution, operated within its territory as the sole, exclusive source of all powers and prerogatives of rule. Since its inception, the single most important characteristic of the United States has been unitary internal sovereignty. All societal activities involving the "authoritative allocation of value"[14] are performed by authority of a single decision center—the State itself (as expressed or implied in the Document of 1787)—without regard to whether those actions may be differentiated (in the federal system) or seemingly private. "No individual or corporate body can engage in activities of rule except as an organ, agent, or delegate of the state; and the state alone assigns and determines the extent of those activities according to its own rules, backed by its own sanctions."[15] Even though many consider the citizenry ("the people") to be the ultimate repository of sovereignty—that is, the idea of "popular" sovereignty—the State nevertheless is monistic. It is *one* unit, with a single currency and a national language and a legal system that, although divided into parts in the federal system, is in fact unified.

For present purposes, the point is that the economy exists—capitalism exists—only because it is permitted by the State. Capitalism, itself a system of power, is therefore derivative rather than autonomous. "The possession of capital is a legally and politically protected means to the creation and reproduction of de facto relations of domination between individuals belonging to different classes."[16] There is an apparent contradiction here: The State that is the source of all power relations within the nation guarantees power relations that emanate from the ownership of capital. (The contradiction is only apparent, not actual, as will be shown.) Private control over capital is possible only because it is permitted by the State, not because of any natural or inherent right to it. Therefore, power exercised by private capital must be considered to be a form of a (tacit) delegation of governing power from the State. In short, the State is the legal abstraction that is designed and operates as a machine whose parts all mesh, both those called public and those called private. "The state organization reached deep into the personal existence of man, forms his being."[17] For example, as Max Weber has argued, it shares with religion the ability to impart meaning to death. "The warrior's death on the battlefield, Weber suggests, is a consecrated one, a consummation vibrant with elevating feeling. Has not the nineteenth-century state appealed all too often and all too successfully to such motifs in order to send young men willingly to die (and to kill)?"[18]

Even though conflicts at times occur, the private law of the Economic Constitution is not at odds with the public law of the Political Constitution. The two systems mesh, each having its own task. Public law gives direction for the operation of official organs of government, whereas private law establishes frameworks for the activities of persons, natural and artificial, pursuing their own interests. Those interests cannot be pursued unless they coincide with the interests of the State itself. They are only apparently autonomous. They include the law of obligations (contract and tort), of property, and of corporations. So it is that the State provides for a system of private agreements by which constitutional persons may enter into horizontal arrangements with each other, a system for the enforcement of liability for private wrongs, and a set of rules for the governance of the private corporation. The State's law-enforcement apparatus is placed at the disposal of persons involved in any or all of those matters.

Under the liberal theory of the Rule of Law, those horizontal transactions, promissory and otherwise, are governed by a neutral body of rules that are impartially administered. That theory, although it has long been exploded, lingers on.[19] Even though Sir Henry Maine could in 1861 assert that the movement of "progressive" societies was from status to contract,[20] that position was invalid when he made it. Since necessitous men cannot be free men, the notion of arms-length bargaining in much of contract law is more fantasy than fact. That point was particularly to be seen in the labor contract, by which an individual sold his time and effort in exchange for a wage. With the advent of collectivization in business, in the drive for incorporation, by no means did the bargaining power of the individual equal that of the enterprise. The law assumed otherwise. So, too, with tort law: In the nineteenth century the dreadful costs of industrial accidents fell on those, the workers, least able to pay. Judges invented rules of assumption of risk, of contributory negligence, and the fellow-servant rule to insulate the corporate enterprise from the human costs of industrialization. It was the private-law counterpart of the Supreme Court's willingness to strike down legislation aimed at ameliorating conditions of the working class.

Those laws were far from neutral. Judges and the law they enunciated were class oriented—in favor of the moneyed and propertied. Holmes knew that well over a century ago. He wrote in 1873 that the notion that law was neutral, impartially imposed by judges, "presupposes an identity of interests between the different parts of a community which does not exist in fact."[21]

The immediate focus of his remarks was the prosecution and conviction of gas stokers who went on strike in London. Holmes claimed that there was not only no unity in law as a whole, but that there was a lack of unity at the social level that eventually was translated into law. With that statement, which was and is almost completely unheeded, he delivered a mortal blow to the liberal theory of the Rule of Law, with its assumptions that known general rules, applied impartially, would produce effects that benefited all. (Those assumptions are a version of Adam Smith economics transferred to the legal system.) Holmes saw that, as did Plato's Thrasymachus, decisions of courts represented the interests of the stronger in society;[22] as he put it, "whatever body may possess the supreme power for the moment is certain to have interests inconsistent with others which have competed unsuccessfully. The more powerful interests must be more or less reflected in legislation [and judicial decisions]; which, like every other device of man or beast, must tend in the long run to aid the survival of the fittest."[23]

Corporation law provides further illustration. Originally, corporations were franchised by government for limited purposes and limited times. Henry Carter Adams said it well in 1896:

Corporations originally were regarded as agencies of the state. They were created for the purpose of enabling the public to realize some social or national end without involving the necessity of direct governmental administration. They were in reality arms of the state, and in order to secure efficient management, a local or private interest was created as a privilege or property of the corporation. A corporation, therefore, may be defined in the light of history as a body created by law for the purpose of attaining public ends through an appeal to private interests.[24]

We have strayed far from that conception. Corporations still must be chartered, but their goal is the pursuit of profits. Only by a transparent fiction can it be said that their actions attain the public good, as by "an invisible hand" (in Adam Smith's language). Private greed is permitted by the State—perhaps on the assumption that Smith, who wrote in 1776 and was influential at the time the Constitution was drafted, was correct in his view of the invisible hand. The Document was written, however, when corporations were not the usual mode of doing business; only about 300 existed in the United States as late as 1800.[25] But the silences of the Constitution provided a framework for capital to operate, and the State also helped in the accumulation of even more capital. The result, in Professor Gianfranco Poggi's words, is "Under capitalism the economy does not operate within the social sphere simply as one 'factor' among and coordinate with others; rather, it imperiously subordinates or otherwise reduces the independent significance of all other factors, including religion, the family, the status system, education, technology, science, and the arts."[26] In sum, *the economy is a system of power.*

As such, capitalism (which has become state capitalism or the Corporate

State) involves the domination of a capital-owning class over other social groups and, of course, over individual persons. That class also has come to dominate large segments of public government. A class society is the inevitable result. To uphold it, the Supreme Court and other organs of government managed for decades to exclude from the formal political process the claims and demands of groups who may have wanted to abolish capital ownership, to modify the distribution of wealth, or to interfere with the accumulation of profits. In other words, property was protected. Only with the spread of the franchise, which came at the same time as greatly increased productivity of labor, were other groups able to gain power. The consequence, as we have seen, is a situation of incipient political paralysis.

I do not wish to push the point further than necessary, save to say that when the public legal order recognized the right of capital to collectivize itself and then went on to equate the economic collectivity with a natural person, something new under the constitutional sun was born.[27] It then became clear beyond peradventure that the economy—certainly, the economy of the corporate juggernauts—is a system of power. Those giant enterprises are quasi-polities, each with a constitutional and legal system of its own. They are at once economic entities and sociological communities, political orders and legal persons. They have created a new social order. H. P. Bahrdt, among others, has argued that they are units of "industrial feudalism":

There are industrial firms that build houses and flats for their employees or make arrangements whereby they can purchase their own homes. They build public parks, schools, churches, and libraries; they arrange concerts and theater outings; they run adult education courses; they look after the aged, widows and orphans. In other words, a range of functions originally carried out by institutions public not only in the juridical but also in the sociological sense are undertaken by organizations whose activities are nonpublic. . . . The "private" sphere of operations of a large firm runs right through the existence of a town where it is located, and brings into being a phenomenon to which one may rightly attach the label of industrial feudalism.[28]

The State in Western nations subordinated itself to the economic process. By being deeply involved in economic tasks, whether those of aiding business growth or of (ostensibly) regulating the excesses of corporate collectivism, the line between politics and economics has, in fact although not in theory, been all but obliterated. The two realms are supposedly separate, as are State and society, but when the workings of the economic fundamental law are perceived as one half, and probably the dominant half, of the State (and thus of the Political Constitution), there can be little question that Americans are governed by two fundamental laws. When President Calvin Coolidge quipped that "the business of the United States is business," he stated not only a historical (and contemporaneous) truism, but also tersely summed up the existence of the Economic Constitution.

But where, one might ask, does sovereignty really lie, if that be so? Under the myth, the United States is characterized by popular sovereignty: "the people" are said to be the ultimate source of all governing power. That idea, however, is not now, nor has it ever been, actually true. Citizen sovereignty exists only to the extent that people have votes and thus in theory can elect anyone they please to public office, with those so elected presumably representing the voters and having the power to govern. In practice, the system does not work that way. People as individuals have no political power; only when they combine into groups, which they often do, is political clout evident. Majority rule, whatever that means, simply does not exist in the United States, if public opinion polls on matters such as wage and price controls, gun controls, and abortion are any criterion. In sum: people do not govern; groups do.

Even the political party is in final analysis a mere sham, a facade. Parties at best are vague electoral alliances, and campaigns are ritualized ceremonies —latter-day Roman circuses. A political party is only nominally a corporate body, and that is so even though at times they have been subjected to constitutional norms (as in the white primary cases).[29]

Sovereignty in the United States lies in the State, rather than the people. (The State, being corporatist, means that sovereignty is shared between the organs of the Political Constitution and those of the Economic Constitution.) That the people, as such, are not sovereign may be seen in the constitutional concept of sovereign immunity. Not mentioned in the formal Document, it is another silence filled by judicial lawmaking. Borrowing from the British rule that the King as sovereign could not be sued in his own courts, the Supreme Court, apparently without much thought, applied the same rule to the United States. (Not that the Justices ever defined "the" United States; they did not— which means that a gap in theory now exists.)[30] Imposing the rule of "sovereign" immunity meant that the federal *government* was immune from suit by a person, despite the widely accepted theory of popular sovereignty, unless Congress in general or specific legislation had consented. As early as 1821, Chief Justice John Marshall, asserted:[31] "the universally received opinion is, that no suit can be commenced or prosecuted against the United States"— and thereby threw the "we, the people" concept of popular sovereignty out of the window. Although Congress has removed much of the immunity of government from suit, it remains true that ultimate power still lies in Congress. What Congress gives, it presumably can take away. The courts will go along. As the Supreme Court said in 1940, the reasons for sovereign immunity "partake of dignity and decorum, somewhat of practical administration, somewhat of the political desirability of an impregnable legal citadel where government, as distinct from its functionaries, may operate undisturbed by the demands of litigants."[32] (The Justices did not say how government can operate "distinct from its functionaries.")

Even though some statutes, mainly in the area of civil rights, and some Supreme Court decisions permit lawsuits against individual government officers for wrongdoings, the general principle still abides. The "sovereign," then, is "the" United States, which in turn is a visible governmental triad of legislative, executive, and judicial powers—with, arguably, the ultimate authority resting in Congress;[33] and it is an "invisible" system of private governments that exists, as Hobbes once said, as "worms in the entrayles" of the body politic. Somewhat more precisely, the State—a disembodied entity existing only in contemplation of law—is sovereign, with the governmental troika beings its apparatus, and with the State being corporatist, a "supergroup-person" consisting of political and economic power being joined together in a condition of syzygy.

The sovereign immunity rulings mean that popular sovereignty has been consigned to a political and legal wastebasket. Replacing it is sovereignty of the State, an amalgam of political and economic power operating coopera- tively. The slogan of popular sovereignty still is used, but it is a mere rhetorical device by which the people are organized and placated. True it is that a combination of the spread of higher education and broadening of the fran- chise have permitted social groups other than the dominant capitalists to in- fluence some narrow segments of public policy. It is precisely for that rea- son—for the fact that the *demos* take the rhetoric of democracy seriously— that neoconservatives and others now decry "the ungovernability of democ- racy."[34] The slow movement toward "participatory" democracy, by which some Americans seek to gain governing power over their own lives, has produced a counter-revolution of latter-day disciples of Edmund Burke.[35] Within the economic sphere, the idea of democracy and of constitutionalism, although bruited by some, is at most a wistful dream. In net, then, Americans are governed by two systems of power—one formal and political and the other informal and economic—both of which are important. The conse- quence: government *of* the people there is, but not *by* the people, and not always *for* the people.

III.

What, then, are the characteristics of the Economic Constitution? They can be given only summary treatment here. The text for this section comes from Adam Smith: "Civil government, so far as it is instituted for the security of property, is in reality instituted for the defense of the rich against the poor, or of those who have some property against those who have none at all."[36] The putative "father" of the American Constitution, John Locke, said in his *Civil Government* that "government has no other end but the preservation of property."[37] We have already noted how James Madison restated that thought in *Federalist No. 10*. There can be little question that the Founding

Fathers believed in Smith and Locke. Furthermore, the Constitution as it has developed, both in its formal and its operative sense, has pursued the same goal. As has been shown in Part I, the Supreme Court historically was in effect, although not in theory, an arm of the business class—those with money and property.

The Economic Constitution has several basic principles, each of which is an inference from the silence of the Document, some important Supreme Court decisions, and the way that the political economy has developed since 1789. Although not incorporated in a written instrument, those principles are as important, perhaps more so, as the provisions of the Document itself. In the ensuing discussion it will be seen that the Political and the Economic Constitutions complement each other, and the institutions of each fundamental law cooperate much more than they conflict.

1. The first principle of the Economic Constitution has already been stated and discussed: *The economy in the United States is a system of power* having significant political consequences for the American people.

2. The second principle is that *governing power was delegated from the State to the owners of property (the capitalists).* That delegation of power was not done in so many words. Rather, it was left to inference and to later judicial and legislative decisions. The economic order, Karl Polanyi has pointed out,[38] was isolated wholly from the jurisdiction of the formal Constitution. When the due process clause was added in 1791, the highest possible protection to private property became a part of the fundamental law. Provisions for protection, however, were in the Document of 1787, in the prohibition against violating contractual obligations (a promise in a contract is a type of property; today, indeed, promises constitute most of the wealth of the nation), and in limiting the franchise almost entirely to male property owners. As written, the Constitution was distinctly "an elitist document."[39]

The process of power transference was subtle: The "delegation" did not take place by Congressional statute, although, as will become evident, corporate charters granted by state legislatures should be considered to be a type of delegation. Indeed, it is generally conceded that *formal* political power cannot be transferred from the legislature to private parties: "The majority rule is that power to legislate may not be delegated by the legislature to the people."[40] That restriction, however, has only a limited meaning—that private parties cannot make *general* rules. It is true now, and has always been true, that legislatures can and do delegate political power to private organizations concerned about a small segment of policy.[41] And of course the electorate as a whole, within a given jurisdiction, can and do make law through the medium of initiatives and referenda.

The delegation of power to organizations of the Economic Constitution did not emanate from the legislature but is to be inferred from the Constitution itself. What was *not* said in the Document becomes, therefore, as important as what was said. The State for centuries has asserted—successfully—that it is the sole source of all power relations within the nation. Nothing can exist without its permission, express or tacit. The Framers, disciples of Locke and Smith, cleverly managed to create the State as the preeminent institution of the Political Constitution and simultaneously made implicit provision for a "self-regulating market economy." Such a market, Polanyi told us, is "nothing less than the institutional separation of society into an economic and political sphere."[42] That separation means that "human society" in a market economy is "an accessory of the economic system."[43] The tail wags the dog.

The market economy, insofar as it existed and still does, is the resultant of *the* major new social force in the Western world—the enormous wealth pouring into Europe following the Great Discoveries. Walter Prescott Webb in *The Great Frontier*[44] has shown the impact that new wealth had upon old institutions. Moreover, the classical market economy, with its alleged natural laws, was a derivative of Newtonian celestial mechanics and Cartesian philosophy—the transference of Newton's famous laws of motion to social affairs. Newton likened the universe to a great clock, with interacting parts that were self-correcting. Classical economists, and their modern descendants, have taken over those ideas—particularly the law of cause and effect—and applied them to the political economy. (A problem with economics today, the study of which Hazel Henderson called "a form of brain damage,"[45] is that economists still proceed on a repudiated cosmology— Newtonian principles of balance—rather than following Darwinian principles of process.)

Our point, however, is not to develop those propositions in detail. Rather, it is to insist that the economy in the United States has always operated by what should be called a privilege granted by the State—in legal terms, there-fore, by a delegation of power from the State. As Robert L. Hale saw in 1935, "the courts have been blind to the fact that much of the private power over others is in fact delegated by the state, and that all of it is 'sanctioned' in the sense of being permitted. This power permeates the entire economic system."[46] Those who wrote the Document of 1787 knew very well what they were doing: The rich and well-born who lived in America during the time of the Articles of Confederation, far from keeping aloof from government, dominated it:

Their power was born of place, position, and fortune. They were located at or near the seats of government and they were in direct contact with legislatures and government officers. They influenced and often dominated the local newspapers which voiced the ideas and interests of commerce and identified them with the good of the whole people, the state, and the nation. The published writing of the leaders of the period are almost without exception those of merchants, of their lawyers, or of politicians sympathetic with them.[47]

Those are the men who wanted and got a free hand in commercial activity, accompanied by repression of attempts of the poor and disadvantaged to better themselves.[48] Looking to a national government to further their interests, at a time when state governments might have been taken over by "the great unwashed," their representatives met in Philadelphia in 1787 with the mission of revising the Articles of Confederation. They went beyond their mission: Instead of revision they produced a structural change in government—a separate executive in the President; Congress was accorded widespread, deliberately nebulous, taxing and spending powers, and, most importantly, the principle of federal supremacy was written into the new Constitution. No longer would the moneyed and propertied have to contend with separate, often balky state governments. By targeting Congress and the courts, they could (and did) make the United States a united State. "The Constitution," Staughton Lynd has noted, "was the settlement of a revolution. What was at stake for Hamilton, Livingston, and their opponents, was more than speculative windfalls in securities; it was the question, what kind of society would emerge from the revolution when the dust had settled, and on which class the political center of gravity would come to rest."[49]

The hindsight of history that makes most people wise after the event gives the answer to that question: Society was to be business dominated, and the propertied class would control the levers of power. The Constitution, in some respects at least, should be perceived as a counter-revolutionary document. Nowhere is that better seen than in the tacit delegation of power from (ironically!) "we, the people" to an elite group. Some observations of Charles Lindblom are apposite:

> Some people believe that wealth or property is the underlying source of power. But property is itself a form of authority created by government. Property is a set of rights to control assets: to refuse use of them to others, to hold them intact, or to use them up. Property rights are consequently grants of authority made to persons and organizations. The wealthy are those who enjoy larger grants of authority than most people do. Just as ecclesiastical authority set limits on secular authority in medieval Europe, entrepreneurial authority in the form of property rights limits governmental authority. But that is because governments authorize such an arrangement.[50]

To those who may argue that power is not granted or delegated by the State in economic affairs, the answer may be tersely stated: that power, for power it is, was seized by fair means or foul.

3. The third principle is that *mechanisms of the State were (and are) used to establish a framework of law without which the propertied class could not rule.*

4. The fourth principle is that *public power—the Political Constitution—was (and is) employed to further the ends of the beneficiaries of the Economic Constitution.*

5. The fifth principle is that *society, as distinguished both the State and government, was (and is) made up of classes: in brief, those who own property (have capital) and those, far more numerous, who are the laborers.*

6. The sixth principle is that *the law, as enunciated by courts, is distinctly not neutral; it had (and has) a class bias — toward those with property*.

These principles, which overlap and complement each other, are discussed together. Under the third principle, the private laws of contracts and torts, of property, and of corporations were, in the nineteenth century and to a large extent still are, a means by which the poor and economically disadvantaged are kept "in their places." My purpose here is not to repeat what has been said previously about the way the Supreme Court protected money and property through a series of decisions involving due process of law and no-impairment-of-the-obligation-of-contracts clauses. Rather, it is to show in brief form the parallel, and arguably more important, development of private-law principles that had the same effect: protection of the creditor class. Take, for example, the law relating to civil obligations. Torts — civil wrongs — provide a classic illustration. There, judges, taken as always from lawyers for the privileged class, invented doctrines such as contributory negligence, assumption of risk, and the fellow-servant rule, so that the awful costs of industrialization would have to be borne by those least able to do so: the workers, the industrial proletariat. Injured workers were said to have contributed to their injury by taking a job or to have assumed the risk of injury, or they were injured by another worker, not their employer. The result was that the owners of capital got a free ride, while those who had only their labor to sell were forced both to work and to pay for injuries suffered. Professor Hale well stated the consequence:

It is . . . seldom recognized that when the state is enforcing contract and property rights at common law it is using its compulsory powers to effectuate the wills of private persons, and doing so in a manner which forces other private persons to forgo the exercise of liberties which the state could not constitutionally deny them in furtherance of any legislative policy of its own other than enforcing contracts or protecting property.[51]

In other words, the power of the State, operating through its apparatus, the government, was placed at the disposal of the moneyed class.

As with torts, so with contracts. Sir Henry Maine's 1861 observation that the movement of progressive societies was from status to contract meant that instead of one's rights and duties being derived from his station in life, they emanated from arms-length bargaining transactions. Maine was inaccurate even as he wrote, simply because of the disproportionate bargaining power between people and particularly between natural persons and corporations. It is far less accurate today, a time when contracts of adhesion (standardized agreements in which little or no bargaining occurs) have become the norm. A contract of adhesion, such as an insurance agreement, is in fact a legislative prescription. Power delegated by a silence in the Constitution to private business makes such "legislation" possible. There is little, often no, bargaining between the parties when standardized contracts are used — as they are throughout American business. A contract of adhesion is a "take it or leave it" proposition; if one leaves it, one soon finds that other businessmen have similar "contracts."

All of this does not violate the Constitution, either the formal or the operative one. Rather, it carries out a provision—what we have called the third principle—of the Economic Constitution. The enforcement of contracts can even override express constitutional terms. Bankruptcy laws are skewed in favor of creditors, and debtors can be forced to work to pay their debts on pain of losing their assets—even though the Thirteenth Amendment prohibits involuntary servitude. (Prison terms for debtors have never been declared unconstitutional.) Furthermore, in *United States* v. *Snepp* (1980),[52] the Supreme Court ruled that a contractual promise to submit planned publications about the Central Intelligence Agency to the CIA for "vetting" prevailed over a former employee's asserted First Amendment rights to write and publish. That exemplified a statement by Justice Holmes: "In order to enter into most of the relations of life people have to give up some of their constitutional rights. If a man makes a contract he gives up the constitutional right that previously he had to be free from the hamper that he puts upon himself. Some rights, no doubt, a person is not allowed to renounce, but very many he may. . . . Every contract is the acceptance of some inequality."[53] (If that remark be so, the theory of contract law, as taught in law schools, is badly out of kilter.) The *Snepp* decision carries Holmes's point a giant step farther.

Property rights require no discussion. They are protected by the due process clauses of the Political Constitution. As such, they approach as nearly as possible being constitutional absolutes. Private property is, without question, highest in the hierarchy of constitutional values. It cannot be taken without just compensation; that is so even though government may take a piece of property from one person and sell it to another. Zoning laws permit limitations on the use of real property, but those laws are notorious for being laxly, even fraudulently, "enforced." Since most wealth today is not tangible (as in land) but intangible, in the form of promises such as stocks and bonds, the place it holds in the constitutional firmament seems impregnable. (Despite the Supreme Court's recent flurry of activity protecting civil rights and liberties, by no means has property been accorded a lesser position. The present Court has even resurrected the long dormant doctrine of the obligations-of-contracts clause to provide a bulwark for owners of some governmental securities.)[54]

How property rights as promises are protected may be seen in the so-called holder-in-due-course rule applicable to negotiable instruments. Under that rule, a good faith purchaser for value is protected and can get payment on a bill or note even though there may have been fraudulent misdealing in the original transaction. Promises are sanctified and business agreements fortified by a private-law counterpart to the constitutional doctrine that contractual obligations cannot be impaired. Under that doctrine, as we have seen, one of the most blatant and infamous frauds in American history, dealing with the Yazoo Lands now a large part of Alabama and Mississippi, was sustained by a Supreme Court that ignored the original fraud and focused on the ultimate purchasers of the land.[55]

Business affairs are facilitated by the power of the State that enforces payment even on a fraudulent note. That means, as we have previously noted, that what government cannot do directly because of the Thirteenth Amendment's prohibition of "involuntary servitude" is permitted in private law. Obligations must be paid off, even if the obligor is forced to work to do so. The holder-in-due-course rule benefits not only the businessman, but supposedly the security of business transactions helps society at large. Whether that is so must be taken on faith; it is not susceptible of empirical verification. Be that as it may, the rule is a clear example of the third principle of the Economic Constitution in operation.

Another example of that principle is the corporate charter. Two points are important here: First, the charter is a means by which the people, acting through government, can get some of the public's business done by private enterprise. Second, historically, the businessman was allowed to collectivize but those who sold labor were not. Corporations began, as Henry Carter Adams said, as special agencies of the State, but they have been transmuted into what lawyers call a *persona ficta*—a fictionalized (constitutional) person. When the Supreme Court called corporations constitutional persons in 1886, it contributed to the belief that even corporate behemoths are both individuals and private. That position enables these firms to exercise some of the powers of public government under the Political Constitution and, indeed, some powers that government does not exercise. Price fixing, for example, through a system of "administered" prices (set not by the market but by the corporate managers) is routine among large corporations, but public government, although it could if it wished, does not do it. There is no system of wage and price controls imposed by government. In addition, corporations can "legislate" the terms and conditions of the "contracts" into which they enter with natural persons. Furthermore, some corporations have waxed so large that they are themselves hierarchical bureaucracies. As such, they are the local self-governments of much of modern society, "the logical successor to manor, village and town."[56] In the well-known words of Arthur Bentley, "A corporation is government through and through. . . . Certain technical methods which political government uses, as, for instance, hanging, are not used by corporations generally speaking, but that is a detail."[57] In sum, then, the public's business may be being done by corporations, but the managers of the enterprises operate without having constitutional restraints placed upon them. As instruments of governance, with authority delegated to them through the corporate charter, corporations not only participate in ruling the people but so do, by and large, on their own terms. Ancillary to that thought is the fact, which no one disputes, that corporations have one and only one principal motivation: making profits. Everything gives way to that objective, even the "public interest," which supposedly is served by permitting corporations to be chartered.

As an abstract matter, it may seem odd that American law for decades permitted, even encouraged, the collectivization of capital but simultaneously discouraged, even forbade, a like movement in the working class. Even though Adam Smith in *The Wealth of Nations* had noted the tendency of associated capital to conspire against the public interest, the law took little notice of that comment. Rather, concentration was on the nascent trade union activity, which was at first viewed as a conspiracy and which suffered a series of blows from the Supreme Court when the Justices declared maximum hours and minimum-wage legislation unconstitutional. Not until 1937, when the Court upheld the Wagner labor relations act, did the unions achieve even a partial constitutional status. The disparity in treatment between capital and labor is not so strange, however, when one remembers that judges are taken from lawyers who represent the business class and who bring their predilections with them to the High Bench. As Justice Samuel F. Miller said in an off-bench statement: "It is in vain to contend with judges who have been at the bar the advocates for forty years of railroad companies, and all the forms of associated capital, when they are called upon to decide cases where such interests are in contest. All their training, all their feelings are from the start in favor of those who need no such influence."[58]

Enough has been said to validate the third principle. The fourth requires only summary treatment. There can be little question that the Economic Constitution, illustrating many of the principles advocated by Alexander Hamilton permitted—perhaps commanded—massive public aid to private business. The United States has always been a Welfare State for those who needed it least—the rich. The federal government, now and in the past, may be likened to a great recumbent sow, with dozens of teats to each one of which some recipient of largesse from the national treasury couples. Billions of dollars are disbursed each year, in the form of grants, direct subsidies, or otherwise. (Even the Queen of England has received $68.00 for not producing anything on her plantation in Mississippi!)[59]

It has always been so. Matthew Josephson, in his classic *The Robber Barons*, asserted in 1934:

> This benevolent government handed over to its friends or to astute first comers, . . . all those treasures of coal and oil, of copper and gold and iron, the land grants, the terminal sites, the perpetual rights of way—an act of largesse which is still one of the wonders of history. To the new railroad enterprises in addition, great money subsidies totaling many hundreds of millions were given. The Tariff Act of 1864 was in itself a sheltering wall of subsidies; and to aid further the new heavy industries and manufactures, an Immigration Act allowing contract labor to be imported freely was quickly enacted; a national banking system was perfected. . . . Having conferred these vast

rights and controls, the ... government would preserve them ... so as to "curb the many who would do to the few as they would not have the few do to them."[60]

That close connection between government and private enterprise is not noted in constitutional law books, perhaps because it was never litigated. The largesse that Josephson discussed came from statutory action, by both Congress and state legislatures, and thus is not constitutional law in the eyes of most lawyers. It should be so considered, both because it is an integral part of the Economic Constitution and because it ramified to affect quite deeply and widely the organs of the Political Constitution.

Consider, in that regard, the regulation of business by the federal government. That began in 1887 with the formation of the Interstate Commerce Commission. Two points merit attention: First was the "capture" of the regulators by the purportedly regulated. Richard Olney, attorney general under President Cleveland, early made the point in some sage and prescient advice he gave to the president of a railroad who inquired about whether it would be advisable to try to get the Supreme Court to invalidate the ICC. Said Olney:

My impression would be that looking at the matter from a railroad point of view exclusively it would not be a wise thing. ... The Commission ... is, or can be made, of great use to the railroads, at the same time that supervision is almost entirely nominal. Further, the older such a commission gets to be, the more inclined it will be [to] take the business and railroad view of things. It thus becomes a sort of barrier between the railroad corporations and the people and a sort of protection against hasty and crude legislation hostile to railroad interests. ... The part of wisdom is not to destroy the Commission, but to utilize it.[61]

So the course of government regulation has gone. The agencies and commissions are more "clients" or "satellites" of the industries they are supposed to control than seekers of the public interest. The first point overlaps the second: business regulation in the twentieth century, far from being a consequence of the Populist and Granger movements, as the popular wisdom would have it, was mainly imposed to *help*, not hinder, business. The "progressive movement" in American history was captured by those against whom it was aimed. Corporate executives and their *apparatchik* lawyers saw in progressivism an opportunity to protect business through the *appearance*, but not the reality, of regulation. Competition, the myth to the contrary, was and is anathema to the men who control the corporations. They wanted to control competition, and succeeded. Gabriel Kolko has shown that increase in competition led to advocacy of regulation:

Competition was unacceptable to many key business and financial leaders, and the merger movement was to a large extent a reflection of voluntary, unsuccessful business efforts to bring irresistible trends under control. . . . As new competitors sprang up, and as economic power was diffused throughout an expanding nation, it became apparent to many important businessmen that only the national government could [control and stabilize] the economy. . . . Ironically, *contrary to the consensus of historians, it was not the existence of monopoly that caused the federal government to intervene in the economy, but the lack of it.*[62] (Emphasis added.)

The antiregulatory movement of the 1980s is largely motivated not to eliminate the ostensible controls on specific segments of American industry, but rather toward across-the-board regulations that hit all industries—such as the Consumer Products Safety Commission, the Environmental Protection Agency, and even the resurgent Federal Trade Commission. Unable to capture the agencies, the business community seeks to have them abolished or, at the very least, to have them manned by "regulators" friendly to business.

Those who wrote the Document of 1787 got the type of government they wished. Chief Justice John Marshall and colleagues saw to that. Congress, too, was the willing ally of that propertied class, a class that simply did not like democracy as such—as Hamilton said in the 1787 Convention:

All communities divide themselves into the few and the many. The first are the rich and the well born, the other the mass of the people. The voice of the people has been said to be the voice of God; and however generally this maxim has been quoted and believed, it is not true in fact. The people are turbulent and changing; they seldom judge or determine right. Give therefore to the first class a distinct, permanent share in government. They will check the unsteadiness of the second and as they cannot receive any benefit from a change, they therefore will ever maintain good government.[63]

The Document of 1787 did just that: It did not permit the propertyless majority to act in concert against the established social order.

"Socialism for the rich" has always characterized American government, but has seldom been controversial. Those Hamilton called "the rich and well born" have always been able to suckle at the teats of the recumbent sow that is the federal treasury. Only when "welfarism" is aimed at alleviating some of the distresses of the poor and disadvantaged do the programs excite controversy. That is so even though the social welfare programs are not at all income or wealth redistributive. The same small percentage of people control the same large amount of wealth today as was true in the past. True, more people have been able to increase their level of living during the post-World War II period, but that improvement is because of rising levels of productivity plus a realization that mass discontent can be distracted by welfare programs.

Finally, as Professor Jerold Auerbach has shown in his brilliant book *Unequal Justice*,[64] the American system of criminal law has been and is being used to control the poor and the disadvantaged. That area is yet another example of the fourth principle in operation: The organs of the Political Constitution dealing with administration of the criminal law for the most part protect those who are the beneficiaries of the Economic Constitution.

The meaning is clear: The United States has always been a class society, the myth to the contrary notwithstanding. That fact is the fifth principle of the Economic Constitution. Classes, to be sure, are not mandated by law, and the American ethos militates against them. But they exist as a derivation from the disproportionate wealth, protected by the State, between the few and the many. Again, little discussion is necessary; a moment's reflection and a little knowledge of history serve to validate the existence of a class system. Those who wrote the Constitution were aware of the stratified nature of American society and produced an instrument that helped to perpetuate it. It is of course true that some social mobility has always taken place and still does take place—but at a lesser rate. Some were able to pull themselves up by their bootstraps and become a part of the "rich." They may not, in Hamilton's terms, have been "well born," but being rich meant that their children were. The Horatio Alger stories were not all mythical.

Furthermore, a subtle legitimation process occurs by which the dominant class is able to assert that it is representative and advocate of all the people. The "governing class"[65] rules by identifying with the people—with the myths and legends of democracy and popular sovereignty. Every nation so conducts itself. The people at large are convinced, by some means—often, as Jacques Ellul has shown, by the use of propaganda[66]—that their interests and those of the ruling class are identical. As is noted below, it is one of the functions of the mass media to persuade the people to accept the American system as defined by the elite. Max Weber knew this, when he maintained that privileged groups have the ability "to have their social and economic positions 'legitimized.'"[67] He went on to say that "They wish to see their positions transformed from a purely factual power relation into a cosmos of acquired rights, and to know that they are thus sanctified."[68] The man of position and fortune is seldom satisfied with merely being fortunate. He knows that if his property is to be secure it must have legitimacy in society. The man of fortune

needs to know that he has a *right* to his good fortune. He wants to be convinced that he "deserves" it, and above all, that he deserves it in comparison with others. He wishes to be allowed the belief that the less fortunate also merely experience their due. Good fortune thus wants to be "legitimate" fortune.

Strata in solid possession of social honor and power usually tend to fashion their status-legend in such a way as to claim a special and intrinsic quality of their own, usually a quality of blood.[69]

A status-legend, as the term was used by Weber, is a myth that both soothes the consciences of the rich and serves to sanctify their dominance in a class-ridden and unequal society.

One way that status-legends are perpetrated and perpetuated is through the Basic Myth of the American legal system—the Rule of Law, impartially created and administered. That leads to the sixth principle of the Economic Constitution: that the law is distinctly not a neutral force in society.

We have already mentioned Holmes's insightful comment in 1873 about the nonneutrality of the law. His brief, though pregnant, statement has never been satisfactorily answered. The tough-minded Holmes perceived all participants in legal affairs struggling to win their self-interests. Although one may hope that compassion would temper self-interest, "all that can be expected from modern improvements is that legislation should easily and quickly, yet not too quickly, modify itself in accordance with the will of the de facto supreme power in the community." If Holmes was correct, as surely he was (and is), the liberal theory of the Rule of Law is thoroughly discredited. Under that theory, the assumption is that *general* rules, applied *impartially*, would produce effects that would benefit all of society. That assumption is the answer that legal theory (and American legal educators, when they thought about it) gave to the brutal question posed by Thrasymachus—that law represented the interests of the stronger. Professor Mark Tushnet has advanced the thesis that "Law in a class society [such as the United States] is one form of the incomplete hegemony of the ruling class."[70] In Holmes's words, law is "a means by which a body, having the power, puts burdens which are disagreeable to them on the shoulders of somebody else."[71]

It will not do to shrug off such comments and thus to proceed on age-old but faulty assumptions about the neutrality of law and the legal process. The hegemony of the ruling class is incomplete, because those with money and property must share some political power with other groups. But it is sufficiently complete for one to be able to say, without fear of valid contradiction, that the ultimate beneficiaries of the legal system are what Hamilton called the "rich and well born." When one analyzes any segment of the corpus of law, one readily finds that, certainly, the law in action—although perhaps not always the law in books—validates that proposition.

The seventh principle of the Economic Constitution has two overlapping facets. *First, the State intervenes when necessary to correct imperfections in the market economy; and second, institutions of the Economic Constitution, mainly corporations, can draw upon organs of the Political Constitution for assistance.* The consequence is a trend toward merger of the two Constitutions into one overarching whole (which we have previously labeled the Corporate State).

That State intervention in the economy is not only necessary but welcome is classically illustrated by the measures taken to combat the Great Depression. Despite a persistent myopia among those with wealth, President Franklin D. Roosevelt's New Deal was a means by which the system of corporate capitalism was preserved at minimum cost. The technique, controversial because the immediate beneficiaries were the poor and powerless, was to siphon off discontent by a series of programs aimed at alleviating the worst aspects of poverty. That the New Deal was a failure is now commonly conceded: Only the advent of World War II and its attendant war economy enabled the nation to pull itself out of the swamp of economic misery that many Americans suffered. (That war economy still exists.) The rhetoric of FDR's first two administrations spoke in terms of helping the common man; the reality of the New Deal was service to the corporate class. "The central dedication of the Franklin Roosevelt administration was to *business recovery* rather than to *social* reform."[72] An immense gap existed between the New Deal's public image and its actual accomplishments. It was not so much the dire misery of millions of Americans that motivated and brought government aid as the threat of political and social unrest. Barton J. Bernstein, speaking of "the conservative achievements of liberal reform," concluded:

The New Deal failed to solve the problem of depression, it failed to raise the impoverished, it failed to redistribute income, it failed to extend equality and generally countenanced racial discrimination and segregation. It failed generally to make business more responsible to the social welfare or to threaten business's pre-eminent political power. In this sense, the New Deal, despite shifts in tone and spirit from the earlier decade, was profoundly conservative and continuous with the 1920s.[73]

Only when war came and the United States began a permanent war economy has a form of economic prosperity been possible. After World War II, as we have noted, the United States entered into a period of its true "golden age" —a time when all things seemed possible and, indeed, many were, a time of economic abundance, and a time of enhancement of civil rights and liberties. (The connection between the Age of Abundance and furtherance of human rights has been little noted and never analyzed.) The Golden Age lasted until about 1970, and then things began to become unraveled.

Since the early 1970s, business once again has been openly seeking government aid. The present difficulties of the Chrysler Corporation (and other automobile firms) have led them to couple on to a teat of the recumbent sow that is the federal treasury or to get assistance against foreign competition.[74] No one should think that Chrysler is aberrational. Because of increasingly obvious errors of corporate management—and they are many—the market economy stutters along. Government is asked to correct mistakes that should not have been made in still another instance of "socialism for the rich," and thus we have an illustration of the seventh principle in operation.

The second aspect of that principle overlaps with the first. Those who control the dominant institutions of the Economic Constitution call upon organs of the Political Constitution for help. An example is the way in which the Army was used to quell labor disputes and other civil disorders in the nineteenth century that threatened the position of the corporate class. (That type of action was not limited to the last century; it lasts well into the present century and, indeed, up to the 1980s). Professor Jerry M. Cooper has concluded that military leaders tried to exploit civilian fears of a disorderly working class to further the Army's interests. They failed, but of much more importance is the fact that troops were used to police labor troubles. "Conflicts over the rights of property in contrast with the needs of individuals," Cooper stated, "inevitably . . . engendered social turmoil. The advocates of property and the new values of [corporate capitalism] . . . controlled the agencies of government and hence the institutions of social control. Police, the National Guard, and the Army were committed to maintaining existing power relationships in the name of law and order."[75] Cooper wrote about the nineteenth century, but he could have broadened his focus.

The Pullman strike of the 1890s provides illustration of how corporate capitalists were able to call upon both the courts and the executive for assistance. There, after federal judges had issued injunctions to prevent interference with the mails, interstate commerce, or railroads in federal receivership, President Grover Cleveland ordered the military to break the strike. They succeeded. In the process, the Supreme Court upheld, in the case of *In re Debs*,[76] the power to send troops into a labor-management conflict; in so doing, the Justices had to create law and thus became perilously close to becoming an arm of the business class.

Many other examples could be mentioned, but need not be. The conclusion is inescapable: Those with money and property had political power and were able to call upon federal agencies, including courts, when their position appeared to be threatened. The same pattern existed in international economic matters. Corporate managers have long been able to define the axiomatic in international economics. It is axiomatic, for example, that United States force (violence) be employed to help American business abroad, as witness this statement by a former Commander of the Marines, General Smedley D. Butler:

I spent thirty-three years and four months in active service as a member of our country's most agile military force—the Marine Corps. . . . And during that period I spent most of my time being a high-class muscle man for Big Business, for Wall Street, and for the bankers. In short, I was a racketeer for capitalism. . . . Thus I helped make Mexico and especially Tampico safe for American oil interests in 1914, I helped make Haiti and Cuba a decent place for the National City Bank boys to collect revenues in . . . . I helped purify Nicaragua for the international banking house of Brown Brothers in 1909-1912. I brought light to the Dominican Republic for American sugar interests in 1916. I helped make Honduras "right" for the American fruit companies in 1903. In China I helped see to it that Standard Oil went its way unmolested.[77]

I do not say that such use of public governmental power to aid business met widespread disapproval. Quite the contrary. The corporate class has been able to achieve general public acceptance and thus a measure of legitimacy.

The use of violence to aid corporations was all perfectly legal—yet another example of the nonneutral character of American law.

Control over the levers of political power, in both the Political and the Economic Constitutions, is helped by the eighth principle: *The mass media of communication are privately owned and are the principal instruments of propaganda in the United States.* To gain public acceptance, those with wealth and property must be able to control or influence the flow of communications to the people. "Not the gun but the word is the symbol of authority."[78] In many respects, Americans have government by persuasion, although it should always be remembered that behind the word is the gun (repression). The mass media in the United States—the three television networks, the major news magazines, the handful of important newspapers— all have similar functions—in essence, making a profit for their owners, helping to sell consumers goods through the medium of advertising, and being a principal means by which the people are socialized by a flow of news and opinion that is supportive of corporate capitalism and the "American way."[79] A number of other publications of course exist, but, generally, they have small circulations and thus little impact on public opinion. It is probably true that the combined readership of non-Establishment magazines such as *The Nation, The Progressive, Mother Jones, Inquiry,* and *Libertarian Review,* even when added to the circulations of "underground" newspapers, is far less than that of only one news magazine: *Time.* Television is 100 percent Establishment oriented. Furthermore, despite the seemingly absolute language of the First Amendment, publications considered to be inimical to the State, and those who control it, have been and are suppressed—by one means or another.[80]

The result is a virtual monopoly on *effective* or *influential* expression in the United States, held by those who are themselves part of the Establishment and thus oriented toward preservation of the system of corporate capitalism. Far from being in an adversarial relationship with government, the media are in fact close allies—so much so that they often appear only too willing to publish or speak the government line without question. Two examples suffice: The media repeated without analysis statements issued by the executive branch in 1981 with regard to the situation in El Salvador; they accepted the line that the guerrilla forces were part of a Communist conspiracy. The same occurred in Iran, both before and after the fall of the Shah, and particularly during and after the long period when the hostages were held captive.

Furthermore, there is very little—almost no—serious criticism of the dominant institutions of the Economic Constitution (the corporations) by the mass media. What criticism there is, as when some firms were caught dumping chemical wastes and endangering lives, is impliedly aberrational. Nothing systemic is attempted. The media seem to be in the position of the fabled monkeys—"see no evil, hear no evil, speak no evil"—unless and until some specific dereliction crops up. They react, and seldom seek; being members of the Establishment themselves, media personnel share the assumptions, the ethos, the expectations and the aspirations of the dominant group in society. Finally, those who control and operate the mass media often engage in a self-imposed system of self-censorship, both about governmental activities (notoriously, those said to involve national security) and about individual members of the moneyed and propertied class. As Clifton Daniel once said, when he was chief of the Washington bureau of the *New York Times*, one would be naive to believe that self-censorship did not occur.[81] Except in times of all-out declared wars, the media barons fight governmental censorship—as in the Pentagon Papers case (1971)[82]—but are not loth to censor themselves when they, in their own discretion, consider it desirable. Nor do they support a non-Establishment periodical when it incurs the government's wrath; witness, for example, the reaction of the *Washington Post* when *The Progressive* was enjoined by court order from publishing an article on the alleged secret of the H-bomb.

The eighth principle leads to the ninth: *The institutions of the Economic Constitution operate with a high degree of secrecy*. The United States is the "bureaucratic state," with those bureaucracies being both public and private. "Every bureaucracy," Max Weber observed, "seeks to increase the superiority of the professionally informed by keeping their knowledge and intentions secret."[83] Weber wrote about public government, but his comments (made circa 1920) are applicable as well to the private governments of the nation. Perhaps more so: there is no Freedom of Information Act for corporations. In the United States and elsewhere there is a tendency to engage in what Professor Christian Bay has called "the democratic make-believe,"[84] by which he meant that every citizen presumably has a chance to influence public policy, and elections determine the will and mandate of the people. That "make-believe" makes enacted laws legitimate and entitled to obedience in a constitutional democracy. The additional assumption is that the citizenry can and will hold the feet of governmental officers to the fire of public opinion for what they do and can hold them accountable for any derelictions. Secrecy, however, often prevents that type of accountability from operating. That statement is true for public government, but much more so for the private governments of the Economic Constitution. Where secrecy reigns, government officials are in a position to rule at virtually their own discretion. Far less is known about the institutions of the Economic Constitution than about those of the Political Constitution.[85]

The tenth principle is: *the institutions of the Economic Constitution are not subject to the limitations of those of the Political Constitution, particularly due process of law and equal protection of the laws*. In other words, the Economic Constitution is one of powers rather than of limitations.

Except as occasionally, but not often, limited by statute or by collective bargaining agreements, managers of corporate capitalism can and do act arbitrarily, in both the due process and equal protection senses; they are not accountable to anyone save themselves for their actions.[86] Boards of directors and top managers are self-appointed oligarchs who answer only to themselves, and not in another place, for their actions. In theory, the market is supposed to control corporate behavior; but the market, while it does exist, is less a constraint than an arena for the exercise of power. No Bill of Rights and no Fourteenth Amendment are applicable to corporations. Power is exercised without important externally imposed *social* controls. Even the crimes of corporations and corporate managers are dealt with as lightly as the peccadilloes of a chicken thief.[87]

Two reasons make immunity from constitutional restraints possible: First, the Supreme Court with remarkable consistency has refused to acknowledge the governing power of the "private" sector's institutions. In technical terms, corporations and other social groups do not fall within the ambit of the concept of state (or governmental) action.[88] The formal Constitution runs against governments only, and the Justices have been almost entirely blind to the governing power of economic entities. John P. Davis could say in 1897 that Americans are "governed more by corporations than by the state" and that corporations "are the major part of the mechanism of government under which they live,"[89] but that knowledge, which should be obvious to anyone who wishes to see, has not penetrated the Temple on the Hill. One corporation—AT&T—has assets of well over $100 billion, which dwarfs those of most of the nation-States of the world, and employs almost one million people. To the Supreme Court, however, it is a person, a constitutional person, and therefore is not accountable to constitutional norms.

The second reason is a variation on the theme previously discussed that law is not, and indeed cannot be, a neutral force, impartially applied. "Equality before the law," Professor Hale maintained, "is not consistent with unequal property rights."[90] Hale spelled that out at greater length:

The premise of legal equality . . . [is] in fact fallacious, for legal rights, privileges and duties depend on property rights and these depend on the law. Each person has a legal duty not to infringe any other person's property rights, a privilege to use what he himself owns and a right to exclude everyone else therefrom except on his own terms. These statements, however, are empty abstractions until it is specified to what particular objects the property rights of each attach; when it is so specified the specious equality disappears. . . . The respective legal rights of A and B are equal only in the most formal and empty sense. . . . The ultimate economic position of each person is not so rigidly predetermined at birth as in the feudal system, but the law still imposes vastly unequal handicaps.[91]

Inequality in the economic sphere is largely taken for granted; it is not only protected by law enunciated in the political domain, it also has become part of the ideology of Americanism. The formal Constitution protects established rights; and the most important of those are the "vested rights" of property. Writing in 1914, Professor Edward S. Corwin said that the basic doctrine of the Constitution was vested rights;[92] that observation is still accurate.

The eleventh principle of the Economic Constitution is that *it is a profound-*

ly undemocratic set of institutions and practices. However the word democracy is defined, itself far from an easy task,[93] by no criterion are corporations and other economic entities democratic. They are authoritarian, exemplifying Michels's "iron law of oligarchy."[94] The only members of the corporate community who can vote are the stockholders; to the extent that Berle and Means are correct, as surely they are for most giant firms, that vote for the mass of stockholders is meaningless.[95] In theory, they own the corporation; in fact, they do not control it. The corporation is a unit of a system of neofeudalism.

The twelfth principle is that of *citizenship*. Two points merit comment: First is the way in which corporations, the giants particularly, appear to owe allegiance to no nation-State. Second is the fact that the allegiance of corporate managers runs more to the enterprise than to the nation-State. The identifications and loyalties—the bundle of rights and duties subsumed under the concept of citizenship—attach to the firm. Corporate managers, and others, operate under a theory of *raison de groupe*, similar to the way that officers of the Political Constitution operate under a theory of *raison d'état*.[96] It is the ends of the company that are important, and corporate managers seem willing to take almost any action to further those goals, no matter how repellent those actions might be in their private capacity as citizens of nation-States. They act on pure Machiavellian principles. The *summum bonum* is the welfare of the enterprise—even, at notable times, over the welfare of the nation-State.

The thirteenth, and final, principle of the Economic Constitution is that *its governing institutions are markedly similar to those of the Political Constitution*. The corporation is a political order, both in its internal operations and in its relationship with other entities in the economic sphere and with public government.[97] Corporations should be studied as political institutions as well as commercial or economic enterprises.

Consider, for example, the widespread use of private judiciaries. Labor arbitration is a clear illustration; so, too, is the employment of arbitrators in international economic affairs. Very little concerning transnational corporations ever gets to court; most disputes are settled by private courts. Consider, too, the increasing use of private police forces—security forces—that might be likened to private armies. There is, in addition, frequent use of intelligence forces, particularly in the area of industrial espionage (and counterespionage).

Finally, the institutions of the Economic Constitution have their own constitutions, either in the corporate charter or, much more so, in the collective bargaining agreement with the labor union. That, too, helps to make them political orders.

IV.

It is no longer possible to think meaningfully of American constitutionalism as being solely concerned with the organs of the Political Constitution. There is more to constitutionalism than the organization and operation of formal political power and limitations on it. Another dimension is necessary: the Economic Constitution, whose institutions both cooperate with those of the public sector and also dominate it. Furthermore, they have as profound, and probably more profound, an impact on the way that people order their affairs than does public government itself. There is nothing in the Document of 1787, or its amendments, that expressly gives such awesome powers to the owners of capital. At most, perhaps, it might be implied from the Ninth Amendment: "The enumeration in the Constitution, of certain rights, shall not be construed to deny or disparage others retained by the people." No one, certainly not the Supreme Court, knows the meaning of that delphic sentence. It is in large part a dead letter. Nevertheless, if the argument of this chapter is accepted, may it not then be said that its fundamental meaning is derived from John Locke: "the preservation of property" and thus the protection of the economic and political power attendant to ownership of property?

During the sixteenth century, John P. Davis asserted, a great change took place that has had great influence on the way that corporations are perceived.

The standpoint from which all institutions were viewed was shifted from society as a whole to the individual. Social forces were conceived as moving from below and not from above. The destruction of tradition and the elevation of reason was one phase of the change. To be sure, the view was not to find full expression in philosophy until the eighteenth century, but the Reformation was a practical application of it. Private contract largely superseded status in the determination of social relations. Corporations were viewed not so much as *divisions of society* as *associations of individuals.* They were now enlarged individuals, not reduced societies.[98]

The task of constitutional law today, and thus of the Supreme Court, is to recognize in formal constitutional theory that corporations, the dominant institution of the American Economic Constitution, are more divisions of society than associations of individuals. Only when that is done will the United States be able to move toward becoming democratic in both theory and practice—as democratic, that is, as any government can be in an uncertain world.

10
Constitutional Fetishism

I.

Americans have a peculiar habit: They view certain social situations, such as relative human freedom, and attribute them to provisions of the formal Constitution of 1787. They thus make a fetish out of the fundamental law, looking to it for surcease from the woes that befall them, and often calling upon the shades of those who wrote it for answers to questions that never entered those men's minds. The Document is believed to have some sort of magical power.

It is more: It is a religious instrument and should be considered as such. No one can understand the American Constitution unless it is perceived to be more than a mere lawyers's document or a means of organizing and allocating political power. That "more" is the Constitution as a part of America's civil religion. This chapter discusses the Document as a sacred text and the Supreme Court as a holy institution in our civil religion. It is necessarily brief, more suggestive than exhaustive.

What, first, is a *civil* religion?[1] Most people think in terms of only one generic type of religion—the formal or the organized. It is identified with churches, temples, synagogues, missionary movements, sects, revivals, and the like. When constitutional lawyers, and others, speak about the separation of church and State, mandated by the First Amendment, it is this type that is the focus of attention. That wall of separation, it should be noted, has never been as high or as impregnable as some think. Even formal, organized religion has ties with the State and with government. State and religion, but not State and church, are closely connected.

The other type, the civil religion, travels under a number of banners—the "democratic faith," the "American way," the "American creed." There actually exists, "alongside of and rather clearly differentiated from the churches, an elaborate and well-institutionalized civil religion in America."[2] In many respects, the myth of the Rule of Law is an integral part of the American civil religion. "Every functioning society," Robin Williams maintained, "has, to an important degree, a common religion. The possession of a common set of ideas, ideals, rituals, and symbols can supply an overarching sense of unity even in a society otherwise riddled with conflict."[3] America's civil religion has several aspects. It is the creed of democracy that exalts and celebrates national unity. A classic illustration came in early 1981 when the fifty-two American hostages in Iran were released; seemingly joyous and spontaneous public outpourings met their return to the United States. (How spontaneous they were is somewhat doubtful, for certainly the mass media contributed greatly to the reception the fifty-two people received.) Our civil religion, however, has more than a political side; it is also economic and social and spiritual.

II.

In times such as the present, when governmental institutions are in disarray, and authority, wherever located, is under challenge, people search for theories and principles and guides. They look to the past in a futile attempt to receive wisdom to help navigate the shoals that lie dead ahead. Questions about economic doctrines are popularly debated, although little understood even by economists. Everyone is uncertain, and everyone seemingly is a reformer or social planner, with a pet scheme or panacea to lead Americans out of the wilderness of the climacteric of humankind. Exhibiting "the arrogance of humanism,"[4] they believe that human problems, no matter how intractable they appear, are both knowable and solvable.

Law and economics are dragged out of technical books and journals, which few read and even fewer heed, to appear in newspapers and on television. Everyone—and no one—is an expert. The received wisdom of the past, in politics and economics and law, is no longer adequate to manifest needs. Novel pressures on ancient institutions produce unbearable strains. Bitterness and intolerance multiply because matters long taken for granted are questioned or, even worse, repudiated. An increasingly frantic search for answers, for solutions, to what ever more seem to be insoluble problems keeps public debate at a cacophonous level.

Some, mainly the unthinking, retreat into religious fundamentalism, seeking in the faith of their fathers answers to questions their fathers never asked and never were asked. Others, knowing the futility of repairing to the dogmas of formal religion, turn to the technocrats—the scientists, natural and behavioral, and technologists—as the new gurus who can, by creating novel devices and vouchsafing new doctrines, resolve the inequities and iniquities of a society that is badly out of kilter. Charles Dickens's famous character in *David Copperfield*, Mr. Micawber, classically exemplified that frame of mind: Mr. Micawber went blithely around, in the midst of appalling conditions, believing that something was sure to turn up to take care of those problems. That he had no evidence for such a belief did not deter him. Nor does it deter today's Micawbers—their number is legion—who want to believe and in wanting do believe that technological "fixes" are the key to the kingdom of heaven on earth.[5] Men and women in white gowns in laboratories have been substituted for men in black robes in pulpits. Still others resolutely refuse to acknowledge that a problem exists. They may realize it, but that does not stop them. Burying their heads in the sands of willful ignorance and blindness, they unwaveringly pursue hedonistic goals. They have but one aim: a grasping materialism, a desire to obtain in personal economic well-being protection from the furies that rage without. Theories and principles are not for them, nor is technology except as a means of personal aggrandizement. "I'm all right, Jack, just let me alone," is their motto.

Those mind-sets, seemingly different, complement and buttress each other. Taken together, they constitute an isosceles triangle of social behavior, each side of which is important to the others, and no side of which could long exist alone. Every American outwardly believes in at least one, and many believe in all three, finding no inconsistency in their beliefs. Each mind-set finds in the Constitution symbols of stability and ancient wisdom and receives reassurance. The hoary Document, the principles stated in *The Federalist Papers*, letters and papers of the never-defined group called the Founding Fathers, and even Washington's farewell address are considered to be sources of special insight and knowledge when cures for today's ills are sought. The methods of physicians in 1787 are no longer studied or followed. But politics and law and economics still look mainly to the past. Their practitioners worship their ancestors. Whatever was (at some unnamed time in the past) is right—and thus to be followed. So the pathetic belief goes.

Every tribe has its myths and fetishes. The United States is not immune. Every tribe, also, adheres to something believed to possess supernatural powers, as a means of trying to control hostile forces in a limitless and unknown universe. Writing almost a half-century ago, Max Lerner said it well:

Men always need something on which to fix their emotions, whether positively in the form of adoration or deification, or negatively in the form of a tabu. Like every people, the American people have wanted some anchorage, some link with the invariant.

"Change and decay in all around I see, Oh, Thou, who changest not, abide with me."

And the Rock of Ages has been as essential in the politics of America as in its religion. In fact the very habits of mind begotten by an authoritarian Bible and a religion of submission have been carried over to an authoritarian Constitution and a philosophy of submission to a "higher law"; and a country like America, in which its early tradition had prohibited a state church, ends by getting a state church after all, although in secular form.[6]

Perhaps some day a scholar will write the complete religious history of America. If so, he will have to pay attention to at least three elements: that of formal churchgoing religion, plus the many sects and hell-and-damnation revivalists; that of worship of technology and the gods of economic enterprise (which help to bind together the Economic Constitution); and the reverence for the Constitution and the Supreme Court. The three are not autonomous; they intersect and overlap, complementing and buttressing each other. In the first, some Americans profess formal religion but in fact are imbued with a rather ferocious religiosity, with the affectation of Christian or Judaic doctrines, but without the substance. The true religions of America are civil or secular. In technology and business enterprise Americans have illustrated the deepest strivings of their nature and character—the quest of what William James called "the bitch-goddess Success." In the Constitution and the Court they have epitomized their expectations and fears for society—in ideal form, their aspirations for a good life for all. America, thus, in G. K. Chesterton's words, "is a nation with the soul of a church."[7]

Americans are a nation of Constitution worshippers. They also revere, albeit unevenly, its most authoritative interpreter—the Supreme Court. The nine Justices have become the High Priests of America's civil religion. The Temple on the Hill is the nearest thing to a latter-day Temple of Apollo—the abode of the Oracle at Delphi—that can be found in the modern world. The priests (the Justices), when asked—and occasionally without being asked in so many words—consult the ancient Document (the Constitution) and deliver portentous pronouncements on public policy. These statements are called law, and since they involve constitutional interpretation, that law is part of what often is called "the fundamental law." It is fundamental because of the myth of the perfect Constitution. The Document of 1787 was ratified at a time of ascending economic prosperity. In a classic example of *post hoc, ergo propter hoc* reasoning, that wave of relative affluence was translated into exultation over the tradition of a perfect Constitution. (In logic, *post hoc* reasoning is the fallacy of thinking that something which follows something else must be its result, in a type of cause-and-effect relationship.)

Both of the first political parties, the Federalists (who were followers of Hamilton) and the Anti-Federalists (who were Jeffersonians), "showed an amazing unanimity in pointing out the perfections of the Constitution, they delighted in honoring it, and they measured their distance from each other by reciprocal charges of violating it and departing from its spirit. Their divergences were those of interpretation."[8] Even though it was far from a revolutionary instrument, its symbolic power was recognized by many people. Even Thomas Paine, writing in 1776, saw the power that lay in a written charter for inculcating the loyalty of the masses to a new regime. Paine laid the groundwork for constitution worship in *Common Sense* (1776): "Let a day be solemnly set apart for proclaiming the charter; let it be brought forth placed on the divine law, the word of God; let a crown be placed thereon, by which the world may know that so far we approve monarchy that in America the law is King."[9] Paine, a brilliant propagandist, well knew that tying a "charter" in with "the divine law, the word of God," would make it much more palatable to people. Paine, later to be called a "filthy little atheist" by Theodore Roosevelt, well knew the irrational power of religious symbols. Almost two centuries after Paine wrote, Reed Benson, a prominent Mormon, was quoted as saying: "It's part of my religious training that the Constitution is an inspired document, that the time will come when it will hang by a thread and it will be our task to save it. . . .We believe that the Lord helped raise up the Founding Fathers to establish the Constitution so there could be the opportunity for religious freedom."[10] An interesting sentiment, showing the persistence of Constitution worship. The Document is both a secular and a theological instrument. As a secular instrument, it is the basic document of the American civil religion.

Torn between reason—the use of rational criticism—and a deep, instinctive belief in hidden, occult powers, Americans look upon the Supreme Court much as the Greeks perceived their oracles. "Oracles helped mankind to find their way on this earth in the face of an unknown and threatening future. The fact that Socrates used to advise his disciples to consult the Pythia [the Oracle at Delphi] in no way detracts from his wisdom. After all, was it not she who proclaimed him the wisest of all men? In this at least she was not mistaken."[11] As with the ancient Greeks, so with modern-day Americans, who ever-increasingly consider the Supreme Court—judges in general—to have answers to some of the most troublous problems of the day. Those answers, quite often, are forthcoming after the Justices consult the Document, which in the rhetoric at least is vested with almost supernatural significance. Surely, it is one way to explain the present explosion in litigation to maintain that Americans look to judges to help them improve their lot ("find their way") when they are faced, as they are, with "an unknown and threatening future." More and more people resort to the Constitution, and thus to judges, when other institutions are unavailing. There is the glimmer of a larger significance here: The Age of Rationalism—the resort to reason as the way to cure human ills—is declining. People want to believe, and in wanting do believe, that there is a force larger than the ordinary human intellect. Whether or not that belief is valid is not the point.

Max Lerner showed in 1937 that the Supreme Court enjoys the nearest thing to a divine right to rule.[12] He attributed this to four factors. First, the Justices sit on a "supreme" court and thus are presumed to be of higher stature than ordinary people or other judges. Second, they are appointed, not elected, and do not have to face the electorate periodically; they *appear* to be above politics and the sweaty mob. Third, the Court has had a great judicial tradition. Some of the Justices "have actually been men of enormous ability; the fact that their ability has not been conspicuously in the direction of detachment is not generally known; what comes down to us is the almost Periclean devotion to their public trust shown by men like Marshall, Taney and Holmes."[13] Finally, the timeless nature of the Constitution, which is considered to be a perfect instrument, is transmuted to the Justices who, in construing it, assert that theirs is the utmost authority. "We are not final because we are infallible." Justice Robert H. Jackson observed in 1953, "but

we are infallible only because we are final."[14] If the Constitution is perfect—
the ultimate wisdom in government—it follows that the Justices must reach
their decisions not as do ordinary men, but by some mysterious processes—
the application of Sovereign Reason. "The judges become, thus, not ordinary
men, subject to ordinary passions, but 'discoverers' of final truth, priests in the
service of a godhead."[15] It is this fact, which even politicians in Congress ever
increasingly seem to acknowledge, that makes the idea of the Justices as
modern oracles so possible. They are, despite the belief to the contrary,
largely in charge of their own agenda and thus are more than passive recep-
tacles of others's demands; they can choose which public-policy issues to
decide from among the 4500 cases presented to them each term; those cases
cover, or could be construed to cover, the entire gamut of public concern.
The Supreme Court, as Michael Walzer has said, together with other federal
courts, "have been the dominant agency for social change in the United
States" during the past three decades, "far outdistancing in both zeal and
effectiveness the Congress, the parties, the unions, interest groups of all
kinds."[16] Walzer does not like this development, but his general point has a
great deal of validity.

The myth of the perfect Constitution could not exist without the two myths
of patriotism: that of unique national origin and that of unique national
destiny. Americans take great pride in their beginnings—in the Declaration of
Independence and the Revolution—and the Document that emerged out of
the fire of controversy. Many appear to think in terms of a "democratic"
revolution and a revolutionary democracy, things at odds with what actually
occurred in the thirteen colonies in the last quarter of the eighteenth century
and equally at odds with what has since taken place. Neither revolution nor
little more than innocuous dissent are tolerated under the scheme of the
formal Document. Heretics are punished under the American civil religion,
not unlike the way they are under formal, organized religion. The State, to be
sure, can invoke the ultimate sanction—capital punishment—something that
churches no longer do; nor can churches imprison. But churches can and do
banish from the sacred congregation—they can excommunicate—which in
psychological terms may be an even more stringent sanction.

Much like Moses coming down from Mt. Sinai with the Tablets (and Com-
mandments), so those who wrote the Constitution are considered to have
produced a sacred document. Emotion and faith, deep seated and essentially
irrational, characterized both those who early on pointed out the purported
perfections of the Constitution and delighted in honoring it; some who
followed saw in that Document "the Ark of the Covenant of our Fathers."
Two centuries later that symbol of national unity is celebrated, even worshipped, first in the bicentennial ceremonies of 1976 and then in various ways
as 1987 approaches—the 200th anniversary of the Convention that
produced it. A few thousand words written on parchment still command not

only admiration but reverence. Lerner has made the point in these pregnant words:

The American people had conquered a domain from its natives, wrested the sover-eignty over it from the greatest power in Europe, fought their way to liberty. They wanted a visible mark of their accomplishment: *ecce signum*. And they wanted it the more strongly as they began to suspect that in the process of consolidating their regime they had lost sight of their original impulsions and the goals they had dreamt of. What they did, to still their doubts, was what *every* man does when troubled about his failure to realize his youthful dreams: they sought a way by which their revolutionary ideals could be worshipped without being followed. They found their peace in the safe haven of the Constitution. Here was the document into which the Founding Fathers had poured their wisdom as into a vessel; the Fathers themselves grew ever larger in stature as they receded from view; the era in which they lived and fought became a golden age; in that age there had been a fresh dawn for the world, and its men were giants against the sky; what they had fought for was abstracted from its living context and became a set of "principles," eternally true and universally applicable. When the Americans began seeing the revolutionary heroes in the hazy light of semi-divinity and began getting them associated or confused with the framers of the Constitution, the work of consolidating the new government was assured. The Golden Age had become a political instrument.[17]

There is an important lesson about human attitudes and behavior here. Some mental, emotional, psychological crutch is needed by people to help stave off the furies of an unknown and unknowable universe. Americans celebrate their revolution, although the Constitution as written was far from a revolutionary document, just as they celebrate their independence. William Maclay noted in acerbic terms in 1791: "It has been usual with declamatory gentle-men, in their praises of the present government, ... to paint the state of the country under the old Congress [the Articles of Confederation] as if neither wood grew nor water ran in America before the happy adoption of the new Constitution."[18] Maclay was of course correct, but was not to prevail. The Constitution served as a symbolic nexus between the revolutionary fervor of the 1770s and the new government—the new *nationalist* government.

"What we have, then, from the earliest years of the republic is a collection of beliefs, symbols, and rituals with respect to sacred things and institution-alized in a collectivity. This religion—there seems to be no other words for it—while not antithetical to, and indeed sharing much in common with, Chris-tianity, was neither sectarian nor in any specific sense Christian."[19] It would be foolish to try to assign relative weights of importance to America's professed formal religions vis-à-vis its civil religion, if for no other reason than that the two closely interact. "We are a religious people," Justice William O. Douglas asserted in 1952, "whose institutions presuppose a supreme being"[20]—thus neatly merging the two types of religion. What can be said is that constitutionalism in the United States is certainly analogous to, and overlaps with, formal religion. As such, it is an attempt by admittedly fallible humans to attain coherency in a chaotic world and an effort to set forth a number of beliefs capable of organizing human behavior. That it, now and in the past, falls short of the idealized goals merely illustrates, once again, that man's aim exceeds his grasp. ("Or what's a heaven for?") In an uncertain world, characterized by extremely rapid social change, there is little other than the dogmas of formal religion to hang on to—save, the Document and the Court, the symbols and the reality of America's civil religion.

III.

A religion—any religion—requires not only a legend (written or unwritten) but an authoritative interpreter, a spokesman of The Word. That function, as has been shown, has been taken over by the Supreme Court. Just as in the Roman Catholic church there is recognition of papal supremacy and, in some circumstances, infallibility, so, too, with the Constitution: "the United States Supreme Court has been happy . . . to reward itself with the title of 'ultimate interpreter of the Constitution,'"[21] with some type of special insight into the meaning of the cryptic language of the Document. That position, taken for granted today, is startling when considered anew; it derives from the facts that the Constitution is considered to be law and that judges are the oracles of the law. As Irving Brant wrote in *The Bill of Rights*, "the written Constitution stands like a tablet on Mt. Sinai, reading 'This is the law.' The problem is to keep the law in the custody of prophets who know how to read the language of liberty."[22] (That assessment is too narrow a view of "the problem," which is to further the ends of human dignity as the ecological trap closes.)

The Supreme Court is a papal-like institution, by its own assertion and by widespread, albeit incomplete, acquiescence. Leo Pfeffer said it well, although not quite correctly:

Under our system the ultimate responsibility for interpreting the Constitution rests with the Supreme Court. Those who disagree with a particular decision can resort to constitutional amendment to overrule it, and that has been done more than once in our history. What they may not do is to disregard the judgments of the Court and proceed as if they had never been handed down or, indeed, as if the Court had reversed itself. When such a path is followed by Congress, it is particularly unfortunate, for each of its members does take an oath to support the Constitution as interpreted by the Supreme Court. If Congress does not follow the Constitution, how can we expect the people to respect and obey it.[23]

Pfeffer's account is faulty on a couple of scores. First, as we have shown, responsibility for interpreting the Constitution, and thus effecting constitutional change, rests at times in the President and even in Congress (and under the Economic Constitution, with the officers of the private governments of the nation). True, the Court asserts that it is the true voice of the Constitution, but in many respects that is more assertion than fact. Second, members of Congress do not swear to uphold the Constitution "as interpreted by the Supreme Court"; their oath is to uphold "the" Constitution—quite a different thing. Finally, Pfeffer's papalist understanding of "our system" is certainly not the only good-faith understanding that an American citizen might make.

Even so, by no means is it clear that Pfeffer is wrong in his general view. The Justices have asserted, and prevailed in that assertion, that theirs is the power to say what the law—the Constitution—is. Learned scholars may not like it, and indeed many do not, but there seems to be no escape from the proposition that "disobedience of the Supreme Court or rejection of its views regarding the Constitution is equivalent to repudiation of the Constitution itself."[24] That proposition, to some—for example, Professors Sanford Levinson and John Hart Ely[25]—is a dubious theory of constitutional construction. But what seems dubious to such commentators is far from so in the minds of most people, including most lawyers and government officers.

The papalist conception of the Supreme Court prevails. Something akin to a divine right of judges has become part of the American ethos. Locating when necessary a "higher law" at once behind and embedded in the Constitution, the Justices have taken over the authority of the church to "grant indulgences" to public officers and, on occasion, to ordinary citizens. The fetishism of the Constitution is a principal segment of that divine right to judge and, in judging, to rule—not always, to be sure, but often enough to make the Supreme Court a highly visible and important instrument of governance.

This "right" has, and will continue to have, enormous political consequences. Recall, again: "Behind the words of the constitutional provisions," Chief Justice Charles Evans Hughes said in 1943, "are postulates which limit and control."[26] Those postulates are presumably best perceived by judges—by their own assertion—and there is no widespread outcry against that bold and bald grasp for power. The public dissent that has surfaced in recent years is over specific decisions, such as school busing and school prayers and abortion, rather than over the power of the courts—the Supreme Court—as an institution. Rather than general dissent over judicial power, there seems to be a wish, even a hunger, for it. That desire, perhaps, lends credence to the Grand Inquisitor's realistic view of humanity—that people long for miracle, mystery, and authority[27] and are willing to forgo the uncertainties and perils of freedom to attain them. If that view is in any degree accurate, as I think it is, the way seems clear for the Justices to undertake an even greater role in the future.

That role will encompass the Court as a latter-day version of the Council of Revision, rejected in the 1787 convention, with one important difference: Whereas the council that was considered but not adopted in 1787 would have had a veto over proposed public policies, the Court today is edging toward being able, in practical effect, to initiate action on its own. That is so, because, as has been mentioned, the large number of cases annually filed at the Court enables the Justices to pick and choose from among them; since almost every policy issue of any consequence may be found among those 4,500 cases, the Court can set its own agenda. True, that the Justices cannot, on their own volition, reach out and take on a given issue; someone—individual or group—must approach it with an inquiry before the Court can give judgment. Once accepted, a case can, however, take on a life of its own: The Justices can (at times, do) move beyond the specific facts of the litigants or the litigation before them, so as to promulgate norms of general applicability.

That ability means that a wholly new dimension of "judicial review" has come into being. "Review" by its very nature suggests a negative, after-the-fact action, with the Court scrutinizing past political actions for their congruence, or lack of it, with the Constitution. The new posture is more affirmative, with legislative norms looking to the future being stated. It is no exaggeration to say that the modern Supreme Court is America's version of Plato's "philosopher-rulers." To be sure, such a posture is fraught with complex problems. But the task of governance has never been easy, and it is even more difficult in a nation that has not only planetary interests but interests that extend far out into space, a nation that cannot and will not escape being an important part of the family of nations in a tightly knit world.

The United States today is on the verge of a profound social transformation. It faces problems of great complexity, for which there are few precedents of any use in guiding policy. To what extent, if at all, can the Supreme Court help in effecting the transition to an entirely different society? Can the ideals of constitutionalism be retained as the ecological trap closes? It is this fundamental question that is discussed in Part IV—how, that is, can the American people get there from here, the "here" being the ecological (and other) crises and the "there" being a humane and ordered society that has human dignity for all as its central goal.

Part IV

THE SUPREME COURT AND THE POLITICAL FUTURE: TOWARD MORE JUDICIAL ACTIVISM

Whether by force of circumstance or deliberate design, we have married legislation with adjudication and look for statesmanship in our courts.
—Woodrow Wilson

The teleological conception of his function must be ever in the judge's mind.
—Benjamin Nathan Cardozo

"The need for judicial action is strongest in the areas of the law where political processes prove inadequate, not from lack of legislative power but because the problem is neglected by politicians." If the legislatures continue to neglect their constitutional responsibilities, we can only hope the [Supreme] Court will do the best it can to fill the gap.
—J. Skelly Wright
(quoting Archibald Cox)

The powers of the [Supreme] Court are a vital and altogether legitimate part of the American Constitution. They should be used positively and affirmatively to help improve the public law of a free society capable of fulfilling the democratic dream of its Constitution in the turbulent second half of the twentieth century.
—Eugene V. Rostow

11
The System in Flux:
The Supreme Court as a
Council of Elders

I.

There are no final answers, no ultimate truths, in problems of governance. So it is with the Supreme Court: Its role and function are constantly being reexamined and reappraised in the light of the social conditions of different eras. After almost two centuries of activity, there is still no settled, widely accepted, conception of what the Justices *should* do as distinguished from what they actually *do*. The reason for this is that the Court, as an instrument of politics, is part of a continuously shifting equilibrium that is the American social order. It is always in motion; therefore, something akin to Werner Heisenberg's "uncertainty principle" in physics can validly be applied to it. Finality, as Disraeli said, "is not the language of politics."[1]

To construct an abstract utopia is relatively easy. Many have done it. Much more difficult—in fact, difficult beyond measure—are feasible prescriptions of how to get there from here; the "here" is the present "time of troubles," the climacteric, in which humankind finds itself, and the "there" is a better, more humane, sustainable world society. Again, no easy answers exist, and none are proposed here. Our focus is much narrower. This chapter draws together the several threads adumbrated before and suggests a role that the Supreme Court, if properly constituted, might undertake to help Americans grapple with the complex problems now facing them and the even more complicated problems sure to come in the future.

Chapter 11, then, is normative. It develops an aspect of what *should be* in the context of what *can be*. My theme is this: The Supreme Court—the judges generally—should be even more activist than they are at present. The time has come not only for candid acknowledgment of "truth in judging"[2]— the view that Supreme Court Justices make up the law as they go along, in accordance with their personal predilections—but for even more intervention by the judiciary into socioeconomic matters. As has been previously argued, judges should not only be negative naysayers, substituting their judgment for the avowedly political branches of government (which is the orthodox definition of activism), but at other times should tell politicians, and thus the American people, what they *should* or *must* do if constitutionalism is to survive. This will require, at the minimum, a different type of person named to the bench and a willingness on the part of judges routinely to immerse themselves in the travail of society. It will also necessitate a reexamination and improvement of the adversary system as a means of making decisions on constitutional questions—and thus of making public policy (law).

I am aware that a call for an even greater normative role for courts to shoulder will not sit well with many people, both those on the "right" who bemoan what they already perceive to be "government by judiciary" or an "imperial judiciary" and those on the "left" like Michael Walzer who maintain:

Among many liberals and leftists, the deepest worry generated by [President] Reagan's victory is the thought of the Supreme Court Justices he is likely to appoint. That seems to me to be a misplaced worry, but it does reflect the enormous importance the Court has come to have in our political process and the generally progressive role it has played since the 1950s. For three decades now, the federal courts have been the dominant agency for social change in the United States, far outdistancing in both zeal and effectiveness the Congress, the parties, the unions, interest groups of all kinds. And there, I think, is a deeper cause for worry. For judicial activism on this scale stands at some remove from democratic politics, and whatever its immediate effects, it doesn't work over the long haul to strengthen democratic institutions.[3]

Because I believe both of those positions to be profoundly in error, I return to them, explicitly or inferentially, from time to time below. Some of the objections to the Court, such as it being an undemocratic institution and making unreasoned decisions, have already been discussed. What follows is, of necessity, more of an outline than an exhaustive delineation of all of the aspects of a more active role for the Court (for federal courts generally). It is based on certain assumptions, which are listed here with little discussion.

First: there can be little question that the formal Constitution of 1787, even as amended and as interpreted by the Supreme Court, has deep flaws that require rectification, and soon. An instrument written in a bygone age, for a vastly different nation existing in a fundamentally different environment, has been sufficiently pliable thus far—but barely so. Only by political officers at times ignoring the Constitution, and by reading content into its silences, has it survived. The problem now is that the Document resembles the Liberty Bell: It has serious cracks and today is more a barrier to adequate government than a means of grappling with the daunting problems now facing Americans. Those problems also confront people elsewhere, to the extent that it no longer is possible to speak merely of a crisis. Rather, it is a climacteric, a profound social transformation. "The world," said Professor Willis Harman, "is headed for a climacteric which may well be one of the most fateful in the history of civilizations. This convulsion is now not far off and most people sense something of it—although interpretations vary widely, like the well-known interpretations of the elephant by blindfolded people who feel different parts of the animal."[4] It is past time that institutions developed for different times and different problems be assessed for their present and future suitability.

Second: humankind must come to terms with nature. That is indispensable. For millenia, Western man, relying on a cosmology that perceived mankind as the center of the universe, exploited nature and nature's creatures. Building on the precepts of the Judeo-Christian religions, which in turn were based on Ptolemaic anthropocentrism, man considered nature to be "red in tooth and claw," and thus to be subdued and exploited. Seeing himself as separate from and superior to the remainder of the natural order, Homo sapiens has with rare exceptions treated nature with avaricious contempt. The book of Genesis bade mankind to exercise dominion over every living thing. That has been, and is, interpreted as a license to exploit Earth and its resources without regard to anything other than man himself. "We are absolute masters," asserted Cicero, "of what the earth produces." That, however, is Western man—the Greeks and Romans and their successors in Europe and its colonies. Aristotle wrote in his *Politics* that "plants were created for the sake of animals, and the animals for the sake of man." John Passmore, in a superb essay, has said that "Christianity has encouraged man to think of himself as nature's absolute master."[5] Professor Lynn White wrote these oft-quoted words in 1967: "Despite Darwin, we are *not*, in our hearts, part of the natural process. We are superior to nature, contemptuous of it."[6]

That view may be changing, however slowly—as, indeed, it has to change if Homo sapiens is to remain on Earth. Professor William A. Galston in *Justice and the Human Good* has written:

Recent years have witnessed a resurgence of interest in the question of moral relations between human beings and animals. Various sources have contributed to this renewed interest: the ecology movement; increased theoretical and moral skepticism about the drive toward the domination of nature characteristic of modern societies; scientific evidence pointing to greater continuity between human and nonhuman animals than hitherto suspected: habits of mind carried over from the contemporary delegitimation of unequal treatment among different human groups: and the extension of the humanitarian tradition that has roots in both Rousseau and classical utilitarianism.

The contention that we are not free to treat animals in any way we choose has great intuitive force. . . .

It is clear that animals cannot be viewed as pure instruments. We may harm them directly. The reason is that animals have *interests*—things that they seek to attain and preserve, the totality of which constitutes their good. This good is independent of human purposes and interests; an animal has a good even if it is not a good for *us.*[7]

Lord Ashby of Brandon has argued, with some force, that a slow evolution of public conscience is occurring from indifference to concern for the environment.[8] His perception, if it is that, may be accurate, although it is necessary to note that a number of competent observers dispute his claim. My point is not to take sides in that argument, but rather to maintain the necessity of changing the millenia-old ethic of the superiority and contemptuous attitude of man toward nature. One would have to be a glandular optimist to believe, with Ashby, that such a reconciliation is in fact taking place. The world, as Thucydides said, is still one where the strong do what they can and the weak suffer what they must, with the weak in this instance being not only those humans with little or no political power but also the flora and fauna of the remainder of nature.[9] One should not be disparaged as an "econut" to assert that the ability of constitutionalism to survive may in the last analysis depend upon the answer to that very problem. The well-known biologists, Paul and Anne Ehrlich, suggested as much in their 1981 volume *Extinction*.[10] As scientists, they join with Ashby (another scientist) and Galston (a philosopher) in verifying the validity of our second assumption.

Third: Another facet of the question of nature lies in the nature of human nature. Political theory must start from a theory of man or it is worthless. Since constitutional law—constitutionalism itself—consists of statements of political theory, it is therefore necessary that any discussion of what the Supreme Court might do, and what the Constitution should become, be initially predicated on "a theory of man." Already discussed is an aspect of the question: When in Part I we showed the myth of neutrality or objectivity in constitutional decision making, we thus rejected "the ideal model of an empty mind passively contemplating pure data presented to pure awareness."[11] (Most discussion of the Court and its work seems to accept that model as a given.) The lack of neutrality or of impartiality, however, is only one segment of a total picture of man and his nature. I should like to suggest, as the third assumption, that all major human enterprises are "value-oriented, goal-directed, and norm-governed."[12] They do not merely exist: They are purposive. That assumption, of course, calls for identification and specification of those values, goals, and norms—both in the sense of what *is* and of what *ought to be*. It will be suggested subsequently that the Supreme Court can help in that task.

Two other aspects of the nature of man merit brief mention: First is the view, now widely accepted, that mankind is far from the rational being that some believe. That fact has long been known, but little acted upon. "The theme of man's irrationality" during the seventeenth and eighteenth centuries, Arthur O. Lovejoy maintained, "and especially of his *inner* corruption was no longer a speciality of divines; it became for a time one of the favorite topics of secular literature."[13] Political theorists thus came to emphasize the dangers rather than the advantages of government. If man was depraved and antisocial, he then required control; but those who controlled, themselves human beings, would mercilessly exploit their subjects unless there was some way to limit their power. Lord Acton's famous aphorism about the corrupting aspects of power simply restated some familiar learning of the seventeenth and eighteenth centuries. There were, to be sure, those who believed that man is not naturally depraved and that he "is capable, guided solely by the light of reason and experience, of perfecting the good life on earth."[14] The first notion derives from the philosophy of Thomas Hobbes, the second from John Locke. In any event, the Framers wrote the Constitution in ways to fragment political power in an effort to prevent despotism.

The second facet of man's nature is that the human being seems to be—likely is—susceptible of almost complete manipulation. As has been said, the ideologist for the development of control measures, subtle and otherwise, is Professor B. F. Skinner.[15] His views provide the intellectual basis for mind control techniques throughout the nation. Skinner had Frazier say in *Walden Two*, his novel about a controlled future:

Most people live from day-to-day. . . . They look forward to having children, to seeing their children grow up, and so on. The majority of people don't want to plan. They want to be free from the responsibility of planning. What they ask is merely some assurance that they will be decently provided for. The rest is day-to-day enjoyment of life. That's the explanation of your Father Divines: people naturally flock to anyone they can trust for the necessities of life.[16]

A moment's reflection about, for example, the manner in which presidential electoral campaigns are waged will readily show that Skinner is correct.

Fourth: The American Dream has ended—the idea that all things are possible to men of goodwill. Charles Beard said it well a half-century ago: To him, American history revealed a concept of progress based upon individual freedom and the humane use of science for democratic purposes and human betterment. "If there is anything which history demonstrates," he maintained, "it is this generalization. All legislation, all individual efforts are founded on the assumption that evils can be corrected, blessings multiplied by rational methods, intelligently applied. Essentially by this faith is American civilization justified."[17] Fifty years later that concept is being perceived to be "the arrogance of humanism"; that man can indeed control his own destiny is by no means self-evident. The contrary is more likely true. Things—external events—are in the saddle, and, as Yeats said, "mere anarchy is loosed upon the world."

Fifth: The ecological trap is once more closing, and the possibility of its being reopened is by no means certain. Humankind in Western societies, including the United States, is now fast approaching the condition of material scarcity relative to (world) population that characterized them before the Great Discoveries opened the New World and poured wealth and treasure into Europe. Americans and others live in a situation, which shows no real signs of abating, of all-too-finite resources on a finite planet. Humankind's patrimony is being depleted at an alarming rate, at the very time that a greatly increased world population attempts to gain a greater share of that wealth.[18] Species, plant and animal, are fast disappearing. The United States came into existence at a time when it appeared to many (for example, John Locke) that Homo sapiens would be able to escape the ecological trap. We now know better: We know that Thomas Hobbes was correct all along. His view that resources are limited and that there would be a continuing struggle for them was merely postponed while Americans and others supped at the tables of opulence that were a direct consequence of the Great Discoveries. Now, there are no more new lands to discover, and the wealth of Earth, including that of the final untapped area, the oceans, is rapidly being depleted. The Age of Scarcity has arrived.

Sixth: Americans are also coming to the end of their "empire," which, as William Appleman Williams has shown, has long been a "way of life."[19] American leaders, said Williams, "recognized the necessity of expansion for the capitalist political economy—industrial and financial as well as agricultural —and deployed their more concentrated and efficient power to define and control the new idiom of empire as a way of life."[20] Throughout American history the drive for more—more wealth, more possessions, more economic growth—has been manifest. Today, however, and surely increasingly so in the future, the wants and demands of Americans collide and will continue to collide against those of others. To the extent that the empire contributed to the American Dream, it can no longer be realized. To the extent that the American Dream was exported, it has contributed to the collision of demands and expectations. The world is no longer our oyster. Try as we might—and try we will—an expansion of the American empire today, or even the retention of what for decades was thought to be America's, is no longer possible. Peoples in other nations the planet over are no longer willing to dance to a tune played in Washington, D.C. We live in a new world in this, the latter part of the twentieth century, but it is the same old world carved up in ways different from the past. Great Britain lost its empire with World War II; the United States is losing its empire at present.

Some American policymakers, particularly those in the Reagan administration and those who control the multinational corporations, seem to think differently. But their ability to translate policy choices into operative reality is fast dwindling (although it has far from vanished at the moment). "No single nation however big and powerful can dominate a world of some 140 interdependent nations and embracing some four billion people."[21] There is an important distinction between world leadership and world domination. The United States no doubt can and will remain a leader—indeed, with its wealth and power it cannot avoid that—but its days of domination are over. Wherever one looks, the foundations of American imperialism are crumbling.

Seventh: A planetary "zero-sum" society has been created.[22] Known and foreseeable resources are insufficient to satisfy the rising demands and expectations of peoples in all nations. The world is in turmoil: From the nauseous barrios of Latin America through Africa to the jungles of Asia, the cry is for more. But there is not enough to go around—hence the zero-sum nature of world society. Hard choices will have to be made—are being made —about who shall be the winners and who the inevitable losers in such a society. What some call *Spaceship Earth* is fast becoming *Slaveship Earth*.

Eighth: The need for mass manpower has ended. With the coming of the third industrial revolution of microprocessing, much of the work that has occupied mankind throughout human history can be performed better and cheaper by automation. If Homo sapiens is also Homo faber, as Hannah Arendt has said,[23] that fact has enormous portents for the species. Mass man has, in sum, become surplus to the politico-economic system of corporate capitalism. His main function is to consume rather than to produce, but the cornucopia from which that consumption flows is, as noted above, fast lessening vis-à-vis the numbers of people. "In a recent issue of the scholarly British periodical Political Quarterly, devoted entirely to the country's unemployment problem, social scientist Jeremy Seabrook warned of a 'terminal sense of extinction of work itself' stalking working-class cities such as Liverpool."[24] My point is that what is occurring in Liverpool and other British cities is fast becoming true of other industrialized nations, not excluding the United States.

Ninth: The United States—the entire world—has entered a period of unparalleled danger. Nuclear war has become ever more possible. If—when —it comes, humanity will be plunged back into the Stone Age. In early 1981 the editors of the *Bulletin of the Atomic Scientists* moved their "doomsday clock" from seven minutes to four minutes to midnight—to, that is, nuclear holocaust. They thus made it clear to all except those who do not wish to see that the possibility of much of the human race being vaporized, or otherwise eliminated, may not be far off. With the proliferation of nuclear weapons to more and more nations, that possibility is fast becoming a probability. When to that is added the enormous overkill capacity of the two superpowers—the United States and USSR—then, as George Kennan has told us, we stand on the precipice of unprecedented disaster.[25]

Tenth: Technology provides the means for complete control over the human being by those in effective control of the State. If it is true, as it seems to be, that what is technologically possible will be done—sooner or later— those control measures are not far away. "Feasibility, which is a strategic concept, becomes elevated into a normative concept, with the result that whatever technological reality indicates we *can* do is taken as implying that we *must* do it." Invention, in other words, is the mother of necessity.

I do not suggest that these ten factors encompass all that Americans must take into account as they count down to the end of the twentieth century. Others may—likely do—exist, but these ten suffice to set the pattern for the ensuing discussion.

II.

In previous chapters enough has been shown to conclude that the notion that every, even any, decision of the Supreme Court follows logically from the formal Constitution must be considered to be a superstition. Morris R. Cohen said it well: "The assumption that the judge's personal opinion does not count and that every decision is in some mystic sense contained in the Constitution is a childish fiction which is irreconcilable with the actual law or body of decisions."[26] That superstition has long been known: The intellectual formalism of the nineteenth century was recognized decades ago for its sterility. Some lawyers (and members of the professoriate), however, over-reacted to what they said was adherence to an excessive formalism. Cohen, perhaps the greatest philosopher of law the nation has produced, knew this; he said in 1936:

In the reaction against mechanical jurisprudence, against the complacent manipulation of legal concepts in utter disregard of the facts of social life, it is well to be on guard against throwing the baby out with the bath....Without the use of concepts and general principles we can have no science, no intelligible systematic account, of the law or of any other field. And the demand for system is urgent not only on theoretical but also on practical grounds. *Without general ideas, human experience is dumb as well as blind.*[27] (Emphasis added.)

This section expounds the need for a break away from the regnant pragmatic temper that has characterized both law and the jurisprudence of the Supreme Court for at least a half-century. Much of that travels under the banner of the intellectual movement called "legal realism."[28] The problem with legal realism was that it was and is almost entirely destructive; it told people what courts and judges actually were but left an intellectual vacuum. Nothing replaced the formalism of the past. The task now is to synthesize legal realism with an intelligent formalism, with, that is, "concepts and general principles" valid for a humane, sustainable society.

Our focus is upon the Supreme Court. Since 1937, although there were some scattered earlier examples, the Justices have been pragmatically inclined. They avowedly "balance interests" in their constitutional decisions. At the very least, that means that they attempt to weigh the societal conse-quences of decisions, rather than deducing their conclusions logically from preexisting (*a priori*) principles. One fault of that approach is that the Justices have never enlightened us about how they identify interests in given cases, how they weigh them, and how one is chosen over another. The Court's opinions tend to be statements of conclusions, rather than reasoned analyses. Another fault is that the Justices usually fail to state the premises from which they begin, in writing their opinions.

Pragmatism has dominated American thought since the latter part of the nineteenth century. In a famous essay, Professor Morton White outlined what he called "the revolt against formalism,"[29] by which he meant an intellectual march away from first principles toward "a philosophy of expedience." White traced the development through law (using Oliver Wendell Holmes as his model), economics (Thorstein Veblen), philosophy (William James and John Dewey), and politics (Arthur Bentley). Law was the last of those "sciences" or "disciplines" to eschew formalism, but the impact of the change in mind-set has been lasting and significant. It changed the nature of the jurisprudence of the Supreme Court. The exponents of the new wisdom, which was given the label of "practicalism" and then "pragmatism" by James, spoke in terms of empiricism, of historicism, and of cultural factors as being much more important than received first principles.

Pragmatism arose at a time when the United States was undergoing a convulsive change from rural to urban, from small shop to mass production, from an era of relative scarcity and deprivation to an Age of Abundance. The "philosophy" of the new era is less a philosophy than a way of making (ad hoc) decisions. To William James, for example, truth was not to be found either by the exercise of pure reason or by scientific observations of nature, but was to be "made": It was "not something that was inert and static but something that happened to an idea or course of conduct." Said James:

The truth of an idea is not a stagnant property inherent in it. Truth *happens* to an idea. It *becomes* true, is *made* true by events: its verity *is* in fact an event, a process: the process namely of its verifying itself, its veri-*fication*. Its validity is the process of its vali-*dation*.... The true is the name of whatever proves to be good in the way of belief, and good, too, for definite assignable reasons.[30]

What those reasons might be James did not say, thus fatally flawing his conclusions. But it is those reasons that must be taken into account—what Morris R. Cohen called "concepts and general principles."

In sum, James argued that if something "works," it is true and good. Theories and abstractions are rejected, and a single standard of workability is established. Again, James:

Grant an idea or belief to be true, what concrete difference does it make in anyone's actual life? How will the truth be realized? What experience will be different from those which would obtain if the belief were false? What, in short, is the truth's cash value in experiential terms? The moment pragmatism asks this question, it sees the answer.

True ideas are those that we can assimilate, validate, corroborate and verify. False ideas are those we can not. That is the practical difference it makes to us to have true ideas; that, therefore, is the meaning of truth, for it is all that truth is known as.[31] (Emphasis added.)

But how is workability to be tested? James did not say. True enough, he and others accomplished a praiseworthy task in succeeding in clearing the underbrush of sterile conceptualistic thought based on logical deductions from assumed first principles. For doing that he and others deserve much credit. Theirs was a major intellectual advance. It enabled, in law, Supreme Court Justices to cut through the miasma of thought that paid no overt attention to actual social conditions, but relied on assumed philosophical principles.

The first overt break away from the traditional formalism of constitutional law and Supreme Court decision making came in *Muller v. Oregon* (1908).[32] There, the Justices, who were confronted with the constitutionality of a state statute regulating the hours that women could work, accepted a brief (a written presentation) from the women's lawyer, Louis D. Brandeis, that contained data showing the deleterious effect on health of working long hours. Thus began the so-called Brandeis brief type of argumentation, in which judges are asked to consider not merely the formalisms of legal concepts, but the social and economic aspects of given constitutional disputes. Thus did pragmatism overtly come to the Supreme Court.

Since 1908, and with accelerating frequency, lawyers routinely present such data to the Court.[33] In legalese, these data tend to be "social" or "legislative" facts, which deal with the societal consequences of decisions, rather than "adjudicative" facts, which are concerned only with the litigants before the Court. As the Supreme Court moves toward an obvious procedure of "legislating" not only for the immediate litigants but for generations yet unborn (see the discussion of the Court as commander in Chapter 5), there is an increasing need for information that goes far beyond "pure" legal concepts. To mention only one example, there was no possible way that the Court could make the *general* ruling it did in the abortion cases (1973) without considering masses of extralegal data. It is, under the adversarial system, the function of lawyers to bring those data to the Court, but the Justices can and do have other techniques of informing themselves. They can request "friend of the Court" briefs[34] from groups that are not litigants but that have an important interest in the outcome of a case. Of perhaps more significance, they can and do have what Justice William Brennan called "independent research" done for them by their law clerks.[35] Also, they can and do take "judicial notice" of matters not presented by counsel.[36] In net, the Justices of the Supreme Court do not rely on only the information brought to them by the parties's lawyers; they, to an immeasurable but nonetheless significant extent, are "self-informers."

In *The American Mind*, Professor Henry Steele Commager stated that pragmatism was not only the philosophy of expedience, it was democratic, individualistic, humane and optimistic, and adventurous.[37] What he did not say is more important: The pragmatic revolt in American thought came at precisely the right moment in history, the time when the idea of progress reigned and all things seemed possible to people of goodwill. It was, therefore, appropriate for an expanding society, for a nation with seemingly endless economic growth based upon what apparently was thought to be an inexhaustible supply of natural resources. Its increasingly obvious shortcomings today can be traced to a far different environment in which Americans live. In the Age of Scarcity a view of truth as being something that is "workable" is simply not enough. More is needed.

As a system of thought, pragmatism was and is no system at all. It is a direct descendant of Darwinian precepts (of process), rather than Newtonian ideas of balance. The world was seen not as a great clock with interacting parts offsetting each other, but as a flow of decisions. It was a river, not a static system. "My generation," James H. Tufts wrote many years ago, "has seen the passing of systems of thought which had reigned since Augustus. The conception of a world as a kingdom ruled by God, subject to his laws and their penalties, which had been undisturbed by the Protestant Reformation, has dissolved. . . . The sanctions of our inherited morality have gone. Principles and standards which have stood for nearly two thousand years are questioned."[38] The impact upon legal thought was tremendous. It spawned, as we have said, the "legal realist" movement.

Oliver Wendell Holmes was perhaps the first, and the leading, exemplar of the new jurisprudence. In his celebrated book *The Common Law* (1881) he stated in oft-quoted words that "the life of the law has not been logic; it has been experience." That was a flashing insight, one that had far-reaching consequences. Consider this well-known passage published by Roscoe Pound in 1909:

Jurisprudence is the last in the march of the sciences away from the method of deduction from predetermined conceptions. The sociological movement in jurisprudence, the movement for pragmatism as a philosophy of law, the movement for the adjustment of principles and doctrines to the human conditions they are to govern rather than to assumed first principles, the movement for putting the human factor in the central place and relegating logic to its true position as an instrument, has scarcely shown itself yet in America.[39]

The problem with realism is the problem of pragmatism: It is indifferent to the "ought" dimension of law; it concentrates on the "is" and assumes that that is enough. It is not. Although the original realists were earnestly concerned "for the discovery of the true and the good," their successors have not been.[40]

Modern realists have little interest in the identification and prescription of general norms or principles. The "is" can be separated from the "ought" for purposes of study, and even of argument, but at some time they must be merged.

The task of jurisprudence today, and thus the task of the Supreme Court as America's first faculty of political theory, is to effect such a synthesis. Legal realists called—rightfully—for candor about the judicial process, about how judges went about doing their job. That was sound counsel for a nation that was, almost literally, bursting its boundaries and entering upon an era of economic abundance. But it cannot be a sustaining factor—it cannot provide the necessary missing element of what law *should* be—as the Age of Scarcity fast approaches. Legal pragmatism, therefore, avoided the problem of judging the goodness or badness of law. It, thus, is insufficient to the manifest needs of the modern era. True it is, as Professor Grant Gilmore has said, the realists "created a professional climate of opinion which immensely facilitated the making of necessary adjustments within the traditional framework of our law. They did much to make of law a more useful and flexible instrument for the resolution of social conflicts."[41] They imprinted in American legal thinking the concept of relativity in the adaptation, in both private law and public law, of positive law to social change.

In recent years, some legal scholars have moved away from legal realism and have begun a search for values, for standards, by which the law can be evaluated. Much of this has concerned the work of the Supreme Court. John Rawls's *A Theory of Justice* is perhaps the most important contribution.[42] His is an egalitarian approach: He proposes as a fundamental principle of justice in a democratic society what he terms "the Difference Principle": "that social and economic inequalities, for example inequalities of wealth and authority, are just only if they result in compensating benefits for everyone, and in particular for the least advantaged members of society."[43] Several others have contributed to the developing dialogue, including Robert Nozick, Alexander Bickel, John Hart Ely, Jesse Choper, Ronald Dworkin, and Myres McDougal.[44] It is fair to say that none of them has effected the necessary synthesis between legal realism and a new type of formalism. But the effort has begun.

We now know that premises that are merely descriptive of what people do cannot provide the basis for deductions, logical or otherwise, of what they should do. "It is folly," Morris R. Cohen said, "to try to banish absolute or rigorous logic." Furthermore, in a passage significant to our discussion below:

While all the material truths we can achieve at any one time are necessarily incomplete or subject to the qualifications of future knowledge, our procedure must be formally rigorous. The direction and goal of our efforts must be relatively fixed if there is to be any significant race. The absolute denial of all constancy or identity in the world of change and variety would make all assertions meaningless. Those who delude themselves with the naive faith of finding refuge in "the facts" are the victims of an uncritical metaphysics which assumes that each fact of existence is complete in itself and independent of every other. In truth, however, there is always a nexus which makes things pass beyond themselves, so that when you begin with one fact and wish to explore its nature you find yourself very soon beyond your starting point dealing with abstract conditions and ideal possibilities. In any case we cannot maintain sound intellectual procedure by turning our backs on critical logic; we cannot attain clear ideas as to the nature of the factual or real world by ignoring the obstinate effort to think clearly which is the core of metaphysics; and we cannot arrive at a clear idea of what we wish to achieve without the clarified vision of the *summum bonum* which is the subject matter of critical ethics. . . . Sound methods and adequate ideas are not attained by wilfully shutting our eyes; and those who have thought that they have succeeded in this by banishing logic, metaphysics and ethics from their view of the law have merely imported them in an uncritical and unavowed form.[45]

Cohen wrote in 1936. His was a call for a merger of empiricism and transcendentalism in law. Are there truths beyond and above the Constitution? If so, what are they? How are they discovered? Who has the capacity of identifying and articulating them? By what criteria?

Law, Justice Felix Frankfurter once said, "presupposes sociological wisdom as well as logical unfolding."[46] So it does. Can the Supreme Court—judges generally—help in the determination of what is sociologically wise? The answer is an emphatic yes. The Court, as Galston has implied, can be an educator:

In the last analysis, . . . the quest for a purely institutional or procedural solution to the practical problem of obtaining justice is futile. Every community, whether democratic or not, must rely on a rudimentary sense of fairness and equity among its members. This sense is not innate, but must rather be fostered [among its members] through some system of education. The traditional American penchant for political engineering or institutional tinkering is thus profoundly one-sided; democratic procedures are almost vacuous in the absence of collectively held moral convictions.[47]

III.

The Justices, that is, are a faculty in a vital national seminar in which national values are, at least to a limited extent, developed.[48] That raises the question of how they interpret the Document of 1787.

We have seen that the Supreme Court is deeply in politics and, indeed, cannot be fully understood unless it is perceived as a major political actor. To be sure, it is more; it is a court, albeit a very special kind of court. Being "in politics" enables the Justices to operate as an authoritative faculty of social ethics, analogous to but not the same as a legislature. There are two basic questions about interpretation of the Document of 1787 and its amendments: How? By whom? "With a numinous document like the Constitution or the

Bible, the principles and methods of correct interpretation are as important as they are problematical."[49] What *are* those "principles and methods"? What *should* they be?

The "by whom" part of the question has already been answered: Suggested above is the proposition that the Court is not the only organ of government that can interpret, and thus update, the Constitution. That is so even though the Court insists that it has the ultimate authority in constitutional interpretation. Such a "papalist" conception must, however, give way to a "Protestant" view of a multiplicity of interpreters. Even though the Court in recent years has asserted its infallibility and has gotten widespread acquiescence, the Justices's authority must be shared with other official, and even some nominally private, decision makers. This position has marked consequences, not the least of which is that the Court, even though an acknowledged policymaker, is enjoined by many to be seen to act like an ordinary court of law. The Justices must simultaneously make policy (law) and pretend that they are not doing so. A cause of intellectual confusion about the Court is precisely the insistence that it hide the fact that it is making law. One would think that when some of the Justices themselves candidly acknowledge their lawmaking proclivities, academic commentators would take them at their word and proceed from there. When, as has been seen, Justice Brennan wrote the following in 1980, it should have caused academics, but did not, to think beyond the judge as "umpire" to the judge as "law-giver":

Under our system, judges are not mere umpires, but, in their own sphere, lawmakers —a coordinate branch of *government*. While individual cases turn upon the controversies between parties, or involve particular prosecutions, court rulings impose official and practical consequences upon members of society at large.

The interpretation and application of constitutional and statutory law, while not legislation, is lawmaking, albeit of a kind that is subject to special constraints and informed by unique considerations. Guided and confined by the Constitution and pertinent statutes, judges are obliged to be discerning, exercise judgment, and prescribe rules. Indeed, at times judges wield considerable authority to formulate legal policy in designated areas.[50]

A major problem of much of the present-day commentary upon the Supreme Court derives from the insistence that the Justices confine themselves to an umpireal or arbitral function. Or if it is conceded that judges routinely make law, the writer usually enjoins them to do so in a "principled" way.

One would think that after almost 200 years of Supreme Court activity, theories of judicial interpretation would be largely settled. The contrary is more nearly the truth. Judges and scholars alike argue not only over the meanings to be given to specific constitutional clauses, but also about the very ways of applying the Document to present problems. What Justice Robert H. Jackson asserted in 1952, concerning President Harry Truman's power to seize the steel mills during the Korean "war," seems to be generally valid about interpretation:

A judge, like an executive adviser, may be surprised at the poverty of really useful and unambiguous authority applicable to concrete problems of executive power as they actually present themselves. Just what our forefathers did envision, or would have envisioned had they foreseen modern conditions, must be divined from materials almost as enigmatic as the dreams Joseph was called upon to interpret for Pharoah. A century and a half of partisan debate and scholarly speculation yields no net result but only supplies more or less apt quotations from respected sources on each side of any question. They largely cancel each other.[51]

As with problems of the reach of presidential powers, so with the other generalities of the Constitution.

What follows in this section is based upon only one assumption: that the Document of 1787 was in effect, although not expressly stated and even not widely recognized today, a delegation of power to later generations of Americans to write their own fundamental laws. That belief is the clear lesson of American constitutional history. It, however, cuts against the grain of the popular wisdom about the Constitution. I cannot prove it in the sense of producing historical data that would show that those who wrote and those who ratified the Document had that *specific* intention. There is simply no other valid way to consider the Document and its evolution. In other words, the actual, the operative, Constitution has always been relative to circumstances and has radically changed through time. Once that is seen, certain principles of interpretation follow logically.

Does that leave the Justices, and thus Americans, adrift without compass or rudder? Perhaps. Raoul Berger, among other constitutional scholars, so believes. Macaulay could call the Constitution "all sail and no anchor." Even federal Judge J. Skelly Wright, far and away America's foremost judicial activist, has maintained: "Constitutional choices are in fact different from ordinary decisions. . . . The most important value choices have already been made by the Framers of the Constitution."[52] That view, however, can scarcely be accurate, as Judge Learned Hand knew:

I venture to believe that it is as important to a judge called upon to pass on a question of constitutional law, to have at least a bowing acquaintance with Acton and Maitland, with Thucydides, Gibbon and Carlyle, with Homer, Dante, Shakespeare and Milton, with Machiavelli, Montaigne and Rabelais, with Plato, Bacon, Hume, and Kant, as with the books which have been specifically written upon the subject. For in such matters everything turns upon the spirit in which he approaches the questions before him. *The words he must construe are empty vessels into which he can pour nearly anything he will.* Men do not gather figs of thistles, nor supple institutions from judges whose outlook is limited by parish or class. They must be aware of the changing social tensions in every society which make it an organism; which demand new schemata of adaptation; which will disrupt it, if rigidly confined.[53] (Emphasis added.)

Those "empty vessels" about which Hand spoke not only permit, they demand that each generation construe the ancient words in the light of current conditions. The Constitution is therefore an appeal to the decency and wisdom of those with whom the responsibility for its enforcement rests. Law in large part being *a posteriori*, the meaning of the Document is altered through time; the words remain the same, but their content changes by dint of circumstance.[54]

Some constitutional absolutes do exist, such as the requirement for a two-house Congress, the President's term of four years, and the like. Those provisions, however, are never litigated, and although some changes are discernible in both the system of federalism and in the separation of powers, they remain frozen in time (some are a barrier to effective government today).[55] Through deliberate employment of ambiguity, those who wrote the Document may be said to have delegated authority to later generations to write their own constitutions. Those parts were left to gain content from experience. So, too, with the silences of the Document (such as executive privilege, Reason of State, and the like). As Justice Holmes put it in 1920: "The case before us must be considered in the light of our whole experience and not merely in what was said a hundred years ago."[56] Purposive use of ambiguity enabled the Framers to set the tone of the Document, without having to spell out in detail what those imprecise words meant. What is "due process of law"? "Commerce among the states"? "Executive power"?

It was that very nebulosity of language that provided the opportunity for Chief Justice John Marshall to make a bold grab for judicial power to put a measure of precision in undefined constitutional language. His successors have followed his example. So, too, have other interpreters of the Document such as the President and Congress. The validity of judicial review is widely accepted today; practically no one disputes its legitimacy. There is, however, considerable controversy over the details of that exercise of governmental power, seen, for example, in 1981 when almost thirty bills were introduced in Congress designed to reduce the power of the Supreme Court specifically, and federal courts generally, by denying them jurisdiction to hear and decide certain matters—abortion, school prayers, mandatory busing, among others.[57]

Delegation, as used here, means constitutional relativism. The nation has survived and waxed strong and prosperous not because of the Constitution, but in spite of it. True, we live under a Constitution, but it, rather than being merely what the judges say it is, reflects the social conditions of different eras. A fundamental law at once sufficiently flexible to tolerate armed resistance to secession, extraordinary measures to combat economic depression, and presidential war making, among other examples, can only be called control-ling as a matter of faith and hopeful theory. Brute practice is otherwise.

So much, then, for the basic assumption of delegation from the constitu-tional Framers to later generations of Americans. Even though it is the clear lesson of American constitutional history, it is stoutly resisted by those who would have modern America repair to the shades of men long dead and allow them—in theory—to rule from their graves. No nation, no society, has ever been ruled that way, certainly not the United States. There can be no dictatorship over the living by the dead.

Nonetheless, we should not throw the baby out with the bath water. The Document is far from irrelevant. Not only is the basic structure of government set forth (even though changes in fact have taken place), even its ambiguous clauses help to set the tone for, though not the specifics of, governmental action. What, then, are the techniques of interpretation that the Justices have used since 1789? Several are worth mention.

First: To repeat for emphasis, it is distinctly *not* a valid principle of constitu-tional interpretation to search for the specific intentions of those who drafted the Document and apply them (if found, which is rare indeed). True enough, the Justices often assert they are invoking the words of the Founding Fathers. That, however, is merely to cloak the opinions in familiar language and thus make them more palatable to lawyers. It also adds an aura of legitimacy to Supreme Court lawmaking: By saying they are merely putting the wishes of the Framers into operation, the Justices can (presumably) achieve a wider degree of acceptance when their decisions change the law. Those who argue for searching for and applying the intentions of the Framers hide their personal preferences behind a screen. They may dislike, for example, the Court's ruling desegregating public schools, but rather than openly saying so they criticize the Justices for not adhering to what they assert were the inten-tions of those who drafted the Fourteenth Amendment. In addition, it is accurate to say that when the Justices outwardly and probably accurately did follow the intentions of the Framers, as in the infamous *Dred Scott* decision (1857), they were severely criticized for doing so.

Once that type of criticism is out of the way, it is possible to determine what the Justices have done—or, at least, what they have said they have done in interpreting the Document (which may be a different matter).

Second: Even though the High Bench is a very special type of court and even though it has to a limited extent become a de facto Council of Elders, it still clothes its opinions in the traditional forms that judges on ordinary courts employ. There are reasons for doing this. The Justices, although fully aware that they are lawmakers (law creators), seem to believe that they should proceed by denying change. An example came in early 1981 in *Democratic National Committee* v. *LaFollette*,[58] where the Court speaking through Justice Potter Stewart asserted that the decision was controlled by the Court's previous decision in *Cousins* v. *Wigoda*.[59] There is a basic trouble with that reasoning: The facts of the two cases are far from similar, and thus *Cousins* was in fact no precedent at all. Stewart merely pretended that it was. That is a typical judicial ploy. Professor Judith Shklar put the matter in effective focus when she observed in 1964:

All judges must sooner or later legislate—create rules either unconsciously or openly. The codes of several European countries directly provide for this possibility, and in the United States it is an accepted aspect of every stage of judicial activity. From Austin to Gray, moreover, writers on jurisprudence have urged judges to face the facts of life candidly, to accept the responsibilities the community has placed upon their shoulders, and to make rules that seem to them useful and intelligent. To the judge, however, these are frightful occasions. By training and professional ideology he is tied to a vision of his function that excludes self-assertion and places a premium on following existing rules impartially. His natural impulse is to find a rule at any cost, or at least to assimilate his decision to a rule as closely as possible. He may even openly evade responsibility. . . . It is obviously of great importance to him that the rules he relies on be based on universal agreement among either the experts, the wise, or the whole people. Otherwise the rule becomes a mere opinion—a thought he does not wish to entertain. . . . In the United States the extent of judicial lawmaking is both greater and more frankly recognized than anywhere else. Nevertheless, this does not mean that our judges like the system. It is well known that Judge Leonard Hand and Justice Frankfurter have expressed a deep aversion to the notion that even in constitutional questions the courts take any legislative initiative. Preferably they should rely on the legislature to have the last say whenever possible, and when that has failed they should place their trust on community sentiment.[60]

Shklar has accurately described the response of many judges. There are few with the courage of, say, federal Judge J. Skelly Wright who will openly acknowledge that they make law. Two members of the present Supreme Court—Justices William Brennan and Byron White—have so admitted. These judges are among the handful who do not delude the citizenry that the burdens imposed by a judgment inevitably flowed from preexisting law. Judges who proceed by denying change, as did Justice Stewart, are refusing to let Americans know who the real architect of our obligations may be.

Third: Despite protestations to the contrary, judges historically have ruled on the wisdom as well as the constitutional propriety of governmental actions. Professor Henry Abraham thinks to the contrary; apparently taking statements of Supreme Court Justices at face value, he called it a "fundamental truth" of the democratic process. Quoting Justice William O. Douglas to the effect that Congress "within its constitutional powers" has the final say on policy issues, Professor Abraham plumped for what he called the overriding need for judicial self-restraint.[61] There are at least two things wrong with that position: First, it does not tell us how the Court, when ruling on the power—the constitutional power—of other segments of government, can avoid considering whether a policy choice by the political branches will or will not have an adverse effect upon the people. The second point overlaps with the first; it was well stated by Justice Holmes:

I think that the judges themselves have failed adequately to recognize their duty of weighing considerations of social advantage. The duty is inevitable, and the result of the often proclaimed judicial aversion to deal with such considerations is simply to leave the very ground and foundation of judgments inarticulate, and often unconscious. I cannot but believe that if the training of lawyers led them habitually to consider more definitely and explicitly the social advantage on which the rule they lay down must be justified, they sometimes would hesitate where now they are confident, and see that really they were taking sides upon debatable and often burning questions.[62]

It is one thing for judges to assert that they are not ruling on the wisdom of governmental actions. That position, as Shklar showed, may be psychologically necessary for the judge. But it is another thing to determine what in fact judges do. That they do weigh "considerations of social advantage" cannot be doubted, and what is socially advantageous is to be equated, at least roughly, with wisdom.

Even a casual reading of Supreme Court opinions will lead, ineluctably, to the conclusion that the Justices since the beginnings have so acted. As a coordinate branch of government—as, that is, what some call a "superlegislature"—the Court has the power to help determine what is or is not good or wise public policy on a wide range of issues. This is not to say, of course, that Court decisions are good or wise in all instances: The Justices's crystal ball may be as cloudy as that of other mortal men. Nor is it to say that the adversary system is sufficient to provide the Justices with all of the data relevant to making wise decisions. Finally, it is not to say that the 101 men and one woman who have sat or are sitting on the High Bench are wise and sagacious. Those shortcomings are not the point. Rather, it is that the Justices, for all of the deficiencies of whatever type, still do utter decisions and write opinions that, despite assertions to the contrary, are statements on the wisdom of governmental policy. Nothing in the law or rules of the Supreme Court prohibits the Justices from assessing the wisdom of public policy. Indeed, Congress probably could not constitutionally deny the Court that power. Since judicial review was established in 1803, the only real restraint on the Justices has been their own sense of self-restraint. That sense of self-restraint, as we have seen, is far from always followed. If the Justices want to rule on the wisdom of a policy, they can usually find a good "legal" reason for doing so.

Fourth: Premises of the Justices, even when inarticulate, are much more important than preexisting rules of law in the decisional process. A constitutional decision, Justice Holmes asserted in 1905, seems to "depend on a judgment or intuition more subtle than any articulate major premise."[63] Recall that in *The Court Years* Justice William O. Douglas quoted Chief Justice Charles Evans Hughes as advising him, "You must remember . . . [that] at the constitutional level where we work, 90 per cent of any decision is emotional. The rational part of us supplies the reasons for supporting our predilections."[64] If that description is accepted, Hughes's "predilections" may be equated with Holmes's "subtle intuition." In any event, it is the premise from which a judge proceeds that is as, and probably more, important than "the law" (the pre-existing rules). As has been seen, Justice Potter Stewart said as much in a dissenting opinion in *Kennedy* v. *Mendoza-Martinez* (1963):

> The Court's opinion is lengthy, but its thesis is simple: (1) The withdrawal of citizenship which these statutes provide is "punishment." (2) Punishment cannot constitutionally be imposed except after a criminal trial and conviction. (3) The statutes are therefore unconstitutional. As with all syllogisms, the conclusion is inescapable is the premise is correct. But I cannot agree with the Court's major premise—that the divestiture of citizenship is punishment in the constitutional sense of that term.[65]

The critical question, as Stewart said, is not the logic or the rule; rather, it is, to use his label, whether the Court majority's premise was "correct." But neither Stewart nor Justice Arthur Goldberg (who wrote the majority opinion) said why his premise was the correct one. Neither set out criteria for choice among premises. Neither informed us about why his premise was superior to the other.[66]

Stewart and Goldberg are not alone; rather, they represent the norm. "General propositions"—that is, preexisting rules of law—"do not decide concrete cases."[67] As Justice John M. Harlan said in 1961, in *Mapp* v. *Ohio*, "In overturning *Wolf* the Court . . . has simply chosen between two constitutional questions. Moreover, I submit that it has chosen the more difficult and less appropriate of the two questions."[68] No need exists to multiply examples of a common phenomenon. Every student of the Court knows that the Justices bring different premises to their consideration of a case and its rationalization in an opinion. Law, including constitutional law, is concerned with regulatory norms rather than descriptions of human behavior. It, therefore, is not scientific and is only partially logical.

A statement of "law," moreover, is one of normative ambiguity—at once a prediction of what a court (the Supreme Court) might do with a given set of facts, a description of how courts have handled disputes of the same nature in the past, and a prescription of what ought to be. Legal rules "do not state what always is, but attempt to decree what ought to be."[69] The "ought" is embedded in the premise a Justice chooses.

Fifth: When rules (principles) do exist, which is usually, they tend to travel in pairs of opposites. This may be called the Principle of Doctrinal Polarity in constitutional decision making.

There is an obvious overlap between the fourth and fifth techniques of interpretation. When one asks how to choose the basic premises of our constitutional order, one enters the realm of ethics, as the "science" of what ought to be. There is no possible way to get a *should* or an *ought* into a judicial conclusion unless there is one in the premise. The basic polarity, therefore, is between identification of law (the judicial decision) with justice. Not that they cannot coincide; of course they can. But it is only when a normative principle is present in the premise.[70]

If, then, the really important thing is the nature of the premises, as Cardozo and others have told us, there are opposite premises in many, perhaps all, constitutional decisions. In litigation, by the very nature of the adversary system, two conflicting major premises, one embodying one set of interests, the other embodying the other, are always present. Those premises end in conflicting conclusions about the appropriate rule (or doctrine), and that duality, then, is the Principle of Doctrinal Polarity. (At times, as in complicated cases, bipolarity becomes multipolarity.) Put another way, that means that the cases the Supreme Court hears tend to be the "hospital" or pathological disputes that cannot be handled by other means of social control. I do not say that all law is in the process of making. Some consistency does exist in the law; people generally are able to know their rights and duties, that is, what they may or may not do in certain situations. The Supreme Court, it may be said, tends to deal with the abnormal and in so doing obscures normality.

What I have called the pathological dispute must, however, be considered in the light of the proliferation of litigation and number of cases brought to the High Bench. That volume means, as has been previously said, that the Justices can to some immeasurable, but surely not small, extent be self-starters: they can pick and choose from among the thousands of cases filed each year to determine which social issue merits their attention. That gives them an open-ended ticket to be law creators. As John Dewey once said, "Whenever there is genuine deliberation, there are alternatives at almost every step of the way."[71] Those alternatives are the polarities of the fifth interpretative technique of the Justices.

Sixth: Supreme Court Justices vary their explanatory techniques from case to case, as they see fit. How they choose to explain or rationalize their decisions, that is, is not set in concrete.

One example will suffice. Chief Justice John Marshall's methods of approaching interpretation of the Document were diametrically opposed in two of his most famous opinions. In *Marbury* v. *Madison* (1803), which set the Court on its way toward judicial review, he treated the Constitution as any ordinary written instrument, such as a contract or a will or a conveyance. He applied time-honored maxims of interpretation, principally that known as *expressio unius est exclusio alterius* ("the expression of one excludes others"). Seeing in Article III certain designated areas of "original" jurisdiction for the Supreme Court, he reasoned that the Court could rule in no other — and, of great importance, that Congress could not enlarge upon the original jurisdiction of the High Bench (it had tried to do so in the Judiciary Act of

1789). Now, there is nothing in the Constitution, or elsewhere, that so limits the Supreme Court or Congress (or, for that matter, gives the Court the power to declare acts of Congress unconstitutional). Marshall treated the Document as if it had been a conveyance of a piece of real property.

When, sixteen years later, Marshall was again faced with a question of the powers of Congress—this time over whether Congress could incorporate a national bank—he forgot that the Document was, as in 1803, a simple legal instrument and intoned that the Supreme Court must never forget that they were construing a constitution—one designed for the ages to come and the various crises of human affairs.[72] So the national bank was upheld; Congress prevailed, because, said Marshall, it had certain "implied powers." Even though the Document did not give Congress the power to incorporate, nonetheless it could do so as a "necessary and proper" incident to its express powers. Even Marshall had to admit that a *national* bank was not strictly necessary; state banks existed. But that did not stop him.

John Marshall was not alone in choosing his explanatory technique to suit the case at bar. Even Justice Felix Frankfurter, the self-appointed advocate of judicial self-restraint, was able to agree in *Brown* v. *Board of Education* that Negroes were protected against invidious discrimination by the equal protection clause of the Fourteenth Amendment; but eight years later, in *Baker* v. *Carr*, he refused to give voters in urban areas similar protection. Strange, one might say, particularly if he adhered, as he did, to the orthodox position of the Rule of Law and the myth of judicial impartiality.

Seventh: The Justices have always gone outside the express language of the Constitution in writing their opinions. Some deny the validity of their doing so,[73] but there is no way they can escape searching beyond the Document itself for principles and precepts. The litigable parts of the Constitution are open-ended invitations to the Justices to write their own notions of constitutional propriety into the Document.

Not only is this done with the great silences of the Document, but it also is true with respect to constitutional rights that have been recognized that do not appear in the Constitution itself. A mere listing of the silences will show the pattern. They include at least the following: where sovereignty lies in the United States; the concept of sovereign immunity; the idea of judicial review itself; constitutional Reason of State; the implied powers of Congress; the inherent powers of the President; cooperation as the norm with the separation of powers of the national government; adherence to multinational institutions; political parties; the right of association; the right to travel; the right to privacy; the application of the Bill of Rights to the states; the application of the equal protection clause of the Fourteenth Amendment to the federal government; the legislative veto; the position of women under the Constitution; the treatment of American Indians; and the economic order.[74]

Each of those silences provides an opportunity for lawmaking, not only by the Supreme Court but by Congress and the President. So, too, with the rights of individuals that have been recognized by the Court, such as privacy, travel, and association. The words of the Document do not really confine the Justices; they instead provide a means for lawmaking by filling in silences and taking cognizance of new rights. Before 1973 the constitutional right to an abortion (during the first trimester of pregnancy) was unknown; after January of that year it became the right of pregnant females to terminate their pregnancies. What is an almost absolute right during the first trimester becomes less so in the second and even less in the third. All of this reasoning was a product of judicial lawmaking. The Justices acted as a "superlegisla-ture," or perhaps as a Council of Elders, in doing so. Having asserted, as we have seen, the power to determine the meaning of the Constitution, it has gone on in controversial matters such as abortion to put its idea of the Consti-tution into effect.

What we have set forth thus far in this section is the "is" of constitutional interpretation—not all of it, perhaps, but enough to show the tenor and tone. Not yet discussed is the "ought"—how should the Justices go about their task of interpreting the fundamental law? On that question opinions differ strongly: After nearly two centuries of Supreme Court interpretation of the sacred document of America's civil religion, there is still no consensus about what is proper for the Justices.

None of the more prominent theories holds water. Raoul Berger, among others, would have the Justices search for, identify (if possible), and then apply the intentions of those who wrote the Document. That idea, as has been said, is not worth serious discussion. Not that the original instrument can be ignored: of course it cannot. But in any situation that reaches the Supreme Court, even if those intentions are known, they should not bind present generations to what was said in yesteryear. Much more is required.

Lord Bryce, and others, have asserted that it is the duty of the Justices to determine "the will of the people" on constitutional issues, and apply it.[75] That view obviously has flaws. There is no such thing as "the" people; the American polity consists of a multiplicity of publics. Even if the people's will could be ascertained, to put it into effect would turn the Court into a mere majoritarian institution. Its function, presumably, would be to employ some sort of public opinion poll when constitutional questions arise and then apply the results of those polls. Furthermore, there is no possible way that the Justices can intuit the "will" of the people. So although it appears likely that they do evaluate in a rough manner the probable acceptance of and thus compliance with specific decisions, that process is a far cry from maintaining that those evaluations should control. Again: much more is needed.

Then there is the school of "judicial self-restraint" that is closely identified with Justice Felix Frankfurter. Although Frankfurter certainly did not deny the legitimacy of judicial review, he advocated its exercise in only extreme cir-cumstances. His preference was to defer to the supposedly democratic branches of government. Many follow similar views. Perhaps the best known was the late Professor Alexander Bickel, who believed in the "morality of process," because, to him, the Supreme Court is a "deviant" institution. Again, however, that course is not enough.

Perhaps the most coherent, sophisticated present-day view is that of Professor John Hart Ely.[76] To him, the Constitution is not a neutral document: "Contemporary constitutional debate is dominated by a false dichotomy. Either, it runs, we must stick close to the thoughts of those who wrote our Constitution's critical phrases and outlaw only those practices they thought they were outlawing, or there is simply no way for courts to review legislation other than by second-guessing the legislature's value choices." To him, the Constitution has two types of clauses: specific and ambiguous. Those vague clauses should not be interpreted, said Ely, either by calling upon the Justices's predilections or by referring to the Founding Fathers. Rather, the Court should look to the entire Constitution and choose its outcomes in particular cases as being the ones that seem most likely to further the democratic process. He called this a "representation-reinforcing" theory, because the results he advocated in the cases he discussed are those that would further the process of representative government. Although sophisticated, Ely's theory presents problems. It does not remove political and moral considerations from constitutional decision making. Furthermore, the theory would approve *First National Bank* v. *Bellotti* (1978),[77] in which the Court accorded a corporation First Amendment rights of expression unrelated to the firm's business; that decision means that the enormous assets of corporations can freely be used politically—and that freedom seems to be the very antithesis of democracy. "The principle of one person/one vote in the political arena . . . confronts the reality of unequal economic rights and an unequal distribution of economic power. The two cannot be separated. The 'free speech' of a General Motors is obviously greater than that of any individual."[78] For the Supreme Court in the *Bellotti* case to speak of "democracy" as if it meant something precise, which emphatically it does not, and to equate the political powers of the natural person with that of a corporate enterprise is, as Justice Robert H. Jackson said in another context, to extend "a promise to the ear to be broken in the hope, a teasing illusion like a munificent bequest in a pauper's will."[79] It is vivid testimony to the poverty of theory about judicial review, and its nature and scope, that Ely's book has been accorded an enormous reception by the professoriate.[80]

V.

What *should* the Supreme Court do? What follows is based on this thesis: *A pressing need exists for an entirely new theory of interpretation.* No useful purpose is served by engaging in debate with any of those mentioned above. None places the Court in socioeconomic context, and none has solved the conundrum first propounded by Chief Justice John Marshall in *Marbury* v. *Madison*, the scope and nature of judicial review.[81] A corollary to the basic thesis is this: *A pressing need exists for improvement of the adversary system, both as to personnel and as to method of operation.*

Said Professor John A. G. Griffith of the London School of Economics:

It is still quite common to hear the constitution described—even lovingly described—as a piece of machinery cleverly and subtly constructed to enable the will of the people to be transmitted through its elected representatives who make laws instructing its principal committee, the Cabinet, how to administer the affairs of state, with the help of an impartial civil service and under the benevolent wisdom of a neutral judiciary. Not only is this the explanation given to thousands of schoolchildren but I have to tell you that it also finds its way—in a more sophisticated form—into the curricula of some institutions of further and higher learning.[82]

Griffith, of course, was talking about the British constitution (which is considered to be unwritten), but his remarks surely are applicable to the United States. The "schoolchildren" version of the Constitution is routinely purveyed in almost all American educational institutions—elementary, secondary, higher, and even in law school. Substitute "the Executive" for Griffith's "the Cabinet," and one sees an accurate description of the United States and the way that Americans are socialized through myths about the Constitution. That description is what is meant by the myth of the perfect Constitution. We have shown the inadequacy of such a conception, mainly in the political order of pluralism. It is time now to propound a new theory of interpretation, one designed to provide for the progressive, *admitted*, in that it is open rather than concealed, updating of the Document of 1787. We ask this question: If the Constitution were to be rewritten today, what would be put in it? Or as Cardozo once said, the interpreter of the Document today has to discern "what today [the Framers] would believe, if they were called upon to interpret . . . that they framed for the needs of an expanding future."[83] In answering this question, it is important that admittedly wide judicial discretion not degenerate into judicial license. Judges must be able to discover "principles sufficiently absolute to give them roots throughout the community and continuity over significant periods of time, and to lift them above the level of pragmatic political judgments."[84]

That objective by no means is an easy task. It may be impossible. But it must be attempted. The values of the past and present must be discerned and linked to the demands of the future. There is no possible way that the art of judging can be reduced to a mathematical or chemical formula; human affairs and disputes are not problems to be solved in the laboratory or on the blackboard. The need is for a dynamic, rather than static, jurisprudence of the Court. The theory of interpretation suggested here is predicated upon the assumptions set out above. It is one, as has been said, of even more judicial activism.

Political scientists have, whether they realize it or not, adopted from Adam Smith economics the idea of the "invisible hand"; they assume that out of the clash of interest groups, consensuses will emerge, each one identified as being in the public or national interest. That idea is what Professor Bickel called "the morality of process."[85] To him, pluralism was sufficient to the need. He thought that out of the bickerings and joustings of the political process wise political decisions would emerge—and, therefore, that there was little reason for the Supreme Court to intervene. But the very statement of that proposition is its own refutation. By hindsight, but doubtless not for many of those who lived through the times, pluralism worked in the past: The result is a large and strong nation. That result, however, should not be attributed to the political system, including the economic order; it is sheer fetishism to accord to the Constitution as such the main causal reason for that size and strength. The system historically was not so much a system as a historical accident; the affluence of the United States was the result of a set of accidental, nonrepeatable, and nonsustainable factors. America is the product of its environment, not its ideology.

The era of abundance is ending, as we have noted, but not with a bang (unless a nuclear war erupts, as it well might) but, in T. S. Eliot's well-known words, "with a whimper." Many still want to believe, and in wanting do believe, that the extraordinary affluence and relative peace and freedom Americans have enjoyed can be repeated given the right amount of will. That, however, is a pathetic, even bathetic, dream; it is Micawberism run riot. We must face the harsh fact that politico-legal mechanisms that were adequate in the past are at least obsolescent. Perhaps they are obsolete. Certainly, a case can be made for the proposition that some of the rigidities of the Document of 1787 are no longer sufficient to the need. A rapidly changing social milieu requires the reexamination and improvement of those mechanisms. In accomplishing this, I will suggest that the Supreme Court, given the proper personnel and an adequate vision of the true needs of the nation, can be of substantial assistance. I will not argue that the judges can do the job alone—we do not have, nor have we ever had in the past, what some purblind commentators persist in calling "government by judiciary"—but they can at least light a candle while the rest of us are cursing the darkness.

With the advent of what can most accurately be called "the politics of self-ishness," a politics that in this generation has become all-pervasive, an immense requirement exists for an authoritative spokesman for national values. There simply is no one today, in either the public or the private sector, who can do that or who is better suited than is the Supreme Court. Never, however, has the task been so demanding. Americans face a harsh environment, both with respect to other nations and with respect to the natural order. We have lived for many years in a type of fool's paradise that made us think as a people that we were something special, that we could avoid, somehow, the tribulations that the less fortunate other nations could not. If the past forty years have taught Americans anything, it is that we, too, are in for it, deeply and irretrievably, and the sooner we realize it the better.

The Court, without announcement, has been groping toward fulfillment of a role as spokesman for national values. A felt need in societal affairs creates a response. Just as nature and politics both abhor vacuums, so too do morals and ethics. Ethical leadership must come, by someone, by some institution. To repeat for emphasis: "The law floats in a sea of ethics," Chief Justice Earl Warren once said.[86] So it does. The Court, as oracle of the law—of constitutional law—has a continuing responsibility to make ethical judgments. It could not be otherwise if the Court is to remain an important organ of American government. It may, as with all human institutions, be imperfect. "The legal machinery," Morris R. Cohen once observed, "never operates apart from human beings, judges, juries, police officials, etc. The imperfect knowledge or intelligence of these human beings is bound to assert itself. It is therefore vain to expect that the legal machinery will work with a perfection that no other human institution does."[87] Surely, that view is accurate; we should not expect perfection from the Supreme Court. But if the Justices are willing to take on an even larger chore in the task of governance, which a large number of Americans, including members of Congress, seem to expect, it can then help the nation navigate the stormy seas that lie ahead. If, that is, they have "the will to discover, the will to enlarge the tiny segment of world we know, the will to learn and to do better, the firm and deepseated conviction that men may, again and again, in everyone's lifetime, see 'thin with distance, thin but dead ahead, the line of unimaginable coasts,'[88] they can play a major role in the transition period toward a sustainable society.

Although the Justices have no real opposition in that task, not even from the President, I do not suggest that their role is now, and surely will not be in the future, an easy one. It is fraught with contention and controversy. That they will meet with contumacy cannot be doubted. But that prospect should not—cannot—be allowed to deter them.

It will do little good to call upon the elected representatives of "the people" in Congress, for that branch is by and large the prisoner of interest groups and of the superior expertise of the executive branch. Nor can the President, as the sole official elected by all the people (albeit indirectly), do much better. Theoretically, he *seems* to be in the best position to fill the need of moral and ethical leadership. But he, too, is the prisoner of the failures of pluralism. The "textbook presidency," of an all-powerful entity, exists only in the textbooks.[89] The President is restrained both by Congress and, mainly, the interplay of decentralized interest groups. He cannot really control even the executive branch; it is too large, too sprawling, too filled with administrators who see presidents and their aides come and go and are able to outlast them. (Richard Nixon knew this well, for one of the major factors in his downfall was the intransigence of the bureaucracy.) The President's power of command is, in last analysis, one of negotiating treaties with the fiefdoms in the branch he purportedly controls. Rather than command, his power tends to be one of persuasion. In this process, which interacts with Congress, the public or national interest is often confused with—is in fact conterminous with—the interests of the groups with the greatest political clout.

Pluralism has always been theoretically faulty. The growth of groups has been perceived, but the most that has been done is to try to assimilate those groups into a notion that, consciously or not, equates them with natural persons. Just as economists have not yet constructed a theory of economic cooperation, a theory, that is, of corporate capitalism, so, too, have political scientists and legal philosophers failed to produce a viable theory of conscious "corporate" political cooperation. The supposition that the public or national interest is a consequence of the clash of interest groups in the political arena is a pathetic fallacy. The "invisible hand" works no better in politics than it does in economics.

It is a socially mischievous situation, one that cries out for sweeping reform. That type of reform, however, is exactly what is not presently possible under the American system of constitutionalism as it has evolved. The system produces what Professor Charles Lindblom has called "the science of 'muddling through,'"[90] which of course is not a science at all but a series of ad hoc adjustments. That type of incremental policymaking does not provide for the anticipation of problems; rather, it is employed after a problem has become an acknowledged crisis, and there is no possibility of rational resolution. American policy, that is, now and in the past, has been a series of cobbled-up compromises. Patches are placed upon the sores of the body politic, without any serious attempt to rectify the causes of those sores. It might be called policymaking by Band-Aid.

The consequence is obvious—and serious: a political and moral vacuum. When bargaining among interest groups is the overriding desideratum of policymaking, the lowest common denominator controls. The need for filling the vacuum has never been more grave. The Supreme Court, as has been suggested in previous chapters, has been moving—haltingly and perhaps without full cognizance of what it was doing—toward fulfilling that need. Some standards have been set, but in a hit-and-miss fashion. There has, thus far, been little consistency in application of norms of what government must do if American constitutionalism is to survive. More by happenstance, it seems, than by design, the Justices draw upon their own consciences to establish standards that in turn become—rather, can become—the conscience of the American people; they articulate values toward which they as a group, but usually not unanimously, believe the American people should strive. Of course, they often disagree, but with some exceptions it is about details, not whether the Court should help to set moral and ethical standards. Since they have no *vade mecum*, no road map by which to steer, they must perforce make up those standards (those rules) as they go along.

The process has been developing since at least 1803. Having to sail upon uncharted seas, picking their way through shoals upon which they might have foundered, the Justices at times have erred, as in the *Dred Scott* decision, but not fatally. That type of self-inflicted wound helped to make the Justices fully aware of the strengths and limitations of their powers, of how they as political actors could take part in "the art of the possible." Today, almost two centuries after the Document was drafted and the Supreme Court came into existence, those whose fate it is to sit on the High Bench are both seen *and* accepted as authoritative spokespersons for national values. As such, they are a modern version of the Oracle at Delphi; in the authority, as well as the opacity, of its pronouncements, the Court tends more and more to resemble that famous institution of ancient Greece. I do not wish to push the analogy too far, but do wish to suggest that there is at least some resemblance between the Court and the Delphic Oracle. Oracles in ancient times helped humans to find their way in the face of an unknown and threatening future—precisely the future that Americans confront today.

That help was on "substantive" issues—what people should or should not do. "The mere fact," said H. W. Parke and D.E.W. Wormell in their *The Delphic Oracle*, "that Delphi provided a center for enquiry on many subjects was of incalculable significance in the Greek world."[91] The Delphic Oracle has often been compared with the papacy, and it is true that there are marked resemblances. But the analogy should not be pressed too far. In many respects the Oracle seems closer to the Supreme Court. The Delphic claim that the Oracle was "without deceit" seems similar to the idea of the Court as ultimate law interpreter or lawmaker under the Constitution—the notion of Supreme Court infallibility. Moreover, the Delphic priesthood, like Supreme Court Justices, had no organized religious system, no established church, but did have close and continuing contacts with local priests—or, in the case of the Court, with the American bar. In each instance, these officials were voluntary agents, and neither Delphi nor the Court could or can exercise more than an influence limited by the fact that the local officials can choose freely to obey the commands issued from on high. "The supremacy which Delphi long maintained over its rivals and all other methods of divination was largely the outcome of an accumulated prestige, and was little supported by dogma or ecclesiastical organization." So it is with the High Bench.

In both instances, those who issued the words of wisdom felt (and feel) the need for proceeding with caution in answering some of the more controversial questions. Their decisions had (and have) to commend themselves to public opinion, even though both could (and can) mold opinion by their decisions. Both have displayed (and do display) a willingness to make pragmatic adjustments to the situations in which they operate. In politics, both were opportunists; they made decisions that were relative to circumstances.

There is, then, more than a slight analogy that can be drawn between the

Oracle at Delphi and the Supreme Court in the Marble Palace. Consider, too, what may be called the procedural characteristics of the Oracle. Parke and Wormell told us:

> The whole activity of the oracle whether in politics, morality or religion was limited by one typical handicap: it could not well initiate action. It had to wait to be approached with an enquiry, before it could give its judgment.... So the oracle's part was more often to suggest risks and offer warnings than to present new ideas or urge on with encouragements....
>
> Still, the Delphian authorities, even though their handling of political problems was sometimes shifting, maintained a firm, even if somewhat negative, position on moral issues. It is this fact which gives an inner rightness to many of their responses, in spite of their mistakes. For the rest, one must remember that in several ways the history of the oracle must always remain difficult for one to understand. Its procedure was mysterious and can never be precisely explained.[92]

So with the Court: as a general rule—although, as we have noted, the abundance of cases today tends to make it different—the Justices have to wait to be approached with an inquiry before they can pronounce judgment. (Once approached, however, the extent of their decision is entirely within their discretion. They can act as "commander," as was shown in Chapter 5.) The Court's procedure, in the sense of its internal workings, remains entirely mysterious despite publication of books such as *The Brethren*.[93]

Until very recent times, a remarkable closeness between politics and religion existed. The history of the Western world cannot be understood without inquiring into that theme. That is so, even though there is an apparent separation, even hostility, between church and State. But such a separation is more ostensible than real: Only in the sense of the church as organized religion, recognized and supported as such by the State, can there be said to be a separation in the United States. A like separation between religion and the State is another matter. The distinction is important. It has a significant consequence when one thinks of the Supreme Court as modern Delphic Oracle. The State has in modern times increasingly replaced the church in determining how we should behave. "Up until our own times," Julien Benda wrote, "men had only received two sorts of teaching in what concerns the relations between politics and morality. One was Plato's, and it said: 'Morality decides politics'; the other was Machiavelli's, and it said: 'Politics have nothing to do with morality.' Today they receive a third. M. Maurras teaches: 'Politics decide morality.' "[94]

If, then, it is conceded, as it must be, that the Supreme Court is a political organ and makes political decisions of importance to the American people, what the Justices say tends to help set the moral tone of the nation. In so doing, they thus merge the concepts of politics and religion—but in the language of the law. The law may have a "specious morality," as Professor

Sanford Levinson has argued,[95] but nonetheless, ethical behavior is mainly a matter of rule making and rule following. The confluence of politics and morality has been well stated by R. M. Hartwell:

> In working, living, and believing the state is now arbiter. It decides about the work place, about the family, and about values. Since the market is no longer allowed to function freely, the state must decide what to produce and how to distribute that production; since the family as a social unit has declined because of the erosion of parental responsibilities largely as a result of state action, the state must decide about education, health, behavior, and all other aspects of growing up and earning a living; and, finally, since the state decides what values should prevail in society, and ensures that such values are embodied in legislation and enforced by bureaucracies, the state has increasingly replaced the church in determining how we should behave. *Politics is now religion.*[96] (Emphasis added.)

Whether one approves of the rise of the State to preeminence (Hartwell does not) is not our present point. Rather, it is that the Supreme Court, as an important part of the political process, cannot avoid making both political and moral decisions. Thomas Dempsey in his study of the Oracle has noted that it was a "legislator and a source of public law"; furthermore: "The Oracle seems to have been consulted in early as well as later times as to the best mode of government."[97] The Spartan constitution of Lycurgus was apparently dictated to him by the Oracle.

It would be wrong to push the analogy too far. There is, of course, an enormous difference between ancient Greece and modern America. Nevertheless, the resemblance is there. Often, commentators will suggest that the Justices are acting like a group of latter-day Platonic philosopher-kings, but that analogy is even more strained. They are not that, although a good and even persuasive argument can be made that they should be. My point, for the moment, is the far lesser one that Americans consult *their* Oracle (in the Marble Palace) much like the Greeks sought counsel from *their* Oracle (at Delphi). I do not say that the Delphic Oracle was the only one consulted; there were other, lesser ones, just as in the United States there is a multiplicity of courts, state and federal, that are consulted by litigants.

The oracular Supreme Court is no modern invention; its roots lie deep in American history. But the full flowering of the concept has come only in the past three or four decades. Beginning in the 1930s, a series of permissive decisions were issued, allowing intervention by the State into socioeconomic affairs that theretofore had been barred. Ancient constitutional language was reinterpreted—redefined—and powers for the federal government were found lurking in Article I that had theretofore been denied it. That led, as we have seen, to the constitutional revolution of the 1930s and 1940s. The Constitution of Powers came into existence, as a translucent layer on the Document of 1787. That development, however, should be seen as one in which the Court constitutionalized political pluralism: The formal law promulgated by the Court reflected the group basis of politics.

The turning point came in the 1937 decision sustaining the Wagner labor relations act: *Jones & Laughlin Steel Corp.* v. *National Labor Relations Board.*[98] There the Justices agreed with the President and Congress that labor could bargain collectively with management, and therefore that the public interest would be served by the pulls and tugs at the bargaining tables between the two decentralized groups. That decision, again, is a version of Adam Smith economics—the "invisible hand"—written into politics (into the Constitution). Not that the Justices wrote their opinion in those words. Rather, they played the lawyers's game of determining the meaning of interstate commerce and of Congress's power to regulate it. But the consequence of *Jones & Laughlin* is not a mere legalism: it meant that the Document of 1787 had been subtly "amended" to reflect the acceptance of the theory that conflicts between "factions" could be beneficent. The political reality of pluralism had been melded into the Constitution.

Perhaps the Justices had no choice, for they were under heavy attack following President Roosevelt's landslide 1936 electoral victory. Perhaps, too, they thus learned a salutary lesson—the Justices may be able to influence the formation of the *zeitgeist*, but they cannot for long withstand the brute force of public opinion. Their capacity to establish norms of behavior is, in other words, limited; they must evaluate what the people, generally, will tolerate. They cannot, in sum, always be a naysayer. Not only must they be permissive—allowing the politicians to do what they wish in some areas—but they must also attempt to state what *should* be done in an affirmative sense. The Court as modern Delphic Oracle does not have a passive role. To constitutionalize political pluralism is one thing; doing that merely involved stepping aside and permitting politicians to have free rein. It is another thing to promulgate affirmatively propositions of what other government officers must or should do. The discovery that the Constitution contains some positive duties, as well as negative limitations, came late in American history—well within the lifetimes of those who sit on the High Bench today. Not before the 1940s was a conception of legally concretized decency read into the Document as a means of aiding those left behind in the political process. The *Jones & Laughlin* decision, and the legislation it upheld, were, however, typical products of a pragmatic frame of mind; they were ad hoc adjustments, legal Band-Aids plastered on the Constitution.

Neither Congress nor the President nor the Supreme Court considered more than the immediate effects. The "second-order" consequences, the long-term effects, were simply not thought of or, when they were, they were assumed away by an assumption, tacit or otherwise, that the new system would inure to the public good. That it has not done so has already been stated. James Madison, by the way, knew that: "By a faction I understand a number of citizens, whether amounting to a majority or minority of the whole, who are united and actuated by some common impulse of passion, or of interest, *adverse to the rights of other citizens, or to the permanent and aggregate interests of the community.*"[99] In other words, interest-group competition (pluralism) to Madison was an evil to be rendered tolerable—to be tamed—rather than a safeguard of democracy to be embraced. Said federal Judge J. Skelly Wright: "we need not accept the pluralists's proposition. We simply are not so helpless that we must blindly equate the outcome of the group pressure process with the public interest.... It is certainly possible to assert—indeed, the case is compelling—that the pluralist process has thwarted the public interest for years."[100] That view, in brief, is the challenge that the desuetude of the political order presents to the Supreme Court.

The Justices began and have continued by recognizing other groups and according them constitutional aid. Justice Harlan Fiske Stone, in a famous footnote in 1938, suggested that the Court should overtly acknowledge that "discrete and insular minorities" left behind in the political group struggle should be given special attention. Professor John Hart Ely has asserted that the tune first composed by Stone was the music to which the Court marched during the tenure of Chief Justice Earl Warren; that Court, he said, was a *Carolene Products* tribunal (the *Carolene Products* case being the one where Stone inserted his influential footnote).[101] Ely's point is valid, although it seems to be too narrow a perspective: The Court marched to other drummers as well.

Racial separation is an example. The first crack in America's de facto caste system came in 1938, in the *Missouri Law School* case,[102] where the Court told Missouri that it could not prevent a black from attending the state's all-white law school even though Missouri was willing to pay his expenses at some law school in another state. That dent in the wall of indecency in the treatment of blacks was soon widened. In *Smith* v. *Allwright* (1944),[103] the linchpin of the so-called white primary cases, blacks for the first time could vote in primary elections of the Democratic party in the South. Then came *Shelley* v. *Kraemer* (1948),[104] in which the Court finally perceived what should have been obvious to all except the willfully blind—that judicial action is state action within the terms of the Fourteenth Amendment, and that, therefore, racially restrictive covenants could not be enforced. (*Shelley* is an immensely important decision, one that, if carried to its logical extreme could literally bring about a revolution in American law. To date, the Justices have not done so.) The movement toward decency in treatment of black Americans reached its apotheosis in the series of education cases that culminated in *Brown* v. *Board of Education* (1954). Neither the Court nor the *formal* law concerning blacks have been the same since—the Court because it made a judgment as to "the best mode of government" and the formal law because the principle of *Brown* was quickly applied in all other actions of government. (The *operative* law often differs markedly.)

In *Brown* and progeny, the Court articulated affirmative principles of morality. It changed the Constitution as it had been known. Blithely sweeping aside the history of the Fourteenth Amendment as being "inconclusive" on the point of racial separation in public schools, a unanimous High Bench found that education was a fundamental right that required equality rather than separateness. The Justices also cited a number of social scientists to buttress their conclusion that separate schools imposed an undue psychological burden on black children. (That type of input, of course, was nothing new; we have already noted that the Court since at least 1908 has overtly used socioeconomic data in its opinions. Those data are as legal as are rules of law.) In fine, the Justices held that "separate but equal," embedded in constitutional law since *Plessy* v. *Ferguson* (1896), was morally insupportable. As the first Justice John Harlan said in his *Plessy* dissent, the Constitution is "color blind." (The pity is that the American people are not.)

The Court's apparent success in questions of racial discrimination emboldened the Justices to move into other areas of social dispute. The condition of urban voters, for example, was made a constitutional matter in 1962 when the decision in *Baker* v. *Carr*[105] held that urban voters could bring a case contesting a disparity in voting powers with rural voters. Two years later, in *Reynolds* v. *Sims*,[106] the Justices went the full mile and enunciated the one person/one vote principle. So, too, in questions of the administration of the criminal law: for the first time in American history, constitutional norms were brought to bear against local police officers. *Miranda* v. *Arizona* (1966)[107] is perhaps the highlight. Then in 1973 the Court recognized the right of a woman to terminate her pregnancy.[108]

Many other decisions were made, but those stated above show the pattern: By design or perhaps by happenstance or possibly because the Justices either had insight into a system of absolute values or asserted that they did, some segments of the populace unable to benefit from the pluralistic political process found a champion in a handful of lawyer-judges. Odd, one might think, particularly when one considers the nature of the legal profession. But perhaps it is not so strange if those decisions are analyzed as a means of helping to distract social discontent. Recall, in this connection, the conclusion of Professor John A. G. Griffith in *The Politics of the American Judiciary*: "the judiciary in any modern industrial society, however composed, under whatever economic system, is an essential part of the system of government and . . . its function may be described as underpinning the stability of that system and as protecting that system from attack by resisting attempts to change it"[109]—not all attempts, of course, but those considered to be minimally necessary to dampen social discontent. I do not say that *all* of the civil rights/civil liberties decisions of the past four decades can be so analyzed.

Enough fit the pattern, however, to be able to conclude that the Supreme Court, in part at least, operates as a social safety valve, bleeding off some of the pustules of social disharmony. Its latent, and at times its manifest, function is to help preserve the socioeconomic status quo. That task can only be done in some instances by government making what seem to be major alterations—but which often turn out to be mere symbolic victories or cosmetic changes.

Brown and *Baker* classically illustrate the point. Even Justice Frankfurter knew that long-suppressed fires of discontent would soon flare up; he was therefore willing—in fact, he was instrumental in getting unanimity in the Court—to strike down racial segregation. (That decision, by any criterion, was his finest judicial hour.) On the other hand, Frankfurter simply could not believe that voters who were victims of the nation's "rotten boroughs" were in the same position as blacks; hence his searing dissent in *Baker*, in which he told urban voters to repair to the very politicians who were the object of the urban voters's discontent and ask that they vote themselves out of office. *Brown* plus *Baker* (plus, as we have seen in Chapter 5, *Cooper* v. *Aaron*) signaled a revolution in the Court's jurisprudence. Whether one agrees with Griffith that judges are Establishment figures whose function it is to stabilize the social order or with those who see the Justices as self-appointed protectors of the disadvantaged and oppressed, there can be no question but that a major milestone in the history of the Supreme Court had been reached— and passed.

To neoconservatives, such as Nathan Glazer and Raoul Berger, the development meant that the Justices have abandoned prudence and are legislating their personal predilections into the Constitution. That belief, however, can hardly be true; or, rather, if it is true, it really is nothing new. Since the inception, the Justices have only been prudent when they perceived a need for it; they have always, as we have repeatedly said, seen in the fundamental law certain principles that (miraculously?) coincide with their personal preferences. The critical points are these: first, the Justices saw a vital need, the political turmoil occasioned by the rise of new groups to power (for example, labor unions and farmers's leagues), and moved to fill it. Second, they did not comprehend that in so doing they were in effect producing either a political vacuum or, better, a stalemate.

The Court as safety valve, as protector of minority interests, has become in some instances (but far from all) "a revolutionary committee."[110] For the first time in American history, non-Establishment plaintiffs, and some defendants, found in the High Bench a safe harbor for claims long denied by a polity that professed to give them (but in fact often did not) some relief. Not only blacks but divers others began to employ the judiciary as a means of working "within the system"; judges became a target, not dissimilar from legislators, of pressure-group tactics.[111] The Supreme Court acted like a third branch of the legislature, and was treated as such. Not everyone agreed, to be sure. Those who had previously dominated politics, and the courts, at times found *their* oxen being gored. They didn't like it. So an intellectual counterattack against the Court—and thus against their permissive decisions (although this was seldom publicly admitted, particularly with respect to questions of racial segregation)—was soon mounted.

If there was any one leader of that counter-revolution, it was Justice Felix Frankfurter. The public point of departure came in 1958 when Judge Learned Hand published *The Bill of Rights*, a mellifluous diatribe against the new role of the courts. Hand called the Justices a group of "Platonic Guardians," which referred to Plato's call for philosopher-kings to rule; Hand was not correct in labeling the Justices as Guardians, for under Plato's plan the Guardians were divided into "rulers" and "enforcers"; he would have been more accurate to use the term "philosopher-kings" or "philosopher-rulers". That, however, is a minor matter. Of far more importance was his error in thinking, however, implicitly, that the political process was adequate to the need. It was on that point that he joined forces with Frankfurter.

Frankfurter and Hand are the leading saints in the hagiology of what may be called the Frankfurter School of Judicial Criticism. Their votaries are many, and their critics are few. The chorus of approval is led by a group of neoconservatives whose dirgelike wails fill some law journals and some magazines (such as *The Public Interest*, *Commentary*, and *The American Spectator*). Rejecting the call for "systematic participation . . . of the judiciary in the travail of society,"[112] they insist that judges follow their own Whiggish, Burkean views of proper public policy—Edmund Burke being the English political philosopher who was the defender of the *ancien regime* after the French Revolution. Modern disciples of Burke—Alexander Bickel,[113] an acolyte of Frankfurter, was perhaps the leading exemplar before his untimely death in 1974—fear what they (erroneously) perceive as judicial participation in a "democratical despotism" (John Adams's label). This group of critics is content to belong to or try to join the Society of Jobbists—that "strange cult . . . which 'undertakes only those jobs which the members can do in proper workmanlike fashion.' . . . It demands right quality, better than the market will pass."[114] (Perhaps the Jobbists do not recognize that they take on only minuscle tasks, because their capabilities permit no more.) They would have their personal feelings submerged and not articulated. They want, in other words, the appearance of objectivity even though they all know it is impossible to attain. They admire what they consider to be good craftsmanship: "Opinions based upon reasoned principle," said one of them, "are necessary to the very self-preservation of the Supreme Court. Assuming that the institution is worth preserving, Justices must sometimes sacrifice what they conceive to be a desirable result, if they cannot logically justify that result."[115] That view—it merits emphasis—is consummate nonsense; it does not take into consideration Frankfurter's own position—that decisions must display sociological wisdom as well as logical unfolding. But that is the way with votaries: Those in the Frankfurter School are pale carbon copies of Frankfurter, just as he was a pale copy of his hero, Oliver Wendell Holmes.

The neoconservative critics may well prevail, sooner or later, depending in large part upon the character and philosophy of those who succeed the present Justices. The Justices have not mastered their new role. One gets the impression that they are foundering, without sail or rudder, as they seek to keep the Constitution current with new demands and new situations. The neoconservative critics, however, have managed to set the terms of the public dialogue about the Court, both in professional journals and in the mass media. Law professors and political scientists alike tend to take their signals from, or at least react to, statements and positions uttered by Frankfurter disciples in the law schools of Harvard, Yale, Columbia, and Chicago. The press, too, when it comments on the Court and wishes an expert opinion will in most circumstances telephone a professor at the same universities (to which other elite law schools such as Michigan, Stanford, and the University of California can be added). That tendency means something important: What the people who read the news or the 60 + percent who get it from television and radio are given is the opinions of those who, with some exceptions, are followers of Frankfurter. "Reporters," Stephen Hess maintained, "are not simply passing along information; they are choosing, within certain limits, what most people will know about government. The freedom given and assumed by these news workers affects the shape of national affairs."[116]

Richard Nixon is doubtless guilty of great crimes, both of omission and commission, but packing the Supreme Court with "strict constructionists" is not one of them. He was entitled, as are all Presidents, to nominate anyone he desired, although one may surely wish that he had found men of greater intellectual capacities. No, it was not a crime to name Burger and Blackmun, Powell and Rehnquist—but a good, even persuasive, case can be made for the proposition that it was a disaster. At the very time when the High Bench is called upon to do more than it ever had before, and at a time when the ecological trap is closing, Nixon chose mine-run lawyers who have little or no sensitivity to the true range and gauge of the problems brought to the Court. They tend on the whole to have minds that were typical of the nineteenth century. Other than a desire to protect the existing system of corporate capitalism, they have no discernible philosophy about either the Constitution or the Court's role in interpreting it.

Even so, the Nixon Court does seem to perceive, at least intuitively, one harsh fact—that the American cornucopia is being emptied, and that hard choices will have to be made, choices that increasingly will involve a zero-sum game. Some group—more precisely, some individual who, expressly or not, represents a group—will have to lose. The Age of Scarcity approaches, and the Justices seem to know it. If so, that does not portend a quietistic role for the Court. Rather, it suggests the need for even more judicial activism. The

Justices can show the way, if only they will seize the opportunity, for even more of the corpus of American public policy to take. They can make choices, hard for officers in the political branches, that cannot be avoided as the Constitution of Control comes into existence.

One such choice that should be addressed, and soon, would be to try to rectify the shortcomings of pluralism. That could be done by "constitution-alizing" the disparate groups of decentralized social and political power. The process is easily accomplished: All that is needed is the perception that those groups, like the business corporation, are "persons" within the meaning of the Fourteenth Amendment. As persons, then, they could be held to constitu-tional duties as well as accorded constitutional rights. Citizenship—the formal status of personhood for natural persons—has its duties and responsibilities, as well as rights, Justice Hugo Black wrote in 1944 (in holding that Japanese-Americans could not constitutionally complain about being penned up in concentration camps during World War II). One of those duties would be the application of norms such as due process of law and equal protection of the laws to the centers of decentralized power—giant corporations, for certain, but others as well. The units of neofeudalism (see Chapter 9) should be brought under control. An Australian, Leicester Webb, has stated the point in these terms:

Since there is as yet no comprehensive and accepted theory of group-State relation-ships to guide legislators and since the association, individual and State are in con-stantly changing equilibrium, it may be that the harmonizing of these three elements, which Acton regarded as "the true aim of politics," is best carried out through the processes of a widely-competent judiciary.[117]

That harmonization, as we have said, has gone this far: The Supreme Court has recognized the constitutional validity of the power of decentralized groups. An autonomous national economy, based on little more than a naive belief that if the groups were approximately equal in power they would arrive at decisions not inconsistent with the public interest, was established. What the Court and political officers alike forgot—or what they probably never thought about—was the second half of the equation of harmonization of in-terests: the realization of the public interest. Political theorists were the same; for example, Professor Robert A. Horn, in *Groups and the Constitution* (1956), maintained that although political scientists had not worked out a valid theory of group-State relations, the Supreme Court has been building a constitutional law of association containing principles that provide the start toward "a theory of liberal democracy that includes . . . [voluntary associa-tions] that makes them indispensable to free, representative government."[118] Again, only the halfway house. Again, the unstated assumption that the public interest would be the result. Group relationships may be "harmonized," as Webb said, but only to the extent that the interests of the State (as spokesman for society at large) are submerged.

Something more is needed. Can the Supreme Court devise some means by which the elites of disparate social groups take the public or national interest into consideration when making decisions? How can that most manifest of the shortcomings of pluralism be overcome? No ready answer is apparent. The Justices might erect a standard toward which Americans could or should aspire, but they must rely on the goodwill of others, at all levels of government, to translate those standards into operational reality. One finds little basis for optimism in American history that a judicial effort to rectify the fundamental fault of pluralism might succeed.

But try the Justices should, even though as with all mortals their reach will probably exceed their grasp. The Court may be a poor substitute for Plato's philosopher-kings, and may be a weak and ineffective Council of Elders, but there is no substitute among existing organs of governance. The time has come for the Justices openly and avowedly to forget Bacon's admonition and move on to try to scale greater heights. Said Bacon: "Judges ought to remember that their office is *jus dicere*, and not *jus dare*; to interpret law and not to make law, or give law. Else it will be like the authority, claimed by the Church of Rome, which under pretext of exposition of Scripture, doth not stick to add or alter; and to pronounce that which they do not find; and by show of antiquity to introduce novelty."[119] Justices Byron White and William Brennan, of the present Supreme Court, have candidly admitted that "their office" tends to be "*jus dare*"—that the Court cannot avoid doing more than mere "interpretation," but must "make" or "give" law. Professor Ray Forrester's bald-faced plea for "truth in judging," by which he meant open acknowledgment that the Justices make up the law as they go along, merely put into print what all observers admit the High Bench does. Some, as we have said, object vehemently, but no one disputes the point.

By that circuitous route, then, we come to one of the most important aspects of what the Supreme Court should or ought to do: develop a conception of the public or national interest and seek in specific cases to further that goal. I do not suggest that this process will be easy, merely that it is necessary.

Thomas Hobbes wrote in 1651 that groups (corporations) could be likened to "worms in the entrayles of a man"; Adam Smith in 1776 warned, in a comment his modern idolators usually forget, that "people of the same trade seldom meet together, even for merriment and diversion, but the conversation ends in a conspiracy against the public in some contrivance to raise prices." The United States, a corporate society, indeed has those groups eating away at the foundations of society; although businessmen may not conspire in the legal sense, surely there is a remarkable coincidence in the way that they act, set prices, and treat consumers. The point is that, particularly with the ecological trap closing, we are back in the same type of social condition that Hobbes and Smith perceived.

The immediate problem is how to bring American social groups within the ambit of the Constitution. That task requires, at the outset, an inquiry into whether they can fit into ancient constitutional language. The answer, at this time, is a qualified yes: Some groups (but not all of them) have received constitutional protection by the Supreme Court calling them "persons" within the meaning of the Fourteenth Amendment;[120] some have had constitutional norms brought to bear against them, mainly because the Court considered them to be sufficiently like a government to come within the meaning of "state action" of the same Amendment.[121] The argument advanced in each instance is that either as a constitutional person or as a segment of "private" government, groups can be held to constitutional duties as well as having rights.

No need exists to repeat the discussion in Chapter 9, save to emphasize that the Supreme Court could in 1886 in effect amend the Document by ruling that business corporations were persons. As such, they apparently have all of the rights of natural persons, including freedom of speech (as the Court held in 1978). No other groups have been given that status, although the Court in 1952 came close to doing so for the Russian Orthodox church. The decision, *Kedroff* v. *St. Nicholas Cathedral*,[122] involved the question of whether secession of the American branch of the church from control of the Moscow patriarch meant that the Americans could, under a New York statute, be the beneficial owner of Russian Orthodox property in New York. The Supreme Court found the statute to be an interference with the free exercise of religion in that it "directly prohibits the free exercise of an ecclesiastical right, the Church's choice of its hierarchy." That meant that the Justices accorded constitutional protection to an international body of believers; the liberty of that group differed from the individual liberties of its members. Of even greater significance, the right of that group was recognized, even though it was an international body with its home office for spiritual government in a foreign nation.

To call an international church, in effect if not in explicit language, a constitutional person is as large a mental leap as calling a disembodied economic entity, the business corporation, a person. Those decisions, however, are open invitations to the Justices to do the same for other groups. Should they do so, social groups, as persons under the Constitution, could be held to duties. That possibility becomes particularly evident when to the concept of personhood is added the notion that these groups are in fact organs of governance—of *private* governance, to be sure, but governance nonetheless. The corporation and church decisions were a means of securing group autonomy. My argument, however, is that personhood can be a device for bringing groups under stricter legal control.

In the modern age, government can operate effectively only through a complex set of interacting groups, each of which performs a vital societal function. At the same time, those groups, which are encouraged and strengthened by the State, and sometimes borrow or employ the State's coercive powers, can be as great a threat to individual freedom as the State itself. "Between all these groups," J. N. Figgis maintained, "there will be relations, and not merely between the individuals composing them. To prevent injustice between them and to secure their rights, a strong power above them is needed. It is largely to regulate such groups and to ensure they do not outstep the bounds of justice that the coercive force of the State exists."[123]

It is the business of courts to consider when "the bounds of justice" have been exceeded. The Supreme Court cannot—at least, should not—fail to confront that need. The time has come for the Justices to recognize that the group basis of politics, which they have done so much to further, requires examination to determine its coincidence with the basic norms of the fundamental law.

John Maynard Keynes, the intellectual father of recognition by Congress and the Court of groups other than the corporation, knew that as long ago as 1926:

> I believe that in many cases the ideal size for the unit of control and organization lies somewhere between the individual and the State. I suggest, therefore, that progress lies in the growth and the recognition of semi-autonomous bodies within the State— bodies whose criterion of action within their own field is solely the public good as they understand it, and from whose deliberations motives of private advantage are excluded, though some place it may still be necessary to leave, until the ambit of men's altruism grows wider, to the separate advantage of particular groups, classes, or faculties—bodies which in the ordinary course of affairs are mainly autonomous within their prescribed limitations, but are subject in the last resort to the sovereignty of the democracy expressed through Parliament. I propose a return, it may be said, towards mediaeval conceptions of particular autonomies.[124]

It is to aid leaders of private groups to exclude "motives of private advantage" that the Supreme Court can be of substantial assistance. My suggestion is that those groups should be "subject to the sovereignty of the democracy," not only as expressed in the legislature but also as expressed in the Supreme Court.

We deal here, in Maitland's words, with a problem where the thoughts of many disciplines are combined—history and political science, philosophy and law; it is a "theme from the borderland where ethical speculation marches with jurisprudence."[125] The powers of corporate organizations—including but not limited to business corporations—of our organized society require curbing in the interests of the greater good—the common good, the good of the community at large. Groups, whether autonomous or semiautonomous, are parts of a community; they owe duties and obligations to that community as well as members of their organizations. One of those duties is, as Keynes said, to act in accordance with "the public good."

That idea of course is abstract and gives much room for coming to different conclusions about what is "the public good." But if the Justices on the Supreme Court would openly and avowedly state that their goal is to enunciate "the public good as they understand it," a first step would be taken on the road to discovery of the details of that all-essential goal. "The key to the discovery of the general good," Robert Paul Wolff told us,

is the concept of community. The severest criticisms of liberal society, both from the left and from the right, focus on the absence of community in even the most efficient and affluent liberal capitalist state. Conservative critics bemoan the loss of tradition and look back longingly to an earlier age when men were bound together by meaningful ties of loyalty and trust; radical critics decry the reduction of all human interactions to the exploitative rationality of the cash nexus, and look forward hopefully to a time when work will unite men in cooperative production rather than setting them against one another in destructive competition.[126]

If that view makes me a "radical critic," so be it; the need is for groups to act "in cooperative production" rather than "destructive competition." The competition of the groups in the American pluralistic society bids fair to destroy the nation. Pluralism is not a self-correcting system; something more is required. The Supreme Court can help fulfill it.

The corporation in history has moved from being an entity that was regarded as an agency of the State, created as an arm of the State for the purpose of achieving public ends through private interests, to an autonomous—at least, semiautonomous—societal-unit (the position it is in now), to a dawning recognition that it is a center of political power and should be treated as such insofar as individuals directly affected by the enterprise are concerned. The latter development, now in its beginning stages, points up what Henry Carter Adams said many years ago—that "the satisfactory working of a society whose moral code is expressed in the formula of rights" requires "that responsibility should attach itself to the exercise of liberty."[127] We are beginning to see responsibilities of corporate entities developed in the main by legislation, as a result of bargaining with other corporate units (such as trade unions), and to a small extent by the application of constitutional limitations to the firms. The latter movement is more incipient than actual; corporations as constitutional persons are still more equal, as George Orwell might have said, than natural persons.

The next step, not yet taken or even talked about save by implication, is for recognition of societal rights in corporate entities, the rights, that is, of the national community toward one of its decentralized agencies. The concept of "responsibility" about which Adams wrote must now consider the claims of the community itself. The liberty of the artificial persons of our corporate society, whether recognized as constitutional persons or not, must encompass a moral code of both rights and duties. Liberty is, in other words, the liberty of an entity in a collective organization. It is time to return to the original conception of corporate enterprises (whether business firms or otherwise) as arms of the State, created for the purpose of doing some of the public's (or society's) business.

The Supreme Court can, if it will, help effect that transmutation. (I am not so naive as to expect that the present group of Justices, consisting in the main of corporation lawyers, will accomplish that end.) The first requirement would be for the Court to acknowledge that leaders of corporate entities "are obliged to recognize a dual code of ethics—one for the business, one for the home."[128] When corporate managers place the financial welfare—the profits—of the enterprise in a preeminent position, they are following what I have called elsewhere a theory of *raison de groupe* (or *raison de compagnie*). By that is meant that they will forgo the practice of personal virtues such as "righteousness, candor, courtesy," and supplant them with profit as the supreme virtue. That course simply will not do. The Court's task as ultimate arbiter of social ethics in the nation is to take action to see that the dual code of ethics becomes one, so that there can be an identity between the "personal" interests of the corporations and social morality.

Should the Supreme Court undertake the task suggested here, no doubt there would be an initial shock. But after that, after the implication of decisions imposing duties on corporate enterprises began to be understood, that shock would wear off. "The quality of the judge's performance," Professor Paul A. Freund once observed, "is at bottom an ethical responsibility."[129] The ethical responsibility of the Justices in the age of what we have called the Constitution of Control is to go beyond historical limitations (mostly self-imposed) on their actions, to see their task large and whole, and to provide moral leadership for a populace that knows not where it is or where it is going. That role, to be sure, is a major step, a large advance (as subsequent discussion will show), but it is necessary. Some oft-quoted language of Alfred North Whitehead suggests the nature of the problem:

It is the first step in sociological wisdom to recognize that the major advances in civilization are processes which all but wreck the societies in which they occur—like unto an arrow in the hands of a child. The art of a free society consists first in the maintenance of the symbolic code; and secondly in fearlessness of revision, to secure that the code serves those purposes which satisfy an enlightened reason. Those societies which cannot combine reverence to their symbols with freedom of revision, must ultimately decay either from anarchy, or from the slow atrophy of a life stifled by useless shadows.[130]

If that opinion is correct, and I think it is, the Supreme Court may be able to do (or help Americans to do) the necessary: maintain the symbolic code (which is the ancient Constitution) while fearlessly revising it.

We have already mentioned one such revision. To develop the larger question, three points are apposite: (1) the problem of historical limitations; this includes both the question of access to the Court and the Court's method of operation, as well as the personnel involved; (2) the need for perceiving the Justices's task as going beyond the immediate problems of the immediate litigants, to take on, that is, a far larger number of public policy questions; and (3) the enunciation of principles of ethical or moral leadership.

Each of these questions is so large that a book could be written about it. For present purposes, it must suffice to sketch the outlines of each and to suggest in general terms a new role for the Justices. Concerning that role, Professor Ronald Downing said:

The fact that the courts are the principal forum for resolving so many political issues is indicative of serious default on the part of our legislative and executive institutions. So long as this default continues, and the courts are responsive to pleas for resolution of such issues, the judiciary (a most fragile institution in the halls of power politics) will continue to be buffeted by the full force of increasingly devastating political conflicts arising in the nation. . . .

There appears to be little prospect that the legislative and executive processes can soon be transformed in such a way as to permit our political system to cope with society's deepest problems. . . .

In short, while it is very doubtful that the courts can save the country, only they may be able to buy the time necessary for revitalization of our other institutions.[131]

Precisely. I do not say that the judiciary can save Americans from their follies, but do say that they can, if they will, help "buy the time" required for other organs of government to refurbish themselves. The Supreme Court as modern Delphic Oracle can—should—be consulted for counsel on the "devastating political conflicts" within the nation.

First, consider the question of access to the courts and to the adversary system, including the personnel of what Jeremy Bentham called "judge and company." In this part, as well as succeeding parts, my position is almost directly contrary to that of Justice Felix Frankfurter. "History teaches," wrote Frankfurter, "that the independence of the judiciary is jeopardized when courts become embroiled in the passions of the day and assume primary responsibility in choosing between competing political, economic, and social pressures."[132] An "intense patriot," Frankfurter was inclined to let what he called the democratic institutions of America have their way except in the very clearest cases of excès de pouvoir. He also took from his intellectual mentor, Oliver Wendell Holmes, the idea of judicial self-restraint, but without full realization of the fact that Holmes's ideas were developed in the context of economic legislation. Frankfurter applied those ideas in entirely different contexts: civil rights and civil liberties. Although he was fully knowledgeable about how government in Washington worked, he nevertheless failed to perceive that the pluralistic system of democracy that he extolled had serious shortcomings. He simply did not think that "discrete and insular minorities" needed judicial protection. His was a simplistic, even naive, conception of the governing process. (Moreover, he was quite willing to defer to the states even in cases that today seem to shock one's conscience. For example, the famous

Francis case,[133] presented the question of whether Louisiana could send a person to the electric chair and kill him, after the first effort failed because the electricity was not powerful enough. Francis merely sizzled the first time. Against an argument that a second attempt would constitute cruel and unusual punishment, Frankfurter's key vote in a 5-4 decision sent Francis to his death. Frankfurter warned that the Court should not enforce its private view, but "the consensus of society's opinion which, for purposes of due process, is the standard enjoined by the Constitution." That simply is not accurate. "The consensus of society's opinion" has never been the standard for due process, if for no other reason than that there is no way that opinion can be determined. Frankfurter knew that, of course, but chose to rule as he did. That decision is one of the reasons why he can accurately be called the most overrated judge in American history. Francis had his "day in court," to be sure, but hardly was treated fairly.)

I speak here of a variation of political justice—the use of legal procedure for political ends—although I do not follow the model employed by Otto Kirchheimer in his classic volume with that title. To him, political justice meant the use of "the devices of justice to bolster or create new power positions." He dealt, however, with political trials, with repression and trial by fiat—and thus what might, at least to many, be termed an improper use of the legal machinery. The United States has had its share of political trials as Kirchheimer spoke of them. But that is not our concern. In highest level abstraction, *political justice* means a "search for an ideal order in which all members will communicate and interact with the body politic to assure its highest perfection."[134] Ideals, however, are unrealizable in this world, so our center of inquiry here is the extent to which the devices or mechanisms of justice, of the legal system, can be used to create a just society. That may, likely will, involve "new power positions," but those positions will be created not by fiat or by *diktat* or by force but by the workings of the system. A large order? Yes, of course. Is it possible? No one can say until it is tried. *If* it is tried.

Who, then, should have access to the courts, particularly to the Supreme Court? The Justices cannot reach out and grasp some public-policy issue and make a judgment upon it. They must await the stimulus of litigation. That is basic. But it is far from a complete account. Two points merit mention: First, as we have already seen, once a case does get to the Temple on the Hill, the Justices may do with it as they wish. They can rule narrowly, sculpting their decision to the immediate parties, or they can rule broadly and thus promulgate a general norm. In this respect, the "who" may be one person, but the ramifications can be nationwide. The second point is even more fundamental: Only those who are seen to present a "case or controversy" may trigger the courts. The litigant, in sum, must present a "justiciable" controversy or question.

That requirement, at least, is the language of the Constitution. Over the years since 1803 the Justices have developed a number of devices to avoid ruling on some matters. They fall into two general patterns: First, the controversy must be "live" (it cannot be "moot"), and the parties before the bench must not be "friendly"; they must be at loggerheads and not present a feigned controversy. Second, the issue presented must not fall within the undefined area of "political questions—those questions that the Constitution commits to Congress or the President (or both). The point is that these restrictions are all self-imposed limitations, there being nothing in the Document or the statutes that requires some cases not to be heard. A "case or controversy" thus is whatever the Justices choose to say it is—in their absolute discretion. Historically, the Supreme Court has had a philosophy of avoiding ruling on constitutional matters except when the clearest case is presented. That stance, at least, is the rhetoric of the Justices.

The rhetoric is not always followed. Nor should it be. The fundamental problem confronting Americans is to have wise public policies promulgated by government. That is so, whatever the source of those policies—in Congress, from the President, or from the judiciary. A refusal to rule on some scabrous problem, because it is asserted to be too "political" or "moot," or to defer unduly to the "democratic" branches of government, serves neither the real needs of the American people nor the constitutional purpose of the Supreme Court. There should be wider access to the courts. In one of his last opinions, one dealing with alleged racial discrimination, Justice William O. Douglas put the matter well: "cases such as this reflect festering sores in our society; and the American dream teaches that if one reaches high enough and persists there is a forum where justice is dispensed. I would lower the technical barriers and let the courts serve that ancient need."[135] Limiting access to the courts can only perpetuate long-felt grievances and eliminate one of the prime checks on the behavior of governmental officers.

The question, emphatically, is not to advocate that the courts intervene into every problem confronting Americans. Rather, it is to propose that the Justices take a liberal view of their own capacities. They should immerse themselves in the travail of society. But such expanded intervention does not, equally emphatically, mean that a complainant should always win when governmental action is challenged. My suggestion, in sum, is an invitation for the Justices to learn and to appreciate their large—indeed, enlarged—role in American society and to learn how to ask, and perhaps to answer, the proper questions. They can help develop what Professor William A. Galston called "a rudimentary sense of fairness and equity" through a system of education carried on at the highest level. Through judicious use of their lawful powers, they can help Americans "to surmise what is possible or probable within a given situation, . . . a feel for what might be called the human and moral center of gravity."[136] The Justices can, in sum, help to further the concept of human dignity in a nation that is rapidly approaching the Age of Scarcity.

That function will, at the outset, necessitate greater access to the courts. But more is required. The Supreme Court's method of operation needs comprehensive reexamination and improvement. We have previously discussed the nature of the "adversary system," the method used by the Supreme Court to make decisions—and thus to make law and establish public policy. That the system, a heritage from feudal days in England when the problems judges decided were the relatively minor disputes between individuals, requires study to determine whether it is sufficient to modern needs is obvious. No effort to do so has thus far been made. Lawyers and judges are content with patching up the system, rather than overhauling it. That overhaul has now become a vital necessity.

Without going deeply into all of the intricacies of the adversary process, two flaws are blatantly evident: first, the means by which the Justices inform themselves; and second, the qualifications of those named to the High Bench. Inquiry into these matters will show the extent of the problem.

"How to inform the judicial mind . . . is one of the most complicated problems," Justice Felix Frankfurter observed during oral argument in *Brown* v. *Board of Education*, the 1954 school desegregation decision.[137] So it is, although the pretense is otherwise. As reflected in judicial opinions and scholarly commentary alike, it is widely assumed—and possibly even believed—that the traditional method of informing the judicial mind through the "normal" operations of the adversary system is sufficient to the need when large issues of public policy (of the constitutional order) are involved. Under this conception, an appellate judge refers to certain documents (briefs and record), to answers gleaned from questions during oral argument, and to "strict" judicial notice. The process is hardly complicated.

That pretense has long been under attack (possibly because it never reflected reality, even historically), particularly during recent decades when the Supreme Court, applying the regnant pragmatic temper, sought to determine what was expedient in the circumstances for the nation. When, as has been shown, the Justices began to issue norms of general applicability—to operate as a "commander"—a different pattern, far different from the orthodoxy, began to emerge. No one, except a Justice himself, can say with any certainty what types of data went into his decisional process—and even then, he would likely not have been aware of the subconscious factors that are present in any decision (in any context). Certain conclusions may be made about how the judicial mind is informed: First, the Justices consider it necessary to go beyond the presentations of lawyers to determine relevant data; second, their opinions purportedly explaining their thinking processes do not fully reveal what they took into consideration; and third, certain personal preferences and predilections consciously or subconsciously have an important role. In sum, very little is known about the flow of information to the High Bench. Enough is known, however, to be able to conclude that the historical method—the orthodoxy—does not comport with reality.

Consider, in this respect, the concept of "judicial notice." As a rule of thumb, courts—including the Supreme Court—may take "notice" of matters "of common knowledge." But what are those matters? Justice Frankfurter went on to say, after his remark quoted above about how complicated it is to inform the judicial mind: "It is better to have witnesses, but I did not know that we could not read the works of competent writers."[138] It is precisely here that the system breaks down. Who are "competent writers?" Should there be ways for the lawyers to test the competency of those writers? At present, those questions are left unanswered.

Writing in 1944, Professor Edmund M. Morgan set forth several "important premises" as background on the problem of "judicial notice." They merit repeating at this time with others added:

As the groundwork for a consideration of the nature and function of judicial notice several important premises must be observed. (1) Our courts are agencies of society for the adjustment of disputes between litigants. The disputes must be real, not moot. Litigants cannot call upon courts to decide hypothetical controversies. (2) Our trial courts of common law are bipartite. Each consists of a judge and jury. Our courts of equity have no juries. The division of functions between judge and jury in courts of common law has set the pattern for the conduct of judges in dealing with questions of law and fact in courts of equity. (3) The judge has exclusive authority to determine the tenor and applicability of rules of law. Neither the judge nor the jury begins a trial with knowledge of any disputed and disputable matter of fact; disputes as to disputable matters of fact must be resolved on the basis of material presented at the trial. (4) The court, whether consisting of judge and jury or of judge alone, has no machinery for discovering, without the aid of the parties, matters of fact which are disputable and disputed. Consequently, the court must apportion between the parties the burdens of making the facts appear in an orderly and reasonable manner. It is the function of the judge to allocate these burdens. (5) The system is designed to produce, so far as practicable, a rational investigation and rational adjustment of disputes as to both law and fact. It necessarily posits a tribunal capable of reasoning rationally.[139]

The very statement of those "premises" is their refutation. The Supreme Court often decides what may be called "hypothetical controversies"; judges in trial courts, about which Morgan spoke, have much greater control than he suggested; often a trial is begun with both judge and jury having some knowledge about matters of disputed fact; judges can by themselves determine matters of fact, and the process is far from rational. There is, at most, only partial validity to Morgan's premises.

Nor is the above list all that is wrong with the underlying assumptions of the adversary process. Each of the following underlying assumptions also is faulty, at least in part. (1) Lawyers appearing before the Supreme Court are sufficiently capable of dealing with complex socioeconomic and technological matters. (2) The lawyers are assumed to be roughly equal in competence or at least to have minimum competence. (3) The Justices, too, are intellectually capable of handling the immensely complicated matters that come before them. They are assumed to be able to deal effectively with the entire range of public-policy problems. (4) The Court's decisions further the "common good." (5) The Justices act as justice blindfolded, with strict impartiality and without predilections or preexisting biases. (6) The Justices rule in accordance with "the law," and do not create law anew with each constitutional decision. (7) The Justices have no interest in who the litigants are or in the social consequences of their decisions. (8) Truth in the legal sense comes from the clash of opposites, in the arena of the courtroom.

Judges, trial or appellate, cannot make decisions without information. My point is that we do not know how judges evaluate such data as comes their way through the adversary process. Enough is known, however, to conclude that the informing process is faulty. That is so without reference to the problem of subconscious motivations (predilections) of the men and women in black robes. One careful study of the system, by Thomas B. Marvell, reached these conclusions: "Appellate judges must make decisions on the basis of incomplete information, as all who hold important decision-making positions must. The adversary system often poorly supplies the information needed, judges' background knowledge is not always helpful, and investigation at the courts is limited."[140] Judges have limited time to gather information and, other than a law clerk or two, plus an occasional staff attorney, have no one to do it for them.

The only possible conclusion is that the system is seriously faulty. That may be seen in the other aspect under discussion: the basic competence of "judge and company." That phrase refers not only to the Justices themselves, but to lower court judges as well, and, of perhaps greatest importance, the lawyers who appear before the High Bench. Again, the conclusion is unavoidable: Lawyers as judges and lawyers as advocates do not have the minimum knowledge or skills to enable them to deal effectively with many of the complex issues of public policy that under the American system of constitutionalism are cast before the Supreme Court for resolution.

There are reasons for that weakness. Some of it may be traced, as we have seen, to blind adherence to the pragmatic temper, the view that "expediency" is the *sine qua non* of decision making. Other reasons exist, including the inadequacy of legal education and practice. Judges tend to be narrow-minded lawyers with little appreciation or even cognizance of the larger issues of public policy with which they are dealing.

Lawyers do not deserve the label of "professional." That self-awarded title is a counterpane covering what lawyers actually are—hired guns, legal mechanics, at best technocrats or *apparatchiks*. They can take orders and can prod subordinates. Their orders come from their clients. Given the fluidity and uncertainty of much of the law, it is a poor lawyer indeed who cannot find a precedent, or at least some colorable analogy, to buttress what his client wants to do. Lawyers, in short, are not so much a group of naysayers as a body of technicians adept in the esoterica of legal procedure. They manipulate the law itself, whether in the legislatures, the administrative agencies, or the courts. Their goal is not justice in the large sense, but victory. Their ideology is "legalism," under which law is separated not only from morals but from politics. They have "tunnel vision," perceiving law as something separate and apart from society, a discrete entity amenable to analysis as such. Legalism means rule following: Moral or proper human behavior is defined in terms of "following the rules." This definition implies that the rules are known and widely acknowledged—precisely what is not true in any matter that gets into litigation.

Legalism as ideology does not accord with reality. Law and politics and morals are inextricably intertwined. Nevertheless, it is still dominant and thus flaws the adversary system and the Supreme Court as a policymaking body. The better lawyers know this when they present, as we have seen, "Brandeis briefs" to the Supreme Court, pamphlets that often are replete with "nonlegal" data (economics, sociology, psychology, among others). Law, moreover, is not simply "there," as the ideology of legalism would have it. Any sociologist knows what lawyers do not (or will not) acknowledge—that the functioning of the State and the legal system are closely entwined. Why is this so? Because, among other things, what passes for education in law school does not teach the interconnection of human matters. Legal education is vocationalism pure and simple. A legal problem is assumed not to differ from, say, a problem faced by an automobile mechanic or a plumber; it is a technical problem and dealt with as such. Nothing could be farther from reality. Legal education, in sum, is a form of brain damage.

Law schools throughout the nation produce legal *apparatchiks*, almost without exception. The schools are in large part service stations for corporations and government. Law professors take pride in the notion that they sharpen a student's mind by narrowing it—at precisely the time that broad-gauged men and women, who see matters whole and truly, are required. Newly minted law graduates must bootstrap their way into even marginally adequate knowledge of economics and politics, of science and technology, any one or all of which may be crucial to their work. Not only their clients but society at large needs more—much more.

Little attention is paid in law school to questions of justice and ethics (even legal ethics!) and about the needs of society as distinguished from clients. Client interest is equated with the public interest—unthinkingly. But since, as Chief Justice Fred Vinson once told the American Bar Association, lawyers represent before the Supreme Court not only their clients but much larger interests,[141] how lawyers are educated and their practice itself does not fulfill obvious needs. In the main, legal education consists of chopping logic with appellate court judges. Students are taught to "distinguish" cases and to construct those sharp quillets of the law that allegedly influence judges. But they learn nothing about law as a system, as perhaps the principal means of social control. This failure results, because the "case method" is employed, with the case being defined as an appellate court opinion. That method is perpetuated, because it is familiar, because it is what the professoriate received, and because it lends itself to examinations similar to state bar examinations. Everyone knows, or should know, that it is an inadequate vehicle for transmitting information and does precious little to hone the skills of a lawyer. All too often, it is merely a luxury by which individual instructors can display their mental agility. The result is that the American people are not getting full value for the hundreds of millions of dollars spent on legal education.

Whether in private practice, as house counsel for corporations, or in government, lawyers have less to offer than they pretend. Most of them, as Chief Justice Warren Burger has said, are not very good in trial courts. The level of oral advocacy before the Supreme Court is depressingly low. The Chief Justice could have gone further: The quality of our judges is also depressingly low. Whether elected or appointed, they tend to be narrow-minded technicians, imprisoned by the ideology of legalism, men and women who perceive human disputes in purely legal terms. "For the most part," Professor Philip Kurland of the University of Chicago Law School has commented, "judges are narrow-minded lawyers with little background for making social judgments."[142] A "social judgment," in Kurland's sense, is not only a legislative prescription; it is one that in last analysis may be said to be a statement of moral or ethical propriety. Some years ago, Dean Roscoe Pound called upon lawyers to be "social engineers,"[143] which is an interesting sentiment but which may be based upon a faulty assumption—that society can in fact be engineered. That is akin to what was called "the arrogance of humanism" by Professor David Ehrenfeld—the notion that humans can control their future. Said Ehrenfeld:

We must come to terms with our irrational faith in our own limitless power, and with the reality that is the widespread failure, in their largest context, of our inventions and processes, especially those that aspire to environmental control. . . .

The core of the religion of humanism [is] a supreme faith in human reason—its ability to confront and solve the many problems that humans face, its ability to rearrange both the world of Nature and the affairs of men and women so that human life can prosper. Accordingly, as humanism is committed to an unquestioning faith in the power of reason, so it rejects other mythologies of power, including the power of God, the power of supernatural forces, and even the indirected power of Nature in league with blind chance. The first two don't exist, according to humanism; the last can, with effort, be mastered.[144]

If for "humanism" we read "legalism," Pound was proposing what might be called, after Ehrenfeld, "the arrogance of lawyers." With overweening conceit, lawyers proceed on the tacit assumption that their activities benefit not only their clients but the public generally. They, thus, whether realized or not, have superstitions (more politely, articles of faith), similar to humanists: *All problems are solvable. Many problems can be solved by technology.*

*Those that cannot have solutions in the social world of politics and eco-
nomics. When absolutely necessary, humankind will buckle down and work
together for a solution before it is too late. Human civilization will survive.*[145]
By calling upon lawyers to be social engineers, Dean Pound allied himself
(and lawyers) with the superstitions of humanism. The problems humans
confront are infinitely greater than Pound, and others like him, assumed. He,
and others, unthinkingly displayed an almost absolute faith in the ability of
humans to control their own destiny.

That they cannot should be obvious. The "social engineering" of President
Franklin D. Roosevelt's New Deal was carried over in all of his successors's
administrations—including, be it emphasized, that of President Reagan.
Reagan ostensibly is trying to reduce the scope of governmental activity (his
success is unlikely), but in so doing he, too, is engaging in a form of social
engineering. It seems that the effort cannot be escaped. Certainly, it cannot
be as the Age of Scarcity draws ever nearer.

Whether society can be "engineered," is one question; whether lawyers
should emphasize the "social" in their actions is another. My suggestion here,
one that is discussed more fully below, is that lawyers and lawyer-judges, if
they are to be true "professionals," must consider more than the immediate
and specific interests of clients or of litigants. In other words, considerations of
social justice should become an integral part of lawyers's work, whether on the
bench or in private practice. There are claims on professionals, such as
lawyers and economists, that transcend the immediate and obvious. Society,
too, has its rights. I do not contend that social justice is an easily defined
concept, nor am I so naive as to think that individuals who are lawyers will
spring to the call for social justice as well as furtherance of their clients's wishes.
The point is merely stated now, and will be elaborated in a moment, that the
guild made up of professional lawyers is, as John P. Davis said about corporations, a division of society rather than a congeries of discrete individuals.

The focus now is not upon lawyers as a guild, but upon those few who
have been chosen (or elected) to wear the black robes of judicial office. What
is the task of a judge? It is to exercise ethical and moral leadership, to search
for and identify principles of justice (not only for the litigants before him but
for the social order). I am not so rash as to delineate those principles. My
point is the lesser but nonetheless enormously significant one that judges
should always consider what is socially just in the community. That need is
particularly true for the Supreme Court, which even though it may be an
undemocratic institution is a part of what often is called the "democratic
process"; as such, it should help, in the language of Professor Frank H.
Knight, in fulfilling "the task, enormously more difficult than enforcing a law
known to all, of deciding what the law ought to be and making any changes
called for."[146] Justice refers to the justice *of* the law itself, not only to what the
existing laws prescribe. That means that reference must perforce be made to

some external standard of judgment. As Oliver Wendell Holmes put it in 1881:

> The very considerations which judges most rarely mention, and always with an apology, are the secret root from which the law draws all the juices of life. I mean, of course, consideration of what is expedient in the community concerned. Every important principle which is developed by litigation is in fact and at bottom the result of more or less definitely understood views of public policy; most generally, to be sure, under our practices and traditions, the unconscious result of instinctive preferences and inarticulate convictions, but nonetheless traceable to views of public policy in the last analysis.[147]

To a considerable extent, Holmes was stating—particularly in speaking about "what is expedient in the community"—what has been criticized as pragmatism (above). His aim was not to pronounce how expediency could be determined or even the meaning of public policy. Rather, he sought—and succeeded very well—to remove some of the intellectual fog that had theretofore characterized descriptions of how judges acted. Nor was he talking about the Supreme Court. But his remarks surely are applicable to the High Bench.

Left unstated in his analysis was the type of mind required to make constitutional decisions, a mind not particularly evident on the Supreme Court today or on the bench generally. One trouble, as has already been suggested, is the failure of legal education. "If law schools are seriously concerned about 'educating,'" said Georgetown University President Timothy S. Healy, "they have to spend time outside the 'training' ambit—with sociology, political science, economics, history, philosophy, theology."[148] So they do, even for the ordinary practitioner.

The meaning, if that be so, is clear: Those who are chosen to be Justices on the Supreme Court need not necessarily be lawyers. There is little in legal education or law practice that suggests that the monopoly of lawyers on judging, particularly on the highest court in the land, is anything other than a heritage of things past. "Of the very nature of the functions of the Supreme Court," Felix Frankfurter once wrote, "each member of it is subject only to his own sense of trusteeship of what are perhaps the most revered traditions in our national system."[149] As Chief Justice Earl Warren put it in his candid valedictory, the Justices have the last word in "great governmental affairs" and are guided only by the Constitution and "our own consciences."[150] We have already seen that the Constitution is little more than a point of departure for legal reasoning; it sets the terms of constitutional adjudication but does not control it. That is the task of the Court. No one can validly say that lawyers have better consciences or better insight into America's "revered traditions" than do others. Not that lawyers should not be in the pool from which Justices are chosen; of course they should. But only if they, and others who do not have the dubious benefit of a legal education, have broad-gauged and compassionate minds. The Justices, in sum, should not pretend that the Supreme Court of the United States is like any other court. It is not. A great distance must be travelled before the Court itself, and members of the bar who practice before it, reach an adequate level of intellectual attainment and attitude.

If lawyers are expert in anything, it is *procedure*—the technical means of adjudication. But constitutional decision making deals with procedure only as an incident toward the greater goal of *substance*. A person with a legal mind may be able to deal comprehensively and effectively with *that* dimension, but not because he or she is a lawyer. Rather, it is because legal education and practice have been transcended.[151] Thus it is that someone not a lawyer is as capable of being a competent Supreme Court Justice as anyone from the legal profession—and perhaps more so: a moral philosopher, perhaps, or even a broad-gauged political scientist. Some individuals can be named, none of whom is a lawyer: Walter F. Murphy of the Princeton political science faculty; philosophers John Rawls and Robert Nozick; economists Robert Lekachman and Robert Heilbroner; diplomat and historian George Kennan; physicist John Platt; and divers others. They may not know the technical procedure, but anyone of a better than ordinary mind can understand it. As a Justice, a law clerk or clerks would always be available to explain it.

In suggesting the need for persons who are not lawyers to sit upon the High Bench, I have distinguished company. In *The Court Years*, his autobiography, Justice William O. Douglas told how he had convinced President Franklin D. Roosevelt to name someone not a lawyer. Douglas asserted that FDR agreed and also that to get Senate confirmation it would be necessary to nominate someone from the Senate. They chose Senator Robert LaFollette of Wisconsin, but FDR died before that nomination could come about.[152] (Even earlier, the superb constitutional scholar and political scientist Professor Edward S. Corwin had entertained the thought that he might be named to the Court in 1937.)[153] In a television interview in 1968, Justice Hugo L. Black also maintained that a nonlawyer should be named to the Court.[154]

I do not wish to labor the point. Suffice it to say that the personnel of the adversary system—judge and company, *as presently constituted*—do not seem to be up to the need in making constitutional judgments.

Concerning revision of the "symbolic code" about the Court and Constitution: if the Justices in fact are legislators, as surely they are, would it not be better for that fact to be candidly acknowledged? The answer is yes; furthermore, the Justices should undertake an even larger legislative role.

Here I tread on quicksand. This is the very center of the controversy about the Supreme Court and its role in modern American governance. The task is to update the Constitution, so as to make both the formal Document and the operative fundamental law current with present needs. Absent another constitutional convention, the Court is the *one* governmental organ with the power and the authority to do that. My point is not that the Justices can

change the actual language of the Document—that either requires an amendment or another convention—but that in its decisions interpreting the ancient
words the Court can alter the psychological climate to make formal change
indispensable. The Justices, once one acknowledges "truth in judging," have
become what Professor Ray Forrester has called America's "legiscourt." They
know it, as do all who study the High Bench. The question is what should be
done in addition to what the nine black-robed High Priests of the American
civil religion are already doing.

In proposing an even greater legislative role for the Court, I am of course
running counter to what many perceive as the proper posture for the Justices.
My position, for example, is contrary to that of Justice Black.[155] Black
asserted that he was bound by the literal words of the Constitution. Justice
William Rehnquist, of the present Court, flatly rejects the idea of a "living"
Constitution.[156] Such assertions must be taken, however, for what they really
are—political gambits whereby judicial lawmaking is denied while the Court is
continuing to make law. The only other conclusion is that Black had, and
Rehnquist has, no real comprehension of what they were, and are, doing.
This, however, cannot be true—except perhaps in a psychological sense.
Recall, in this connection, Shklar's observation about judicial lawmaking
being a "frightful" occasion for judges. Their background and professional
ideology both contribute to a perception of their function as excluding self-
assertion. So they hide their own activities even from themselves.[157] How
anyone, on or off the bench, can think that the Constitution contains answers
to all of the manifold problems brought to the Supreme Court is completely
mysterious. It does not. To repeat a previous comment: The Justices make
up the law as they go along.

In so doing, they apparently believe that they are acting in accordance with
the democratic principle and thus giving either the legislature or community
sentiment the ultimate say in constitutional decisions. That view is intellectual
fraud. For that matter, it is not "democratic," as Professor Julius Stone said:
"Citizens left to believe that burdens flowing from a judgment inevitably
flowed from pre-existing law, when in fact decision on the law might have
been the other way, are in a sense being deceived. The right to know the
architect of our obligations may be as much a part of liberty, as the right to
know our accuser and our judge."[158] Hiding the fact of judicial discretion
serves only to obfuscate, not to explain, the very real problems of judging.

For judges to take on an avowed legislative function requires one thing—
the identification of men and women willing to face up to the task—and has
one major obstacle—the identification and delineation of the limits (if any) on
judicial legislation. (Also required, as is shown below, is the identification of
judges who have the philosophy, the mind-frame, requisite to the vigorous
use of judicial power to further the concept of human dignity.) We have
already suggested that the pool of men and women who should be considered for the task of being Justices should encompass much more than the

legal profession. Breaking the lawyers' monopoly on the Supreme Court is an indispensable first step, difficult in itself but greatly less so than devising some means by which men and women of the necessary qualifications can be selected. I do not propose here to probe that problem in depth. It is enough to suggest the need. A moment's reflection should demonstrate its validity. Nomination to the Supreme Court has always been a political task, all the more so because of the need for Senate confirmation. I am aware that it may be impossible, or at least surpassingly difficult, to take the politics out of politics. Nevertheless, the emergence of the High Bench as an acknowledged de facto third, and highest, legislative chamber points up the need.

Even more intellectually forbidding is the task of establishing limits to judicial legislation. Some commentators, as has been shown, have sought to do this by insisting that the Justices pay undeviating attention to the intentions of those who wrote the Document. They deny the validity of judicial creativity. Joined by those who strongly advocate judicial self-restraint, this school of thought plumps for "the passive virtues." By that is meant a severely restricted Supreme Court. In other words, they would limit judicial legislation by maintaining that the Justices should take on tasks of only the clearest type of (un)constitutionality. There can be no question but that this view is the dominant philosophy of judicial behavior extant today. They are content with the workings of the political process.

Others are not so content, but still adhere to a restricted role for judicial activism. Professor John Hart Ely's theory of "representation-reinforcement," by which he means that the Court should decide cases that involve the furtherance of participation in politics, is perhaps the leading exemplar.[159] In this limited—too limited, in my judgment—view of the proper scope of judicial action, Ely joins the judicial passivists in exhibiting a fear of judges having too much power. There is, to be sure, ample evidence in history to buttress such an apprehension. But it is wrong to engage in what Felix Frankfurter called "the great either-or": There is a third alternative. That alternative is having judges who openly and avowedly pursue the concept of human dignity. Professor Walter F. Murphy has observed: "With typical Germanic thoroughness, justices of the Federal Constitutional Court [in Western Germany] have parsed the underlying theory and values of constitutional democracy with far more care than their colleagues in other countries. The Court's oft-repeated statement that 'the dignity of man is the supreme value' of the constitutional order was facilitated, not compelled, by the words of the Basic Law's initial article."[160] This is not to say, however, that human dignity is an overriding criterion of German judicial policy. For example: in 1970 the German Court sustained a constitutional amendment that permitted the government to wiretap without judicial supervision. The majority of the judges conceded that the amendment restricted some basic rights (privacy) but insisted that it did not contravene human dignity. Said the majority: "Wherever the Basic Law restricts basic rights, it is always to protect effectively another individual or supra-individual legal interest which has priority. . . . *The existence of the Federal Republic and its liberal constitutional order are a predominant legal interest for whose effective protection basic rights may, if absolutely necessary, be restricted.*"[161] (Emphasis added.) The point the Court majority was making is this: Survival of the social order—that is, national survival—is essential; human dignity cannot be furthered without it. (That thought, it should be noted, puts the German Court on a parallel line with the American Supreme Court, which has made "national security"—national survival—the ultimate value.)[162]

There is, then, an entirely possible alternative to the great either-or that is usually posited. Neither free-wheeling judicial decision making nor severely circumscribed judicial behavior need be followed. If the Justices were openly to announce that they were pursuing the concept of human dignity as the ultimate value of American constitutionalism, they would still have much freedom, but would be required to confront the fact that values outside of the express terms of the Document do exist.

To ask the human dignity question is a method, not a set of answers. Justices have been dealing with similar abstractions since the inception of the republic. In many respects, the United States does not have a written constitution. "The great clauses of the Constitution, just as the more important provisions of our fundamental statutes, contain no more than an appeal to the decency and wisdom of those with whom the responsibility for their enforcement rests."[163] To say that protection of the laws must be "equal," punishments not "cruel" or "unusual," and bails or fines not "excessive," or to say that Congress has power to "regulate commerce," or that "the executive power" rests in the President is merely to license lawmaking (constitution making) by judges (and others) who must put content into those terms. The Justices to date have not lent precision to those (and other) terms. That fact, among other things, has led Murphy to conclude that the United States has a political system with two political theories in tension—democracy and constitutionalism.[164] Democracy aims toward popular rule and makes the process of lawmaking crucial, but constitutionalism emphasizes limitations on governmental power.

Murphy may be accurate. Certainly, a tension between the idea of judicial review and the ideal of representative democracy exists. Judges historically have never openly pursued the concept of human dignity. Rather, they have couched their decisions in language such as the following:

the evolving standards of decency that mark the progress of a maturing society[165]

disinterested inquiry pursued in the spirit of science[166]

considerations "deeply rooted in reason"[167]

the traditions and conscience of our people[168]

history and tradition[169]

the deposit of history[170]

notions that go to "the very essence of a scheme of ordered liberty"[171]

the decencies of civilized conduct[172]

conduct that shocks the conscience[173]

the premise of individual dignity and choice upon which our political system rests.[174]

No need exists to multiply quotations such as the foregoing. Examples may be found sprinkled throughout the official reports of the Supreme Court. It is enough to say, with Murphy, that "judges may properly look beyond the purity of the political processes and protect substantive values."[175]

Indeed, they cannot escape doing so. There are, however, dangers and risks. To contend that the Justices should openly ask and seek to answer the human dignity question requires satisfactory answers to a number of objections. But they can be surmounted. In doing so, we can borrow from the Irish Supreme Court, which in 1974 stated that the provisions of the Irish constitutional document "emphatically reject the theory that there are no rights without laws, no rights contrary to the law and no rights anterior to the law. They indicate that justice is placed above the law and acknowledge that natural or human rights are not created by law but that the Constitution confirms their existence and gives them protection. The individual has rights over which the State has no authority."[176] The Constitution of the United States appears to express a similar sentiment in the Ninth Amendment: "The enumeration in the Constitution, of certain rights, shall not be construed to deny or disparage others retained by the people."

True, the Ninth Amendment has been seldom invoked by the Supreme Court. But that may be taken to mean only that the Justices have found sufficient room to maneuver within the nebulous terms of the Document that it has not been necessary to attempt to put content into that amendment. Mentioned above are some of the ways that the Court has done that. In last analysis, the Justices have invoked the core principle of due process of law and employed it as a means of ruling on the advisability and wisdom of governmental policies. As Justice Lewis Powell wrote in 1977:

> Substantive due process has at times been a treacherous field for this Court. There *are* risks when the judicial branch gives enhanced protection to certain substantive liberties without the guidance of the more specific provisions of the Bill of Rights. As the history of the *Lochner* era demonstrates, there is reason for concern lest the only limits to such judicial intervention become the predilections of those who happen at the time to be Members of this Court. That history counsels caution and restraint. But it does not counsel abandonment.[177]

Indeed it does not, Justice Black to the contrary notwithstanding.

Objections to the Justices asking and answering the human dignity question involve three groups of ideas, which may be summarized as follows. First, it will be argued that the human dignity question should be asked by legislators, not by judges. Second, it may be objected that even when a judge has full awareness of his goal, that awareness does not necessarily mean that the goal will be attained. More specifically, asking the question will not make the judge a good or better lawgiver. Finally, there is no agreement upon what human dignity means; the social and behavioral sciences can provide little guidance as to its specific content; and, therefore, it serves no useful purpose.

These objections have a superficial validity, but they can be countered. All that a jurisprudence of human dignity requires is that where the lawmaking process has not been exhausted by legislatures, or where legislatures have obviously gone astray, the courts act in accordance with their role in a *constitutional* democracy and not according to a fable that in fact permits irresponsible government. Those lawmaking activities may be "frightful occasions" to judges, but that merely points up the need for selection of men and women with the mental and moral stamina sufficient to enable them to face the fact of "truth in judging."

Law, and the Supreme Court, are too serious a business to be left to the lawyers. There is no such thing as a purely "legal" answer to any human problem. Embedded in every "law," every legal precept, are considerations of social morality, of human welfare, of human dignity writ large. I am not suggesting that a jurisprudence of human dignity is *the* answer to the problems of our time (and of the future). Rather than being an answer, it is a method of inquiry—an invitation to learn; a suggestion concerning the ways that questions about the Court and Constitution should be asked; "a call," as Alexander Pekelis put it, "for the growth of a systematic participation of the judiciary—burdened with responsibility and stripped of its pontifical robes—in the travail of society." There are no easy solutions to the very real problems of the human condition.

Nevertheless, the effort can—and should—be made. In that effort, judges, including those on the Supreme Court of the United States, cannot be aloof. It is the rejection of an issueless life and an issueless jurisprudence, the rejection, that is, of the inadequacies of pragmatism. In the context of specific litigation between private parties or between government and an individual, the Justices can—and should—recognize that they are making judgments (even when they refuse to rule) on burning questions of public policy. Their pronouncements are viewed, whether liked or not, by the populace as the formulation of law. They cannot properly perform their high duties unless they see beyond the immediate and consider—openly and comprehensively—the age-old problems of the human condition that are brought to them for decision.

There is nothing really new about those problems, except, of course, the context in which they are brought. They are as old as known human history. Many of the best minds known to humankind have grappled with them.

They far antedate the rise of the nation-State as the characteristic form of political order. Those who wrote the Document of 1787 were concerned with them.

The fact that those problems, which may be summed up in the realization of the slogan "equal justice under law" that is carved on the facade of the Supreme Court building in Washington, are still with us shows their inherently intractable nature. But being difficult should not be taken to mean that they should be ignored. The Supreme Court, as an important political actor, cannot—indeed, should not—be immune from attempts to achieve the ideal. Americans have been subjected to an incessant barrage of propaganda about "democracy" and about the "Rule of Law": there should be little wonder, therefore, that they believe in litigation—in the courts as expositors of "the law"—and call upon them to do more and more. When to that is added the indubitable fact that the system of mass higher education, into which the United States has slipped seemingly without plan or design in the past several decades, it may readily be seen why more and more is demanded from government. It is asked not only to be a caretaker but to be "responsible," responsible for an entire range of goods and services. The *demos*, in sum, takes the propaganda about democracy seriously, so seriously, indeed, that some commentators of neoconservative persuasion now speak about the basic "ungovernability" of democracy. Democracy, that is, is said to be ungovernable, simply because it is, in part at least, successful.

That sentiment (that democracy has become ungovernable) was flatly stated in 1975 by Professor Samuel Huntington of Harvard University's department of government.[178] Writing for the Trilateral Commission, he thus echoed what many had said before. For example, Walter Lippmann asserted in 1955:

In ordinary circumstances voters cannot be expected to transcend their particular, localized and self-regarding opinions. As well expect men laboring in the valley to see the land as from a mountain top. In their circumstances, which as private persons they cannot readily surmount, the voters are most likely to suppose that whatever seems obviously good to them must be good for the country, and good in the sight of God.

. . . That a plurality of the people sampled in [the public opinion polls] think one way has no bearing upon whether it is sound public policy. For their opportunities of judging great issues are in the very nature of things limited, and the statistical sum of their opinions is not the final verdict on an issue. It is, rather, the beginning of the argument.[179]

Lippmann's call was for a stronger executive power in government, one that would defend and promote the public interest. The task of the courts, to Lippmann, was to protect the executive from the representative assemblies and from mass opinion. The executive was to be guided by a conception of the *public interest*, defined by Lippmann as "what men would choose if they saw clearly, thought rationally, acted disinterestedly and benevolently."[180]

I do not propose to argue the merit of Lippmann's views. They are, of course, an early recognition of the failures of pluralism. My point is simply this: that the Supreme Court can have an important role to play in helping Americans navigate the stormy seas that lie ahead. The task is great: The Justices should not shirk their responsibility of helping the creation of a just social order, to the extent, that is, that it is within their capacity to do so. That capacity is limited by two hard facts: The ecological trap is closing, and the community itself has interests, as the German Court recognized. There can be no human dignity absent a harmonious internal social order and absent freedom from external dangers. Those things government must supply: There is no alternative. Lippmann called for the assertion of "a public interest against private inclination and against what is easy and popular." If "the governors of the state . . . are to do their duty, they must often swim against the tides of private feeling."[181] But as we have seen in Part II, often "the governors of the state" are unable to "swim against the tides of popular feeling."

I do not argue for what Lippmann called "the public philosophy," even though there is much to be said in favor of his views. Rather, the call is for a jurisprudence of human dignity. Survival of the State may be necessary for the achievement of that goal, but it should be perceived for what it is—a means to a greater end. Although much of Supreme Court history is to the contrary, national survival, *as such*, cannot and should not be taken as the ultimate value. Those who make decisions of constitutional dimension should always remember that, Machiavelli to the contrary notwithstanding, the State (the political order) is a means to an end, not the end itself. There may be, as there is, much constitutional law that makes the State preeminent over the individual. That, however, merely points up the staggering immensity of the problem: "Constitutional law," Professor Aviam Soifer maintained, "requires a sense that the way things are, and even the way they were, is not the way they should be."[182]

"The way they should be": that's the question. It has thus far received no satisfactory answer from those who write on constitutional matters. A few have tried—John Rawls, Ronald Dworkin, and Robert Nozick come to mind —but none has proposed that the Constitution, rather than being a set of eternal verities to be gnawed and worried over much like medieval scholastics analyzed Aristotle, is a delegation of power to subsequent generations to write their own fundamental law(s). But once it is perceived that the Constitution is not a static instrument, that far from being frozen in time it is always in a state of "becoming," there can be no question but that the original Document (and its amendments) are connected to the actual fundamental law only in a meta-phorical sense. That perception calls for a different type of analysis and scholarship about the Constitution than has been thus far evident.

It also demands a Supreme Court of a substantially different nature from the one that has been seen historically. Justices on the High Bench should be men and women of probity, high moral and mental stamina, courage, perception, compassion without sentimentality—men and women who can see things true and see them whole; who can surmount the petty passions of the day; who know that human dignity can come (or be preserved) only within the confines of a harmonious social order; who are willing to joust with politicians; who, in short, have the capacity to see what is right and the courage to state it. If that demand is a call for a group of superhumans, as perhaps it is, so be it. The need is there and should not be ignored. Americans should no longer tolerate the appointment of mine-run lawyers to the Supreme Court.

Since Plato's *Republic*, written well over 2,000 years ago, the question of how to identify, select, and then educate an intellectual elite who would govern has been the subject of contention and controversy. Plato wanted "an aristocracy of talent," and *The Republic* delineates both the reasons for that conclusion and the means of attaining such a group. I do not propose to take over the Platonic concept of "philosopher-rulers." There are serious objections to such a notion—even if by some chance it could come into fruition. My point, rather, is to *adapt* Plato's idea, meld it with two other ideas—that of the Delphic Oracle (previously discussed) and of the Council of Revision, which was considered and rejected in the 1787 Constitutional Convention. I propose, in sum, the transmutation of the Supreme Court into a modern Council of State (or Council of Elders), vested with the authority to make pronouncements on political theory and moral philosophy. That authority should be open and acknowledged, rather than hidden. The proposal is not that the Council of State should rule in the sense of administration; rather, its function would be to make oracular pronouncements on matters of public concern. Those pronouncements would then have to be translated into operational reality by the legislatures and the public administrations.

To understand this proposal, it is necessary to make brief reference to the idea of the Council of Revision and to Plato's philosopher-rulers (or philosopher-kings). As is well known, the Framers of the Constitution not only rejected the need for such a Council, but made no provision whatsoever for judicial review of the acts of other governmental organs, federal or state. That omission, however, did not prevent the Court from becoming the puissant tribunal in the American system.

The idea of the Council of Revision was one of establishing a body that would exercise "prior" judicial review—that would, in other words, review the acts of Congress for constitutionality *before* they went into effect. In the 1787 Convention, the eighth resolution of the Virginia Plan provided in part:

That the Executive and a convenient number of the National Judiciary, ought to compose a council of revision with authority to examine every act of the National Legislature before it shall operate . . . and that the dissent of the said council shall amount to a rejection, unless the Act of the National Legislature be passed again . . . by ( ) of the members of each branch.[183]

The problem that this resolution addressed may be simply stated: that although the framers were committed to inclusion of the democratic principle in some part of American government (it ended in the House of Representatives), they thought that the principle was so dangerous that it should be checked by all possible means—hence, the Senate; hence, the Supreme Court; hence, the presidential veto. The advantages seen in a Council of Revision were several.[184] First, it would, by combining the executive and the judicial, help to stop legislative (that is, democratic) encroachment. Second, it would make the presidential veto more effective. Third, it would in effect permit the issuance of advisory opinions and thus help the President stave off unwise legislation. (It must be remembered that government under the Articles of Confederation was legislative, without a separate executive; no one knew for sure just what powers the President would actually have.) Fourth, it would discourage the legislature from enacting unwise and improper laws, by making legislators think in advance about possible vetoes by the Council. Finally, the Council would preserve stability and continuity in the laws by making them conform with the basic values, principles, and purposes of the Constitution.

Those reasons are weighty, but they were not enough to carry the day. James Madison, sometimes called the "father" of the Constitution, favored it, but that was not enough. Fearing laws that might impair the position of the propertied classes, he thought that:

It would be useful to the Judiciary department by giving it an additional opportunity of defending itself against Legislative encroachments. It would be useful to the Executive, by inspiring additional confidence and firmness in exerting the revisionary power. . . . It would moreover be useful to the Community at large as an additional check against a pursuit of those unwise and unjust measures which constituted so great a portion of our calamities.[185]

There can be no question but that Madison was worried about the House of Representatives.

But the proposal failed. Precisely why it did cannot be determined. Some argued in the Convention that making the Supreme Court in effect a part of the formal political process, permitting its "prior" judicial review, would bias its judgment and would also undermine the confidence of the people in its role. Others—Rufus King, for example—opposed the Council, because it would conflict with the idea of a unitary executive.

Two hundred years later, the objections do not seem nearly so meritorious as perhaps they were. With the recognition of the fact of constitutional dualism—between the formal and operative—has come the realization that the true danger in government emanates mainly from an uncontrolled bureaucracy and an executive who has almost unfettered discretion. That fact, plus the acceptance of the idea that the Supreme Court has a valid political role to play, makes it desirable for serious thought to be given to resurrection of the idea of a Council of Revision. But I am not suggesting that such a modern Council should be formally combined, as in the Virginia Plan, with the executive.

The requirement is for some institutional means by which public policies, proposed by either Congress or the President, can be scrutinized before their promulgation. In Plato's *Republic*, the key problem addressed is how to unite *power* and *wisdom*. How, that is, can those who govern—those who exercise formal governing power—also issue the wisest policies? Alexander Hamilton argued that the electoral system established by the Constitution was well designed to bring forth to the presidency persons "pre-eminent for ability and virtue."[186] That statement seems to mean that Hamilton thought that a preeminently wise person would be chosen to be Chief Executive. In other words, Hamilton had a Platonic conception of the presidency. Consider his language in *Federalist No. 72*:

The administration of government, in its larger sense, comprehends all the operations of the body politic, whether legislative, executive, or judiciary; but in its most precise signification, it is limited to executive *details*, and falls peculiarly within the province of the executive department. The actual conduct of foreign negotiations, the preparatory plans of finance, and the application and disbursement of the public moneys in conformity with the appropriations of the legislature, the arrangement of the army and navy, the direction of the operations of war, —these, and *other matters* of a like nature, constitute what seems to be most properly understood by the administration of government. (Emphasis added.)

Note what Hamilton called mere "details" of administration and undefined "other matters." That expression suggests that in Hamilton's view the executive and legislative, and perhaps even the judicial, powers of government meld into each other. They may be distinct in the rhetoric, but are closely interlocked in practice. As Madison said in *Federalist No. 37*, "Experience has instructed us that no skill in the science of government has yet been able to discriminate and define, with sufficient certainty, its three great provinces— the legislative, executive, and judiciary."

Before, during, and after the 1787 Convention, the idea of a Council of State to advise the President was often bruited. Benjamin Franklin, for example, believed that "a Council would not only be a check on a bad President, but be a relief to a good one."[187] No vote, however, was ever taken on the matter of a Council in the Convention. The Founding Fathers could not have foreseen the enormous changes in the nation that have profoundly altered the constitutional structures of power established by the Constitution. Not only has there been a flow of power toward the executive branch, and a consequent diminution of legislative power, but for various reasons the states have become mere administrative districts for centrally established policies. The meaning is clear—both in the separation of powers and in the federal system, structural changes have occurred. The President is not merely *primus inter pares* ("first among equals"); he is *primus*. Period. "He has the power," Benjamin V. Cohen (one of President Franklin Roosevelt's closest advisers) observed in 1974, "to make important decisions which may profoundly affect the course of human events in this country and in the world without checking in advance his views with any responsible and informed group of persons of political stature and importance."[188] Cohen advocated the creation of an Executive Council within the executive branch as a means of guarding against improvident action: "Quiet consultation by our Presidents before they make their momentous decisions with a small Council of wise and respected persons may protect our Presidents, our nation and our world from much of the hazards of fateful decisions which ultimately must be made by one man."[189]

My proposal is to make the Supreme Court into such a council, but with a broader focus. Not only presidential but Congressional actions would be submitted to it before promulgation—plus, of course, its traditional function of hearing the complaints of individual persons about governmental action. The Court as Council of State (or of Elders) would not necessarily have a veto on proposed policies. Rather, it would insure that all aspects of a proposed policy had been thought through and given due consideration. The Court as Council would not, of course, be a set of philosopher-rulers in Plato's sense of the term. Its function *prior* to policies going into effect would be advisory. But when any policy was issued, and complaints arose, it would then revert to its historical function of *subsequent* judicial review and determine whether the governmental action was in accord with constitutional principles. To be more specific I draw on an analysis by the late Emile Benoit:

Through a policy of dynamic equilibrium, humanity may escape the apparent conflict between rising living standards and ecological stability. It is dynamic in that it assumes a continued rapid growth of science, technology, real living standards, and human welfare. But the equilibrium involved is not like a conventional economic equilibrium where a stable relationship among economic variables is automatically maintained or restored by the free market. This particular equilibrium is between the economy as a whole and the natural environment. It is maintained not automatically but by deliberate policy. And it consists essentially of a balance between the economy and the environment such that the economy may be sustained by the environment far into the indefinite future.[190]

Benoit believed that, properly administered, the concept of dynamic equilibrium would enable humankind to escape from the ecological trap. The concept calls for three basic policies: conservation/simplification, the wise use of technology, and negative population growth. To him, that need meant the creation of "a very different sort of government, one that regards helping humanity turn the corner and avoid its threatened self-destruction as its primary mission."[191] That role in turn calls for "a very different set of persons to run such a government—persons with a passion for intellectual integrity, with an abiding curiosity for how things work, and with a fundamental commitment to helping mankind survive." That blueprint is a large order and one that is more than faintly reminiscent of Plato and also of the abortive "technocracy" movement of the 1930s. Benoit believed that "The crisis is too grave to be left to the politicians";[192] instead, he would have us governed by scientists, engineers, artists, architects, educators, and the like. His is a call for government by experts, but with expertise defined not in the purely technical sense but in a humanistic sense.

My proposal for the Supreme Court to operate not only as the nation's highest judicial body but also as a Council of State is one that moves beyond where the nation is today, but that does not accept Benoit's prescription in toto. If the Court were to be manned by men and women "with a passion for intellectual integrity, with an abiding curiosity of how things work, and with a fundamental commitment to helping mankind survive," men and women who are not necessarily lawyers, it could through time assume a new posture. Its pronouncements would provide moral and ethical leadership in a nation that falters and stumbles because of the absence of such leadership. It would forgo the pragmatic approach to the problems brought before it and take, as Benoit pointed out, the long view—the view that is concerned with the survival of the species and with the dignity of individual members of the species.

The Supreme Court as Council of State, as well as the Court in its traditional role of a court of law, can, if the desire is there, transcend parochialism and even the Constitution itself. We have seen how the Justices at times have gone beyond the written words to determine rights of individuals (for example, the right to privacy recognized in the abortion cases) or of government (as in the concept of sovereign immunity) and have made legislative pronouncements. Since the Court is in charge of its own agenda, it can if it wishes entertain requests from both Congress and the President for advice on proposed public policies. If the request is not forthcoming, the Justices can in the context of litigation issue similar advisory opinions. They thus can alter the mix of politics. Not only can they take a sober first or second thought on governmental actions, they can by making substantive decisions require that both Congress and the President consider the full implications of their actions in advance of their being put into effect.[193] All of the above can be done without amendment to the Constitution, by the Justices seeing the essential problem as Benoit (and others) have seen it and acting accordingly. The Court, that is, can be a Council of State if it so desires by simply assuming the task and evolving the judicial power to a new plateau of relevance. There are dangers, to be sure, as well as objections and resistances that are certain to surface. Even more than in the past, the High Bench will be the center of controversy. (The dangers, objections, and resistances are considered in the next chapter.) There is nothing in the Constitution, the statutes, or the rules of Court to prevent it from assuming an even larger role than it has in the past. The limitations on the Justices come, that is, from politics rather than from law.

To illustrate: the Supreme Court can become a latter-day Council of Revision, exercising *prior* judicial review, merely by reversing a precedent announced in George Washington's tenure as President—that the Court would not, even on request, issue any advisory opinions. Such a request can come from anywhere—from a government officer, executive or legislative, or from an individual or group of individuals. Again, all that would be required would be a reassessment of the "case or controversy" requirement of Article III, a requirement that is peculiarly within the province of the Justices to define. The Justices would not perforce be kept within the strict boundaries of constitutional language for two reasons: First, much of the Document is written in high-level abstractions that require creative interpretation, which, indeed, has been true since 1803; and second, because the Justices have never been limited, save when they wished, by a strict "interpretivist" conception of the Constitution. They have been freewheeling lawmakers and still are. The point is obvious and needs no documentation. Dean Terrance Sandalow put it well: "the evolving content of constitutional law is not controlled, or even significantly guided, by the Constitution, understood as an historical document."[194] Professor Philip Kurland said: "We are repeatedly told by the courts that the current egalitarianism which they are helping to impose derives from the Constitution. That, I think, is arrant nonsense. It is not being taken from the Constitution, it is being put into it."[195] Professor Paul Brest remarked: "Many of what we have come to regard as the irreducible minima of rights, are actually supraconstitutional; almost none of the others are entailed by the text or original understanding."[196]

Except for self-imposed restrictions, there are no limits upon what the Supreme Court can do. It can cut as wide a swath as it wishes and can narrow its actions, also as it wishes. During the early part of the nineteenth century, the Justices moved with caution. Only twice before the Civil War was an act of Congress invalidated. Since the Civil War, the pattern has been one of steadily aggrandizing power to the High Bench—not always, to be sure, and not on all issues—so today it has become an acknowledged oracle of the fundamental law.

During the past quarter-century or so the Justices have moved with alacrity to fill a political power vacuum that was created by the pent-up demands of many groups that were not satisfied by the ordinary workings of the political process. A combination of mass higher education, plus a relative economic Golden Age during the 1945-70 period, so raised the expectations of groups previously deeply submerged in society that they began to surface and demand more. The trade union movement flowered. Black Americans, long under the thumb of a rigid caste system, became insistent that they, too, were persons under the Constitution and entitled to its protections. Add the incessant propaganda about democracy, plus widespread expansion of the franchise, and another factor may be seen. Then, too, the United States fought World War II with conscripts, many—perhaps most—of whom, came from the working class. A tacit perception that those who fought and won a war would not remain quiescent in the face of either economic deprivation or denial of democratic rights may, as in Great Britain, have been significant in the enhancement of personal rights. The Justices of the Supreme Court saw the need and moved to fill it. Neither the country nor the Court has been the same since.

An even greater role beckons—and is possible. I do not say that the Court will move to a function such as that outlined above, but do say that the Justices can and should make the attempt. As an integral part of an "aristocracy of talent," they can deal with areas such as the following:

First: The Justices can help formulate a new public philosophy, in Benoit's sense of a dynamic equilibrium. This course will mean, at the very least, that the pragmatic temper must give way to a conscious philosophy or ideology. One of the most important aspects of that philosophy would be to recognize that humankind is a part of nature and will survive or become extinct only to the extent that there is cooperation with nature. The millenia-old Judeo-Christian ethic of man's dominance over nature and nature's creatures can no longer prevail.

Second: The Justices can, as has already been suggested, help to alleviate some of the shortcomings of the pluralistic political order. The need is for public- or national-interest decisions. In the context of particular litigation, or at the request of some official to render an advisory opinion, the Court could erect a standard that would help Americans move toward a conservation/simplification ethic. "In ordinary circumstances voters cannot be expected to transcend their particular, localized and self-regarding opinions," Walter Lippmann told us.[197] If that be so, and I think it is, the task of the Supreme Court becomes obvious—determine what the larger interests of the community are and, to the extent possible, enforce those larger interests. This conclusion is not a plea for the interests of the State or of society to be over-riding. Rather, it is to note that human dignity for individuals is only possible within the confines of a harmonious social order. As Emile Benoit and others have said, harmony is precisely what is not likely to characterize any nation, including the relatively free or open nations of the West, in the future. Sir Henry Maine, writing in 1886, knew that: "the actual history of popular government since it was introduced, in its modern shape, into the civilized world," does "little to support the assumption that popular government has an indefinitely long future before it. Experience rather tends to show that it is characterized by great fragility, and that since its appearance, all forms of government have become more insecure than they were before."[198] That modern American government has "great fragility" cannot be gainsaid.

Third: The Court could continue to aid those not favored by fortune or inheritance, by stricter enforcement of the equal protection clause of the Fourteenth Amendment. The trend toward equality, long ago noted by Alexis de Tocqueville in his classic *Democracy in America*, has, as is well known, accelerated in recent years. But there is much yet to be done, particularly in the operative Constitution. For example, black Americans have full equality under the formal Constitution, but the living or operative reality shows quite the contrary. The Justices dared to strike a blow for decency, for human dignity, when in 1954 they decided *Brown* v. *Board of Education*. They addressed the core of what Gunnar Myrdal called in the book with that title *An American Dilemma*, when all other governmental officials, federal and state, were not only refusing to do so but, in the case of many, were insisting that blacks be kept in a permanently subservient position. But they have not gone far enough—not for blacks, not for women, not for members of other disadvantaged groups—even though the formal Constitution has for blacks become "color blind." There is much to be done, much, that is, before the slogan of "equal justice under law" that is carved in the facade of the Marble Palace becomes a living reality. The Justices could, for example, "enact" the Equal Rights Amendment into the Constitution through the technique of deciding sex discrimination cases, as they have cases involving racial discrimination. The fact that the Court has not done so displays the enormous distance yet to go before the promise of the Declaration of Independence is realized. The Court has erred not in trying too much, but in trying too little. The Augean stables of centuries of discrimination have yet to be cleansed.

The problem, to repeat, is not only to bring the *formal* law into consonance with a concept of human dignity, but also to tackle the far more difficult task of delving beneath the surface and attempting to alter the *living* or *operative* Constitution. Opportunity for those long under the thumb of informal but rigid caste systems should be the goal; equality should come in fact as well as in theory. Human dignity requires no less. No one expects that discriminations that have characterized Homo sapiens since the dawn of time can or will be eradicated overnight. The Court, however, can continue what it started in *Brown* v. *Board of Education*, remembering of course that, as T. S. Eliot put it, there is always a gap between the ideal and the reality.[199] The Justices are not required to do everything, but they cannot stand aside and see injustice without trying to do something about it.

Fourth: A significant aspect of human dignity is the need to be needed. The Justices could further that goal by holding that a constitutional right to a job is derivable from the Constitution. The argument is easily made. A necessitous man is not a free man. Liberty is protected by due process of law. That provision, as Chief Justice Hughes said in 1937, at times may *require* affirmative governmental action. Finding a constitutional right to a job, or at least a right to minimum economic well-being, would mean that a concomitant duty would be imposed on government to take action designed to create those job opportunities. That government does have obligations to the populace is beyond argument, although some commentators (for example, Robert Nozick, George Gilder) would severely limit that role. Justice Felix Frankfurter said it well in 1949: "It is of the very nature of a free society to advance in its standards of what is deemed reasonable and right. Representing as it does a living principle, due process is not confined within a permanent catalogue of what may at a given time be deemed the limits or the essentials of fundamental rights."[200] Surely, a part of what is "reasonable and right" is the creation of conditions of economic well-being for the citizenry. That step, of course, must be seen in the context of the Age of Scarcity and of the need, perhaps pressing need, for a more frugal existence.

Fifth: Ancient institutions can be adapted to fit modern demands. The basic divisions of power established by the Document—the tripartite separation in the national government, the federal system, and foreign and domestic—have all been structurally altered in the operative Constitution since 1787. There has been a flow of power toward the presidency and, in part, toward the Supreme Court; the national government is more equal than the states, and a slow but seemingly steady adherence to multinationalism is apparent in governmental policies. How far the Court can go in actually altering long-established patterns of power in the formal Constitution is dubious at best. But there can be no question about what it has done to constitutionalize alterations in power relationships. For example, the Justices have approved a form of presidential prerogative (in the Civil War) and have legitimized the exercise of executive privilege—in two examples of enhancement of presidential power.[201] Furthermore, they have approved Congressional actions that, as in the exercise of the power over interstate commerce, have had a substantial impact upon the federal system. They have found no constitutional impediment in adherence of the United States to multinational institutions such as the International Monetary Fund and the North Atlantic Treaty Alliance (although it must be noted that these never got to the Court for decision). But by upholding the President's authority to enter into international agreements without consent of Congress—a noteworthy example came in 1981 in the decision sustaining President Carter's agreement on the Iranian hostage crisis[202]—they have enabled the United States to adhere to multilateral economic organizations such as the General Agreement on Tariffs and Trade.

The problem today is whether further adaptations of the Document can occur without constitutional amendment. Possibly, the answer is no—that any thoroughgoing commitment to, say, internationalism must come by amendment. But that answer lies in the formal document. The operative Constitution may well differ. The Court could point the way by stating needs (in all three divisions of power) that would not be enforceable in the legal sense but would alter the mix of politics. That act, alone, would be a major contribution.

Sixth: The Justices could develop a theory of American constitutionalism suitable for the present and the foreseeable future. That theory must take full cognizance of the political economy of the nation; of the terrible vulnerabilities that humanity faces; of the closing of the ecological trap; of, in sum, the adaptation of ancient theories to modern conditions. Professor Richard D. Parker of the Harvard Law School has pointed the way (although his is a call for legal scholars, rather than the Supreme Court, to construct the badly needed new theory).²⁰³ Parker suggested that there should be a deep critique of orthodox theory (this volume is a preliminary attempt to do that) and a critique of the flaws in our political life (it should not be taken "for granted that the constitution of our polity is fundamentally sound, subject only to an occasional malfunctioning"). His conclusion merits fuller quotation; "the final aspect of the job" in building a new constitutional theory is the most important but . . . the most opaque":

> It involves elaboration of a new—a much more ambitious—conception of what our polity could and should be, a critique of our actual polity in the terms of that conception and then an analysis of its possible implications for the substantive values to be vindicated, and doctrines through which to vindicate them, in various areas of constitutional law. We shall have to be willing to speculate freely about these matters without making the conventional assumption that anything we advocate necessarily must be capable of immediate enforcement by the courts. Judicial enforcement and its timing may depend . . . on all sorts of prudential concerns; and unless we segregate those concerns and insist on their clearly subsidiary status, we shall allow—just as our predecessors have allowed—our perception of the present condition of our polity and of what can immediately be accomplished within it to stunt our vision of what our polity might, one day, become and our criticism of what it now is.
> There is no predicting now what the constitutional theory of the future will be. But, at least, it is ours—for the time being—to make. And it is our mission . . . to make it something very different—an expression of the possibilities of democracy instead of an apology for its corruption—from the constitutional theory of the past.²⁰⁴

Parker's call for new constitutional theory must encompass a reassessment of what the Supreme Court can and should do. That need is what this book is all about. Of course legal scholars and political philosophers should heed his call. My point is that the Justices of the Supreme Court cannot avoid taking part in that very necessary endeavor.

What I have suggested in this chapter is, of course, fraught with problems. In sum, it is an effort to point the Supreme Court in its capacity of America's first faculty of political theory and social ethics in a new and higher direction. It eschews judicial restraint and advocates the vigorous and continuing use of judicial power to further the cause of human dignity and to help Americans effect the transition from an economy of abundance to one of scarcity.

Some, of course, will recoil in dismay, even horror; many will think the prescription I make to be intellectually unsound. Those who disagree, however, should do so on the merits of the analysis and proposals, not on the dangers of judicial activism, anytime, anywhere, against any power, and toward any end. But those objections must be discussed, and that is the task of the next chapter.

12
Why the Supreme Court?

This volume is an unabashed plea for a more activist, result-oriented Supreme Court—activist in the sense of it intervening more often into the political process and result oriented in the sense that the Justices should openly pursue a concept of human dignity in their decisions. That position, of course, calls for a fundamental change from what the Court has been in the past and even the present—the protector of the moneyed elite—to a new permanent plateau of the heights reached in *Brown v. Board of Education*. There, nine Justices dared to act to achieve a new birth of freedom for black Americans. That freedom still exists in the formal Constitution but is apparently being dashed in the operative fundamental law. But *Brown* did set the Court on a new course; it "was the beginning,"[1] the beginning of a new role for the High Bench. *Roe v. Wade*, the 1973 abortion decision, merely carried on under Chief Justice Warren Burger what had started under Chief Justice Earl Warren. My plea, thus, is for the continuation *and* expansion of the *Brown/Roe* constitutional breakthroughs. The Justices should ask the human dignity question and answer it in the context of the coming Age of Scarcity. I am not so naive as to believe that that proposal *will* happen, but do say that it *should*. If *Brown* was the beginning, *Roe* should not be the end. To achieve this objective, the Justices should move toward becoming a Council of State (or of Elders, the precise label being meaningless).

The Supreme Court has come a long way since John Marshall essayed his rather tentative thrust into political affairs in 1803. It can, and should, go even further. If the Constitution and the Court are the most important institutions of America's civil religion, the Justices thus are in a position to give moral and ethical guidance to a nation that flounders from crisis to crisis without any guiding star. People no longer look to the leaders of orthodox religious sects for that guidance. Nor do they get it from the President. Unless new institutions are to be created, only the Supreme Court remains. I fully realize that, as Aristotle maintained, a mere change in institutions will in all likelihood not be enough. The essential problem for the Justices is not to try to change the nature of human nature, but to take those actions that through time can alter the social milieu in which humans operate and to which they react. In time, then, the hope is that the Justices can demonstrate to the strong that they are in the same basket as the weak and that they will prosper (or fall) together, not separately. It is in the interests of the strong—they who have always been favored by the legal system and the constitutional order—to help protect the weak and the disadvantaged. That attitude is not a matter of altruism but of enlightened selfishness. Law, as Machiavelli said and as has been shown in previous chapters of this volume, may well be a function and product of power relationships. "In political affairs, Machiavelli believed that law is devoid of independent significance on its own account. As Thucydides correctly observed two thousand years before, *right* is only in question between equals in power. Law becomes irrelevant in the face of power politics."[2] My point is that it serves the interests of power politics—rather more precisely, the interests of those who are able to exercise power in political situations—to see that politics is not the "quintessential zero-sum game"[3] that it was for Thucydides, Machiavelli, Hobbes, and other exponents of power politics. My view is based on an analogy to international politics and the theory of "mutual assured destruction" (MAD) under which the superpowers are restrained from using nuclear weapons because of the certainty that the first who uses such a weapon will also be destroyed. As in world politics, so in domestic affairs (and so, for that matter, in the well-known "North-South" debate[4] between the affluent and the poor nations of the world) a MAD theory also may be applied. Of that, more below. First, it is necessary to outline the chief objections to the theory of the Supreme Court as a Council of State and to show the merit, or lack of merit, of each.

Judge Learned Hand once asserted, in an attack on an activist judiciary, that he would find it irksome to be governed by a group of Platonic Guardians, even if he knew how to choose them (which he didn't).[5] That matter of choice, then, is the first of several objections: How would the Council of State be named? By whom? Once selected, how can it be insured that the councillors will pursue the goal of human dignity? These questions ask much and must be answered. In seeking those answers, we must be wary of trying to achieve perfection. We live in an imperfect world. That fact, however, should not be taken to mean that it cannot be made better. Even under the system as it now is, perhaps "It was not reasonable to expect judges to be heroes" in civil rights matters during the 1950s and 1960s, "but the truth of the matter," Professor Owen M. Fiss of the Yale Law School maintained, "is that many lived up to these unreasonable expectations—they fought the popular pressures at great personal sacrifice and discomfort. The average judge turned out to be more heroic than the average legislator (or juror)."[6] Federal judges in the South—John Minor Wisdom, Richard Rives, Elbert Tuttle, John R.

Brown, J. Waties Waring, J. Skelly Wright—were able to rise above caste and background and translate the Supreme Court's decree in *Brown* v. *Board of Education* into operational reality.

So the men and women *are* available—even in the legal profession—and the need is to devise means by which they can be identified and appointed. Heretofore, the system has worked by accident and happenstance rather than by design. No systematic effort has ever been made to create ways by which truly superior Justices of the Supreme Court can be named. Appointment has been a political maneuver. Can it in some way be removed from politics? In all probability, no. There are, however, degrees of political behavior. The effort should be made, and soon, to improve upon the ways that judges are selected. I do not propose any method here, but merely point out the pressing need.

Once selected, by what means can the Justices be required to consider the human dignity criterion in their decisions? That is the second objection. Enough is known about the selection of Supreme Court Justices in American history to be able to say that, once on the High Bench, they can and often do go their own ways. Several examples may be cited. President Theodore Roosevelt was so irritated by a decision of Justice Oliver Wendell Holmes that he snorted that he could carve a judge with more backbone out of a banana. President Harry Truman said that naming a man to the Supreme Court made twelve enemies and one ingrate. President Dwight Eisenhower called his appointment of Chief Justice Earl Warren as "the biggest damfool mistake I ever made." Even three of the four "strict constructionists" named by President Richard Nixon soon joined in making the most latitudinarian decision in recent memory—in the abortion cases of 1973.

An independent judiciary means just that: independence. The Justices, Chief Justice Warren said in his valedictory, answer only to their "own consciences." The objection, therefore, is not frivolous. It, too, must be confronted. The answer, if answer there be, would seem to lie in the quality of the person chosen to be a Justice. In the last analysis, this second objection merely points up the need for a selection process that differs from the one presently employed. Once the Justices are freed from even nominal adherence to the constitutional text, the problem becomes one of determining how unfettered judicial discretion can be prevented from degenerating into judicial license. Here, again, I concede the problem and do not pretend to have an answer. Surely, however, the answer does *not* lie in judicial passivity.

Third, the Supreme Court as Council of State would be taking on too many tasks, for which the Justices have neither time nor special expertise. By doing too much, they would dissipate their ability to protect civil rights and liberties in the areas that come within their cognizance at present. This objection is less meritorious. The Court has not even begun to explore ways to lighten its work load. There is no reason, for example, that the nine Justices could not operate in panels of three, as do the courts of appeals, subject to the proviso that a losing party could always petition for an *en banc* (the entire Court) hearing. By that one device alone, what seems to be a staggering burden of work could be split into three parts. There is, furthermore, no reason for the Justices to write (or to approve what their clerks have written) such long opinions or to write so many concurring and dissenting opinions (often quite lengthy).[7] For that matter, there is no requirement that opinions be written in any case. They are not in the 4,400 + decisions made each year not to review a lower court decision; only in the 140 or so decisions "on the merits" are opinions written—and then not always by a named Justice but by a *per curiam* technique (an unsigned opinion, usually for the entire Court). Most *per curiam* opinions tend to be short and to the point; by no stretch of the imagination are they more opaque in their language than are signed opinions. The conclusion is obvious: There are ways to give the Justices more time.

Opinions are supposed to explain the reasoning process by which the Justices reached their decisions. That, at least, is the pretense. But no one really believes it. The federal courts of appeals have in recent years begun to issue decisions, although not all of them, without opinion. Were the Supreme Court to do so, there would be at least one major benefit: Lawyers would have to concentrate on the results of decisions, on who won and who lost, rather than on the explanation or rationalization. That change would mean that in time lawyers would become more and more outwardly result oriented. In many of its affirmances or reversals of lower court decisions, the Supreme Court merely states "appeal dismissed" or "affirmed" and then goes on to cite one or two previous decisions. At times—more often than many realize—an appeal may be dismissed for "want of a substantial federal question." Those rulings, even without elaborate opinions, have the force of law.[8]

As to whether the Justices have any special expertise to decide complicated and oft-times controversial questions submitted to them, the answer is easy. They have been doing so since the beginnings of the republic. Although no doubt it is true that they could become more expert in some of the areas, means are available to have the requisite data submitted to them. Furthermore, surely Justices, even today, are as expert as are members of Congress and, indeed, are more expert—almost by definition—on the questions, the ultimate questions, of political theory and social ethics with which they deal.

Fourth, it will be objected that the Supreme Court today, and surely the Justices as a Council of State, would be an undemocratic institution. That hoary criticism, however, does not wash. Only those with a simplistic view of the political process can call American politics truly democratic. Certainly, it is the results reached, rather than the means of attaining them, that is the crucial criterion. If those results further the concept of human dignity, whether or not the Court is seen as a democratic organ of government fades into insignificance. It should always be remembered, the Frankfurter School of Judicial Criticism to the contrary notwithstanding, that Americans in general care about results, about who wins or loses, and not about the way those results were reached—or by whom.

There is, to be sure, a pressing requirement for the Justices to be able to evaluate the probable second-order, as well as the first-order, consequences of their decisions. They have few means of doing so now; they must make educated guesses. Alexander Bickel asserted in 1962 that "the Court should declare as law only such principles as will—in time, but in a rather foreseeable future—gain general assent. . . . The Court is a leader of opinion, not a mere register of it, but it must lead opinion, not merely impose its own; and—the short of it is—it labors under the obligation to succeed."[9] Indeed it does. Bickel pointed up the problem. Changes in the ways in which the adversary system operates could go far toward fulfilling the need.

Finally, it will be argued that the recommendation that the Supreme Court become a Council of State would in effect cast it adrift from the Constitution itself and thus make the Document a mere artifact—a revered artifact, to be sure—but only that. The answer to that objection may be bluntly stated: That position is precisely where we are now. Why not recognize that fact?

II.

So much for the major objections. Are they insuperable? Should the Court pursue "passive virtues"? Should Americans concede that the Constitution is what Congress, the President, and officials of state government say it is—save in the most extraordinary situations? I think not.

Why the Supreme Court? Why should it do more? One reason is that it is an *existing* institution and requires the formation of no new governmental organ. The Court also, as we have shown, is an *evolving* institution. It takes actions today that would have been beyond the comprehension of Justices during most of the nineteenth century. It has filled, at least in part, a power vacuum that existed and still exists in the political order.

Why the Supreme Court? Because it can fulfill communal needs by tendering at least token or cosmetic or symbolic gains to the underclass, gains that have the latent function of stifling social discontent. Even though the Court is, and no doubt will continue to be, controlled by those of conservative persuasion, the High Bench cannot escape being in the forefront of major segments of public policymaking. The question, as always is which values should—must?—be furthered. Can it not be postulated that the Justices will exemplify the essence of true "conservatism," perhaps as Edmund Burke saw it, by emphasizing law and order but with enough change—enough attention paid to the human dignity question—to siphon off some of the hydraulic pressures of social discontent? Federal Judge Frank M. Johnson, Jr., has made the point well: The traditional model of litigation, he said, is *bipolar*: "it takes place between two diametrically opposed interests which initiate the lawsuit and define the issues."[10] Litigation thus is retrospective—about what happened in the past—and also is supposedly self-contained (its impact limited to the parties before the court). All that has changed, Judge Johnson asserted, so that the "new model of litigation must account for the following:

—the subject matter often is not a private dispute but a public policy;
—the party structure is not rigidly bilateral but multilateral;
—the factual inquiry is not retrospective, but predictive; and
—the relief is not compensatory but ameliorative."[11]

If federal judges are more activist, said Johnson, it is less because they have appointed themselves "roving commissioners to do good" than it is because new procedures have opened the courthouse doors to new interests. The lawsuit, thus, has become "an instrument of reform." Criticizing that phenomenon as judicial activism shows a lack of historical perspective. "The courthouse door has always been open to the powerful," Johnson went on to say, "and the lawsuit has always been a ready instrument of the affluent. I suggest ...that *activist judges may be the true conservatives.* As Edmund Burke recognized: 'People, crushed by law, have no hopes but from power. If laws are their enemies, they will be enemies to laws.'"[12] (Emphasis added.)

If the Supreme Court continues as the protector of the moneyed and the privileged, it will have to help effectuate adjustments to make the position of the privileged impregnable. Those adjustments, in final analysis, can come in only two ways—either through savage, ruthless repression, by violence if need be, or by social change that represents what the privileged can tolerate while staving off major "revolution." That the oppressed and disadvantaged will not remain quiescent forever is the clear lesson of history.

It is by no means clear which of the two avenues of adaptation will be taken. Repression in America is not a historical oddity: A principle of constitutional relativism runs through American history. Government has always been as strong as circumstances required. Repression, however, is a short-term "solution"; it can work in a limited area for a limited time. Even totalitarian nations, such as the Soviet Union, have not been able to stifle dissent permanently. Sooner or later, the irrepressible spirit of Homo sapiens will assert itself.

It is, therefore, wholly in the interests of the moneyed and propertied—they who have always profited from the legal system—to be sufficiently rational to perceive that their long-term interests lie in the reasonable satisfaction of the reasonable expectations of the masses of people. With the enormous increase in population, with widespread education and literacy, with the incessant propaganda about democracy, those masses will continue to demand more from the political order. (Those demands, of course, must be balanced against what is possible in the political economy.) The need, thus, to paraphrase Thucydides, is for the strong to continue to do only what they can after seeing to it that the weak are not unduly suffering. (In his classic *The Peloponnesian War*, Thucydides asserted the preeminence of power politics: "you know as well as we do that right, as the world goes, is only in question between equals in power, while the strong do what they can and the weak suffer what they must.")[13] My point is that the strong's ability to do "what they can" has been sharply and probably permanently altered by the weak's ability to bring counterpressures. Consider the following statements and ask whether it is definitely in the interests of those with property and power to take into consideration the whole of humanity:

A political theorist:

...the free way of life depends to an extent...not yet dreamed of, on the Western nations remedying the inequality of human rights as between ourselves and the poor nations.[14]

An economist:

As we head into the 1980s, it is well to remember that there is really only one important question in political economy. If elected, whose income do you and your party plan to cut in the process of solving the economic problems facing us?[15]

A biologist:

The Iron Laws of Ecology

You can't win.
You can't break even.
Things are going to get worse before they get better.
They are not going to get better.
And you can't get out of the game.[16]

A professor of religion:

We are sadly forced to conclude that we live in a world that is *functionally* godless and that human rights depend upon the power of one's community to grant or withhold them from its members....

It is an error to imagine that civilization and savage cruelty are antitheses. On the contrary, in every organic process, the antitheses always reflect a unified totality, and civilization is an organic process. Mankind moves from one type of civilization involving its distinctive modes of both sanctity and inhumanity to another. In our times the cruelties, like most other aspects of our world, have become far more effectively administered than ever before. They have not and they will not cease to exist.[17]

A political philosopher:

The organizer of industry who thinks he has "made" himself and his business has found a whole social system ready to his hand in skilled workers, machinery, a market, peace, and order—a vast apparatus and a pervasive atmosphere, the joint creation of millions of men and scores of generations. Take away the whole social factor and we have not Robinson Crusoe, with his salvage from the wreck and his acquired knowledge, but the naked savage living on roots, berries, and vermin.[18]

My point is that democracy as constitutionalism cannot survive with a restive and repressed underclass. To do something about that restiveness does not call for altruism—for a change in human nature—by the moneyed and propertied, but only a recognition of where their true interests lie.

That requirement has been seen by more perceptive members of the privileged classes in the past. Unlike the Bourbons, who could learn nothing and forget nothing, nations such as Bismarck's Germany, Great Britain after World War II, and the United States have been able to effect adjustments in the social order to ameliorate some of the brutalities of life. As Professor C. B. Macpherson has said, the Welfare State came because of "the sheer need of governments to allay working-class discontents that were dangerous to the stability of the state. It was Bismarck, the conservative Chancellor of Imperial Germany, and no great democrat, who pioneered the welfare state in the 1880s, for just this purpose."[19] In Great Britain, one should remember how speedily Britons turned Winston Churchill out of office once the War was won. He was replaced by Clement Attlee, a leader of the Labor party. The lesson is that the British Establishment knew that it was in its interests to reward those who had fought a bloody war.

So it was in the United States: World War II was largely fought with conscripts. Surely a tacit recognition that men who were asked to fight and often to die for their country, in the name of freedom and democracy, would not remain idly quiescent was one of the factors underlying both the Employment Act of 1946, with its commitment to maximum employment, and the series of civil rights decisions that emanated from the Supreme Court. So, too, with the "Great Society" programs of the federal government during the Vietnam "war." Again, young men were forced to fight in a far-off land in the name of democratic principles. The Great Society programs were a means of paying the nation's debt to them. An ever clearer example came in the New Deal programs of President Franklin D. Roosevelt. FDR, a patrician, set in motion a system similar to Bismarck's to allay working-class discontent. Only when World War II came did the President cease that thrust. Putting on his "Dr. Win-the-war" hat, he announced that victory had been won in the battle against economic depression and turned his attention to defeating the Axis powers. (It is one of the supreme ironies of history that Roosevelt was, and still is, hated by the very people—the moneyed and propertied—who were the latent and, indeed, the principal beneficiaries of New Deal actions.)

Whether those who wield actual governing power in the nation will see the point at this time is by no means certain. Perhaps they will, as the few examples just mentioned tend to demonstrate. Perhaps, that is, matters are sufficiently different from Thucydides's Greece to make ruling elites defer some of their own self-interests to the interests of the entire polity. In Pericles's well-known speech before the Athenian assembly, he made the profound, but perhaps supremely cynical, remark that harmony in the social order rests in last analysis upon power and self-interest.[20] If members of ruling elites are able to foresee, to intuit rationally, that the furtherance of their own long-term interests requires protection of the masses's welfare, if, that is, they perceive the symbiotic relationship between their own interests and those of all citizens, they will see to it that governmental power is exercised in that direction. Mankind's unrelenting "lust for power arising from greed and ambition"[21] would then be tempered.

This view, to repeat, is not altruism; it does not require a change in human nature. If that type of response is not made, by whatever institutions of government, including but not confined to the Supreme Court, what we have called above a domestic version of "mutual assured destruction" may well occur. The Athenians did not follow Pericles's advice and lost the Peloponnesian War because of their own internal disorders. My point has been put in classic terms by Niccolò Machiavelli:

Prudent men always and in all their actions make a favour of doing things even though they would of necessity be constrained to do them anyway. The Roman Senate made good use of prudence deciding to use public money to pay men on military service. It had been the custom for soldiers to pay their own expenses, but the senate saw that in such case they could not make war for long, and, in consequence, would neither be able to lay siege to towns, nor to lead their armies far afield. Since, therefore, they thought it necessary to be able to do both these things, they decided that the troops should be paid a stipend; but did it in such a way that they made a favour of doing what necessity constrained them to do.

So acceptable was this gift to the plebs that Rome went mad with delight; for it seemed to them that they had received a great benefaction which they had never expected, and which they would never have asked for themselves. And, though the tribunes tried hard to remove this impression, pointing out that it would increase the burden on the plebs instead of lightening it since it would be necessary to levy taxes to be able to defray the cost; none the less they were quite unable to prevent the plebs welcoming the change. It was made the more welcome, too, by the way in which taxes were distributed; for those imposed on the nobility were heavier and greater, and they had to be paid first.[22]

Make, Machiavelli said, a virtue out of necessity: "A republic or a prince should ostensibly do out of generosity what necessity constrains them to do."[23] Today, people the world over are asking for themselves what their predecessors did not (as Machiavelli said). That they will not long tolerate penury and want, even starvation, seems to be as clear a proposition as can be stated. The riots that swept several British cities in the summer of 1981 had their counterparts in disturbances on the European continent. The danger is the continuation of such violent actions: "When the populace has thrown off all restraint," Machiavelli cautioned, "it is not the mad things it does that are terrifying, nor is it of present evils that one is afraid, but of what may come of them, for amidst such confusion there may come to be a tyrant." Furthermore: "The brutalities of the masses are directed against those whom they suspect of conspiring against the common good."[24] The matter, then, of the ruling elites perceiving that "mutual assured destruction" may well result from stomping too long and too hard on the people generally is not a matter of morality or of law, including constitutional law, but of self-preservation.

III.

We live in a time of continuing crises, of a climacteric of humankind that threatens to engulf the species. On a *planetary* scale, we live in a period that shows no signs of cessation similar to the turbulence that Thucydides wrote about in history of the Peloponnesian War, that Machiavelli chronicled about the discord of Renaissance Italy, and that Hobbes perceived during the time of the English revolution. Small wonder, then, that each was driven to a profoundly despairing view of human nature as selfish and even despicable. Little that has occurred since they wrote leads one to take a different position. We should not, therefore, expect moral perfection in humans or in human destiny. To believe in such perfection, in the moral perfectibility of man, is a figment of some utopian's imagination.

But that belief, as has been suggested, is not necessary. The need is for those who wield effective power within the nation—indeed, the world over—to recognize that life on this tiny speck called Earth must in significant part be cooperative. People will have to hang together, not because they will hang separately if they do not, but because of mutual assured destruction.

The role, then, of law—and of the Supreme Court, to the extent that it can make authoritative social pronouncements that have the force and effect of law—is to assist in making the adjustments necessary for a sustainable society. In saying that, I am not suggesting that the Court, or law itself, can do the job without cooperation from other institutions. As former Attorney General Edward Levi said, "Law is not everything in society. Law is one of a number of institutions through which we express ourselves and which in turn influence us, maintain our customs and change our habits. Thus, law takes a place along with family structures, religious beliefs, the expressions of art and the explanations of science."[25] Even so, it does seem to be accurate to say that law is the most important means of social control; it may not be sovereign but it is preeminent. Witness Roscoe Pound:

Since the sixteenth century political organization of society has become paramount. It has, or claims to have and on the whole maintains, a monopoly of force. All other agencies of social control are held to exercise disciplinary authority subject to the law and within bounds fixed by the law. . . . The household, the church, the associations which serve to some extent to organize morals in contemporary society, all operate within legally prescribed limits and subject to the scrutiny of the courts. Today social control is primarily the function of the state and is exercised through law.[26]

In sum, law provides—and courts enforce—the means by which other agencies of social control operate.

It will be perceived, no doubt, that what I have said in this book adds up to the conclusion that there is a false dichotomy between law and politics. Law is always instrumental, not an end in itself. It is purposive human behavior, not at all dissimilar from politics. To ask about the limits of law and of courts is in fact to ask a much deeper question: What, if anything, are the limits of politics? Law is the means by which political decisions are put into effect. That fact means that law achieves justice to the extent that the political order is itself devoted to that end. Law thus has value to the extent that it attains desirable ends, just as politics has value insofar as it is employed to further the essential worth and dignity of the human being.

IV.

We should not indulge ourselves any longer with the threadbare and bank-rupt notion of a government of preexisting laws, not of men. The human element cannot be divorced from either lawmaking or law enforcement. It is of course true that law is a means of social order, that the expectations it creates do circumscribe and guide human behavior—particularly at the lowest levels of administration. But it should never be forgotten that he who has authority to interpret laws is more truly the lawgiver than he who first uttered it.

Our interest in this volume lies in the high level of constitutional interpreta-tion, mainly by the Supreme Court. There it becomes utterly obvious that the Justices have almost unfettered discretion. They know, as Justice Louis Brandeis once put it, that "Our Constitution is not a strait-jacket. It is a living organism. As such it is capable of growth—of expansion and of adaptation to new conditions. . . . Because our Constitution possesses the capacity of adaptation, it has endured as the fundamental law of an ever-developing people."[27] (That statement is not quite correct: It has an anthropomorphic flavor. The Constitution can be, and is, adapted—but by identifiable human beings.) Some contemporary Justices, however, reject the Brandeis formula-tion. Justice Hugo L. Black, for example, stated in 1965:

I realize that many good and able men have eloquently spoken and written, sometimes in rhapsodical strains, about the duty of this Court to keep the Constitution in tune with the times. The idea is that the Constitution must be changed from time to time and that this Court is charged with a duty to make those changes. For myself, I must with all deference reject that philosophy. The Constitution makers knew the need for change and provided for it. Amendments suggested by the people's elected representative can be submitted to the people or their selected agents for ratification. That method of change was good for our Fathers, and being somewhat old-fashioned I must add it is good enough for me.[28]

It is difficult to believe that Black was serious. After all, he was the Justice who in a memorable dissent in *Adamson v. California* (1947)[29] asserted that the

Fourteenth Amendment's due process clause was intended to make all the Bill of Rights applicable to the states. No one has been able to discover the same history as did Black in maintaining that such was the intention of those who wrote the amendment. That his view has by later Supreme Court law-making become constitutional law means at most that Black had an idea whose time had come and, therefore, that the Court was keeping "the Constitution in tune with the times."

Justice William H. Rehnquist of the present Supreme Court is without question the leader of the antiactivist view of the Court's function. He rejects "the notion of a living constitution" insofar as it meant that the "non-elected members of the federal judiciary" were to serve as the "voice and conscience of modern society" and "articulate the modern conception of human dignity."[30] Rehnquist must, of course, be taken seriously; he is the leader of a Court dominated by Richard Nixon's appointees. Although he is not always able to carry the day, as the decisions in the abortion cases attest, nevertheless his views on judicial self-restraint and deference to elected officials are probably the prevailing philosophy of a majority of the present Court. Not that he is consistent in self-restraint or deference. He defers when he wishes to do so, apparently when elected officials have reached decisions compatible with his own, but does not defer in others. Consider, in that respect, two recent decisions: In *Miami Herald Co. v. Tornillo* (1974),[31] Rehnquist joined a unanimous Court in striking down Florida's "right of reply" statute that permitted those attacked by newspapers to have equal space to reply. In his judgment, such a statute was "commandeering" the newspaper's property. In *United States Trust Co. v. New Jersey*, Justice Rehnquist joined a 4-3 majority to invalidate New Jersey's alleged attempt to impair the obligation of a contract. That 1977 decision was underscored in 1978 in *Allied Structural Steel Co. v. Spannaus.*[32]

The point is clear beyond doubt: Justice Rehnquist is willing to legislate his notions about the meaning of the Constitution when the matter involves something his personal philosophy favors. In the three illustrative decisions just mentioned, he favored those who owned property. When human rights are at issue, the deference posture becomes visible. All of that merely underscores what was said in the first chapter of this volume: Americans like to believe that they have a government of laws, not of men, but that is not true insofar as the Supreme Court is concerned.

V.

The Supreme Court is, I believe, an indispensable institution, all the more so as the terrible vulnerabilities of the fast-coming climacteric of humankind places greater and greater demands upon ancient institutions of governance.[33] It is indispensable in the sense that if Americans wish to retain (regain? attain?) the values of constitutionalism, only the Court is in a position to see the need and to erect a standard toward which the nation can strive.

It will not do for the Justices to pursue passive virtues and to defer un-thinkingly to the elected officials of government (federal and state). Those officers are the prisoners of the failures of the political order. The Supreme Court should (I do not say will, because of the Rehnquist-type mentality now on the bench) take its cue from Judge Frank Johnson's path-breaking mental hospital and prison cases in Alabama. Johnson found a constitutional right to treatment due those incarcerated in mental hospitals and later found that prison conditions in Alabama violated the cruel and unusual punishment provision of the Constitution.[34] He thus was able to do what elected officers presumably (probably: actually) could not do. Johnson pointed the way toward a fuller realization of human dignity.

That surely was not law in an interdictory sense, but it was a moral judg-ment, a courageous foray into the jungle of politics by a judge with a lifetime appointment. Americans would indeed be fortunate if they were served as well by all judges, including those on the Supreme Court of the United States. Why the Supreme Court? Because there is no alternative. Federal Judge J. Skelly Wright said it well: "It is regrettable that in deciding this case this court must act in an area so alien to its expertise. It would be far better for these great social and political problems to be resolved in the political arena. . . . But there are social and political problems which seem at times to defy such resolution. In such situations, under our system, the judiciary must bear a hand and accept its responsibility to assist in the solution when constitutional rights hang in the balance."[35]

Notes

CHAPTER 1

1. W. Wilson, Congressional Government par. 10 (1885).
2. In his concurring opinion in Richmond Newspapers, Inc. v. Virginia, 100 Supreme Court Reporter 2814, 2838 (1980).
3. W. Bagehot, The English Constitution (1867) (2d ed. 1872), 267 (pagination to 1963 paperback edition of 2d ed.). Justice William Rehnquist of the present Supreme Court seems to reject the idea of a living Constitution. See Rehnquist, *The Notion of a Living Constitution*, 54 Texas Law Review 693 (1976). But his views are not shared by any thoughtful student of the Court and, indeed, are not put into practice by Rehnquist himself. See, for example, his opinion for the Court in the Iranian hostage case, Dames & Moore v. Regan, No. 80-2078 (July 2, 1981).
4. Quoted in W. Bagehot, supra note 3.
5. In Marbury v. Madison, 1 Cranch (5 U.S.) 137 (1803). See R. McCloskey, The American Supreme Court (1960).
6. Quoted in R. Jackson, The Struggle for Judicial Supremacy 59 (1941).
7. For an argument that the United States should revert to a type of government similar to that under the Articles of Confederation, see W. Williams, America Confronts a Revolutionary World: 1776-1976 (1976).
8. The Constitution of Control is discussed in A. Miller, Democratic Dictatorship: The Emergent Constitution of Control (1981).
9. J. Commons, Legal Foundation of Capitalism 7 (1924).
10. Brown v. Board of Education, 347 U.S. 483 (1954); and 349 U.S. 294 (1955) (setting forth the famous "with all deliberate speed" formula for racial desegregation).
11. Compare J. Auerbach, Unequal Justice (1975) with J. Griffith, The Politics of the Judiciary (1977).
12. J. Griffith, supra note 11, at 213.
13. In his dissenting opinion in Nebbia v. New York, 291 U.S. 502 (1934).
14. In his famous footnote in United States v. Carolene Products Co., 304 U.S. 144 (1938). For discussion, see J. Ely, Democracy and Distrust (1980).
15. For discussion of Douglas, see J. Simon, Independent Journey (1980) and Douglas's autobiography, The Court Years (1980); and for Johnson, see R. Kennedy, Judge Frank Johnson (1977) and J. Bass, Unlikely Heroes (1981).
16. Quoted in M. Cohen, American Thought: A Critical Sketch 163 (1954).
17. Ibid.
18. Wright, *Professor Bickel, the Scholarly Tradition and the Supreme Court*, 84 Harvard Law Review 769 (1971).

19. F. Cohen, Ethical Systems and Legal Ideals 113 (1933).

20. Aristotle, Politics, Book 7, ch. 1. Felix Cohen said, supra note 19, at 113: "legal criticism must be based upon an adequate description of what this [the good] life is, and . . . all the uncertainties and inaccuracies which attend our formulation of this ideal are likely to reappear in our valuation of law."

21. W. Williams, Empire as a Way of Life (1980).

22. For an account of the reception one law professor received after his plea for a more activist Supreme Court, see Black, *Toward a Judicial Role for the Twenty-first Century*, 52 Washington Law Review 791 (1977). The term *result orientation* seems to be a neologism of Justice Felix Frankfurter; it is used by one of his acolytes (among many other examples) in Griswold, *Of Time and Attitudes: Professor Hart and Judge Arnold*, 74 Harvard Law Review 81 (1960).

23. See H. Abraham, The Judicial Process (3d ed. 1975).

24. Quoted in M. Mayer, The Lawyers 497 (1967) (pagination from 1968 paperback ed.).

25. Ibid. For discussion of Vinson's point, see Miller, *Constitutional Decisions as De Facto Class Actions: A Comment on Cooper v. Aaron* (to be published in University of Detroit's Journal of Urban Law).

26. Bakke's case may be found at 438 U.S. 265 (1978); the Nixon tapes case at 418 U.S. 683 (1974); and the school case at 347 U.S. 483 (1954).

27. Quoted in Youngstown Sheet & Tube Co. v. Sawyer, 343 U.S. 579 (1952) (Frankfurter, J., concurring).

28. For discussion, see Saphire, *The Value of The Brethren: A Response to its Critics* 58 Texas Law Review 1475 (1980).

29. Traynor, *Badlands in an Appellate Judge's Realm of Reason*, 7 Utah Law Review 157 (1960).

30. F. Frankfurter, Of Law and Men 32 (1956).

31. See Raskin, *Democracy Versus the National Security State*, 40 Law & Contemporary Problems 189 (1976); Bay, *Access to Human Knowledge as a Human Right*, in I. Galnoor (ed.), Government Secrecy in Democracies 22 (1977).

32. As discussed in A. Miller, supra note 8.

33. Warth v. Seldin, 422 U.S. 490 (1975) (dissenting opinion).

34. An annual review of Supreme Court decisions for the previous terms (which run from October of one year until June or July of the next) may be found in the November issues of the Harvard Law Review.

35. Terminiello v. Chicago, 337 U.S. 1 (1949).

36. See Lewis, *Is the Supreme Court Creating Unknown and Unknowable Law? The Insubstantial Federal Question Dismissal*, 5 Nova Law Journal 11 (1980). See also R. Stern & E. Gressman, Supreme Court Practice (4th ed. 1978).

37. See Ohio v. Wyandotte Chemicals Corp., 401 U.S. 493 (1971).

38. See W. Murphy, Elements of Judicial Strategy (1964).

39. See W. Douglas, supra note 15.

40. This was told to me in a personal conversation with Justice William O. Douglas.

41. Federal Judicial Center, Report of the Study Group on the Caseload of the Supreme Court 42 (1972).

42. Brennan, *Working at Justice*, in A. Westin (ed.), An Autobiography of the Supreme Court 300 (1963).

43. See Miller & Sastri, *Secrecy and the Supreme Court: On the Need for Piercing the Red Velour Curtain*, 22 Buffalo Law Review 799 (1973).

44. In F. Dostoevsky, The Brothers Karamazov.

45. Lewis, *Supreme Court Confidential*, New York Review of Books, Feb. 7, 1980.

46. See L. Hand, The Spirit of Liberty (1959).

47. Quoted in O. Kirchheimer, Political Justice 175 (1961).

48. For example, A. Bickel, The Supreme Court and the Idea of Progress (1970).

49. The few definitions that are proffered are inadequate. See, for example, Golding, *Principled Decision-making and the Supreme Court*, 63 Columbia Law Review 35 (1963): "Briefly put, the requirements for principled decision are: (1) that a reason for the disposition of the case be given; and (2) that the case be so decided because it is held to be proper to decide cases of its type in this way." Golding does not say either what the ingredients of "a reason" are or the criteria for determining when it is "proper" to decide cases in a certain way.

50. See M. Shapiro, Law and Politics in the Supreme Court (1964); Shapiro, *Political Jurisprudence*, 52 Kentucky Law Journal 294 (1964).

51. See Kurland, *"Brown v. Board of Education was the Beginning": The School Desegregation Cases in the United States Supreme Court, 1954-1979*, 1979 Washington University Law Quarterly 309.

52. Mason, *Myth and Reality in Supreme Court Decisions*, 48 Virginia Law Review 1385 (1962).

53. Justice William O. Douglas in Gori v. United States, 367 U.S. 364 (1961) (dissenting opinion).

54. See G. Myrdal, Value in Social Theory (1958).

CHAPTER 2

1. The best is A. Mason, Harlan Fiske Stone: Pillar of the Law (1956).

2. See J. Shklar, Legalism (1964).

3. So labeled in Tushnet, *Truth, Justice, and the American Way: An Interpretation of Public Law Scholarship in the Seventies*, 57 Texas Law Review 1307 (1979).

4. T. Arnold, The Symbols of Government 5 (1935).

5. Frankfurter, *The Supreme Court and the Public*, 83 Forum 329 (1930).

6. M. Shapiro, Law and Politics in the Supreme Court (1964).

7. Mishkin, *The High Court, the Great Writ, and the Due Process of Time and Law*, 79 Harvard Law Review 56 (1965).

8. Ibid.

9. Plato, The Republic, Part Four, Sec. 1.

10. Lee, *Introduction*, Ibid., p. 177 (pagination from 1974 paperback ed. translated by Desmond Lee).

11. Ibid.

12. L. Hand, The Bill of Rights (1958).

13. M. Cohen, Law and the Social Order 380 (1933).

14. A. Gasquet (ed.), Lord Acton and His Circle 166 (1906).

15. Quoted in C. Warren, The Supreme Court in United States History 653 (rev. ed. 1935).

16. New York Times Co. v. United States, 403 U.S. 713 (1971).

17. See the opinions by Frankfurter, J., in Rochin v. California, 342 U.S. 165 (1952), Adamson v. California, 332 U.S. 46 (1947), and Louisiana ex rel. Francis v. Resweber, 329 U.S. 459 (1947).

18. H. Gerth & C. Mills (eds.), From Max Weber: Essays in Sociology (1946).

19. Quoted in M. Mintz & J. Cohen, Power, Inc. 77 (1976).

20. In 1886. See Miller, *A Modest Proposal for Helping to Tame the Corporate Beast*, 8 Hofstra Law Review 79 (1979); Ratner, *Corporations and the Constitution*, 15 University of San Francisco Law Review 11 (1980).

21. M. Kammen, People of Paradox 58 (1972).

22. W. Wilson, Constitutional Government in the United States (1908).

23. See note 2, chapter 1, supra, for Brennan's statement; Miranda v. Arizona, 384 U.S. 436 (1966) for White's; and 395 U.S. *vii* for Warren's.

24. O. Holmes, The Common Law 35 (1881).

25. Quoted in A. Miller, The Supreme Court: Myth and Reality 8 (1978).

26. Quoted in L. Henkin, Foreign Affairs and the Constitution (1972).

27. J. Acton, Lectures on Modern History 295 (1906) (paperback ed. 1960).

28. M. Cohen, American Thought: A Critical Sketch (1954).

29. Quoted in W. Douglas, Stare Decicis 31 (1949).

30. R. Miles, Awakening from the American Dream: The Social and Political Limits to Growth (1976).

31. Ibid.

32. See A. Miller, supra note 25, c. 8.

33. Professor Philip B. Kurland, quoted in Oster & Doane, *The Power of Our Judges*, U.S. News & World Report, Jan. 19, 1976, p. 29.

34. B. Cardozo, The Growth of the Law 62 (1924).

35. Quoted from Oliphant & Hewitt, *Foreword* to H. Rueff, From the Physical to the Social Sciences *xv* (1929). See A. Miller, supra note 25, c. 5.

36. Hand, *Book Review*, 35 Harvard Law Review 479 (1922).

37. E. Thompson, Whigs and Hunters: The Origins of the Black Act 266 (1975).

38. Frankfurter, *The Judicial Process and the Supreme Court*, in F. Frankfurter, Of Law and Men 35 (P. Elman ed. 1956).

39. L. Hand, The Spirit of Liberty 81 (1953).

40. Clor, *Constitutional Interpretation: An Interview With Justice Lewis Powell*, 3 Kenyon College Alumni Bulletin No. 3, p. 14 (Summer 1979).

41. Chief Justice Warren Burger and Justices Harry Blackmun, Lewis Powell, and William Rehnquist.

42. Marshall, C. J., in Osborn v. Bank of the United States, 9 Wheaton (22 U.S.) 738 (1824).

43. L. Hand, The Bill of Rights (1958).

44. J. Shklar, supra note 2.

45. E. Thompson, supra note 37.

46. Arnold, *Professor Hart's Theology*, 73 Harvard Law Review 1298 (1960).

47. Bailey v. Drexel Furniture Co., 259 U.S.20 (1922).

48. B. Cardozo, The Nature of the Judicial Process (1921).

49. Wirth, *Preface* to K. Mannheim, Ideology and Utopia: An Introduction to the Sociology of Knowledge *xx* (1936).

50. See R. Cushman, Therapeia: Plato's Conception of Philosophy (1958).

51. P. Bridgman, The Way Things Are (1959).

52. M. Polanyi, Personal Knowledge (1958) and The Study of Man (1958).

53. K. Mannheim, supra note 49.

54. G. Myrdal, Value in Social Theory (1958).

55. Niebuhr, *The Dilemma of Modern Man*, The Nation, Feb. 22, 1947.

56. A. Whitehead, Modes of Thought (1938). See also A. Whitehead, Process and Reality (1929).

57. See J. Frank, Courts on Trial (1949).

58. Quoted in Soifer, *Complacency and Constitutional Law*, 42 Ohio State Law Journal 383 (1981).

59. See the unsigned comment (now known to be written by Holmes) entitled *The Gas-Stokers' Strike*, 7 American Law Review 582 (1873). For discussion, see Tushnet, *Truth, Justice, and the American Way: An Interpretation of Public Law Scholarship in the Seventies*, 57 Texas Law Review 1307 (1979).

Chapter 3

1. O. Holmes, Collected Legal Papers 292 (1920).

2. See R. McCloskey, The Modern Supreme Court (1972).

3. Brown v. Board of Education, 347 U.S. 483 (1954). See R. Kluger, Simple Justice (1976).

4. J. Galbraith, The New Industrial State (1967).

5. See Santa Clara County v. Southern Pacific Railway, 118 U.S. 394 (1886); Ratner, *Corporations and the Constitution*, 15 University of San Francisco Law Review 11 (1980).

6. J. Ely, Democracy and Distrust (1980), discussed in *Symposium: Judicial Review Versus Democracy*, 42 Ohio State Law Journal 1-434 (1981).

7. In saying this about American "ruling classes," I accept the analysis of C. Mills, The Power Elite (1956) and G. Domhoff, Who Rules America? (1967). Of course, I recognize that it is a controversial point.

8. United States v. Nixon, 418 U.S. 683 (1974).

9. See Miller, *Reason of State and the Emergent Constitution of Control*, 64 Minnesota Law Review 585 (1980); A. Miller, Democratic Dictatorship: The Emergent Constitution of Control (1981).

10. A. Bickel, The Least Dangerous Branch 103 (1962).

11. The Federalist Papers were written by Alexander Hamilton, James Madison, and John Jay.

12. See A. Sofaer, War, Foreign Affairs and Constitutional Power: The Origins (1976); A. Miller, supra note 9.

13. Quoted by James Reston, New York Times, Aug. 21, 1964, p. 28.

14. Shapiro, *Political Jurisprudence*, 54 Kentucky Law Journal 294 (1964).

15. Quoted in P. Freund, On Understanding the Supreme Court (1949).

16. Address by Chief Justice Warren at the Louis Marshall Award Dinner of the Jewish Theological Seminary, New York, N.Y., November 11, 1962. He went on to say: "Each is indispensable to civilization. Without law, we should be at the mercy of the least scrupulous; without ethics, law could not exist. Without ethical consciousness in most people, lawlessness would be rampant. Yet without law, civilization could not exist."

17. For the history, see C. Swisher, American Constitutional Development (rev. ed. 1954); R. McCloskey, The American Supreme Court (1960).

18. R. McCloskey, supra note 17.

19. Marbury v. Madison, 1 Cranch (5 U.S.) 137 (1803); Fletcher v. Peck, 6 Cranch (10 U.S.) 87 (1810); Woodward v. Dartmouth College, 4 Wheaton (17 U.S.) 518 (1819); Martin v. Hunter's Lessee, 1 Wheaton (14 U.S.) 304 (1816); McCulloch v. Maryland, 4 Wheaton (17 U.S.) 316 (1819); Cohens v. Virginia, 6 Wheaton (19 U.S.) 264 (1821); Gibbons v. Ogden, 9 Wheaton (22 U.S.) 1 (1824).

20. 2 Dallas (2 U.S.) 419 (1793).

21. For discussion, see Ratner, *Congressional Power Over the Appellate Jurisdiction of the Supreme Court*, 109 University of Pennsylvania Law Review 157 (1960). The leading judicial expression is Ex Parte McCardle, 7 Wallace (74 U.S.) 506 (1869). In early 1981, more than twenty bills had been introduced into Congress with the aim of limiting judicial power. See Miller, *The Supreme Court Under Fire*, Miami Herald, June 28, 1981, p. 4E.

22. Quoted in R. Jackson, The Struggle for Judicial Supremacy (1941).

23. A quirk of fate gave Marshall his opportunity. Had Marbury brought his suit in the *trial* court, the Supreme Court then would have had to deal with it as a matter of its *appellate* jurisdiction—and that would have prevented Marshall from declaring the statute invalid. On such accidents, great matters of state turn.

24. Dred Scott v. Sandford, 19 Howard (60 U.S.) 393 (1857), holding that Americans of African descent were not "citizens" in the constitutional sense, even though freed from slavery, and thus not entitled to constitutional protections.

25. See C. Magrath, Yazoo: Law and Politics in the New Republic (1966).

26. See Huntington, *The United States*, in M. Crozier, S. Huntington & J. Watanuki, The Crisis of Democracy (1975) for a discussion of the fears of the Founding Fathers about democracy.

27. R. Jackson, supra note 22, at 8. Jackson wrote this book while Solicitor General; he was

later to become an Associate Justice of the Supreme Court. The context of the quoted material in the text comes from this paragraph: "The men who framed the Constitution were, in the main, men of property, having a conservative background and interest, and believing generally in 'government by the wise, the good and the rich.' The doctrines of equality set forth in the Declaration of Independence had been hard-tested by the trying times that had followed and the Constitution represented something of a counter-revolution. While the Declaration was directed against an excess of authority, the Constitution was directed toward anarchy."

28. See, for discussion of Madison's essay, G. Wills, Explaining America (1980).

29. For insightful discussion, compare T. Lowi, The End of Liberalism (2d ed. 1979) with L. Thurow, The Zero-Sum Society (1980).

30. For discussion, see H. Hart & H. Wechsler, the Federal Courts and the Federal System (1953).

31. Quoted in M. Cohen, The Faith of a Liberal 185 (1946).

32. Quoted in G. Gunther, Cases and Materials on Constitutional Law 48 (9th ed. 1975).

33. In Martin v. Hunter's Lessee, supra note 19.

34. See Levinson, *The Specious Morality of the Law*, Harper's Magazine, May 1977, p. 37. See also J. Shklar, Legalism (1964).

35. Roe v. Wade, 410 U.S. 113 (1973); Doe v. Bolton, 410 U.S. 179 (1973).

36. R. Jackson, supra note 22 at 18.

37. Younger v. Harris, 401 U.S. 37 (1971).

38. For example, National League of Cities v. Usery, 426 U.S. 833 (1976).

39. Warren, *Legislative and Judicial Attacks on the Supreme Court of the United States — A History of the Twenty-fifth Section of the Judiciary Act*, 47 American Law Review 1 (1913).

40. See C. Warren, The Supreme Court in United States History 555 (Vol. 1, 1926).

41. 349 U.S. 375 (1955). See B. Prettyman, Death and the Supreme Court (1956).

42. Minnesota v. Clover Leaf Creamery Co., 101 Supreme Court Reporter 715 (1981).

43. T. Lowi, supra note 29, at 295.

44. See Norman v. Baltimore & Ohio Railroad Co., 294 U.S. 240 (1935), discussed in R. Jackson, supra note 22.

45. For signs that the Court is reentering the economic policy field, see United States Trust Co. v. New Jersey, 431 U.S. (1977) and Allied Structural Steel Co. v. Spannaus, 438 U.S. 234 (1978); the cases are discussed in Phillips, *The Life and Times of the Contract Clause*, to be published in the American Business Law Journal in 1982.

46. National Labor Relations Board v. Jones & Laughlin Steel Co., 301 U.S. 1 (1937).

47. Smith v. Allwright, 321 U.S. 649 (1944).

48. See R. McCloskey, supra note 2. See also R. McCloskey, supra note 17.

49. Federalist No. 22.

50. 4 Wheaton (17 U.S.) 122 (1819).

51. R. Jackson, supra note 22.

52. Quoted in L. Berg, H. Hahn & J. Schmidhauser, Corruption in the American Political System (1976); see also N. Miller, The Founding Finaglers (1976).

53. See the books cited in notes 25 and 52, supra.

54. Monaco v. Mississippi, 292 U.S. 313 (1943).

55. C. Curtis, Lions Under the Throne (1947).

56. G. Gunther, Cases and Materials on Constitutional Law 110 (9th ed. 1975).

57. Osborn v. Bank of the United States, 9 Wheaton (22 U.S.) 738 (1824).

58. 15 Writings of Thomas Jefferson 278 (A. Libscomb & A. Burgh eds. 1904-7). See Miller, *The Elusive Search for Values in Constitutional Interpretation*, 6 Hastings Constitutional Law Quarterly 487 (1979).

59. 395 U.S. *x-xii* (retirement address of Chief Justice Warren, June 23, 1969).

60. See G. Gunther, supra note 56, at 604. See also H. Maine, Popular Government (1885): The contract clause "secured full play to the economical forces by which the achievement of

cultivating the soil of the American continent has been performed; it is the bulwark of American individualism against democratic impatience and socialistic fantasy."

61. W. Mendelson, Capitalism, Democracy, and the Supreme Court 24 (1960).

62. See, for example, Griswold, *Of Time and Attitudes: Professor Hart and Judge Arnold*, 74 Harvard Law Review 81 (1960).

63. Golding, *Principled Decision-Making and the Supreme Court*, 63 Columbia Law Review 35 (1963).

64. 3 J. Cambell, Lives of the Chief Justice of England 481 (3d ed. 1874).

65. W. Douglas, The Court Years (1980).

66. 12 Howard (53 U.S.) 290 (1851).

67. Hood v. DuMond, 336 U.S. 525 (1949).

68. Quoted in R. Jackson, supra note 22.

69. F. Frankfurter, Law and Politics: Occasional Papers of Felix Frankfurter 62 (A. MacLeish & E. Pritchard eds. 1962).

70. F. Neumann, The Democratic and the Authoritarian State 8 (1957).

71. P. Jones, The Consumer Society: A History of American Capitalism 99 (1965).

72. See B. Mitchell, Alexander Hamilton: The National Adventure, 1788-1804 (1962).

73. Ibid.

74. See A. Miller, The Modern Corporate State: Private Governments and the Constitution (1976).

75. See S. Bruchey, The Roots of American Economic Growth, 1607-1861: An Essay in Social Causation (1965).

76. Discussed in A. Miller, The Supreme Court and American Capitalism (1968).

77. T. Lowi, supra note 29, at 5.

78. A. Kelly & W. Harbison, American Constitutional History (5th ed. 1975).

79. See, for example, Munn v. Illinois, 94 U.S. 113 (1877).

80. Santa Clara County v. Southern Pacific Railway, supra note 5. See Ratner, supra note 5.

81. Cf. B. Twiss, Lawyers and the Constitution (1942); J. Auerbach, Unequal Justice (1976).

82. Plessy v. Ferguson, 163 U.S. 537 (1896).

83. This statement from *The Federalist Papers* merely states a truism, of course, but it is one that the Supreme Court neglected for many years.

84. In cases such as Lochner v. New York, 198 U.S. 45 (1905); Adair v. United States, 208 U.S. 161 (1908); Coppage v. Kansas, 236 U.S. 1 (1915); Adkins v Children's Hospital, 261 U.S. 525 (1926).

85. Ibid.

86. Ibid.

87. Quoted in C. Fairman, Mr. Justice Miller and the Supreme Court 374 (1939).

88. L. Thurow, supra note 29.

89. Quoted in A. Nevins, John D. Rockefeller 622 (1940).

90. Standard Oil Co. of New Jersey v. United States, 221 U.S. 1 (1911).

91. See T. Arnold, The Folklore of Capitalism (1937). Although more than forty years old, the book still is accurate.

92. 158 U.S. 564 (1895).

93. United States v. Nixon, supra note 8.

94. Pollock v. Farmers' Loan & Trust Co., 157 U.S. 429 *1895).

95. Dissenting in the Lochner case, supra note 84.

96. See Parenti, *The Constitution as an Elitist Document*, in R. Goldwin & W. Schambra (eds.), How Democratic is the Constitution? 29 (1980).

97. Quoted in B. Twiss, supra note 81, at 149.

98. T. Veblen, The Theory of the Leisure Class 231 (1899).

99. IV T. Roosevelt, Presidential Addresses and State Papers May 10, 1905, to April 12, 1906 at p. 419 (1910).

100. R. Smith, Justice and the Poor (1919).

101. See J. Auerbach, Unequal Justice (1976).

102. Ibid.

103. R. Jackson, supra note 22.

104. See H. Pringle, The Life and Times of William Howard Taft 853-54 (Vol. 2, 1939).

105. Ibid. See also R. Jackson, supra note 22, at 184-87.

106. R. Jackson, supra note 22, at 187.

107. Ibid., at 190.

108. 110 U.S. 421 (1884); 79 U.S. 457 (1871).

109. West Coast Hotel Co. v. Parrish, 300 U.S. 379 (1937). See Miller, *An Affirmative Thrust to Due Process of Law?* 30 George Washington Law Review 399 (1962).

110. In the Parrish case, supra note 109.

111. See Phillips, *Status and Freedom in American Constitutional Law*, 29 Emory Law Journal 3 (1980).

112. National Labor Relations Board v. Jones & Laughlin Steel Co., supra note 46.

113. Steward Machine Co. v. Davis, 301 U.S. 548 (1937); Helvering v. Davis, 301 U.S. 619 (1937).

114. See, for example, Kluger, supra note 3.

115. Buck v. Bell, 274 U.S. 200 (1927).

116. Quoted from Civil Liberties (publication of the American Civil Liberties Union), Feb. 1981, p. 6.

117. Powell v. Alabama, 287 U.S. 45 (1932).

118. Missouri ex rel. Gaines v. Canada, 305 U.S. 337 (1938).

119. For example, Fullilove v. Klutznick, 100 Supreme Court Reporter 2758 (1980); United Steel Workers v. Weber, 443 U.S. 193 (1979). But see Miller, *The Court and Racial Bias: The Second Reconstruction Is Ending*, Miami Herald, May 24, 1981, p. 1E; G. Gill, Meanness Mania (1980).

120. See L. Ruchames, Race, Jobs and Politics (1953).

121. Monaco v. Mississippi, supra note 54.

122. Smith v. Allwright, supra note 47.

123. 334 U.S. 1 (1948).

124. Baker v. Carr, 369 U.S. 186 (1962).

125. Reynolds v. Sims, 377 U.S. 533 (1964); Wesberry v. Sanders, 376 U.S. 1 (1964).

126. For discussion, see Perry, *Modern Equal Protection: A Conceptualization and Appraisal*, 79 Columbia Law Review 1023 (1979).

127. Trop v. Dulles, 356 U.S. 86 (1958).

128. A. Cox, The Role of the Supreme Court in American Government (1976).

129. For example, A. Bickel, The Supreme Court and the Idea of Progress (1970).

130. Quoted in N. Graglia, Disaster by Decree 17 (1976).

131. 358 U.S. 1 (1958). See P. Kurland, Politics, The Warren Court, and the Constitution (1970).

132. See E. Rostow, The Sovereign Prerogative (1962).

CHAPTER 4

1. For the cases and discussion, see W. Lockhart, Y. Kamisar & J. Choper, Constitutional Law: Cases—Comments—Questions 1267-1333 (5th ed. 1980).

2. For discussion, see Baker, *Neutrality, Process, and Rationality: Flawed Interpretations of Equal Protection*, 58 Texas Law Review 1029 (1980).

3. See G. Gill, Meanness Mania (1980); F. Jones, The Changing Mood in America: Eroding Commitment? (1977).

4. Soifer, *Complacency and Constitutional Law*, 42 Ohio State Law Journal 383 (1981).

5. See T. Lowi, The End of Liberalism (2d ed. 1979). See also P. Green, The Pursuit of Inequality (1981).

6. W. Sumner, Folkways (1906). See also M. Berger, Equality by Statute (1952).

7. See I. Jenkins, Social Order and the Limits of Law (1979); Phillips, *Status and Freedom in American Constitutional Law*, 29 Emory Law Journal 3 (1980).

8. Phillips, supra note 7.

9. See Miller, *Judicial Activism and American Constitutionalism: Some Notes and Reflections*, in J. Pennock & J. Chapman (eds.), Constitutionalism 333 (1979).

10. Quoted in H. Hirsch, The Enigma of Felix Frankfurter 118 (1981).

11. E. Nagel, The Structure of Science: Problems in the Logic of Scientific Explanation (1961).

12. Quoted in G. Stent, The Coming of the Golden Age: A View of the End of Progress x (1969). See also A. Wheelis, The End of the Modern Age (1971).

13. For an update of the Paley Commission Report, see The Global 2000 Report to the President: Entering the Twenty-First Century (in 3 volumes, Gerald O. Barney, Study Director, 1980).

14. See W. Ophuls, Ecology and the Politics of Scarcity: Prologue to a Political Theory of the Steady State (1977).

15. Baker v. Carr, 369 U.S. 186 (1962) (dissenting opinion).

16. Reynolds v. Sims, 377 U.S. 533 (1964).

17. Berger's preposterous views are discussed in Miller, *The Elusive Search for Values in Constitutional Interpretation*, 6 Hastings Constitutional Law Quarterly 487 (1979).

18. Glazer, *Towards an Imperial Judiciary?* The Public Interest, no. 41, p. 104 (Fall 1975).

19. Murphy, *An Ordering of Constitutional Values*, 53 Southern California Law Review 703 (1980).

20. H. Hirsch, supra note 10.

21. G. Gilmore, The Ages of American Law (1977).

22. G. Jacobsohn, Pragmatism, Statesmanship, and the Supreme Court (1977).

23. T. Hobbes, Leviathan (1651).

24. G. Poggi, The Development of the Modern State: A Sociological Introduction (1978).

25. For discussion, see D. Cater, Power in Washington (1964); Heclo, *Issue Networks and the Executive Establishment*, in A. King (ed.), The New American Political System 87 (1978).

26. See, for brief discussion, G. Gunther, Cases and Materials on Constitutional Law 429 (9th ed. 1975).

27. See, for example, Wilson, *The Rise of the Bureaucratic State*, The Public Interest, no. 41, p. 77 (Fall 1975).

28. See A. Miller, Democratic Dictatorship: The Emergent Constitution of Control (1981).

29. See Cox, *Executive Privilege*, 122 University of Pennsylvania Law Review 1383 (1974); Dorsen & Shattuck, *Executive Privilege: The Congress and the Courts*, 35 Ohio State Law Journal 1 (1974).

30. Discussed in Miller & Bowman, *Presidential Attacks on the Constitutionality of Federal Statutes: A New Separation of Powers Problem*, 40 Ohio State Law Journal 51 (1979).

31. Ex parte Merryman, 17 Federal Cases 114 (No. 9487) (1861).

32. For discussion, see Miller & Knapp, *The Legislative Veto: Preservation of the Constitutional Framework*, 52 Indiana Law Journal 367 (1977).

33. See J. Ellul, The Political Illusion (1967); H. Arendt, On Revolution (1965); M. Duverger, Political Parties: Their Organization and Activity in the Modern State (1961).

34. Cf. J. Lieberman, The Litigious Society (1981).

35. See Mintz, *The Supreme Court: Remaining Silent on Homosexual Rights*, Washington Post, Dec. 11, 1979, p. A3.

36. Naim v. Naim, 350 U.S. 891 (1955); Loving v. Virginia, 388 U.S. 1 (1967).

37. See L. Tribe, American Constitutional Law 71-79 (1978).

38. Griswold v. Connecticut, 381 U.S. 479 (1965).

39. Roe v. Wade, 410 U.S. 113 (1973); Doe v. Bolton, 410 U.S. 179 (1973).

40. See J. Ely, Democracy and Distrust (1980), discussed in *Symposium*, 42 Ohio State Law Journal 1-434 (1981).

41. See A. Bickel, The Supreme Court and the Idea of Progress (1962).

42. Orwell, *Politics and the English Language*, in G. Orwell, Collected Essays 353 (1961).

43. See M. Rejai, Democracy: The Contemporary Theories (1967). See also E. Schatt-schneider, The Semisovereign People (1960).

44. Crick, *Introduction*, to N. Machiavelli, The Discourses 27 (B. Crick ed. 1970) (paperback ed.).

45. See Wright, *Politics and the Constitution: Is Money Speech?* 85 Yale Law Journal 1001 (1976). Judge Wright said in part: "We simply are not so helpless that we must blindly equate the outcome of the group pressure process with the public interest." See also Barry, *The Public Interest*, in W. Connolly (ed.), The Bias of Pluralism 159 (1969).

46. Linde, *Due Process of Lawmaking*, 55 Nebraska Law Review 197 (1976).

47. Y. Simon, Philosophy of Democratic Government 123 (1951).

48. The Economist (London), Vol. 277, No. 7165, Dec. 27, 1980, p. 22.

49. R. Michels, Political Parties (1911).

50. A. Bentley, The Process of Government (1908); D. Truman, The Governmental Process (1951); T. Lowi, supra note 5.

51. G. McConnell, Private Power and American Democracy 139 (1966).

52. Cf. R. Pious, The American Presidency (1979).

53. The Federalist No. 51.

54. M. Mintz & J. Cohen, Power, Inc. (1976). See also B. Smith & D. Hague, The Dilemma of Accountability in Modern Government (1971).

55. A. Bickel, The Least Dangerous Branch (1962).

56. P. Murphy, World War I and the Origin of Civil Liberties in the United States (1979).

57. C. Friedrich, The Pathology of Politics (1973).

58. Ibid.

59. For a discussion of the two types of functions, see R. Merton, Social Theory and Social Structure 115-22 (rev. ed. 1968).

60. See Cohen v. California, 403 U.S. 15 (1971).

61. J. Griffith, The Politics of the Judiciary 213 (1977). See Miller, *The Politics of the American Judiciary*, 49 Political Quarterly 200 (1978).

62. Cf. Miller, *On Politics, Democracy, and the First Amendment: A Commentary on First National Bank v. Bellotti*, 38 Washington & Lee Law Review 21 (1981).

63. B. Skinner, Beyond Freedom and Dignity (1971).

64. W. Thompson, Evil and World Order 24 (1976).

65. C. Lindblom, Politics and Markets (1977).

66. A. de Tocqueville, Democracy in America, quoted in ibid., at p. 53.

67. P. Schrag, Mind Control xi (1978). See also A. Scheflin & E. Opton, The Mind Manipulators (1978).

68. A. Huxley, Brave New World Revisited (1958).

69. Hart, *The Time Chart of the Justices*, 73 Harvard Law Review 84 (1959), criticized in Arnold, *Professor Hart's Theology*, 73 Harvard Law Review 1298 (1960).

70. See Forrester, *Are We Ready for Truth in Judging?* 63 American Bar Association Journal 1212 (1977).

71. R. Dworkin, Taking Rights Seriously (1977).

72. O. Holmes, The Common Law 35 (1881).

73. Kennedy v. Mendoza-Martinez, 372 U.S. 144 (1963).

74. United States v. Snepp, 100 Supreme Court Reporter 763 (1980). See Miller, *Reason of State and the Emergent Constitution of Control*, 64 Minnesota Law Review 585 (1980).

75. R. Funston, Constitutional Counter-revolution? 29 (1977).

76. R. Dworkin, supra note 71. For discussion, see Delgado, *Active Rationality in Judicial Review*, 64 Minnesota Law Review 467 (1980).

77. P. Diesing, Reason in Society: Five Types of Decisions and Their Social Conditions (1962).

78. H. Hirsch, supra note 10.

79. Quoted in Soifer, supra note 4.

80. G. Dickinson, The Meaning of Good 86 (1901), quoted in B. Toulmin, An Examination of the Place of Reason in Ethics 225 (1950).

81. T. Marvell, Appellate Courts and Lawyers: Information Gathering in the Adversary System (1978). See Miller & Barron, *The Supreme Court, the Adversary System, and the Flow of Information to the Justices: A Preliminary Inquiry*, 61 Virginia Law Review 1187 (1975).

82. B. Cardozo, The Growth of the Law (1924).

83. O. Holmes, The Common Law (1881).

84. Oral Argument, Brown v. Board of Education, 347 U.S. 483 (1954), reprinted in L. Friedman, Argument 63 (1969).

85. The "marketplace of ideas" is the judicial theory of the First Amendment's freedom of speech and press provisions, first articulated by Holmes, J., in Abrams v. United States, 250 U.S. 616 (1919).

86. Brennan, *Working at Justice*, in A. Westin (ed.), An Autobiography of the Supreme Court (1963).

87. The best is T. Marvell, supra note 81.

88. Santa Clara County v. Southern Pacific Railway, 118 U.S. 394 (1886). See also Erie Railroad Co. v. Tompkins 304 U.S. 64 (1938).

89. 358 U.S. 1 (1958).

90. Discussion may be found in K. Davis, Administrative Law Treatise (1958).

CHAPTER 5

1. Richmond Newspapers, Inc. v. Virginia, 100 Supreme Court Reporter 2814, 2838 (1980) (concurring opinion). See also White J., dissenting in Miranda v. Arizona, 384 U.S. 436 (1966).

2. Cf. J. Commons, The Economics of Collective Action (1950).

3. 391 U.S. 430 (1968), discussed in Miller, *Toward a Concept of Constitutional Duty*, 1968 Supreme Court Review 299.

4. I speak here of the high-level decisions in government, whether legislative or executive or judicial, and, indeed, much of the activities of the public administration. See K. Davis, Discretionary Justice (1969).

5. Quoted in M. Mayer, The Lawyers 497 (1967) (paperback ed. 1968), discussed in Miller, *Constitutional Decisions as De Facto Class Actions: A Comment on Cooper v. Aaron*—University of Detroit Journal of Urban Law—(1981).

6. So labeled in A. Miller, The Supreme Court: Myth and Reality c. 8 (1978).

7. Quoted in M. Mayer, supra note 5, at 490.

8. G. Gilmore, The Ages of American Law (1977).

9. Rummel v. Estelle, 100 Supreme Court Reporter 1133 (1980).

10. Bakke v. Regents of the University of California, 438 U.S. 265 (1978).

11. Quoted in Kelly, *Who Needs a Theory of Citizenship?* in 108 Daedalus No. 4, p. 21 (1979).

12. Ibid.

13. Horwitz, *The Emergence of an Instrumental Conception of Law*, in M. Horwitz, The Transformation of American Law, 1780-1860 at 1 (1977).

14. Wolf v. Colorado, 338 U.S. 25 (1949).

15. L. Duguit, Law in the Modern State 26 (H. Laski trans. 1919).

16. W. Wilson, Constitutional Government in the United States (1908).

17. See A. Miller, The Supreme Court and American Capitalism (1968).

18. Galbraith, *How To Get Ahead*, New York Review of Books, July 19, 1979.

19. L. Thurow, The Zero-Sum Society (1980).

20. P. Duignan & A. Rabushka, The United States in the 1980s *xxxix* (1980). See also L. Brown, The Twenty-Ninth Day (1978).

21. See R. Barnet, The Lean Years (1980).

22. International Congress of Jurists, The Rule of Law in a Free Society (1960). See Thorson, A New Concept of the Rule of Law, 38 Canadian Bar Review 239 (1960); Miller, An Affirmative Thrust to Due Process of Law? 30 George Washington Law Review 399 (1962).

23. Y. Simon, Philosophy of Democratic Government 123 (1951).

24. 300 U.S. 379 (1937).

25. 349 U.S. 294 (1955).

26. E. Corwin, Liberty Against Government 161 (1948).

27. H. George, Progress and Poverty c. 8 (1879).

28. 426 U.S. 833 (1976). But see Fry v. United States, 421 U.S. 542 (1975).

29. Quoted in M. Mayer, supra note 5, at 516.

30. T. Green, Works: Miscellanies And Memoir 371 (1888), discussed in Miller, supra note 22.

31. See H. Hirsch, The Enigma of Felix Frankfurter (1981).

32. R. Nozick, Anarchy, State, and Utopia (1974); G. Gilder, Wealth and Poverty (1981).

33. T. Green, supra note 30.

34. See N. Machiavelli, The Discourses, Book I, Sec. 51: "A republic or prince should ostensibly do out of generosity what necessity constrains them to do."

35. 321 U.S. 649 (1944); 334 U.S. 1 (1948); 347 U.S. 483 (1954).

36. Hobson v. Hansen, 269 Federal Supplement 401 (1967).

37. 100 Supreme Court Reporter 1490 (1980).

38. Soifer, Complacency and Constitutional Law, 42 Ohio State Law Journal 383 (1981).

39. Hill, The Illusion of Black Progress, 9 Social Policy No. 3 at 14 (1978). See Miller, Brown's 25th: A Silver Lining Tarnished With Time, 3 District Lawyer No. 5 at 22 (1979).

40. Cf. L. Lusky, By What Right? A Commentary on the Supreme Court's Power to Revise the Constitution (1975); Lusky, "Government by Judiciary": What Price Legitimacy? 6 Hastings Constitutional Law Quarterly 403 (1979).

41. Cf. P. Kurland, Politics, the Constitution, and the Warren Court (1970).

42. Wyatt v. Stickney, 344 Federal Supplement 387 (1972); Pugh v. Locke, 406 Federal Supplement 318 (1976).

43. See J. Wilkinson, From Brown to Bakke (1979); Fullilove v. Klutznick, 100 Supreme Court Reporter 2758 (1980).

44. A. Miller, Democratic Dictatorship: The Emergent Constitution of Control (1981).

45. Quoted in Oka, A Crowded World: Can Mankind Survive in Freedom? Christian Science Monitor, Feb. 10, 1975, at 5.

46. E. Mishan, The Economic Growth Debate: An Assessment 265 (1977).

47. R. Berger, Government by Judiciary (1977).

48. But see City of Mobile v. Bolden, supra note 37.

49. Reynolds v. Sims, 377 U.S. 533 (1964) (dissenting opinion).

50. Morgan v. Kerrigan, 388 Federal Supplement 581 (1975).

51. Robinson v. Cahill, a series of five decisions by the highest court in New Jersey.

52. Glazer, Towards an Imperial Judiciary? The Public Interest, no. 41, p. 104 (1975).

53. See Miller, Judicial Activism and American Constitutionalism: Some Notes and Reflections, in J. Pennock & J. Chapman (eds.) Constitutionalism 333 (1979).

54. See Murphy, Lower Court Checks on Supreme Court Power, 53 American Political Science Review 1017 (1959).

55. Quoted in W. Lockhart, Y. Kamisar & J. Choper, Constitutional Law: Cases—Comments —Questions 1 (5th ed. 1980).

56. I am developing this idea in a forthcoming volume, tentatively entitled Getting There from Here: Toward a Constitution of Human Needs (in progress).

57. See M. Crozier, S. Huntington & J. Watanuki, The Crisis of Democracy (1975).

58. For example, A. Bickel, The Supreme Court and the Idea of Progress (1970); A. Bickel, the Morality of Consent (1975).

CHAPTER 6

1. W. Yeats, The Second Coming (1924).

2. See M. & R. Friedman, Free to Choose: A Personal Statement (1979).

3. H. Maine, Ancient Law (1861).

4. A. Bentley, The Process of Government (1908).

5. F. Tannenbaum, The Balance of Power in Society 25 (1969).

6. T. Lowi, The End of Liberalism 48 (1969).

7. Quoted in Odegard, *Introduction* to A. Bentley, supra note 4, at *ix* (1967 ed.).

8. Kelly, *Mediation Versus Compromise in Hegel*, in J. Pennock & J. Chapman (eds.), Compromise in Ethics, Law, and Politics 87 (1979).

9. E. Burke, quoted in Golding, *The Nature of Compromise: A Preliminary Inquiry*, in ibid., at 3.

10. F. Hayek, Law, Legislation and Liberty, vol. 2, *The Mirage of Social Justice*, at 15 (1976).

11. Hallowell, *Compromise as a Political Ideal*, 54 Ethics 173 (1944).

12. R. Wolff, The Poverty of Liberalism c. 4 (1968).

13. Ibid., at 160.

14. H. Kariel, The Decline of American Pluralism (1961).

15. R. Wolff, supra note 12, at 156.

16. See, for discussion, A. Miller, Democratic Dictatorship: The Emergent Constitution of Control (1981).

17. D. Ehrenfeld, The Arrogance of Humanism (1978).

18. A. Comte, System of Positive Polity (1851).

19. P. Rhinelander, Is Man Incomprehensible to Man? 13 (1973).

20. Thucydides, The Peloponnesian War, Book 3, Sec. 82-83.

21. L. Fuller, The Morality of Law 19 (1964).

22. P. Rhinelander, supra note 19, at 1.

23. D. Ehrenfeld, supra note 17.

24. Ibid.

25. McWilliams, *A Figurehead Presidency for an Authoritarian Establishment*, The Progressive, Sept. 1980, p. 9.

26. See W. Connolly (ed.), The Bias of Pluralism (1969).

27. A. Bentley, supra note 4, at 389-90.

28. K. Boulding, The Organizational Revolution (1953).

29. A. de Tocqueville, Democracy in America. Quoted in Connolly, *The Challenge to Pluralist Theory*, in W. Connolly, supra note 26.

30. L. Thurow, The Zero-Sum Society (1980).

CHAPTER 7

1. Sundquist, *The Crisis of Competence in Government*, in J. Pechman (ed.), Setting National Priorities: Agenda for the 1980s at 531 (1980).

2. See A. Miller, The Modern Corporate State: Private Governments and the American Constitution (1976).

3. See the discussion in ibid.

4. Missouri v. Holland, 252 U.S. 416 (1920).

5. Hamilton, *On the Composition of the Corporate Veil*, quoted in R. Eells & C. Walton, Conceptual Foundations of Business 132 (1961).

6. Galbraith, *Power and the Useful Economist*, American Economic Review, March 1973, p. 2, quoted in Samuels, *Introduction* to W. Samuels (ed.), The Economy as a System of Power *iii* (1979).

7. Galbraith, supra note 6.

8. E. Rostow, Planning for Freedom: The Public Law of American Capitalism (1959).

9. The Federalist No. 51.

10. F. Neumann, The Democratic and the Authoritarian State 8 (1957).

11. Ibid.

12. Discussed in A. Miller, Democratic Dictatorship: The Emergent Constitution of Control (1981). See also Miller, *Reason of State and the Emergent Constitution of Control*, 64 Minnesota Law Review 585 (1980).

13. Miller, *Accountability and the Federal Contractor*, 20 Journal of Public Law 473 (1971).

14. See the account in chapter 5, supra.

15. F. Cohen, Ethical Systems and Legal Ideals 261 (1933).

16. Ibid., at 42.

17. Ibid., at 41.

18. B. Bentham, 1 Works c. 2, at 1.

19. Pound, *The Limits of Effective Legal Action*, 27 International Journal of Ethics 150 (1917).

20. H. Maine, Popular Government 60 (1886).

21. W. Lippmann, Essays in the Public Philosophy (1955).

22. For example, R. Nozick, Anarchy, the State and Utopia (1974).

23. Quoted in J. Stone, Social Dimensions of Law and Justice 671 (1966).

24. K. Kapp, The Social Costs of Private Enterprise (1971) (paperback ed.).

25. Ibid., at 13.

26. A. Whitehead, Science and the Modern World 25 (1925).

27. See I. Jenkins, Social Order and the Limits of Law (1980).

28. K. Kapp, supra note 24, at 245.

29. These are analogous to the environmental impact statements mandated by the National Environmental Policy Act of 1969. For brief discussion, see Miller, *A Modest Proposal for Helping to Tame the Corporate Beast*, 8 Hofstra Law Review 79 (1979).

30. Knight, *Foreword*, to A. Macfie, Economic Efficiency and Social Welfare *vi* (1943).

31. N. Machiavelli, The Discourses, Book II, Sec. 2.

32. T. Lowi, The End of Liberalism (2d ed. 1979).

33. T. Carlyle, Past and Present 29 (Everyman's ed. 1941).

CHAPTER 8

1. R. McCloskey, The American Supreme Court 252 (1960).

2. C. Friedrich, Transcendent Justice: The Religious Dimension of Constitutionalism 17 (1964).

3. Ibid.

4. T. Lowi, The End of Liberalism (2d ed. 1979).

5. Murphy, *The Art of Constitutional Interpretation*, in M. Harmon (ed.) Essays on the Constitution of the United States 130 (1978).

6. Addresses and Papers of Charles Evans Hughes 139 (2d ed. 1916).

7. 6 Messages and Papers of the Presidents 9-10 (J. Richardson ed. 1896), quoted in J. Choper, Judicial Review and the National Political Process 212 (1980).

8. See Miller, *Notes on the Concept of the "Living" Constitution*, 31 George Washington Law Review 881 (1963).

9. See Kolakowski, *Permanent and Transitory Aspects of Marxism*, quoted in C. Frankel, The Democratic Prospect 189 (1962).

10. Cf. W. Wilson, Constitutional Government in the United States (1908).

11. P. Bridgman, The Way Things Are 308 (1959).

12. A. Bentley, The Process of Government (1908).

13. G. Garvey, Constitutional Bricolage 91 (1971).

14. Ibid.

15. Passenger Cases, 7 Howard 283 (1849).

16. G. Garvey, supra note 13.

17. Levinson, *Self-Evident Truths in the Declaration of Independence*, 57 Texas Law Review 847 (1979).

18. H. Lasswell & A. Kaplan, Power and Society 75 (1950).

19. R. Tawney, Equality (1931). See B. Russell, Power (1938).

20. F. Neumann, The Democratic and the Authoritarian State 8 (1957).

21. W. Williams, America Confronts a Revolutionary World (1976).

22. See A. Miller, The Supreme Court and American Capitalism (1968).

23. Ibid.

24. E. Corwin, A Constitution of Powers in a Secular State (1951).

25. See Miller, *Reason of State and the Emergent Constitution of Control*, 64 Minnesota Law Review 585 (1980) for discussion and citations.

26. N. Machiavelli, The Discourses, Book I, Sec. 34 (1531).

27. H. Brown, The Human Future Revisited 227 (1978).

28. See Oka, *A Crowded World: Can Mankind Survive in Freedom?* Christian Science Monitor, Feb. 10, 1975, at 5.

29. B. Gross, Friendly Fascism (1980).

30. A. Miller, Democratic Dictatorship: The Emergent Constitution of Control (1981).

31. O. Gierke, Natural Law and the Theory of the State, 1500-1800 (E. Barker trans. 1933).

32. Quoted in New York Times, March 8, 1962, at 14.

33. Quoted in Miami Herald, Jan. 15, 1981, at 17A.

34. E. Barker, *Introduction* to O. Gierke, supra note 31.

35. See Raskin, *Democracy Versus the National Security State*, 40 Law & Contemporary Problems 189 (1976).

36. Weber, *Religious Rejections of the World and Their Directions*, in H. Gerth & C. Mills (eds.), From Max Weber: Essays in Sociology 323 (1958).

37. See A. Wolfe, The Seamy Side of Democracy: Repression in America (1973).

38. J. Ellul, Propaganda (1965).

39. McWilliams, *A Figurehead Presidency for an Authoritarian Establishment*, The Progressive, Sept. 1980, p. 9.

40. H. Lasswell, The Analysis of Political Behaviour 146 (1948).

41. See Raskin, supra note 35.

42. H. Lasswell, National Security and Individual Freedom (1950).

43. E. Mishan, The Economic Growth Debate: An Assessment 265 (1977).

44. F. Church & C. Mathias, *Foreword* to H. Relyea, A Brief History of Emergency Powers in the United States v (U.S. Senate, 93d Congress, 2d Session 1974).

45. E. Mishan, supra note 43, at 265.

46. B. Skinner, Beyond Freedom and Dignity (1971).

47. The first quote may be found in L. Andres & M. Karlins, Requiem for Democracy? An Inquiry Into the Limits of Behavioral Control 1 (1971); the second comes from A. Huxley, Brave New World Revisited (1958).

48. R. Seidenberg, Posthistoric Man (1950).

49. See P. Bachrach, The Theory of Democratic Elitism (1967).

50. Sobolewski, *Electors and Representatives: A Contribution to the Theory of Representation*, in J. Pennock & J. Chapman (eds.), Representation 95 (1968).

51. See I. Galnoor (ed.), Government Secrecy in Democracies (1977).

52. See Miller, *The Resurgent Presidency: A Comment on Dames & Moore v. Regan*—UCLA Law Review—(forthcoming, in 1982). See also R. Pious, The American Presidency (1979).

53. What Frankfurter, J., termed "the unifying forces of modern technology," Freeman v. Hewit, 329 U.S. 249 (1946), have diminished and at times obliterated the political importance of the several states; so, too, has the creation of a national, even multinational, economic system

dominated in large part by the giant corporations. See R. Barnet & R. Muller, Global Reach (1974); S. Rolfe, The International Corporation (1969).

54. See the insightful discussion in J. Auerbach, Unequal Justice (1976).

CHAPTER 9

1. M. Lerner, America as a Civilization 289 (1948).

2. Cf. W. Serrin, The Company and the Union (1973).

3. See W. Samuels (ed.), The Economy as a System of Power (1979).

4. The term "the Political Constitution" is borrowed from Griffith, *The Political Constitution*, 42 Modern Law Review 1 (1979); my reading of Dam, *The American Fiscal Constitution*, 44 University of Chicago Law Review 271 (1977) prompted my thinking about "the Economic Constitution."

5. J. Commons, Legal Foundations of Capitalism 47-64 (1924).

6. License Tax Case, 5 Wallace (72 U.S.) 462 (1866).

7. Recognized, for example, in United States v. Butler, 297 U.S. 1 (1936). See Dam, supra note 4.

8. Most cases deal with the power of state governments to spend under the First Amendment's "establishment clause." For discussion of the general problem, see W. Lockhart, Y Kamisar & J. Choper, Constitutional Law: Cases—Comments—Questions 1163-1214 (5th ed. 1980).

9. R. Tawney, Equality (1931).

10. Barron v. Baltimore, 7 Peters (32 U.S.) 243 (1833).

11. C. Lindblom, Politics and Markets 8 (1977).

12. See K. Renner, The Institutions of Private Law (1949); J. Commons, The Economics of Collective Action 302 (1950); Berle, *The Developing Law of Corporate Concentration*, 19 University of Chicago Law Review 639 (1952).

13. Gross, *The Peace of Westphalia: 1648-1948*, in R. Falk & W. Hanrieder (eds.), International Law and Organization: An Introductory Reader 53-54 (1969).

14. G. Poggi, The Development of the Modern State: A Sociological Introduction 92 (1978).

15. Ibid.

16. Ibid., at 94-95. See J. Commons, supra note 12.

17. Hermann Heller, quoted in G. Poggi, supra note 14, at 99.

18. G. Poggi, supra note 14, at 99. See Weber, *Politics as a Vocation* and *Religious Rejections of the World and Their Directions*, in H. Gerth & C. Mills (eds.), From Max Weber: Essays in Sociology 77, 323 (1946).

19. See Tushnet, *Truth, Justice, and the American Way: An Interpretation of Public Law Scholarship in the Seventies*, 57 Texas Law Review 1307 (1979). Professor Tushnet comments on Oliver Wendell Holmes's observations, *The Gas-Stoker's Strike*, 7 American Law Review 582 (1873).

20. H. Maine, Ancient Law (1861).

21. Holmes, supra note 19.

22. See Plato, The Republic, Book I, 338.

23. Holmes, supra note 19.

24. H. Adams, Relation of the State to Industrial Action and Economics and Jurisprudence 145 (1954) (originally written as two essays in 1887 and 1897).

25. See the discussion in A. Miller, The Modern Corporate State: Private Governments and the American Constitution c. 3 (1976).

26. G. Poggi, supra note 14, at 120-21.

27. For discussion, see C. Stone, Where the Law Ends (1975).

28. Quoted in G. Poggi, supra note 14, at 128.

29. For example, Smith v. Allwright, 321 U.S. 649 (1944).

30. See Miller & Bowman, *Presidential Attacks on the Constitutionality of Federal Statutes: A New Separation of Powers Problem*, 40 Ohio State Law Journal 51 (1979).

31. Cohens v. Virginia, 2 Dallas (2 U.S.) 419 (1821).

32. United States v. Shaw, 309 U.S. 495 (1940).

33. Cf. Van Alstyne, *The Role of Congress in Determining Incidental Powers of the President and of the Federal Courts*, 36 Ohio State Law Journal 788 (1975); Miller & Bowman, supra note 30.

34. See M. Crozier, S. Huntington & J. Watanuki, The Crisis of Democracy (1975).

35. For discussion, see P. Steinfels, The Neo-conservatives (1979); P. Green, The Pursuit of Inequality (1981).

36. A. Smith, The Wealth of Nations 674 (1937 Modern Library ed.) (first published in 1776).

37. Discussed in ibid.

38. See K. Polanyi, The Great Transformation 225-26 (1944).

39. See Parenti, *The Constitution as an Elitist Document*, in R. Goldwin & W. Schambra (eds.), How Democratic is the Constitution? 29 (1980).

40. 1 J. Sutherland, Statutes and Statutory Construction Sec. 306 (3d ed. F. Horack, Jr. 1943), quoted in Liebmann, *Delegation to Private Parties in American Constitutional Law*, 50 Indiana Law Journal 650 (1975).

41. See Hanslowe, *Regulation by Visible Public and Invisible Private Government*, 40 Texas Law Review 88 (1961); Wirtz, *Government by Private Groups*, 13 Louisiana Law Review 440 (1953).

42. K. Polanyi, supra note 38, at 71.

43. Ibid., at 75.

44. W. Webb, The Great Frontier (1952).

45. H. Henderson, Creating Alternative Futures (1978), discussed in Robertson, *Perils of Dictatorship by High Technology*, Manchester Guardian Weekly, April 15, 1978, p. 22.

46. Hale, *Force and the State: A Comparison of "Political" and "Economic" Compulsion*, 35 Columbia Law Review 149 (1935).

47. M. Jensen, The New Nation 178 (1950).

48. See Parenti, *The Constitution as an Elitist Document*, in R. Goldwin & W. Schambra, supra note 39.

49. S. Lynd, Class Conflict, Slavery and the United States Constitution (1967).

50. C. Lindblom, supra note 11.

51. Hale, *Our Equivocal Constitutional Guarantees*, 39 Columbia Law Review 563 (1939). See Cohen, *Property and Sovereignty*, 13 Cornell Law Quarterly 8 (1927).

52. 100 Supreme Court Reporter 763 (1978).

53. Power Manufacturing Co. v. Saunders, 274 U.S. 490 (1927).

54. See Phillips, *The Life and Times of the Contract Clause*—American Business Law Journal—(1982).

55. See C. Magrath, Yazoo: Law and Politics in the New Republic (1966).

56. Drucker, *The Meaning of Mass Production*, 57 Commonweal 547 (1953).

57. A. Bentley, The Process of Government 268 (1908).

58. Quoted in C. Fairman, Mr. Justice Miller and the Supreme Court 374 (1939).

59. New York Times, July 11, 1973. See M. Parenti, Democracy for the Few 77 (3d ed. 1980).

60. M. Josephson, The Robber Barons 52 (1934).

61. Quoted in L. Jaffe, Judicial Control of Administrative Action 11 (1966).

62. G. Kolko, The Triumph of Conservatism 4-5 (1967).

63. Quote taken from 1 M. Farrand (ed.), Records of the Federal Convention (1935). Elbridge Gerry called democracy "the worst of all possible evils," and Madison warned against "the danger of the leveling spirit." Ibid. See M. Parenti, supra note 59, at c. 4.

64. J. Auerbach, Unequal Justice (1976).

65. See. G. Domhoff, The Higher Circles (1972); C. Mills, The Power Elite (1956); M. Parenti, Power and the Powerless (1978).

66. J. Ellul, Propaganda (1965).

67. Weber, *The Meaning of Discipline*, in H. Gerth & C. Mills (eds.), From Max Weber: Essays in Sociology 262 (1958).

68. Ibid.

69. Weber, *Social Psychology of World Religions*, in ibid., at 271.

70. Tushnet, supra note 19.

71. Holmes, supra note 19.

72. M. Parenti, supra note 59, at 71.

73. Bernstein, *The New Deal: The Conservative Achievements of Liberal Reform*, in B. Bernstein (ed.), Towards a New Past 264-65 (1963).

74. Chrysler Corporation Loan Guarantee Act of 1979, Public Law No. 96-185.

75. J. Cooper, The Army and Civil Disorder *xiv* (1980).

76. 158 U.S. 564 (1895).

77. Quoted in S. Lens, The Forging of the American Empire 270 (1971).

78. C. Lindblom, supra note 11, at 52.

79. See Lazarsfeld & Merton, *Mass Communication, Popular Taste, and Organized Social Action*, cited in N. Chomsky, For Reasons of State 205 (1973).

80. For example, United States v. The Progressive, 467 Federal Supplement 990 (1979). See Cheh, *The Progressive Case and the Atomic Energy Act: Waking to the Dangers of Government Information Controls*, 48 George Washington Law Review 163 (1980).

81. In a conversation with me.

82. 403 U.S. 713 (1971).

83. H. Gerth & C. Mills, From Max Weber: Essays in Sociology (1958).

84. Bay, *Access to Human Knowledge as a Human Right*, in I. Galnoor (ed.), Government Secrecy in Democracies 22 (1977).

85. See R. Stevenson, Corporations and Information: Secrecy, Access, and Disclosure (1980).

86. See Miller, *A Modest Proposal for Helping to Tame the Corporate Beast*, 8 Hofstra Law Review 79 (1979).

87. See M. Clinard & P. Yeager, Corporate Crime (1980).

88. For discussion of the "state action" concept, see L. Tribe, American Constitutional Law 261-275, 1147-74 (1978).

89. J. Davis, Corporations 268 (1897) (1961 paperback ed.).

90. Hale, *Economics and Law*, in W. Ogburn & A. Goldenweiser (eds.), The Social Sciences and Their Interpretation 131 (1927).

91. Hale, *Labor Law, Anglo-American*, 8 Encyclopedia of the Social Sciences 669 (1932).

92. Corwin, *The Basic Doctrine of American Constitutional Law*, in A. Mason & G. Garvey (eds.), American Constitutional History: Essays by Edward S. Corwin 25 (1964).

93. See M. Rejai, Democracy: The Contemporary Theories (1967); E. Schattschneider, The Semisovereign People (1960).

94. R. Michels, Political Parties (1911).

95. A. Berle & G. Means, The Modern Corporation and Private Property (rev. ed. 1968).

96. See A. Miller, Democratic Dictatorship: The Emergent Constitution of Control (1981).

97. See E. Mason (ed.), The Corporation in Modern Society (1960).

98. J. Davis, supra note 89, at 246.

CHAPTER 10

1. See R. Richey & D. Jones (eds.), American Civil Religion (1974).

2. Bellah, *Civil Religion in America*, in ibid., at 21.

3. R. Williams, American Society: A Sociological Interpretation 312 (1952).

4. D. Ehrenfeld, The Arrogance of Humanism (1978).

5. See P. Bereano (ed.), Technology as a Social and Political Phenomenon (1976); J. Ellul, The Technological Society (trans. 1964).

6. Lerner, *Constitution and Court as Symbols*, 46 Yale Law Journal 1290 (1937).

7. Quoted in R. Bond (ed.), The Man Who Was Chesterton 125 (1960).

8. Lerner, supra note 6, at 1297.

9. T. Paine, Common Sense (1776), quoted in Corwin, *The Constitution as Instrument and as Symbol*, 30 American Political Science Review 1071 (1936).

10. The New Republic, May 8, 1965.

11. R. Flaceliere, Greek Oracles 87 (1965).

12. Lerner, supra note 6.

13. Ibid.

14. Brown v. Allen, 344 U.S. 443 (1953).

15. Lerner, supra note 6, at 1312.

16. Walzer, *The Courts, the Elections, and the People*, Dissent, Spring 1981, p. 153.

17. Lerner, supra note 6, at 1299.

18. Quoted in Schechter, *The Early History of the Tradition of the Constitution*, 9 American Political Science Review 707 (1915).

19. Bellah, supra note 2, at 29.

20. Zorach v. Clauson, 343 U.S. 306 (1952).

21. Levinson, *"The Constitution" in American Civil Religion*, 1979 Supreme Court Review 123.

22. I. Brant, The Bill of Rights 8 (1965).

23. Leo Pfeffer, Letter to the Editor, New York Times, Feb. 16, 1978.

24. Levinson, *Law as Our Civil Religion*, 31 Mercer Law Review 477 (1980). Levinson attributes the view in the text to Chief Justice Warren Burger's opinion in United States v. Nixon, 418 U.S. 683 (1974).

25. Levinson, supra note 24; J. Ely, Democracy and Distrust (1980).

26. Monaco v. Mississippi, 292 U.S. 213 (1943).

27. F. Dostoevsky, *The Legend of the Grand Inquisitor*, in The Brothers Karamazov.

CHAPTER 11

1. Quoted in W. Murphy, Congress and the Court 268 (1962).

2. Forrester, *Are We Ready for Truth in Judging?* 63 American Bar Association Journal 1212 (1977).

3. Walzer, *The Courts, the Elections, and the People*, Dissent, Spring 1981, p. 153.

4. Quoted in R. Dubos, So Human an Animal 200 (1968).

5. J. Passmore, Man's Responsibility for Nature (1974).

6. White, *The Historic Roots of Our Ecologic Crisis*, 155 Science 1204 (1967).

7. W. Galston, Justice and the Human Good 124 (1980).

8. E. Ashby, Reconciling Man with the Environment (1978).

9. See P. & A. Ehrlich, Extinction (1981).

10. Ibid. For more extended discussion, see P. Ehrlich, A. Ehrlich, and J. Holdren, Ecoscience: Population-Resources-Environment (2d ed. 1977).

11. P. Rhinelander, Is Man Incomprehensible to Man? 98 (1973).

12. Ibid.

13. A. Lovejoy, Reflections on Human Nature 15 (1961).

14. C. Becker, The Heavenly City of the Eighteenth-Century Philosophers (1932).

15. See B. Skinner, Beyond Freedom and Dignity (1971).

16. B. Skinner, Walden Two (1948).

17. C. Beard, The American Spirit 580 (1942). See W. Williams, Empire as a Way of Life c. 6 (1980).

18. See S. Eyre, The Real Wealth of Nations (1978).

19. W. Williams, supra note 17.

20. Ibid., at 100.

21. Quoted in ibid., at 219.

22. See L. Thurow, The Zero-Sum Society (1980); W. Brandt, North-South: A Program for Survival (1980).

23. H. Arendt, The Human Condition (1958).

24. Miami Herald, June 7, 1981, p. 7B.

25. Kennan, *The Only Way Out of the Nuclear Nightmare*, 124 Manchester Guardian Weekly, May 31, 1981, p. 1.

26. M. Cohen, Reason and Law 150 (1950) (paperback ed. 1961).

27. Ibid., at 73.

28. See W. Rumble, American Legal Realism: Skepticism, Reform, and the Judicial Process (1968).

29. M. White, Social Thought in America: The Revolt Against Formalism c. 2 (1957 enlarged edition).

30. Quoted in H. Commager, The American Mind 94 (1950).

31. Ibid., at 94-95.

32. 208 U.S. 412 (1908).

33. See P. Rosen, The Supreme Court and Social Science (1972).

34. See Krislov, *The Amicus Curiae Brief: From Friendship to Advocacy*, 72 Yale Law Journal 694 (1963).

35. Brennan, *Working at Justice*, in A. Westin (ed.), An Autobiography of the Supreme Court 300 (1963).

36. See Morgan, *Judicial Notice*, 57 Harvard Law Review 269 (1944); Roberts, *Preliminary Notes Toward a Study of Judicial Notice*, 52 Cornell Law Quarterly 210 (1967).

37. H. Commager, supra note 30, c. 5.

38. Quoted in ibid., at 106.

39. Pound, *Liberty of Contract*, 18 Yale Law Journal 464 (1909).

40. E. Patterson, Jurisprudence: Men and Ideas of the Law 552 (1953).

41. Gilmore, *Legal Realism: Its Cause and Cure*, 70 Yale Law Journal 1048 (1961). See also Yntema, *American Legal Realism in Retrospect*, 14 Vanderbilt Law Review 329 (1960): "The significant achievement of American legal realism has been to imprint in legal thinking the concept of relativity in the adaptation of positive law to social change."

42. J. Rawls, A Theory of Justice (1971).

43. Ibid.

44. See *Symposium: Judicial Review Versus Democracy*, 42 Ohio State Law Journal 1-434 (1981).

45. M. Cohen, supra note 26, at 113-14.

46. Frankfurter, *The Judicial Process and the Supreme Court*, in F. Frankfurter, Of Law and Men 35 (P. Elman ed. 1956).

47. W. Galston, Justice and the Human Good (1980).

48. See E. Rostow, The Sovereign Prerogative (1962).

49. E. Hirsch, The Aims of Interpretation 20 (1976).

50. Richmond Newspapers, Inc. v. Virginia, 100 Supreme Court Reporter 2814 (1980).

51. Youngstown Sheet & Tube Co. v. Sawyer, 343 U.S. 579 (1952).

52. Wright, *Professor Bickel, the Scholarly Tradition and the Supreme Court*, 84 Harvard Law Review 769 (1971).

53. L. Hand, The Spirit of Liberty 81 (I. Dilliard ed. 1953).

54. See R. McCloskey, The American Supreme Court (1960).

55. See Cutler, *To Form a Government*, 59 Foreign Affairs 156 (1980).

56. Missouri v. Holland, 252 U.S. 416 (1920).

57. See Miller, *The Supreme Court Under Fire*, Miami Herald, June 28, 1981, p. 4E.

58. 101 Supreme Court Reporter 1010 (1981).

59. 419 U.S. 477 (1975).

60. J. Shklar, Legalism 101-2 (1964).

61. H. Abraham, The Judicial Process c. 9 (3d ed. 1975).

62. Holmes, *The Path of the Law*, 10 Harvard Law Review 457 (1897).

63. Lochner v. New York, 198 U.S. 45 (1905).

64. W. Douglas, The Court Years (1980).

65. 372 U.S. 144 (1963).

66. See Miller, *On the Choice of Major Premises in Supreme Court Opinions*, 14 Journal of Public Law 251 (1965).

67. Holmes, J., in Lochner v. New York, supra note 63.

68. 367 U.S. 643 (1961).

69. M. Cohen, Law and the Social Order 205 (1933).

70. M. Cohen, supra note 26.

71. J. Dewey, Logic: The Theory of Inquiry 163 (1938).

72. McCulloch v. Maryland, 4 Wheaton (17 U.S.) 316 (1819).

73. Cf. Soifer, *Complacency and Constitutional Law*, 42 Ohio State Law Journal 383 (1981).

74. See Miller & Bowman, *Constitutional Silences in the "Perfect Constitution"* (forthcoming, to be published in a legal periodical).

75. Quoted in Glazer, Towards an Imperial Judiciary? The Public Interest, no. 41, p. 104 (1975).

76. J. Ely, Democracy and Distrust (1980).

77. 435 U.S. 765 (1978).

78. M. Carnoy & D. Shearer, Economic Democracy 131 (1980). See Miller, *On Politics, Democracy, and the First Amendment: A Commentary on First National Bank v. Bellotti*, 38 Washington & Lee Law Review 21 (1981).

79. Edwards v. California, 314 U.S. 160 (1941).

80. See *Symposium*, supra note 44.

81. See Peebles, *A Call to High Debate: The Organic Constitution in its Formative Era, 1890-1920*, 52 Colorado Law Review 49 (1980).

82. Griffith, *The Political Constitution*, 42 Modern Law Review 1 (1979).

83. Quoted in Murphy, *Constitutional Interpretation: The Art of the Historian, Magician, or Statesman?* 87 Yale Law Journal 1752 (1978).

84. Murphy, *An Ordering of Constitutional Values*, 53 Southern California Law Review 703 (1980).

85. A. Bickel, The Morality of Consent (1975).

86. Address by Chief Justice Warren at the Louis Marshall Award Dinner of the Jewish Theological Seminary, New York City, Nov. 11, 1962.

87. Cohen, *Positivism and Idealism in the Law*, 27 Columbia Law Review 237 (1927).

88. Pekelis, *The Case for a Jurisprudence of Welfare*, in M. Konvitz (ed.) Law and Social Action 1 (1950).

89. Cf. T. Cronin, The State of the Presidency (1975).

90. C. Lindblom, The Policy-Making Process (1968).

91. H. Parke & D. Wormell, The Delphic Oracle 416 (1956).

92. Ibid., at 420.

93. B. Woodward & S. Armstrong, The Brethren (1979).

94. J. Benda, The Treason of the Intellectuals 110 (1969 paperback ed.) (first published in 1927 in France). See Hartwell, *Introduction* to K. Templeton (ed.), The Politicization of Society 7 (1979).

95. Levinson, *The Specious Morality of the Law*, Harper's Magazine, May 1977, at 37.

96. Hartwell, supra note 94.

97. T. Dempsey, The Delphic Oracle 105 (1918).

98. 301 U.S. 1 (1937).

99. Federalist No. 10.

100. Wright, *Politics and the Constitution: Is Money Speech?* 85 Yale Law Journal 1001 (1976).

101. J. Ely, supra note 76.

102. 305 U.S. 337 (1938).

103. 321 U.S. 649 (1944).

104. 334 U.S. 1 (1948).

105. 369 U.S. 186 (1962).

106. 377 U.S. 533 (1964).

107. 384 U.S. 436 (1966).

108. Roe v. Wade, 410 U.S. 113 (1973).

109. See Miller, *The Politics of the American Judiciary*, 49 Political Quarterly 200 (1978).

110. A. Berle, Power 342 (1969).

111. See C. Vose, Constitutional Change (1972).

112. Pekelis, supra note 88.

113. His views were best expressed in A. Bickel, The Supreme Court and the Idea of Progress (1970).

114. Taken from Kurland, *Equal in Origin and Equal in Title to the Legislative and Executive Branches of the Government*, 78 Harvard Law Review 143 (1964).

115. R. Funston, Constitutional Counterrevolution? 29 (1977).

116. S. Hess, The Washington Reporters (1981).

117. L. Webb, Legal Personality and Political Pluralism 194 (1958).

118. R. Horn, Groups and the Constitution 152 (1956).

119. Bacon, Of Judicature, quoted in Miller & Scheflin, *The Power of the Supreme Court in the Age of the Positive State*, 1967 Duke Law Journal 522.

120. Mainly business corporations. Santa Clara County v. Southern Pacific Railway, 118 U.S. 394 (1886).

122. 344 U.S. 94 (1952).

121. The principal example is the Democratic party. See Smith v. Allwright, 321 U.S. 649 (1944).

123. J. Figgis, Churches in the Modern State 89 (2d ed. 1914).

124. J. Keynes, The End of Laisser Faire 41-42 (1926).

125. Maitland, *Moral Personality and Legal Personality*, in F. Maitland, Selected Essays 223 (1936).

126. R. Wolff, The Poverty of Liberalism 183 (1968).

127. H. Adams, Relation of the State to Industrial Action, and Economics and Jurisprudence 151 (J. Dorfman ed. 1954) (reprinted from 1886 statement of Adams).

128. Ibid., at 147.

129. P. Freund, The Supreme Court of the United States 189 (1961).

130. A. Whitehead, Symbolism: Its Meaning and Effect 88 (1927).

131. Downing, *Judicial Ethics and the Political Role of the Courts*, 35 Law & Contemporary Problems 94 (1970).

132. In Dennis v. United States, 341 U.S. 494 (1951).

133. Louisiana *ex. rel.* Francis v. Resweber, 329 U.S. 459 (1947).

134. O. Kirchheimer, Political Justice *vii* (1961).

135. Warth v. Seldin, 422 U.S. 490 (1975).

136. W. Galston, supra note 7.

137. *Oral Argument*, Brown v. Board of Education, 347 U.S. 483 (1954), reproduced in L. Friedman, Argument 63 (1969).

138. Ibid.

139. Morgan, *Judicial Notice*, 57 Harvard Law Review 269 (1944).

140. T. Marvell, Appellate Courts and Lawyers: Information Gathering in the Adversary System (1978).

141. Quoted in M. Mayer, The Lawyers 497 (1967) (paperback ed.).

142. Quoted in Oster & Doane, *The Power of Our Judges*, U.S. News & World Report, Jan. 19, 1976, p. 29.

143. In a number of articles and books. See, for example, R. Pound, Social Control Through Law (1942); and see D. Wigdor, Roscoe Pound: Philosopher of Law (1974).

144. D. Ehrenfeld, The Arrogance of Humanism (1978).

145. Adapted from ibid.

146. Knight, *On the Meaning of Justice*, in C. Friedrich & J. Chapman (eds.), Justice 1 (1963).

147. O. Holmes, The Common Law 35-36 (1881).

148. Quoted in Miller, *There Are Too Many Lawyers on the High Court*, Washington Post, July 20, 1980, p. E1.

149. Frankfurter, *The Process of Judging in Constitutional Cases*, in A. Westin (ed.), An Autobiography of the Supreme Court 267 (1963).

150. 395 U.S. *vii* (1969).

151. See Tushnet, *Legal Scholarship: Its Causes and Cure*, 90 Yale Law Journal 1205 (1981).

152. W. Douglas, supra note 64.

153. See Garvey, *Scholar in Politics: Edward S. Corwin and the 1937 Court-packing Battle*, 31 Princeton University Library Chronicle 1 (1969).

154. See *Text of Historic TV Interview of Justice Black*, Congressional Quarterly, Jan. 3, 1969, p. 6.

155. See Griswold v. Connecticut, 381 U.S. 479 (1965) (Black, J., dissenting).

156. See Rehnquist, *The Notion of a Living Constitution*, 54 Texas Law Review 693 (1976).

157. J. Shklar, supra note 60.

158. J. Stone, Social Dimensions of Law and Justice 678 (1966).

159. J. Ely, supra note 76.

160. Murphy, supra note 84.

161. Ibid.

162. As the Supreme Court said in Dennis v. United States, supra note 132.

163. Pekelis, supra note 88.

164. Murphy, supra note 84.

165. Trop v. Dulles, 356 U.S. 86 (1958).

166. Rochin v. California, 342 U.S. 165 (1952).

167. Ibid.

168. Snyder v. Massachusetts, 291 U.S. 97 (1934).

169. Griswold v. Connecticut, 381 U.S. 479 (1965).

170. Rochin v. California, supra note 166.

171. Palko v. Connecticut, 302 U.S. 319 (1937).

172. Rochin v. California, supra note 166.

173. Ibid.

174. See, for discussion of this and other similar statements, Murphy, *The Art of Constitutional Interpretation*, in M. Harmon (ed.) Essays on the Constitution of the United States 130 (1978).

175. Murphy, supra note 84.

176. Quoted in W. Murphy & J. Tanenhaus, Comparative Constitutional Law: Cases and Commentaries (1977).

177. Moore v. City of East Cleveland, 431 U.S. 494 (1977).

178. Huntington, *The United States*, in M. Crozier, S. Huntington & J. Watanuki, The Crisis of Democracy (1975).

179. W. Lippmann, Essays in the Public Philosophy (1955).

180. Ibid.

181. Ibid.

182. Soifer, *Complacency and Constitutional Law*, 42 Ohio State Law Journal 383 (1981).

183. Quoted in P. Eidelberg, The Philosophy of the American Constitution 204 (1968).

184. Ibid.

185. Ibid.

186. Ibid.

187. C. Tansill (ed.), Documents Illustrative of the Formation of the Union of the American States 567 (1927).

188. B. Cohen, Presidential Responsibility and American Democracy (1974) (photocopy of Royer Lectures, University of California Berkeley).

189. Ibid.

190. E. Benoit, Progress and Survival: An Essay on the Future of Mankind 63 (1980).

191. Ibid., at c. 4.

192. Ibid.

193. This suggestion is for a type of "social impact statement" analogous to the environmental impact statements now required by the National Environmental Policy Act of 1969, 42 United States Code Sec. 4332.

194. Sandalow, *Judicial Protection of Minorities*, 75 Michigan Law Review 1162 (1977).

195. Kurland, *Ruminations on the Quality of Equality*, 1979 Brigham Young University Law Review 7. See Brest, *The Misconceived Quest for the Original Understanding*, 60 Boston University Law Review 204 (1980).

196. Brest, supra note 195.

197. Lippmann, supra note 179.

198. H. Maine, Popular Government 20 (1886).

199. T. Eliot, The Complete Poems and Plays 58-59 (1952).

200. Wolf v. Colorado, 338 U.S. 25 (1949).

201. See Miller, *Reason of State and the Emergent Constitution of Control*, 64 Minnesota Law Review 585 (1980).

202. Dames & Moore v. Regan, 49 United States Law Week 4969 (1981).

203. Parker, *The Past of Constitutional Theory—And Its Future*, 42 Ohio State Law Journal 223 (1981).

204. Ibid.

CHAPTER 12

1. "Brown v. Board of Education was the beginning." A. Bickel, The Supreme Court and the Idea of Progress 7 (1970).

2. Boyle, *The Law of Power Politics*, 1980 University of Illinois Law Forum 901.

3. Ibid.

4. See W. Brandt, North-South: A Program for Survival (1980).

5. L. Hand, The Bill of Rights (1958).

6. O. Fiss, The Civil Rights Injunction (1978). See J. Bass, Unlikely Heroes (1981).

7. Cf. A. Bickel, The Caseload of the Supreme Court (1973).

8. For discussion, see Lewis, *Is the Supreme Court Creating Unknown and Unknowable Law? The Insubstantial Federal Question Dismissal*, 5 Nova Law Journal 11 (1980).

9. A. Bickel, supra note 1.

10. Johnson, *In Defense of Judicial Activism*, 28 Emory Law Journal 901 (1979).

11. Ibid. See Chayes, *The Role of the Judge in Public Law Litigation*, 89 Harvard Law Review 1281 (1976).

12. Johnson, supra note 10.

13. Quoted in Boyle, supra note 2.

14. C. Macpherson, The Real World of Democracy 14 (1966).

15. L. Thurow, The Zero-Sum Society (1980).

16. Professor Paul Ehrlich of Stanford University, in a personal conversation with the present author.

17. R. Rubenstein, The Cunning of History: The Holocaust and the American Future (1975).

18. L. Hobhouse, The Elements of Social Justice (1922), quoted in W. Galston, Justice and the Human Good (1980).

19. C. Macpherson, supra note 14.

20. See Boyle, supra note 2.

21. Ibid.

22. N. Machiavelli, The Discourses, Book I, Sec. 51.

23. The title to ibid.

24. N. Machiavelli, supra note 22, Book I, Sec. 58.

25. Quoted in I. Jenkins, Social Order and the Limits of Law (1980).

26. R. Pound, Social Control Through Law (1942).

27. Brandeis, *Proposed Dissent to United States v. Moreland*, 258 U.S. 433 (1922), as quoted in A. Bickel, The Least Dangerous Branch 107 (1962). See Peebles, *A Call to High Debate: The Organic Constitution in Its Formative Era, 1890-1920*, 52 Colorado Law Review 49 (1980).

28. Griswold v. Connecticut, 381 U.S. 479 (1965).

29. 332 U.S. 46 (1947).

30. See Rehnquist, *The Notion of a Living Constitution*, 54 Texas Law Review 693 (1976).

31. 418 U.S. 241 (1974).

32. For discussion, see Phillips, *The Life and Times of the Contract Clause*—American Business Law Journal—(1982).

33. See A. Miller, Democratic Dictatorship: The Emergent Constitution of Control (1981).

34. Discussed in Miller, *The Elusive Search for Values in Constitutional Interpretation*, 6 Hastings Constitutional Law Quarterly 487 (1979).

35. Hobson v. Hansen, 269 Federal Supplement 517 (1967).

A Note on Further Reading

The Supreme Court of the United States is one of the most studied, yet least understood, governmental institutions in the world. An immense literature discusses aspects of its work. Relatively little, however, is directed toward viewing the Court as a political organ. That dearth of literature is because the prevailing ideology of lawyers and even of many political scientists considers the Court to be a "legal" rather than a "political" body. That it is both should be, but is not, obvious to all.

This bibliographical note highlights and supplements the materials cited in the notes to each chapter of this volume. Many of the works cited in those notes contain extensive bibliographical data. Only books are mentioned in this essay. References to the massive periodical literature, mostly on constitutional law rather than the High Bench as a segment of American government, may be found in the *Index to Legal Periodicals, Social Sciences Index, Readers Guide to Periodical Literature*, and the *New York Times Index*.

The leading American student of the politics of the judiciary is Professor Martin Shapiro. See his *Law and Politics in the Supreme Court* (New York: Free Press, 1964); *The Supreme Court and Administrative Agencies* (New York: Free Press, 1968); *The Courts: A Comparative and Political Analysis* (Chicago: University of Chicago Press, 1981). Walter F. Murphy, *The Elements of Judicial Strategy* (Chicago: University of Chicago Press, 1964) is a keen insight into the internal dynamics of the Supreme Court. J.A.G. Griffith, *The Politics of the Judiciary* (Manchester: Manchester University Press, 1977) is a political analysis of the British judiciary, useful and provocative. Henry J. Abraham, *The Judicial Process: An Introductory Analysis of the Courts of the United States, England and France* (New York: Oxford University Press, 3d ed. 1975) is a thoughtful contribution. Victor Rosenblum, *Law as a Political Instrument* (New York: Doubleday & Co., 1955) is a useful brief introduction. See also Sheldon Goldman & Thomas P. Jahnige, *The Federal Courts as a Political System* (New York: Harper & Row, 2d ed. 1976) and Jack Peltason, *Federal Courts in the Political Process* (New York: Doubleday & Co., 1955).

Important studies of the Justices may be found in Leon Friedman & Fred L. Israel (eds.), *The Justices of the United States Supreme Court, 1789-1969: Their Lives and Major Opinions* (New York: R. R. Bowker Co., 1969) (updated with an additional volume in 1978); John R. Schmidhauser, *Judges and Justices: The Federal Appellate Judiciary* (Boston: Little, Brown & Co., 1979); James F. Simon, *In His Own Image: The Supreme Court in Richard Nixon's America* (New York: David McKay Co.,

1973); and in the following biographies: Alpheus Thomas Mason, *Harlan Fiske Stone: Pillar of the Law* (New York: Viking, 1956); J. Woodford Howard, *Mr. Justice Murphy: A Political Biography* (Princeton: Princeton University Press, 1968); Joseph P. Lash (ed.), *From the Diaries of Felix Frankfurter* (New York: W. W. Norton & Co., 1975); James F. Simon, *Independent Journey* (New York: Harper & Row, 1980) (biography of Justice William O. Douglas); H. N. Hirsch, *The Enigma of Felix Frankfurter* (New York: Basic Books, 1980); and Gerald T. Dunne, *Hugo Black and the Judicial Revolution* (New York: Simon & Schuster, 1977). The books by Mason and Howard are particularly rewarding for providing glimpses of the Court's internal operations. On that point, see the keyhole view in the bestseller by Bob Woodward & Scott Armstrong, *The Brethren: Inside the Supreme Court* (New York: Simon & Schuster, 1979).

See Richard Kluger, *Simple Justice: The History of Brown v. Board of Education and Black America's Struggle for Equality* (New York: Alfred A. Knopf, 1976) for a detailed and revealing account of the legal strategy pursued by black Americans that culminated in the *Brown* case. Jack Bass, *Unlikely Heroes* (New York: Simon & Schuster, 1981) is a well-written account of how federal appeals judges in the South put the principle of the *Brown* case into operational reality. Also see J. Harvie Wilkinson, *From Brown to Bakke: The Supreme Court and School Integration, 1954-1978* (New York: Oxford University Press, 1979).

The best single-volume history of the Supreme Court is Elder Witt (ed.), *Guide to the U.S. Supreme Court* (Washington: Congressional Quarterly, 1979). Older but still useful histories include Charles Warren, *The Supreme Court in United States History* (Boston: Little, Brown & Co., rev. ed. 1935); Homer C. Hockett, *The Constitutional History of the United States* (New York: Macmillan Co., 1939); Carl B. Swisher, *American Constitutional Development* (Boston: Houghton Mifflin Co., rev. ed. 1954); Robert McCloskey, *The American Supreme Court* (Chicago: University of Chicago Press, 1960); Wallace Mendelson, *Capitalism, Democracy and the Supreme Court* (New York: Appleton-Century-Crofts, 1960); Charles Black, *The People and the Court* (New York: Macmillan Co., 1960); and Bernard Schwartz, *A Commentary on the Constitution of the United States* (New York: Macmillan Co., 1963). In the process of being written is a multivolume study of the Supreme Court, commissioned under the terms of the will of Justice Oliver Wendell Holmes. Three volumes have been published: Julius Goebel, *Antecedents and Beginnings to 1801*; Charles Fairman, *Reconstruction and Reunion, 1864-88*; and Carl B. Swisher, *The Taney Period, 1836-64* (all three volumes were published by Macmillan Co. in New York).

For a careful and important study of the adversary system, see Thomas B. Marvell, *Appellate Courts and Lawyers: Information Gathering in the Adversary System* (Westport: Greenwood Press, 1978). Other aspects of the Court's work and influence are discussed in Theodore L. Becker & Malcolm M. Feeley (eds.), *The Impact of Supreme Court Decisions* (New York: Oxford University Press, 2d ed. 1973); William K. Muir, *Prayer in the Public Schools: Law and Attitude Change* (Chicago: University of Chicago Press, 1967); Arthur Selwyn Miller, *The Supreme Court: Myth and Reality* (Westport: Greenwood Press, 1978); and Stephen L. Wasby, *The Impact of the United States Supreme Court: Some Perspectives* (Homewood, Ill.: Dorsey Press, 1970).

The legitimacy of the Supreme Court's lawmaking proclivities is discussed in Raoul Berger, *Government by Judiciary: The Transformation of the Fourteenth Amendment*

(Cambridge: Harvard University Press, 1977); Louis Boudin, *Government by Judiciary* (New York: Godwin & Co., 1932); John R. Commons, *Legal Foundations of Capitalism* (New York: Macmillan Co., 1924); Herbert Wechsler, *Principles, Politics and Fundamental Law* (Cambridge: Harvard University Press, 1961); Louis Lusky, *By What Right? A Commentary on the Supreme Court's Power to Revise the Constitution* (Charlottesville: Michie Co., 1975); Philip B. Kurland, *Politics, the Constitution and the Warren Court* (Chicago: University of Chicago Press, 1970); and Lino A. Graglia, *Disaster by Decree* (Ithaca: Cornell University Press, 1976).

Insightful analyses of the Court and its work may be found in Alexander M. Bickel, *The Least Dangerous Branch* (Indianapolis: Bobbs-Merrill Co., 1962), *Politics and the Warren Court* (New York: Harper & Row, 1965), and *The Supreme Court and the Idea of Progress* (New York: Harper & Row, 1970); John Hart Ely, *Democracy and Distrust* (Cambridge: Harvard University Press, 1980); Jesse H. Choper, *Judicial Review and the National Political Process* (Chicago: University of Chicago Press, 1980); and Archibald Cox, *The Role of the Supreme Court in American Government* (New York: Oxford University Press, 1976) and *The Warren Court: Constitutional Decision as an Instrument of Reform* (Cambridge: Harvard University Press, 1968); John P. Roche, *Courts and Rights: The American Judiciary in Action* (New York: Random House, 2d ed. 1966); and Learned Hand, *The Bill of Rights* (Cambridge: Harvard University Press, 1958). Each of these books takes a point-of-view different from the present volume. Scheduled for publication in the near future is Michael Perry, *The Constitution, the Courts, and Human Rights: An Inquiry into the Legitimacy of Constitutional Policymaking by the Judiciary* (to be published by Yale University Press, New Haven, Conn.).

Additional books of value in the study of the judiciary as a political institution include the following: Samuel Krislov, *The Supreme Court and Political Freedom* (New York: Free Press, 1968); Robert Scigliano, *The Supreme Court and the Presidency* (New York: Free Press, 1971); David F. Forte (ed.), *The Supreme Court in American Politics: Judicial Activism vs. Judicial Restraint* (Lexington, Mass.: D. C. Heath & Co., 1972); Donald L. Horowitz, *The Courts and Social Policy* (Washington: Brookings Institution, 1977); Glendon Schubert, *The Constitutional Polity* (Boston: Boston University Press, 1970); Robert McCloskey, *The Modern Supreme Court* (Cambridge: Harvard University Press, 1972); Dean Alfange, *The Supreme Court and the National Will* (Port Washington, N.Y.: Kennikat Press, 1967); Arthur Selwyn Miller, *The Supreme Court and American Capitalism* (New York: Free Press, 1968); Ward E. Elliott, *The Rise of Guardian Democracy: The Supreme Court's Role in Voting Rights Disputes, 1945-1969* (Cambridge: Harvard University Press, 1974); Richard Funston, *Constitutional Counter-revolution? The Warren Court and the Burger Court: Judicial Policy-Making in Modern America* (Cambridge: Schenkman Publishing Co., 1977); Leonard Levy (ed.), *Judicial Review and the Supreme Court: Selected Essays* (New York: Harper & Row, 1967); Paul L. Rosen, *The Supreme Court and Social Science* (Urbana: University of Illinois Press, 1972); and Clement E. Vose, *Constitutional Change* (Lexington, Mass.: D. C. Heath & Co., 1972). Scheduled for publication in 1982 is a collection of essays by leading scholars that touch upon many of the points in the present volume: Stephen Halpern & Charles Lamb (eds.), *Supreme Court Activism and Restraint* (Lexington, Mass.: D. C. Heath & Co., 1982).

The following books may be consulted for discussions of the philosophical issues concerning judicial review: Wilfred E. Rumble, *American Legal Realism* (Ithaca:

Cornell University Press, 1968); Ronald Dworkin, *Taking Rights Seriously* (Cambridge: Harvard University Press, 1977); William A. Galston, *Justice and the Human Good* (Chicago: University of Chicago Press, 1980); Bruce Ackerman, *Private Property and the Constitution* (New Haven: Yale University Press, 1977); Richard Brandt (ed.), *Social Justice* (Englewood Cliffs: Prentice-Hall, 1962); Ross Fitzgerald (ed.), *Human Needs and Politics* (Rushcutters Bay, Australia: Pergamon Press, 1977); Robert Nozick, *Anarchy, State, and Utopia* (New York: Basic Books, 1974); John Rawls, *A Theory of Justice* (Cambridge: Harvard University Press, 1971); J. Pennock & J. Chapman (eds.), *Constitutionalism* (New York: New York University Press, 1979); and Gary J. Jacobsohn, *Pragmatism, Statesmanship, and the Supreme Court* (Ithaca: Cornell University Press, 1977). Also well worth reading are Owen M. Fiss, *The Civil Rights Injunction* (Bloomington: Indiana University Press, 1978); Paul Eidelberg, *The Philosophy of the American Constitution* (New York: Free Press, 1968); Charles A. Beard, *An Economic Interpretation of the Constitution* (New York: Macmillan Co., 1954); Robert Brown, *Charles Beard and the Constitution* (Princeton: Princeton University Press, 1956); Iredell Jenkins, *Social Order and the Limits of Law: A Theoretical Essay* (Princeton: Princeton University Press, 1980); Michael Parenti, *Democracy for the Few* (New York: St. Martin's Press, 3d ed. 1980); and Robert A. Goldwin & William A. Schambra (eds.), *How Democratic Is the Constitution?* (Washington: American Enterprise Institute, 1980).

Finally, a four-volume *Encyclopedia of the American Constitution*, containing some 2,000 articles, will be published in 1987 by Macmillan Company in New York; it is edited by Leonard Levy and Kenneth Karst.

Index

About the Author

ARTHUR SELWYN MILLER is a Professor Emeritus of Law at George Washington University and Leo Goodwin, Sr. Distinguished Visiting Professor of Law at Nova University's Center for the Study of Law. Among his earlier publications are *The Modern Corporate State* (Greenwood Press, 1976) and *Democratic Dictatorship* (Greenwood Press, 1981).

DATE DUE
